The New Values-Based Safety

Using Behavioral Science to Improve Your Safety Culture

The New Values-Based Safety

Using Behavioral Science to Improve Your Safety Culture

Terry E. McSween & Adam S. Hockman

KeyPress Publishing
www.keypresspublishing.com

KeyPress Publishing

This book is a work of nonfiction. Unless otherwise noted, the author and the publisher make no explicit guarantees as to the accuracy of the information contained in this book, and in some cases, names of people and places have been altered to protect their privacy.

Copyright © 2024 by KeyPress Publishing
All rights reserved. No part of this publication may be reproduced, stored in a retrieval system, or transmitted in any form or by any means, electronic, mechanical, photocopying, recording, or otherwise, without the prior permission of the publisher or in accordance with the provisions of the Copyright, Designs and Patents Act 1988 or under the terms of any license permitting limited copying issued by the Copyright Licensing Agency.

Authors: Terry E. McSween and Adam S. Hockman

The New Values-Based Safety: Using Behavioral Science to Improve Your Safety Culture

Published by: KeyPress Publishing
Publisher: Alice Darnell Lattal
Brand Integrity: Jana Burtner
Production Manager: Adele Hall
Editors: Ashley Johnson, Amanda Jackson, Stefanie Carr, and Mary Sproles Martin
Designers: Jana Burtner and Kim Harding

ISBN: 979-8-9886548-4-1

The terms *Values-Based Safety* and *VBS* are registered service marks of ABA Technologies, Inc.

Distributed by:
ABA Technologies, Inc.
930 South Harbor City Blvd, Suite 402
Melbourne, FL 32901
www.abatechnologies.com

KeyPress Publishing books are available at a special discount for bulk purchases by corporations, institutions, and other organizations. For more information, please email keypress@abatechnologies.com.

Table of Contents

Foreword by Julie M. Smith, PhD xi
Foreword by E. Scott Geller, PhD xiii
Preface xiv
Acknowledgments xv
Introduction: Rethinking Behavior-Based Safety 17
    0.1 The Evolution of Behavior-Based Safety 17
    0.2 BBS: The Proven Potential. 17
    0.3 Broadening the Perspective: Beyond Peer-to-Peer Observations .. 18
    0.4 The Way Forward: Values-Based Safety. 18
Chapter 1: Understanding the Role of Behavior in Safety 20
    1.1 Traditional Safety Programs 20
    1.2 Early Studies in Behavioral Safety. 21
    1.3 DuPont's Success. 24
    1.4 Our Findings. 26
    1.5 The Safety Triangle 27
    1.6 Complacency. 29
    1.7 Safety as a Team Process 29
    1.8 Common Problems With Typical Safety Efforts. 31
    1.9 Problems With Punishment 33
    1.10 Appropriate Use of Punishment 35
    1.11 Components of a Proven Safety Process 36
    1.12 More Recent Research Studies 37
Chapter 2: The Vision. 40
    2.1 Scenario One: An Organization With Strong VBS Leadership .. 40
    2.2 Scenario Two: An Organization Implementing a VBS Process .. 42
Chapter 3: Safety Culture, Part 1: Assessment and Alignment 44
    3.1 What Is Company Culture? 44
    3.2 What Is Safety Culture? 45
    3.3 Elements of a Safety Culture. 45
    3.4 Breakdowns in Culture 46
    3.5 Great Plains Railroad: The Culture You Don't Want 47
    3.6 What to Do About Culture. 48
    3.7 Assessing the Safety Culture 49

  3.8 Steps Toward the Shared Vision 56
  3.9 Final Thoughts. 58

Chapter 4: Safety Culture, Part 2: Safety Leadership 60
  4.1 Leaders, Managers, and Supervisors: Is There a Difference? 60
  4.2 MasterBuild: The Culture You Want 61
  4.3 Barriers to Safety. 63
  4.4 Promoting Safety Through Organizational Alignment 64
  4.5 Communicate the Importance of Safety 69
  4.6 Build Participation and Support 70
  4.7 Review and Study Safety in the Workplace 71
  4.8 Manage the Consequences for Safety Practices 75
  4.9 An Implementation Plan to Improve Safety Leadership 76
  4.10 Final Thoughts. 78

Chapter 5: Leadership Safety Improvement Projects. 80
  5.1 Element 1: Build Management Commitment and Leadership . . 82
  5.2 Element 2: Involve Employees. 83
  5.3 Element 3: Understand the Risks 83
  5.4 Element 4: Identify Critical Work for Controlling the Risks . . . 83
  5.5 Element 5: Establish Performance Standards 84
  5.6 Element 6: Maintain Measurement and Feedback Systems. 84
  5.7 Element 7: Reinforce and Implement Corrective Actions 84
  5.8 Element 8: Improve and Update the Process. 85
  5.9 Implementation of a Leadership Safety Project:
    Pipeline Operations Case Study 85

Chapter 6: The Values-Based Safety Process. 90
  6.1 Values-Based Safety. 90
  6.2 What's in a Name? 90
  6.3 Team-Based Process 91
  6.4 Programs Versus Process 93

Chapter 7: Safety Assessment. 95
  7.1 What Is a Safety Assessment? 95
  7.2 Why Conduct a Safety Assessment? 96
  7.3 Who Should Conduct the Assessment?. 97
  7.4 Objectives of the Assessment. 98
  7.5 Outcome of the Assessment 101
  7.6 Safety Assessment Process. 102

Chapter 8: Management Overview and Design Team Workshop 112
  8.1 What Is the Management Overview? 113
  8.2 What Are the Objectives of the Management Overview? 113

8.3 What Is the Design Team Workshop?.................... 114
   8.4 What Are the Objectives of the Design Team Workshop? 114
   8.5 What Is the Agenda?................................. 114
Chapter 9: Final Design **116**
   9.1 What Are the Objectives of This Phase? 117
   9.2 Design Team Process.................................. 117
   9.3 Role of the Management Team 119
Chapter 10: Step 1: Establishing Mission, Values, and Milestone Targets..... 121
   10.1 Clarifying Values: A Structured Approach................ 122
   10.2 Step 1: Brainstorm Actions Likely to Impact the Process 123
   10.3 Step 2: Pinpoint Those Practices 123
   10.4 Step 3: Sort These Practices Into "Value" Categories 124
   10.5 Step 4: Use Values in Designing Your Safety Process........ 124
   10.6 Step 5: Discuss Values During Kickoff Meetings and Training. . 125
   10.7 Step 6: Use Values as Criteria for Evaluation............... 126
   10.8 Establish a Milestone Schedule 126
Chapter 11: Step 2: Creating the Safety Observation Process................ 128
   11.1 How Do You Create the Observation Process? 130
   11.2 Analyze Past Incidents and Injuries..................... 130
   11.3 Develop a List of Critical Safe Practices 131
   11.4 Identify Safe Practices That Prevent Serious Incidents 140
   11.5 Draft and Revise Checklists 143
   11.6 Develop the Observation Procedure 150
   11.7 Feedback on Observations............................ 156
   11.8 Trial Run the Observation Checklist and Process 158
   11.9 Conduct Management Review 160
Chapter 12: Step 3: Designing Feedback and Involvement Procedures 162
   12.1 Develop Guidelines for Using Graphs................... 163
   12.2 Plan Review of Safety Process Data..................... 166
   12.3 Develop Guidelines for Setting Improvement Goals........ 166
   12.4 Establish Guidelines to Expand Involvement in Observations. . 167
   12.5 Checklist for Planning Feedback and Involvement 169
Chapter 13: Step 4: Developing Recognition and Celebration Plans......... 170
   13.1 Overview of Safety Awards and Incentives 172
   13.2 Safety Recognition................................... 172
   13.3 Simple and Concurrent Safety Awards 174
   13.4 Tiered Safety Awards................................. 175
   13.5 Opportunities for Professional Development.............. 185
   13.6 Support Through Promotions and Traditional Compensation . . 185

13.7 Safety Incentive Compensation 186
13.8 General Guidelines on Supporting Safety Motivation 187
13.9 Checklist for Ensuring the Effectiveness of Recognition
 and Celebrations 187

Chapter 14: Step 5: Planning Training and Kickoff Meetings 191

14.1 Observer Training 192
14.2 Plan Kickoff Meeting(s) 193
14.3 Plan Training Needed to Support the Process 194

Chapter 15: Step 6: Conducting Management Review 196

Chapter 16: Implementing the Values-Based Safety Process 199

16.1 Conduct Training for the Steering Committee 200
16.2 Establish a Process Owner 200
16.3 Steering Committee's Responsibilities 201
16.4 Management's Responsibilities 204

Chapter 17: Maintaining the Values-Based Safety Process 206

17.1 Steering Committee Members' Responsibilities 207
17.2 Common Situations 210
17.3 Steering Committee's Responsibilities 211
17.4 Management's Responsibilities 213

Chapter 18: Some Final Suggestions on Implementation 215

Chapter 19: Special Topics: The Self-Observation Process 217

19.1 What Must I Do to Successfully Carry Out My Job? 218
19.2 How Am I Doing? 218
19.3 What's in It for Me? 219
19.4 How to Implement a Self-Observation Process 220
19.5 Final Suggestions on Self-Observations 224

Chapter 20: Special Topics: The Steering Committee 225

20.1 Creating the Steering Committee 225
20.2 Training the Steering Committee 226
20.3 Steering Committee Responsibilities 226
20.4 Responsibility Summary 232

Chapter 21: Advanced Topics: Behavioral Basics 233

21.1 Pinpointing 233
21.2 ABC Analysis 235
21.3 Consequences 236
21.4 Antecedents 239
21.5 Individual Learning History 239
21.6 Behavioral Analysis Worksheet 241

21.7 Developing an Action Plan to Address Behavioral Causes ... 241

Chapter 22: Advanced Topics: Steering Committee Improvement Projects ... 243

22.1 Problem-Solving Steps ... 243
22.2 Methods of Gathering Additional Information ... 245
22.3 Identifying Weak or Missing Contingency Elements ... 246
22.4 Guidelines for Setting Goals ... 249
22.5 Conclusion ... 250

Chapter 23: Other Support Programs ... 251

23.1 Additional Safety Process Components ... 251
23.2 Supplemental Safety Programs ... 251
23.3 Additional Safety Process Components ... 252
23.4 Supplemental Safety Programs ... 254
23.5 Coordinate Special Programs ... 257

Chapter 24: Long-Term Case Studies ... 258

24.1 Values-Based Safety in a Refinery ... 258
24.2 Employee Safety Process at an Ore-Processing Facility ... 262

Chapter 25: Self-Observation Case Studies ... 266

25.1 Canadian Gas Production and Pipeline Company ... 266
25.2 Electric Utility ... 269
25.3 Logging Industry ... 272

Chapter 26: Small-Company Case Studies ... 277

26.1 Pipeline Company ... 277
26.2 Polyolefin Plant ... 278
26.3 Food-Processing Plant ... 280

Chapter 27: The Observer Effect ... 283

27.1 The First Study ... 284
27.2 A Second Study ... 291
27.3 Conclusion ... 297

References ... 298

Index ... 302

Foreword

by Julie M. Smith, PhD

When I read the first edition of *The Values-Based Safety Process*, I was the cofounder and Managing Partner of CLG (now ALULA), a consulting firm that specializes in strategy execution through the application of behavior science. I reached for Dr. McSween's book not because I was looking for a way to implement safety programs, but because I was looking for a practical organizational change approach to execute a total quality management (TQM) system.

My firm was in the throes of helping two Fortune 100 firms reinvigorate their stalled TQM programs. To problem-solve what was happening, we turned to every change management book and quality guru available. It wasn't until we discovered Dr. Terry McSween's step-by-step guide that we found the answers we needed.

I found the first edition of *The Values-Based Safety Process* to be a great, great book. Here, Dr. McSween provided a practical, no-nonsense handbook to help organizations clearly articulate their safety vision and values, and then bring them alive through specific behaviors that propel the organization toward its goals. The book was complete with forms, checklists, stories, and essential elements necessary for implementing your own processes, or as we did, adapting them to other performance improvement programs. It served as the foundation for us to confidently elevate any targeted performance with our clients, helping ALULA to become one of the premiere behavior-based performance improvement consultancies in the world.

Building on the success of Dr. McSween's previous edition, this edition deepens the exploration into culture and leadership. It offers innovative strategies for fostering a safety culture that not only enhances organizational performance but also secures the well-being of every associate. Dr. McSween's culture and leadership work actively engages employees in safety walk-arounds and coaching peers based on the natural value they bring to the safety and well-being of their associates. The blend of practical advice, theoretical underpinning, and real-world examples makes this book a must read. It stands out as a pinnacle in the safety field, offering straightforward, practical, and effective guidelines for developing companywide action plans that resonate with values and propel organizations toward excellence.

When I first came across Dr. McSween's work, I was struck by the fact that he so openly shared all of his secrets. Most consultants never do that—they want to protect their intellectual property. So, I had to learn more about the man behind the book. After all, he was our company's unsung hero.

I found Terry to be a true altruist, selflessly concerned for the well-being of others. It wasn't about fame or fortune for Terry; it was about ensuring everyone went home to their loved ones every night. To do that, Terry's mission became one of disseminating as broadly as possible the lessons he had learned in applying behavior science during his decades of hands-on consulting work. He wanted everyone, from executives to frontline workers, to understand and embrace a Values-Based Safety process.

I unequivocally recommend Dr. McSween's *The Values-Based Safety Process* as the most successful and practical safety book available. It is not just a safety book; it's a transformative tool that has shaped the landscape of organizational change efforts. The new edition will have a lasting impact on how leaders go about creating and sustaining safety cultures.

—Julie M. Smith, PhD
    CEO, Performance Ally

Foreword

by E. Scott Geller, PhD, for the first and second editions of *The Values-Based Safety Process*

One of my primary professional goals has been to encourage people to actively care for the safety and well-being of others in their communities and work settings. For the past two decades I have been traveling around the country promoting the concept of actively caring in both communities and organizations. In the context of organizations, actively caring is defined as employees acting to optimize the safety of other employees (e.g., giving rewarding feedback to an employee working safely or giving corrective feedback to a coworker working at risk). That's what *The Values-Based Safety Process: Improving Your Safety Culture With Behavior-Based Safety* is all about. It teaches both the mechanics of how to design and implement a behavioral safety process in any organization and the importance of creating an environment where everyone actively cares about his or her fellow employees or associates.

In discussing the importance of values, Terry McSween embraces my concept of actively caring while also addressing a number of other cultural practices that are crucial to the success of a behavioral safety process. Many of these elements are quite familiar to those involved in total quality efforts. For example, he emphasizes the importance of eliminating blame from the workplace. He suggests that data be used for problem-solving, not victim blaming. He also cautions us about using data from the safety observation process (i.e., "percent safe") as a basis for personnel evaluations for either individuals or supervisors, suggesting that such practices will destroy the integrity of the process. In addition, he warns us of the dangers of mandating standards for such observational data, again because such practices will destroy the integrity of our improvement efforts.

Dr. McSween shows the reader how to plan and implement a behavioral safety process. All of us realize the difficulty of developing a cookbook implementation, but he clearly describes what must be done while including potential design options and issues to consider when selecting from those options. In short, while I do not believe anyone will ever write the perfect safety cookbook for managing safety, this one is as close as I have seen.

In the safety field, it is rare to find well-written books with straightforward, practical, and effective guidelines for developing companywide action plans. This is one of those books. Read it carefully. It will help you make a beneficial difference in your organization.

—E. Scott Geller, PhD

Preface

In 2003, I authored the second edition of *The Values-Based Safety Process*. I aimed to update the recommended approach for using behavioral techniques to enhance workplace safety. My goal was to bring the recommended approach into alignment with the latest behavior-based safety research. Since then, I have implemented Values-Based Safety[SM] (VBS[SM]) across various organizations. While many efforts succeeded, some did not.

During those safety improvement efforts, I discovered VBS's robust and effective approach to employee engagement might not fit every organization. Many organizations can ensure safe operations by focusing on safety leadership and cultivating a safety culture. However, heavy industrial and construction sectors often require formal workforce engagement in safety efforts. This edition aims to support those seeking to boost their safety culture and leadership efforts. **Chapter 3: Safety Culture, Part 1: Assessment and Alignment** delves into enhancing safety culture. **Chapter 4: Safety Culture, Part 2: Safety Leadership** builds on the previous edition's discussion of safety leadership by outlining strategies to develop and sustain safety leadership behaviors at all levels of your organization.

I have worked to align the implementation guidelines with the latest research. For example, readers will notice a strategic shift: Instead of urging all employees to join safety walk-arounds, we now advocate for a select, well-trained group of VBS observers. This group will rotate, allowing other employees to eventually take on the safety observer role, marking a significant change from our 2003 strategy. These adjustments, among others, ensure our VBS design remains in line with the most current research findings.

—Terry E. McSween, PhD

Acknowledgments

I owe a debt of gratitude to my teachers and mentors and to the behavioral researchers who originally developed the ideas presented in this book. In particular, Richard W. Malott of Western Michigan University has been, and continues to be, my teacher, manager, coach, and friend. Several friends and customers also deserve special thanks. Among them, Rixio Medina, previously of CITGO Corporation in Tulsa, Oklahoma, has been a special supporter and friend for many years. Anthony "Corky" Carter and Kim McVey have been strong supporters of Values-Based Safety in their companies, and friends for many years.

My coauthor, Adam Hockman, has been a joy to work with and remained positive both on this book and throughout my brief tenure with ABA Technologies, Inc. In particular, he was a great asset in helping me clearly define the approach taken in the culture and leadership chapters.

For their work and input on our approach, I thank my past associates at Quality Safety Edge, especially Angelica Grindle, Grainne Matthews, and Judith Stowe. They were exemplary consultants and helped in the evolution of the techniques employed throughout this book.

I remain indebted to the early researchers whose work validated and helped define today's approach through their research and writings on the topic of safety. Their good work remains foundational for those studying organizational behavior management. Among them, Beth Sulzer-Azaroff, Bill Hopkins, and Dwight Harshbarger were each significant in my education and development. I had the joy of working with each of them through our involvement with the Cambridge Center for Behavioral Studies.

Also, I am particularly indebted to my editor, Ashley Johnson, for holding my hand through the entire process of writing the third edition. Her thoughtful comments and suggestions made my job as an author as easy as it could possibly be. Through the entire process, she was supportive and encouraging, and she never once missed a commitment!

—Terry E. McSween, PhD

Introduction

Rethinking Behavior-Based Safety

0.1 The Evolution of Behavior-Based Safety

Behavior-based safety (BBS), the approach to safety that typically involves peer-to-peer observations and feedback designed to increase safe behaviors in the workplace, emerged as a proven tool for fostering a safe workplace. It tapped into the behavioral aspects of safety, emphasizing how employee and leader behavior led to safety outcomes. Like many promising tools, the widespread adoption of BBS led to myriad interpretations and applications, not all of which were effective.

In the early days of BBS, organizations, intrigued by the promise of improved safety, eagerly integrated it into their safety protocols. But rapid adoption led to several challenges.

The Overselling of BBS. One of the foremost initial issues was the overselling of what BBS could do for an organization. Many leaders were sold on BBS even if it wasn't the best fit for their workplace and company culture. Its universal appeal overshadowed the fact that customizing BBS to the workplace is what makes it effective. Effective BBS accounts for the nuances of an industry, the work, and the company's workforce. Adding to the issue of overselling, many safety practitioners and consultants also jumped on the BBS bandwagon. Some offered BBS services without a comprehensive grasp of behavioral science—the very foundation of *behavior*-based safety. Their superficial understanding led to implementations that, while well-intentioned, often missed the mark.

A Shift in Focus: Behavior Over Environment. In their haste to implement BBS, leaders, practitioners, and consultants stressed employee behavior, rather than the work environment surrounding that behavior. By focusing on employee behavior, they lost sight of a critical aspect of BBS: Behavior does not exist in a vacuum; if you wish to improve behavior, start with the environment. In practice, having a faulty focus meant that organizations tried to change an individual's actions rather than reengineer a job to reduce employees' exposure to hazardous conditions. Throughout this process, most organizations drifted away from the primary goal of using BBS: to foster a compassionate and caring work culture that looks out for everyone's safety and well-being.

0.2 BBS: The Proven Potential

Despite challenges with maintaining an effective focus during implementation, BBS, at its core, holds immense potential. When executed properly, BBS produces safe workplaces with fewer injuries (see Alavosius & Burleigh, 2022; Spigener et al., 2022). BBS encourages employees to actively communicate about safety issues, which fosters a culture of mutual respect and concern. In this culture of mutual respect, dialogue between employees and their supervisors improves, and safety becomes a collaborative effort.

0.3 Broadening the Perspective: Beyond Peer-to-Peer Observations

BBS is not just about peer-to-peer observations and coaching, although many people view it as such. It is a comprehensive, systems-based approach to safety that involves every level of an organization. From top-tier leadership to frontline employees, everyone plays a pivotal role.

Leadership is the bedrock of a BBS initiative. If an organization is to create a safe culture and produce positive outcomes from it, leadership must consistently support safety. Leaders need to engage in behaviors that demonstrate their value for safety. Taking the time to gain a deep understanding of behavioral science—how the environment influences behavior and what leadership does that promotes or hinders safety—is an important first step. It paves a path toward a more effective implementation of BBS.

In designing a BBS process, leaders must examine an organization's values. We think values are so important that we consider those an integral part of a successful and sustainable peer-based safety observation and feedback process, commonly referred to as behavior-based safety. With that in mind, we will use the term Values-Based Safety (VBS) throughout our discussion of implementing a BBS process. It is a VBS process when you formally ensure that your process is built on a defined set of values, such as a value for openness and honesty, respect among colleagues, and concern for the safety and well-being of everyone. See Chapter 10 for more on values and values clarification exercises.

0.4 The Way Forward: Values-Based Safety

The mission of this book is to help organizations rethink and redefine their approach to safety. First, VBS and a values-based orientation to safety culture are introduced. A culture of safety often starts with what leaders say and do. Leaders who are clear on their values around safety can help shape the safety values of their organization. They can communicate the values of the organization and engage in safety-critical behaviors that align with those values. A compassionate, caring culture is the result of safety values aligning with employee and leader behavior. The leadership section of this book discusses the importance of defining leadership behaviors that demonstrate leaders' personal value for safety, which is VBS for leaders. It provides an ideal foundation for implementing BBS as a VBS process.

After the introduction to VBS, chapters are dedicated to the details of creating, implementing, and sustaining a VBS process. Whether you choose to continue your BBS programs in their traditional form or decide to modify aspects of your programs based on what you learn in this book, keep employee well-being top of mind. Every employee deserves to work for an organization that values their health and safety and ensures they return home at the end of each workday. The discussion and clarification of values in VBS helps ensure that your process creates a culture of caring and concern built on compassion and encouragement, rather than on discipline and enforcement.

Thanks for joining us on this VBS journey.

CHAPTER 1

Understanding the Role of Behavior in Safety

Improving organizational safety is often a challenge, partly because of the excellent safety records of today's businesses and industries. In 2022, organizations lost an average of 1.2 workdays to injury for every 200,000 hours worked (National Safety Council Injury Facts, n.d.). On average, one in three American employees can expect to lose one workday to injury in 33 years of working. While these statistics are positive, excellent safety records can create complacency among employees and leaders—employees shortcut safety procedures, managers emphasize productivity over safety, and organizations reduce the frequency of observation and feedback. When incidents and injuries are low, maintaining 100% compliance with safety procedures is sometimes nearly impossible.

Behavior is heavily influenced by the events that immediately follow it. If taking a safety shortcut produces immediate comfort or convenience, that behavior is likely to continue in the future. Similarly, if employees are praised for achieving a particular result, regardless of how unsafe they were in getting there, those behaviors will also continue. When an organization experiences a serious incident, employees may temporarily perform their jobs more cautiously. But that often wears off if incidents remain low and the organization changes nothing else about the work environment.

An organization with an excellent safety record is not an environment free of unsafe acts. It means that unsafe acts haven't led to an incident detectable on safety reports and metrics. In fact, unsafe acts may occur at very high rates for the reasons mentioned earlier, and serious incidents that result from those actions are predictable.

This chapter reviews the history of behavior-based safety (BBS): how organizations have handled the behavioral side of safety issues and the results of those efforts.

1.1 Traditional Safety Programs

Most companies embrace the following programs and initiatives to improve safety compliance:
- informal feedback on an employee's compliance with safety procedures
- safety meetings and training
- safety awards
- safety audits

- written procedures
- special initiatives (posters, newsletters, off-the-job safety training, etc.)

All of these initiatives are important, often required components of a safety process. They contribute, to some degree, to safe performance. How consistently they are implemented affects the rate of injuries. But today, these elements alone often define only average safety efforts and outcomes. Every company does them. If a company does them well, it achieves an average level of safety within its industry. Relying on these components as the sole safety system of a company typically results in outcomes that are near the industry average. Some years, outcomes are better than average; other years, they are worse.

To reach excellence in safety, companies must do more than what is listed above. Very few companies that focus on unsafe conditions alone achieve consistently high levels of compliance from employees. Consistently high levels of safety compliance require attention to behavior and conditions.

1.2 Early Studies in Behavioral Safety

Early research from DuPont, a chemical company, suggested that safe behavior can prevent 80%–90% of worker injuries, while addressing unsafe conditions alone might prevent only 25%–30% of injuries. (More of its findings will be discussed in the next section.)

The following studies were done from the 1980s to mid-1990s, early in the history of BBS. In each of the cases described, companies had previously implemented the elements of traditional safety programs.

In 1980, a major U.S. drilling company reduced its Occupational Safety and Health Administration (OSHA) recordable injury rate by 48%. The company moved from performing at the industry average to the top five companies in its field. Its improvements were achieved by managers monitoring employee behavior. This early example demonstrates success in adding behavioral elements, even without the higher engagement of employees involved in today's implementation efforts (Figure 1.1).

In another case, a solids-handling chemical company with incident rates more or less typical of other companies at the time went from three or four OSHA-recordable injuries per year to no recordable injuries for a period of more than 18 months (Figure 1.2). This case comes from a union plant where hourly employees were "tired of being beaten up for safety" and initiated a behavioral approach on their own. They wanted to create a positive safety process that was employee driven.

In the final study, a division of a large pipeline company achieved zero injuries for 3 years, a vast improvement from the previous 6 years (Figure 1.3). This company initially planned to implement a self-observation process. During planning, they discovered that employee shifts could be scheduled to accommodate peer observations. This approach was highly effective.

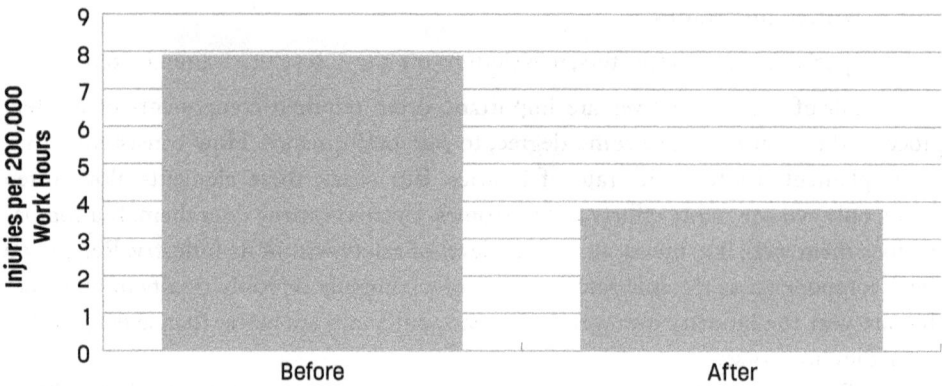

Figure 1.1. *Reduction in recordable injuries achieved by a drilling company using a BBS process.*

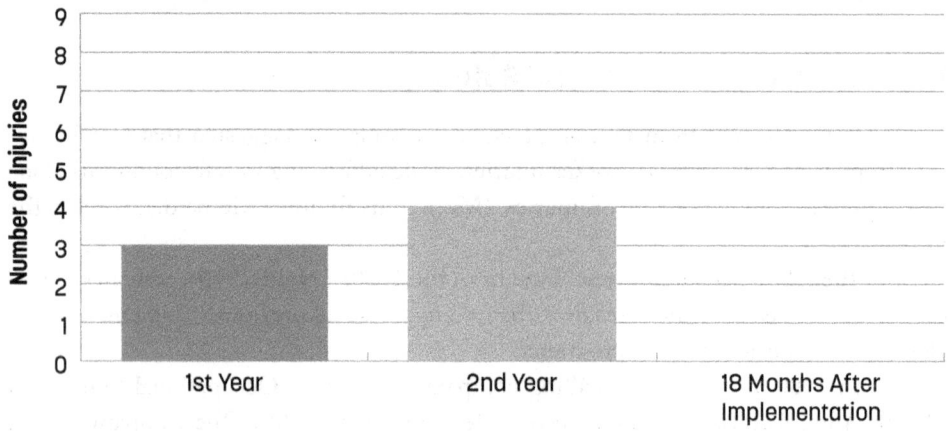

Figure 1.2. *Reduction in recordable injuries achieved by a chemical plant using a BBS process.*

Each case represents positive changes that came from moving away from traditional safety programs to a behavior-based approach. In experimental studies and in practice, these key elements form a foundation for success:

- implementing a behavioral observation and feedback process
- reviewing observation data
- setting improvement goals
- recognizing employees for their improvements and attainment of goals

These key elements seem so simple and logical that many people underestimate how difficult it is to consistently apply them in the workplace to create a BBS process. Leadership, in particular, often fails to anticipate the challenges of consistent application and does not put forth appropriate resources and support to make such approaches

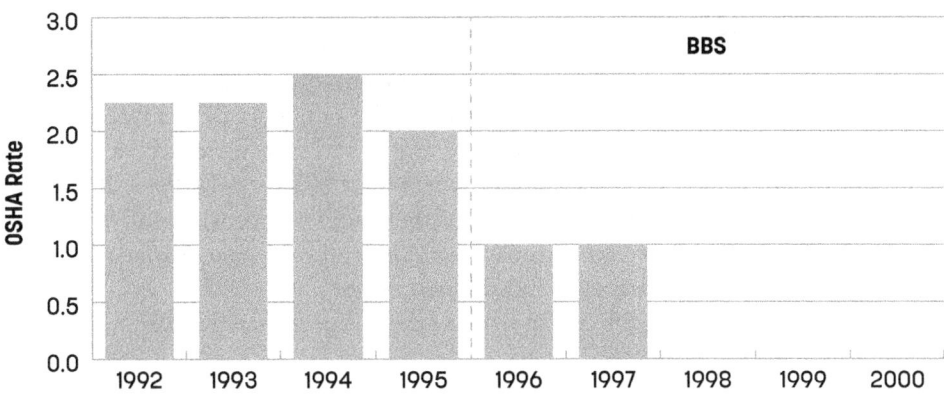

Figure 1.3. Reduction in recordable injuries achieved by a division of a pipeline company using a BBS process.

successful. The chapters on culture and leadership attempt to debunk myths about promoting safety at work and present deliberate actions and systems that create the kinds of results represented in the studies we have reviewed so far.

By 1999, more researchers reported consistent improvements using BBS. In the most comprehensive study of its time, Krause et al. (1999) reported statistically significant reductions in injury for 73 companies, comparing their success to industry averages as a control. Improvements steadily continued for 4 years following the start of a BBS implementation (Figure 1.4).

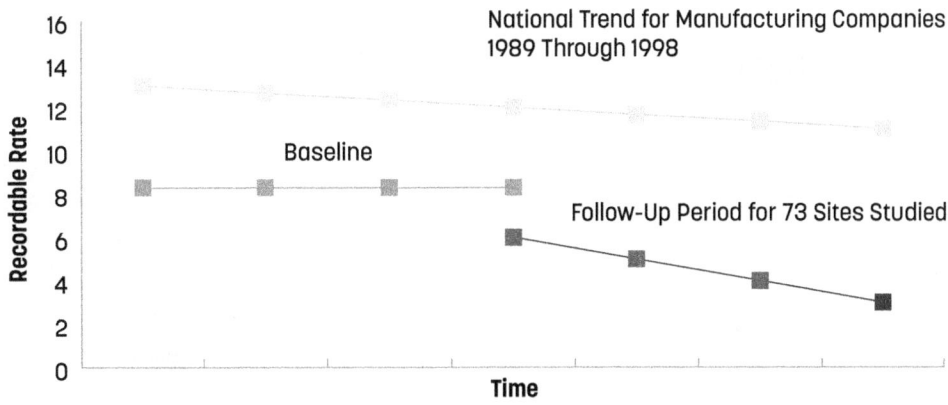

Figure 1.4. Reduction in incident rate among manufacturing companies implementing BBS. Adapted from Krause et al. (1999).

Before examining the BBS process in more detail, let us take a closer look at some of the key elements of modern safety improvement efforts.

1.3 DuPont's Success

During colonial times, the DuPont Company produced black powder. The DuPont family planned and built their factory on the side of a hill in a direction that would move the force of an explosion over the Delaware River. Their architectural plan protected the workers' homes and the village behind the factory (DuPont, 2019). The risks associated with their line of work meant they needed to consider safety in every decision; their lives depended on it. Today, DuPont continues to emphasize safety. The company also champions innovation in industrial safety.

DuPont was among the first to develop the following practices, among others:

- layered safety audits
- safety audits focused on behavioral factors rather than environmental housekeeping ones (e.g., handrail height, permits)
- specific feedback techniques during audits

Over a 10-year period, DuPont's study on lost-workday cases led to the development of these three practices and others. Its findings suggested that 96% of DuPont's injuries resulted from unsafe *acts* rather than unsafe *conditions* (Figure 1.5). This study supported findings in H. W. Heinrich's 1929 research, which suggested that 88% of all injuries were the outcome of unsafe employee actions rather than unsafe work conditions (Heinrich, 1959). (For additional details, see the discussion of Heinrich's work in Section 1.5.)

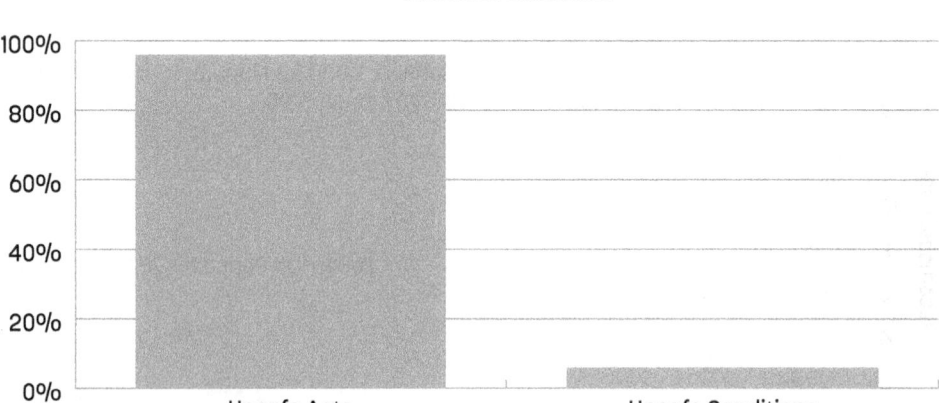

Figure 1.5. DuPont found that 96% of its lost-workday accidents during a 10-year period resulted from an unsafe act by an employee.

DuPont's findings helped the company refine its approach to safety, which evolved into its current-day Safety Training Observation Program (STOP). DuPont promotes STOP extensively, both within and outside the company. STOP involves a process of *layered safety audits* in which each layer of management typically conducts a weekly safety audit, cascading them throughout the organization. At the start of an audit, a site manager enters a work area and finds the area's manager. The two managers then complete a safety audit together. During a different week, the area manager chooses an area supervisor, and together, they conduct a safety audit. All managers conduct a formal audit every week in one of the work areas for which they are responsible. Of course, throughout the week, they conduct informal observations of safety practices and work conditions anytime they are in the work area.

During audits, managers and supervisors fill out a STOP card to document any unsafe acts they observe without documenting the names of the observed employees. As soon as it is convenient, they approach the employee who performed an unsafe act and ask two questions:

1. "What could happen?" This question prompts discussion about the unsafe actions the observer noted.
2. "How could you do the job safely?" This question prompts the employee to select the correct steps to avoid an unsafe act or incident.

Alongside STOP, DuPont emphasizes safety in other ways. The company has extensive materials to support safety meetings, planning sessions, and on- and off-the-job training. For example, Take Two is a safety program that encourages employees to take 2 minutes to consider the safety aspects of each job before they begin their work. DuPont also tracks off-the-job injuries that prevent employees from working their jobs as designed.

If a safety incident occurs and results in a lost workday, a company executive visits the worksite to personally review the incident and its investigation. They interview personnel involved in the incident and take appropriate actions to avoid the situation in the future. An employee's safety record follows them throughout their DuPont career.

DuPont's approach creates a "safety culture" that routinely results in the outcomes shown in Figure 1.6. For many years, DuPont had the best safety record in the chemical industry, and often, its record was twice as good as the next safest company. In 2020, the Bureau of Labor Statistics reported that the chemical industry experienced 1.8 cases of nonfatal occupational injuries and illnesses per 100 full-time equivalent (FTE) employees (U.S. Bureau of Labor Statistics, 2021). By comparison, in 2019, DuPont reported 0.311 cases of nonfatal injuries or illnesses per 100 FTE workers, clearly an exemplary level of safety (DuPont, n.d.).

Although DuPont's safety record is excellent, the average record of the entire chemical industry is also commendable. Figure 1.6 depicts this comparison and shows that chemical plant employees are at low risk of getting hurt—on average, they might be injured one time in 30 years of work. By the same measure, a DuPont employee would only suffer an injury requiring medical attention once in 100 years of work.

This is an example of how the low probability of injury makes improving safety a challenge. Since numbers are low, leadership puts attention on other areas of the business.

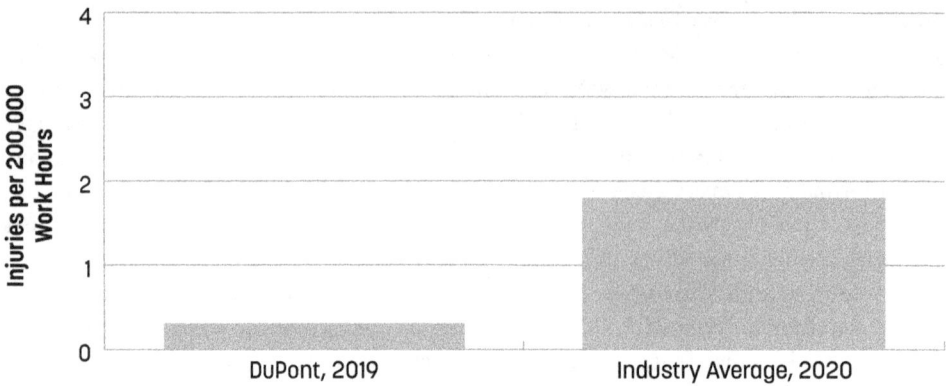

Figure 1.6. DuPont has an exemplary safety record in the chemical industry.

1.4 Our Findings

Our studies on the extent to which unsafe behavior contributes to injuries are similar to those found at DuPont. Over the past 40 years, we have analyzed injuries at hundreds of organizations to develop checklists that help prevent injuries. In most organizations, we found that behavior contributes to 86%–96% of all injuries. Figure 1.7 presents data from one of the studies we conducted with a client that replicates DuPont's findings that behavior contributes to 96% of all injuries.

These data do not suggest that employees are to blame for 96% of their injuries. Our behavioral perspective suggests that all behavior is a function of the environment in which it occurs. Therefore, unsafe work behavior is the result of (1) the physical environment, (2) the social environment, and (3) workers' experience within those environments.

Several other lessons were learned from this analysis. First, when we examined serious injuries and fatalities, almost all of them fell into the category of "behavior and conditions." That is, serious injuries and fatalities most often came from a combination of engaging in unsafe behaviors and being in unsafe conditions. Safety professionals commonly discuss the

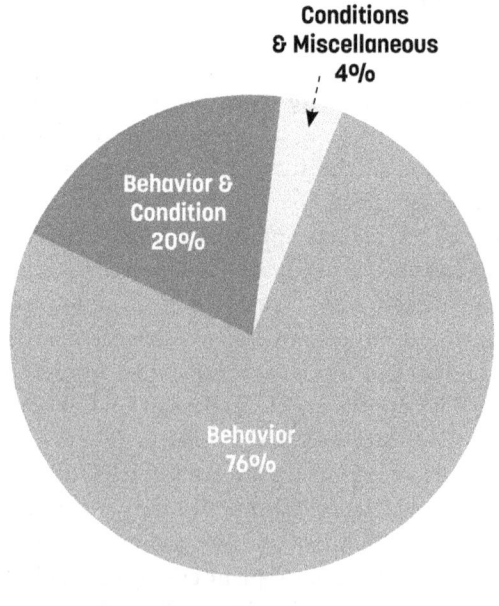

Figure 1.7. These data represent the extent to which behavior contributed to injuries for one of our clients.

chain of events that lead to an injury. Some of the links of the chain are behaviors; others are conditions. We can prevent many injuries by breaking any one of those links.

In our experience, one story stands out as a clear example of how behavior and conditions interact. Early one morning at a 40-year-old coker unit at a major oil refinery in Lake Charles, Louisiana, a train derailed from the tracks and exposed a 5-foot pit under a grate used as a walkway. (Coker units are huge facilities from which finished coke, a coal-like substance, is cut from huge drums and unloaded into rail cars.) Workers immediately placed barricades on each side of the railroad tracks to indicate there was danger on the walkway. A few hours later, a pump failed and flooded the area with boiling water. Three employees, who were just beginning their shift for the day, approached the scene. These employees had not been briefed about the train derailment and resulting pit that occurred earlier in the day. When the employees approached the area, the flooding water overshadowed the open pit, and the employees proceeded beyond the barricades. They assumed these were intended to prevent employees from walking through the water. Two of the three employees walked around the area. The other employee, wearing knee-high rubber boots, walked around the barricade, stepped between the railroad tracks, and fell to his chest in boiling water. He suffered significant burns and was off the job for over 14 months.

This story depicts how treacherous conditions and unsafe behaviors contribute to an unimaginable injury. Let's review the chain of events: The barricades were inadequate after the area flooded. Incoming employees were not briefed about the condition of the unit. The injured employee walked around one of the barricades, and his coworkers allowed him to do so. Prior to these events, management cut budget funds to upgrade the unit, which would have prevented the unit from flooding. Instead of spending the money to upgrade, management built a platform where operators could control valves when flooding occurred. It was a bandage solution.

The point of this story is to show that breaking any one of the links in the chain of events could have prevented this serious incident from occurring.

1.5 The Safety Triangle

DuPont's emphasis on correcting unsafe acts, rather than fixing conditions alone, aligns with the lowest section of Heinrich's safety triangle depicted in Figure 1.8. DuPont's data lend credibility to Heinrich's work, even though various authors later criticized his methodology. Heinrich's original triangle reporting the ratio of injuries was expanded to extend the concept of a ratio of events, as presented in Figure 1.9. Today, the ratios presented in such diagrams are not considered useful in predicting injuries. Very simply, no fixed ratio applies to all organizations, but the model still has descriptive value (McSween & Moran, 2017). While we do not know the ratio in any given organization and cannot predict one value from the others, the ratios help us understand the importance of addressing the bottom rows of the triangle. Further, the triangle suggests that because most of the time employees do not get injured, unsafe acts are part of the problem. When employees perform an unsafe act and are not injured, they become just a bit more complacent about the risk involved in the shortcuts they take. This problem is discussed in more detail in Section 1.6.

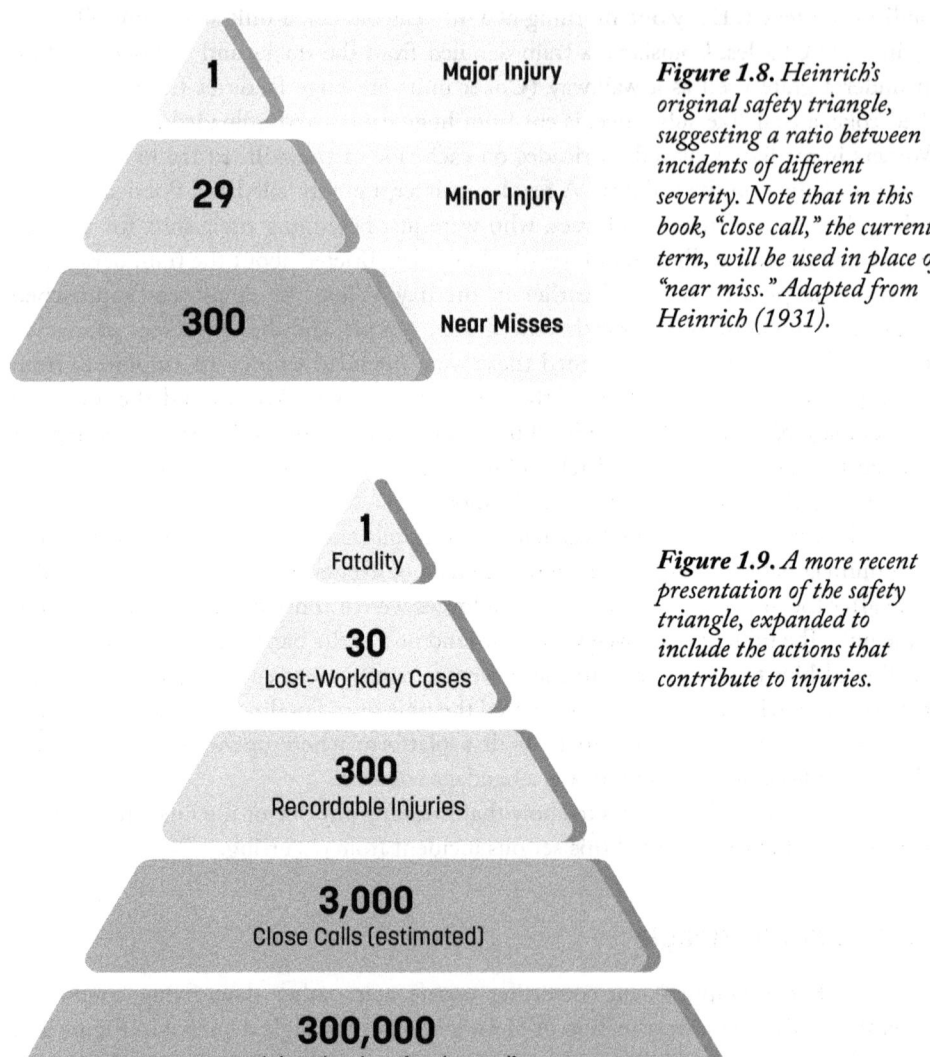

Figure 1.8. Heinrich's original safety triangle, suggesting a ratio between incidents of different severity. Note that in this book, "close call," the current term, will be used in place of "near miss." Adapted from Heinrich (1931).

Figure 1.9. A more recent presentation of the safety triangle, expanded to include the actions that contribute to injuries.

Geller (1988) suggests that intervening on unsafe acts and conditions alone is a reactive approach: You are intervening on what caused the other remaining sections of the triangle. As an alternative, Geller suggests a preventive method focused on increasing and maintaining safe acts.

Reber and Wallin's findings (1983) support Geller's logic. In a heavy manufacturing environment, the authors used an observational procedure to measure safe and unsafe acts, the rate of injuries, and time lost due to injuries. Reber and Wallin reported a significantly negative correlation between the percentage of safe behaviors and the rate of injuries and lost-workday injuries (i.e., fatality, permanent disability). In other words, a higher rate of injuries occurred when people performed fewer safe behaviors in the workplace. This suggests that increasing safe behavior should result in lower incident and injury rates. The empirical studies found in the previous sections confirm the effectiveness of this preventive approach.

1.6 Complacency

In safety, we find that employees become complacent when they are neither rewarded for performing safe acts nor fear the risk of getting injured from performing unsafe acts. People who fear injury work safely to avoid the pain, suffering, or lost wages that come from injury. If the risk of injury is low, employees may no longer believe it is possible to get hurt and thus begin to shortcut their jobs: They experience the immediate rewards of efficiency, comfort, and ease. If fatalities, lost-workday injuries, or first aid cases are unlikely to occur, unsafe acts and conditions are likely to prevail.

In situations where the probability of getting injured is high, complacency is not a problem. Welding is a good example. We seldom have a problem getting welders to use appropriate eye protection. In the first seconds of turning on a welding machine, sparks, splatter, and fumes are emitted and can irritate the welder's eyes. Unfailingly, using a welding machine produces immediate risk, so welders wear eye and body protection.

In other areas of work, harm is less likely to occur, which is the premise of the safety triangle. With some jobs, you can perform unsafe acts in unsafe conditions for extended periods of time without a close call, first aid incident, or fatality. The low probability of events is too small to sustain a consistent level of safe work practices. Each time employees shortcut a safety procedure and avoid injury, they lose a bit of the fear that typically motivates people to work safely.

Clinical psychologists use a technique called *systematic desensitization* to help people overcome phobias or irrational fears of flying, snakes, spiders, heights, and so forth. The desensitization process involves gradually exposing the person to the item or activity they fear. The same process seems to occur in the natural environment and works against our efforts to promote safe work habits.

For example, when an employee first works at height, the fear of falling provides strong motivation to consistently use appropriate fall protection. After years on the job, an employee often has greater comfort with heights and does not fear falling. In turn, the employee is more likely to work without appropriate fall protection. The BBS process is designed to offset that phenomenon.

1.7 Safety as a Team Process

To improve safety and fight complacency, many organizations establish safety initiatives that involve many employees in safety improvement. It's an approach similar to the one used in quality improvement. The idea is that if employees have ownership over the safety process, they are more likely to abide by the process.

To execute this approach, teams of employees are formed that are then directed to find safety problems and develop solutions to address those problems. Each team has control over the improvement efforts initiated in its work area. Not only do employees have greater ownership within this approach, but they also have accountability for safety initiatives, which shifts the responsibilities from management to employees. This shift reduces the perceived threat of punishment found in mandated safety programs and results in a more positive work environment.

But team approaches aren't perfect; they struggle with several problems. First, teams often shift their priorities as they begin to feel safety is under control. This results in a cycle of incidents. Figure 1.10 explains this phenomenon. When attention drifts away from safety, safe behavior also drifts. This problem is found in team-based safety efforts whether the team consists of managers or employees.

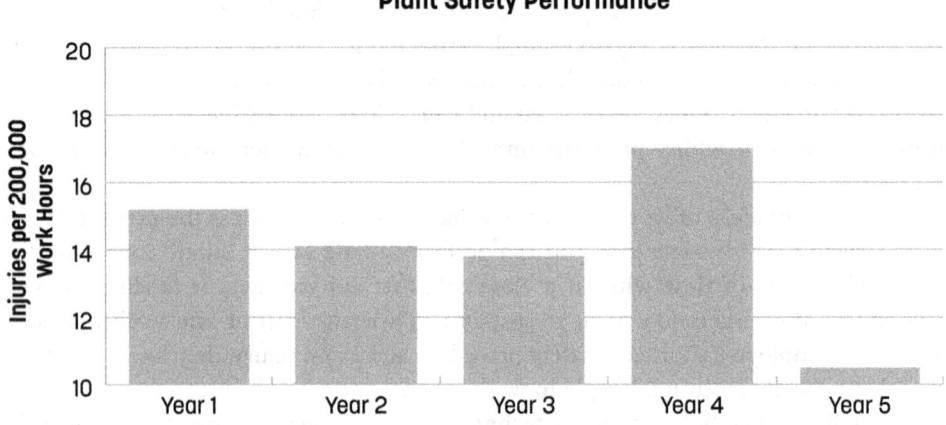

Figure 1.10. A cycle of accidents often characterizes safety improvement efforts.

Figure 1.10 presents data for a plant with safety teams comprising managers and supervisors. Teams were given responsibility for the continuous improvement of safety in different areas of the facility. The graph shows the teams' successes and the cycle of injuries that prompted renewed interest in safety. In some cases, companies using traditional safety programs experience a regular cycle of injuries. In other cases, variation in injuries correlates with inconsistent levels of attention paid to safety.

Teams can also struggle to design a process. They may spend inordinate amounts of time identifying safety problems and, in doing so, either generate suboptimal solutions or find new problems for other people to resolve. Additional problems identified by teams usually result from a poorly designed team process that fails to achieve the following:

- ongoing communication with management
- a structured process for selecting problems and developing solutions
- a good understanding of how to deal with human performance issues

Employee teams seldom know about or have skills in proven safety improvement methods, such as those in the behavioral research on safety improvement. Without specific training in such methods, teams create systems and procedures that do not build sustainable, positive changes. Instead, they repeat the types of programs they have seen in the past (e.g., safety posters or safety awards). Teams may also hyperfocus on work conditions and propose expensive changes to facilities or equipment. Sometimes they simply compile a laundry list of safety items that need attention.

Our experience suggests that the team approach to safety can achieve an incident rate in the range of 5 to 10 recordable incidents per 200,000 hours worked, for certain industries. Organizations in which management pays frequent attention to safety and implements a traditional behavior-based safety process consistently achieve results better than 5 to 10 recordable incidents per 200,000 hours worked.

1.8 Common Problems With Typical Safety Efforts

Current safety improvement efforts also suffer from a common set of problems:
- Employees may encounter severe consequences for reporting incidents.
- Safety awards are not related to on-the-job behavior.
- Management or staff make all the safety-related plans and decisions.
- Organizations rely on punishment to reduce unsafe acts.

Employees may encounter severe consequences for reporting incidents. The foundation of a safety process is the accurate reporting of incidents. If people are not reporting when an incident or injury occurs—no matter how small—leadership cannot improve safety programs.

Underreporting is a problem that organizations experience when formal or informal policies penalize managers or employees for reporting an injury. In this kind of environment, even the well-intentioned supervisor may listen to an employee's claim and respond with something like this: "It's really nothing serious. I wouldn't think twice about this kind of injury." In other cases, an injured employee may lie and report that the injury occurred at home rather than at work, especially if the injury does not require time off.

Employees may feel similar pressure not to report minor incidents if safety awards and incentives are significant. This is often an issue with systems that provide individual awards based on the group's performance. Such incentive programs contribute to peer pressure that can encourage false reporting and thereby give the appearance that the rate of recordable injuries is going down. Organizations should look at steady rates of lost workdays as red flags representing people underreporting incidents, as the organization's clean record does not align with injuries causing missed work.

Every incident—whether an employee grabs a bandage and submits a first aid case, or a more serious incident takes place—is a lesson in teaching the organization what is and is not working. Minor situations, such as an employee needing a bandage, should be studied before they can contribute to a larger problem, such as a crushed hand. But to learn from minor incidents, they must be properly reported. Poorly designed awards programs and the threat of disciplinary action can jeopardize the integrity of systems designed to document such events. Unfortunately, some less-than-knowledgeable consultants continue to recommend the use of such safety incentives in ways that expose their clients to added liability.

One of our prospective clients had arranged an incentive program that provided a $25 bonus for employees of work groups that went 4 months without an injury. They also received 4 paid hours off if their work group went 6 months without a recordable injury. Predictably, the rate of recordable injuries went down while the rate of lost-workday injuries remained unchanged. The incentive program reduced minor injury reporting but did not encourage employees to work more safely.

The outcomes of court decisions in recent decades are one reason simplistic approaches, such as easy-to-implement incentive programs, continue. In the 1990s, an employee in Texas won a worker's compensation case against an employer that had a safety bingo program that discouraged employees from accurately reporting injuries (*Paragon Hotel Corp. v. Ramirez*, 1990). In a case from the early 2000s, a court ruled that a cash incentive discouraging employees from reporting on-the-job injuries could provide evidence of an employee being terminated for filing for worker's compensation on an incident not reported in accordance with company policy (*Glass v. Amber Inc.*, 2002). An incentive knowingly or inadvertently encouraging employees to hide incidents can increase a company's liability when an employee is injured. Safety incentive systems also increase an employee's ability to successfully file a compensation claim well after the normal allotted time.

Safety awards are not related to on-the-job behavior. Most approaches to safety awards do not reinforce safe behavior on the job. Instead, the typical program bases its awards on individual or team performance. Individual awards are usually earned after working a month, quarter, or year without an injury. Awards based on group performance are generally earned at the same cadence for working without injury to anyone in the group. Companies already track injuries for regulatory purposes, so this type of awards system easily leverages that data. The problem with these approaches is that they base awards on outcome measures rather than on process measures and safe behaviors.

Many employees roll the dice with this approach: They take shortcuts that allow them to complete jobs quickly and comfortably. Today's low incident rates mean most employees won't experience an injury. Employees working unsafely do so alongside fellow employees who always follow safety procedures—wearing a safety harness above 4 feet, wearing appropriate protective equipment, or getting appropriate permits. At the end of the year, if no injuries occur, the safest and least safe employees earn the same award. In fact, the likelihood of receiving the award is roughly the same as the likelihood of not getting hurt. In a typical U.S. company, an unsafe employee could receive a safety award 32 out of 33 years of work, on average. In this way, safety awards become little more than a gift to safe employees and those who take risks. While the awards promote some awareness of safety, they do little to motivate employees to work safely in the future.

Management or staff makes all plans and decisions regarding safety. Many safety programs are led by executives, managers, and supervisors. They may assign hourly employees to participate on safety committees, but managers and supervisors are responsible for enforcing safety rules and procedures. Many companies use some version of a layered safety audit, like that of DuPont. Managers have the responsibility for enforcing the audit and correcting the actions of employees, which invariably comes as a form of punishment. Manager-led programs result in employees relying on their managers to ensure safe practices occur rather than watching out for their coworkers' safety. Employees have little motivation to achieve safety improvements and don't feel a sense of accomplishment from improvements in their work areas. Employees in these organizations see other people responsible for safety and become inactive in the safety process.

Organizations rely on punishment to reduce unsafe acts. Safety programs typically rely on punishment-based approaches to address safety problems. In these organizations, punishment is used to reduce unsafe acts rather than encourage safe actions. The problem with such an approach is that the consequence (punishment) cannot be delivered until an unsafe act occurs. Waiting for an unsafe act increases the risk of injury—the very issue we try to avoid. Focusing on safe acts, on the other hand, reduces the risk of injury. Punishment also has side effects that are not readily apparent.

1.9 Problems With Punishment

We use punishment for a simple reason: It works and does so quickly. The immediate payoff for the person using punishment increases the odds that they will use it in the future. This is particularly true of people in positions of power.

You can see punishment everywhere: in homes, schools, communities, and at work. When a child makes too much noise, their parent may respond with yelling, threats, or physical forms of punishment. The child becomes quiet as a result, and the parent's behavior is reinforced. The noise went away. In the future, the parent is likely to use punishment to resolve other annoyances. The same dynamic occurs in adult relationships: The critical spouse punishes a behavior of their spouse or the supervisor punishes a behavior of an employee, and the behavior stops. Too often, punishment characterizes a relationship.

On the other hand, using positive feedback results in future improvements, but it doesn't have the same immediate impact. For instance, when a manager provides positive feedback to an employee for adhering to a safety protocol, the result of that consequence is visible in the future. If the employee continues using the safety protocol, we know that the consequence was effective. For busy leaders, managers, and supervisors, punishment may seem like a better option—an immediate change in the moment. But too much punishment or negative feedback can affect relationships and morale.

Overusing punishment in the safety process has several disadvantages:

- Punishment must be severe enough to get the behavior to stop.
- Punishment is only effective if the punisher is present.
- Punishment often teaches the wrong lesson.
- Punishment damages relationships and suppresses people's involvement in the safety process.
- Punishment runs contrary to the philosophy of quality improvement efforts.
- Punishment is difficult to maintain.

Punishment must be severe enough to get the behavior to stop. People behave as they do for a reason. Their behavior is understood by examining what occurred before it and what will occur after it. If an employee takes a safety shortcut, the event is followed by comfort or convenience. If you wish to punish that behavior, the punishment must be severe enough to get it to stop and be applied consistently. If not, the natural incentives (convenience, comfort) will win every time. Research on punishment, outside of safety, supports this notion (Malott et al., 2000).

To consistently apply punishment, managers must supervise carefully. If they aren't supervising, employees will take risks because their chance of being punished is low. In today's economy, most companies cannot afford to maintain a management staff large enough to ensure compliance with safety procedures and provide careful enough supervision to dole out punishment.

Policies stating that employees must work safely to remain employed also do not lower the chance of employees taking shortcuts or engaging in unsafe behaviors. Instead, such policies have two undesirable effects: (1) They discourage employees from reporting minor incidents and close calls, and (2) they discourage frank discussions about factors that contribute to injury.

Punishment is only effective if the punisher is present. Punishment only works when applied consistently. If management is unable to supervise every moment of a shift, the punisher (i.e., supervisor) is not always present. For punishment to work, the punisher must be present when the behavior occurs. Employees quickly learn to follow procedures only when certain supervisors or managers are nearby. They find times when they can bend the rules without fear of correction or discipline. The adage that "when the cat's away, the mice will play" directly pertains to this concept. Educational systems often struggle with the same problem. When a teacher relies on punishment as their primary motivator for good behavior, misbehavior takes over when the teacher leaves the classroom for any length of time. With leaner management, organizations must encourage employees to self-manage and share responsibilities for all aspects of safety.

Punishment often teaches the wrong lesson. Punishment teaches people how to avoid being punished instead of how to perform what is desired. Returning to our classroom example, students learned to be quiet when the teacher was present. Employees learn to generate reasonable excuses to explain why they act in a certain way. When it comes to reporting, an employee learns not to report minor injuries or close calls, and it affects the accuracy of incidents that are reported. An employee who gets something in their eye may claim to have been wearing safety glasses, for fear of punishment if they were to tell the truth.

Punishment damages relationships and suppresses people's involvement in the safety process. People dislike those who routinely criticize or punish them. Supervisors who rely on punishment harm their relationships with employees. As a result, employees may respond with emotional behavior, such as counterattacks, avoiding the punisher, or getting even. The adage that "what goes around comes around" applies to people who use punishment. When someone is publicly criticized or punished in a meeting, they may retaliate in the meeting or afterward. Punishment can lead to slow or poor-quality work and a lack of teamwork. It can also lead an employee to seek revenge by doing exactly what the supervisor told them to do even in inappropriate circumstances. Punishment destroys relationships, which are the bedrock of teamwork and the safety process.

Cooperation and problem-solving suffer on teams when punishment is frequently used. Rather than problem-solve or work diligently to improve the operation, people who have been criticized may become defensive. They begin making excuses, rationalizing, or explaining why they could not do the work differently.

Managers, instead of relying on punishment, must create a work environment that encourages personal responsibility and minimizes blame. Damaged relationships prevent management and employees from partnering for safety.

Punishment runs contrary to the philosophy of quality improvement efforts. Deming (2018), one of the gurus of the quality movement, exhorted companies to "drive out fear, so that everyone may work effectively" (p. 22) and "remove barriers that rob … workers of pride in workmanship" (p. 342). Overuse of punishment is one of the barriers to quality efforts. In an environment motivated by fear, employees work because they have to, not because they want to. When people do something because of threats, nagging, or criticism, they seldom feel a sense of accomplishment or pride in the quality of work they produce.

Punishment is difficult to maintain. Audits that may result in punishment are no fun for the auditor or those being audited. Managers generally do not like punishing employees, and employees do not like being punished. Corrective feedback is almost always punishing, regardless of the method or severity of its delivery.

Instead of punishment, organizations should learn other methods for promoting safe behavior. For safety efforts to effectively improve outcomes, leadership and employees must partner and share the responsibility. When people across the organization work together to promote safety, they are more likely to find ways to create safe environments for everyone.

1.10 Appropriate Use of Punishment

While an overreliance on punishment is a serious problem, discipline does have a place in safety programs. Punishment works and works quickly. If employees are doing something that endangers themselves or others, they must stop immediately. If employees repeatedly violate a safety policy, the company must review their understanding of the policy and their ability to adhere to and align their actions with the policy. The employees must understand that their career and health are at risk and change their behavior. Whether it comes in the form of corrective feedback or more stringent disciplinary action, enacting punishment is appropriate for life-threatening situations.

Some practitioners suggest that disciplinary action is rarely appropriate in safety situations. Geller (1997) believes employees should only be disciplined if they intentionally break a safety rule. The problem with this recommendation is that the only way to know if a worker intentionally violated a safety policy is to ask them. When faced with the prospect of disciplinary action, few workers are likely to admit to the unsafe act.

In society, we expect people to be responsible for both knowing and complying with laws. For example, not knowing the speed limit is not a sufficient reason to avoid a speeding ticket. We expect people to be conscious of their activities, whether driving at the speed limit or following safety rules. Disciplinary action is appropriate for violating a requirement such as lockout/tagout, even if the employee did not make a conscious decision to take the risk. Of course, this assumes the company's procedure is clear and employees have received adequate training and support for lockout/tagout.

Every employee needs to know their company's "rules of life" and understand that breaking any of those rules will result in disciplinary action. Rules of life are those that the company will always enforce. They are rules critical for protecting lives. Supervisors and managers who fail to enforce rules of life are subject to disciplinary action.

When considering whether to punish or reward, keep these things in mind: Punishment produces immediate feedback, but when used excessively, it can degrade relationships and become ineffective over time. It is often effective to reserve punishment for extreme situations, such as those that endanger health or life. In comparison, rewards have less immediate effects than punishment, but they lead to positive relationships and real and lasting safety in the workplace.

1.11 Components of a Proven Safety Process

Research from the past 40 decades helps us identify key components of a more positive system for addressing safety. Two noted researchers in the field of behavioral psychology, Judith Komaki and Beth Sulzer-Azaroff, identified several features of an effective safety process. Komaki, Sulzer-Azaroff, and their associates demonstrated and proved the effectiveness of using these components to improve safety:

- a behavioral observation and feedback process
- formal review of observation data
- improvement goals
- reinforcement for improvement and goal attainment

Both researchers began their studies by pinpointing safe behaviors in the workplace that would reduce the likelihood of an incident. Next, they developed an observation procedure to provide feedback to employees on the pinpointed behaviors. Managers reviewed observation data, set improvement goals, and arranged reinforcement in the form of celebrated recognitions. (See References for a list of Komaki and Sulzer-Azaroff's research; Sulzer-Azaroff & Austin, 2000, provide an extensive review of behavioral safety literature.)

Since those studies were conducted, research has been done on the importance of individual components of a safety system. But research on the effectiveness of individual components is difficult to conduct in practice, as each component only partially contributes to the effectiveness of the intervention package.

Komaki, Sulzer-Azaroff, and colleagues conducted three studies that examined components that have implications for the design of an effective safety improvement effort. The first study proved that on-the-job feedback in conjunction with safety training produced a much higher level of safety compliance than training alone (Komaki et al., 1980). In the second study, researchers looked at what effect goal setting had on performance (Fellner & Sulzer-Azaroff, 1985). This study showed that explicitly setting goals improves the effectiveness of safety feedback; whether those goals are set by the supervisors or employee was not a critical factor. The third study examined whether observations should be performed by supervisors or safety personnel (Fox & Sulzer-Azaroff, 1990). This study found that conducting safety observations and providing feedback was more important than who conducted the observations.

Tom Krause, a well-known figure in BBS, documented the first long-term successes in behavioral safety. His data demonstrated that 73 companies were able to sustain BBS for 5 years. This study was significant because earlier interventions appeared to be short lived, often only lasting for the duration of the study (Krause et al., 1999).

Multiple studies have documented the long-term effectiveness of intervention packages that include behavioral observation, feedback, improvement goals, and reinforcement for those improvements. Empirical data on the components of this approach further demonstrate the importance of those components in maximizing safety performance.

1.12 More Recent Research Studies

After 40 years of research, Alavosius and Burleigh (2022) concluded in their book that surveys the application of behavioral psychology in organizations that BBS is an established and replicable technology.

Studies have continued to replicate and expand existing data in BBS. A report by Spigener et al. (2022) showed similar results to those of Krause et al. (1999). Across 88 organizations, all of them demonstrated statistically significant reductions in injuries (see Figure 1.11 on the following page). Spigener et al.'s study included a statistical analysis of the design considerations for safety programs that we present in the chapters on design.

In a separate analysis, 76 sites with 5 years of safety culture survey data reported significant improvements in safety culture based on survey responses (see Figure 1.12). After 6 years, organizations showed a full standard deviation improvement in overall

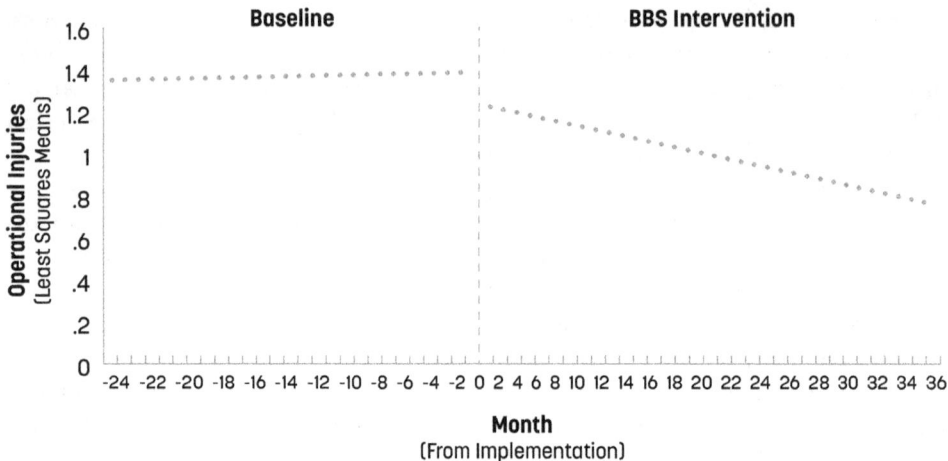

Figure 1.11. *Least squares means of injuries in 88 organizations, showing 2-year baseline versus 36 months following BBS implementation (Spigener et al., 2022).*

survey scores. Figure 1.13 presents the categories of that survey. Notice that the first six factors are related to the importance of relationships and trust. Only the last three factors are specific to safety.

The changes in culture scores suggest important changes in the perception of employees. Figure 1.13 shows baseline versus final scores for each category in the survey. Notice the improvements shown on the last three safety-related items: 21% more employees reported that their organizations valued safety, 15% more employees were more likely to talk with their supervisor about safety issues, and 30% of employees

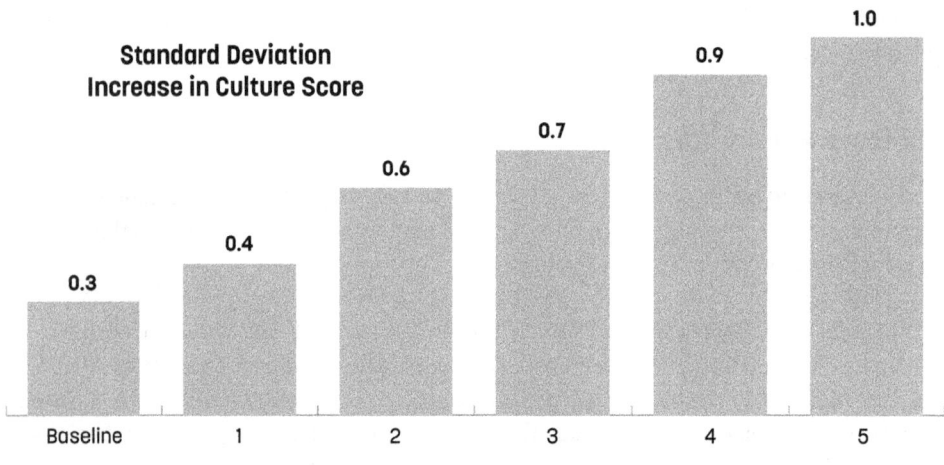

Figure 1.12. *Changes in culture survey scores occurring 5 years after BBS implementation (Spigener et al., 2022).*

were more likely to talk with other employees about safety issues. These data suggest that BBS contributes to significant changes in the culture of organizations that implement it successfully. Chapter 3 addresses culture in greater detail.

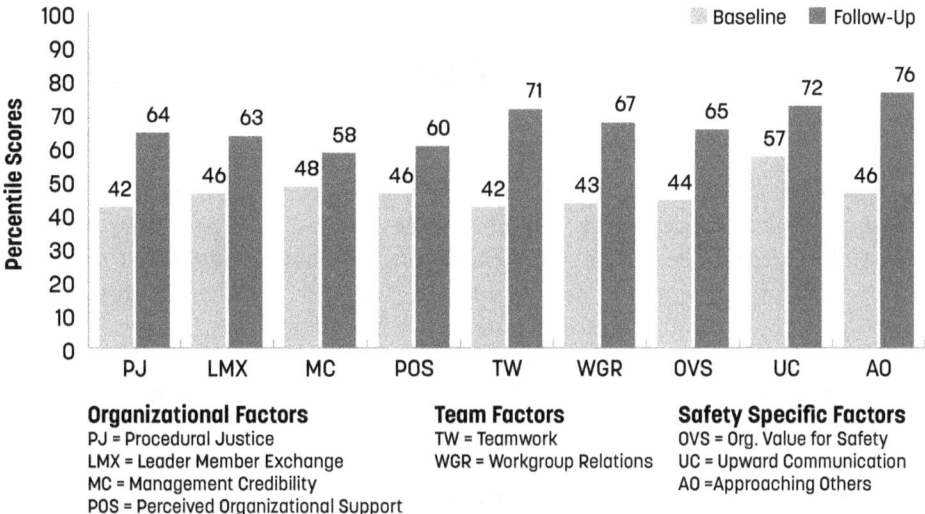

Organizational Factors
PJ = Procedural Justice
LMX = Leader Member Exchange
MC = Management Credibility
POS = Perceived Organizational Support

Team Factors
TW = Teamwork
WGR = Workgroup Relations

Safety Specific Factors
OVS = Org. Value for Safety
UC = Upward Communication
AO = Approaching Others

Figure 1.13. The percentage of responses in each category 5 years after successful BBS implementation (Spigener et al., 2022).

CHAPTER 2

The Vision

In Chapters 3 and 4, the principles and tactics of building an organization's leadership capabilities and safety culture will be detailed. The remaining chapters, which outline steps for designing and implementing a Values-Based Safety (VBS) process, are built around strong leadership and the culture that leadership creates. Poor leadership and poor company culture undermine safety efforts every time.

This edition of the book places greater emphasis on VBS leadership, and the reason for that is twofold. VBS leadership is important for all organizations that have potential hazards in the workplace. For some organizations, leadership alone is sufficient to keep employees safe. For other organizations, VBS leadership is a necessary prerequisite for the VBS process to thrive. When leadership is strong, it serves as a building block for employee engagement.

This chapter presents two scenarios illustrating how an organization that includes VBS can positively influence employees. Scenario one depicts safety leadership on its own, without using a full-blown behavior-based safety (BBS) process. Scenario two combines VBS leadership with a VBS process. Both hypothetical examples provide a big-picture look at the vision we're aiming for. As you read the scenarios, consider if they align with the current safety efforts of your organization.

2.1 Scenario One: An Organization With Strong VBS Leadership

Friday meetings

Rick Gallant, plant manager at Big Tex Production, holds a staff meeting every Friday. Department managers attend and participate in these sessions. Unlike typical organizations where the talk about safety ends once safety metrics have been reviewed, Rick's group takes the time to go deeper.

First, the safety manager presents injury reports and close-call data. Afterward, the group generates a list of actions for addressing issues that may put someone at risk of severe injury or death.

Next, each department manager shares a weekly update, reporting on the actions they took to promote safety during the previous week. They also indicate how those actions demonstrate a personal value for safety. After the department managers give their updates, the managers describe, in equally specific detail, what actions they plan to take to promote safety in the coming week.

Monday meetings

On Mondays, the company starts with a layer of meetings involving supervisors. Supervisors carry out safety observations to ensure employees are compliant with safety procedures. In these meetings, supervisors scrutinize the past week's incidents and outline their safety plans for the week ahead. Special focus is paid to jobs that demand lockout/tagout procedures, fall protection, and confined-space entry—tasks Big Tex Production has identified as high risk for leading to severe injuries.

Daily meetings

Every day, supervisors huddle to plan their actions for the day. Part of the huddle is a discussion of unexpected safety issues from the previous day and hazards expected to occur on the current day. This dialogue invites input from everyone by providing a platform for employees to voice concerns they have.

It should be noted that outside of team meetings, Rick makes it a point to walk through the plant multiple times a week. He talks with supervisors and employees, particularly those on the safety committee. He asks about their current projects and their concerns, and he always offers to support their efforts and improve conditions.

Situations

One day, Brad, the day-shift maintenance supervisor, hears about an unscheduled shutdown on press number one. Brad heads to the area and finds maintenance mechanic Sally and press operator Billy Joe in a heated conversation. Sally advocates for a quick repair without a full lockout. She's concerned about meeting delivery schedules. "Besides," she says, "we've always done it this way. Otherwise, we'd have to shut the whole line down. We can't isolate one press from the other machines. They run on the same circuit." Billy Joe insists they shut the electrical power off for the entire line to promote safety as they address the one press.

Brad supports Billy Joe's stance and immediately contacts the production supervisor. Together, they schedule the best time to shut down the line and safely repair press number one. Brad follows up with Sally about the incident. They decide to work with the electrical department to plan a project that allows them to lockout each press independently when issues arise.

Interactions such as these occur weekly. They form the backbone of the robust safety culture at Big Tex. Every individual—from leadership to frontline workers—understands and acts on the value of safety. When profits challenge the company, their commitment to safety remains steadfast. Safety is a backbone value for everyone.

Scenario one describes the importance of VBS leadership. Big Tex Production isn't implementing a full-blown BBS process, but the attention to safety from leadership promotes a culture that ensures safe outcomes.

2.2 Scenario Two: An Organization Implementing a VBS Process

Observation process

At the end of Monday's safety meeting, Randy, a safety representative for the maintenance unit, announces he will conduct an observation of the maintenance crew working in unit one.

On Tuesday afternoon, Randy finds another maintenance employee, Jim, to join him for the observation. "Come with me to unit one. I want to do a safety observation of that crew and would like you to see how these are done. Eventually, you can do them on your own. Your participation is totally voluntary, but it'll help us maintain a safe workplace."

Jim agrees to go with Randy to conduct the observation. As they head to unit one, Randy and Jim discuss the fact that soon everyone in the plant, including the site manager and supervisors, will finish observation training and volunteers will conduct safety observations. Everyone will partner in the safety effort and share responsibility for achieving safe outcomes.

Randy and Jim arrive at unit one, where Randy takes out a detailed, one-page checklist. First, they scan the work area to locate where the employees are working and check for hazards. Next, Randy explains the observation procedure to Jim. They begin the procedure by asking themselves this question: "What do we see these employees doing that could cause someone to get hurt?" They note one such practice on the checklist. They continue to review the checklist and note where they see safe practices and areas of concern. No names are recorded on the checklist.

At the end of the observation, Randy and Jim approach the observed employees and review the checklist with them: "We noticed all of you were using personal protective equipment. Your work areas are neat, your tools are well organized, and you use the right tools for the work you're doing. That's great! We did notice a lack of barricades to prevent people from passing through your work area." Randy and Jim take time to answer a few questions about the situation and then ask employees to rope off the work area.

The two men return to Randy's office, where Randy puts the completed checklist into a three-ring binder. The two men spend 20 minutes completing the observation and documentation process. After Jim returns to work, Randy spends another 5 minutes entering checklist data into the company's safety software.

Weekly meeting

At the safety meeting on Monday morning, Randy shows employees data from the previous week's safety observations. He acknowledges what the group is doing well and encourages them to keep up the good work. He then turns to the issue of barricading work areas. As a group, employees agree to shoot for 100% compliance with adding proper barricades in their areas for the next 4 weeks.

Monthly meeting

On Friday afternoon, the behavioral safety steering committee holds its monthly meeting. The team of 10 includes Randy and representatives from each work area, the safety department, and the management team.

The committee reviews graphs of planned observations: What percent of employees conducted observations and which practices are cause for concern? After reviewing the data, the committee decides to focus on fall protection for the next month. While falling is not the most frequent issue, it contributes to severe injuries when it does occur. John, one of the committee members, agrees to chair a subcommittee to study the problem and develop an action plan that will be discussed at the next meeting. Their plan for the month simply includes sharing data about fall protection with employees and discussing what can be done to improve the safety practice.

The steering committee also reviews the data from several excellent observations from the previous month. After selecting the highest-quality observations, the team decides to review those observations at upcoming safety meetings and provide a "Safety Champion" T-shirt to the employees who conducted the observations. The committee adjourns, and its members return to their work duties.

This month, like many months that came before it, did not have even a minor safety incident recorded or reported.

Scenario two demonstrates strong safety leadership. But this time, it's embedded in a VBS process with an observation and feedback system. You can see that adding observation and feedback allows greater involvement of employees. Within this system they have a say in how safety goes in their organization.

CHAPTER 3

Safety Culture, Part 1: Assessment and Alignment

"Culture eats strategy for breakfast," a statement often attributed to Peter Drucker, rings especially true for organizational safety. A robust culture where leaders, managers, and employees act in alignment with established values and business objectives produces superior safety outcomes compared to companies without such a culture. Conversely, a meticulously designed safety strategy and corresponding programs will fail if the company culture is toxic, unsupportive, or dysfunctional. Recognizing the role culture plays in safety efforts is a first step toward enabling safety leaders and managers to design and implement programs that will produce a safer, more productive workplace.

Future chapters will explore the Values-Based Safety (VBS) process. Both VBS and behavior-based safety (BBS) are more successful when implemented in organizations with a strong safety culture. Developing a culture involves (1) aligning formal and informal systems with company values and (2) aligning leadership practices with company values. Formal systems are the written components of organizational operations that establish official procedures (appraisal systems, compensation, etc.). Informal systems refer to the social norms around how leaders and employees interact with one another and how those interactions guide behavior. Aligning leadership behavior and formal/informal systems with organizational safety values will create a safe workplace for everyone within the organization.

3.1 What Is Company Culture?

Edward Hall (1976) often described societal culture using an iceberg analogy. When an iceberg floats in the water, a small portion is visible above the waterline, but most of the iceberg is underwater. Hall's analogy shows that people often associate culture with the surface-level items at the tip of the iceberg: language, cuisine, clothing, and overt behavior. But culture is more than that. It's made up of values, beliefs, norms, and so forth. Those elements are the 90% below the surface of the water, and they comprise the majority of culture.

Josh Bersin and colleagues (2022), at the Josh Bersin Academy, are among the organizational experts who adapted Hall's model to describe the elements of *company* culture. People often associate the physical office, employee attire, pay, benefits, and perks with company culture. But these are only part of the equation and aren't usually mentioned when someone is asked: *What's it really like to work around here?* Elements below the waterline—such as trust, core purpose, mission, vision, values, and learning opportunities—are what executives, managers, supervisors, and employees do daily. Some of the most important elements below the waterline are the norms supported by both leadership and fellow associates.

Company culture encompasses the entire iceberg. Looking at the tip alone gives you an incomplete picture of what is supporting or hampering the employee experience, productivity, and safety outcomes.

3.2 What Is Safety Culture?

The cultural iceberg analogy also applies to safety. Companies that have incident reporting systems, hazard communication practices, safety committees, emergency preparedness, and formal safety training are often believed to have a "safe culture." But many of these elements are just the tip of the iceberg. These are *formal systems* that are necessary, but not sufficient for keeping people safe. You can have the right reporting methods, committees, and processes in place and still have employees who take shortcuts, leaders who overemphasize productivity, and managers who don't complete work observations. These are the kinds of behaviors that lead to injuries and fatalities.

An ideal safety culture is one in which employees take care of one another. They encourage and reinforce safe activities, call out and put a stop to unsafe actions, and require leader engagement to sustain safety efforts for the long haul.

3.3 Elements of a Safety Culture

The first step toward creating a safe culture—or tightening up the current one—is to get the company aligned with a shared vision. That vision must be clearly defined and understood by everyone. To create or adjust that vision, consider these key elements:

- **Purpose:** Why does the organization exist?
- **Mission:** What does the organization do, for whom, and how?
- **Vision:** What does the organization want to achieve in the long term?
- **Values:** How will the employees conduct themselves as they work, and how will they interact as a group (e.g., behavior, attitudes, ethics)?

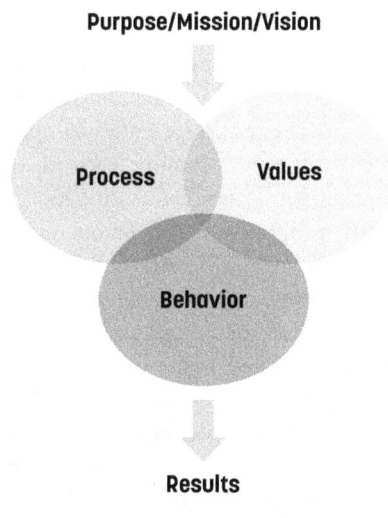

Figure 3.1. *A simplified model of culture.*

Figure 3.1 illustrates the four elements working together alongside work processes, employee behavior, and business results.

Executives at the top help establish and maintain the **purpose, mission,** and **vision**. These statements describe the ideal state of what the company works toward. Once those are set, **values** are defined to specify how employees ought to carry out their work. **Processes**—or the steps for how people get work done—are created and aligned with the values so that processes never override values, and values are realized through effective processes. People behave inside processes and their behavior leads (or doesn't lead) to meaningful results. Notice that process, values, and behavior overlap to signify how the three create synergies in a safe, employee-centered workplace.

Organizations that balance their approach to implementing and encouraging each of these elements are far more likely to create happy, healthy employees and desired business results.

3.4 Breakdowns in Culture

Once the elements of culture are defined, it's up to executives and managers to put them into action. Unfortunately, many leaders over- or under-emphasize certain elements of the diagram, which leads to an unsafe culture. Some of those problems are overemphasizing results and/or process.

Overemphasizing results. When executives overemphasize results, a company's success hangs on the herculean effort of a few top managers and key employees. People will work long hours and tolerate high levels of stress to produce desired results. In turn, companies will have higher rates of employee burnout and turnover and higher than average rates of participation in employee assistance programs. Employees who stay at the organization may believe that "all management really cares about is the numbers," meaning they will do anything in the name of having good budget figures, production records, efficiency targets, and safety statistics.

The results-oriented company tends to blame its employees when desired results aren't achieved. Blaming leads to a culture where people fear managers and distrust top leaders. For safety teams, this kind of culture impedes efforts to implement and sustain safety programs. Safety teams must work around resistant employees who are skeptical of initiatives such as establishing effective performance measures, often because they are unsure of how managers will use such measures. Or employees may become frustrated when their company seems more concerned with the number of injuries than the health and well-being of its employees. Such factors damage the relationship between managers and employees and make cultural change all that much harder.

Overemphasizing process. In process-oriented companies, managers look closely at the processes used to achieve results. Managers use process improvement methods to clarify requirements, standardize procedures, and establish measures of key steps. This approach tends to achieve consistent execution of processes and establish continuous improvement of those processes.

While these efforts address process problems, they do not repair poor employee-manager relationships that pervade organizations and negatively impact culture.

When cultural problems arise, the tendency is to create a new process or fine-tune an existing one. To accomplish this, problem-solving tools are often used to look for the root cause of a cultural issue. But these tools mostly focus on process issues, not behavioral ones. Problem-solving tools assume all company problems are a function of the system and try to resolve those problems by inadvertently adding complexity, bureaucracy, and paperwork. As a result, changes to process make work cumbersome and don't solve the root behavioral or relationship problem.

In process-oriented organizations, employees may believe that "all management really cares about is the paperwork." In our experience, cultural problems arise when what the company says about its care for safety does not align with what leaders do in relationship to it. Said another way, the organization's values and its leaders' behavior are disconnected.

3.5 Great Plains Railroad: The Culture You Don't Want

Let's look at the kind of culture Great Plains Railroad, a fictional railroad company, inadvertently created for its employees by not placing sufficient emphasis on safety relative to other outcomes. Notice some of the problems we've just discussed.

Production over safety. Terrell is an experienced railroad car inspector for Great Plains Railroad. He takes pride in spotting defects before a vehicle leaves the yard. Terrell's attention to detail reduces the risk of malfunction and injury. One morning, he flagged a car with its GPS dangling from the roof. To Terrell, it looked as if the unit would fall off during transport and potentially injure someone, so he wanted to stop the car from going out of the rail yard.

His boss, Andy, prioritized efficiency above safety: "We get paid to move cars, not fix them," he scolded. Andy pressured Terrell and other inspectors to overlook minor issues so trains could leave on time. Terrell was conflicted—was Andy right that slowing down for "nitpicky" safety issues wasn't worth it?

A few weeks later, Terrell spotted imminent danger: faulty brakes on a car that was about to leave the yard. He flagged the car, but Andy overrode his decision and sent it out anyway. Terrell felt he had no choice but to report the violation. Andy retaliated by closing up the repair shop, which put Terrell and his colleagues out of work.

Chilling effect that creates underreporting. In another yard at Great Plains, supervisor Keith pushed track inspector Ang to underreport safety issues. "I'm about to lose my job and my family's welfare over your reports!" Keith yelled. He feared the number of reports would cause concern to management. Ang knew that ignoring chronic problems could cause a serious incident, so he reported the safety issues to regulators. Keith fired him and received praise from corporate for his "record low" safety delays.

Close calls, fatigue, and a culture of fear. Conductor Gloria loves her job but struggles to stay attentive during long shifts. One foggy night, Gloria dozed off, narrowly avoiding a derailment (note: this is a close call). When she asked to rest before her next shift, management denied her request, despite a federal law requiring a 12-hour-maximum rule for operators. She and her coworkers said nothing; they were scared of retaliation. Gloria developed severe anxiety, afraid each day would be her last. The close call went unreported and was never investigated as a systems and leadership issue.

The result? Great Plains Railroad created a dysfunctional culture that prioritized efficiency and profits over employee safety and well-being. While everyone plays a role in company culture, managers have a major impact on the quality of that culture. At Great Plains, the threats and punishments of managers Andy and Keith motivated employees to shortcut safety procedures to meet metric goals. In response, inspectors, conductors, and other railroaders ignored chronic issues, remained silent about violations, and operated equipment in dangerous conditions. These activities eroded the company's regard for public safety and the psychological safety of its employees.

In a dysfunctional culture, like that of Great Plains, employees are caught between speaking up about issues and losing their livelihoods. Until a company shifts its mentality from profit- or productivity-first to people-first, everyone's safety is at risk.

We don't know the purpose, mission, vision, and values of Great Plains Railroad, but we do know that the behavior of its leaders produced a culture that was not aligned with whatever formal elements had been established.

3.6 What to Do About Culture

There are several steps one could take to improve company culture. In our experience, the following steps are recommended when your culture is underdeveloped or in need of revitalization:

1. **Learn about your company's culture.** Using the cultural iceberg, identify elements above and below the waterline that define your current company culture. Identify the elements that are represented in your formal and informal systems and those that need to be established or worked on. Do formal systems, such as appraisal, compensation, and promotion processes, provide solid support for safety? Do informal practices, especially those surrounding leadership behavior, align with those of your company's value for safety? Assess how well each level of leadership supports safety. Look for pockets of the organization where production takes priority over safety, then assess the elements that impact the culture in those groups. (Note: You may need to study Chapter 4 to clarify which leadership behaviors you should look for throughout the assessment.)

2. **Devise above-the-line items if they are missing.** As you learn about the company's culture, you may uncover that purpose, mission, vision, and values statements do not exist or are outdated. If that is the case, you can work with leadership to develop and refine those elements. At this point, it's important to involve leadership. They must know what's happening and buy into it. Leadership also helps bring formal safety systems to life.

3. **Develop an action plan for improving safety leadership.** When formal safety systems and the purpose, mission, vision, and values are established, you can identify leadership behavior that will build and maintain that culture. Depending on your assessment findings, leadership could be close to or very far from the target. Develop an action plan accordingly. That plan might include leader-

ship training and accountability practices. Suggested leadership behaviors and accountability practices are addressed in Chapter 4.

4. **Implement a VBS process.** If you are in a high-risk organization, implement VBS to get employees actively involved in promoting safety in all aspects of their work.

While not all organizations need to have the peer-to-peer observation and coaching process that characterize the VBS process in Step 4, all organizations should constantly strive to improve their safety leadership practices and create a strong safety culture.

3.7 Assessing the Safety Culture

A full assessment of an organization's safety culture is beyond the scope of this book. Our goal here is to provide a simple yet practical framework for assessing key aspects of safety culture, those that enable organizations to identify improvement opportunities. We focus specifically on assessing factors that impact employees' safety actions and their willingness to voice concerns about safety issues to supervisors and peers.

Key areas for assessment

Formal systems and policies

Begin by assessing the organization's formal, documented policies and systems related to safety:

- **Safety statements and documentation:**
    - Is safety reflected in the company's values statements?
    - Does the company have clear safety policies and procedures covering critical on-the-job safety practices?
    - Does leadership express their commitment to safety through formal company communications (e.g., town halls, emails, documents)?
- **Safety metrics:**
    - What safety performance and incident data are available?
    - Who is held accountable for safety performance and incident metrics and how?
- **Data review processes:**
    - How are those safety metrics reviewed?
    - Who participates in reviews of safety metrics?
    - How are safety statistics and incidents shared with employees?
- **Performance and HR systems:**
    - Is safety accounted for in performance appraisals, promotion decisions, compensation, and disciplinary procedures?

- Does the organization integrate safety into formal HR processes?
- Are employees and leaders held accountable for safety?
- Is the disciplinary process clearly defined in policies and procedures?

Informal culture and behaviors

Next, look at the equally important elements of the informal culture and behaviors that impact safety:

- **Leadership:**
    - Do leaders demonstrate a commitment to safety through what they say and do?
    - What decisions do leaders make that work for or against safety?
    - Do employees see their leaders taking actions every week that clearly demonstrate a value for safety?
- **Social contingencies:**
    - What are social norms or practices that impact trust?
    - How willing are employees to speak up about safety concerns?
    - What happens when people voice their concerns?
- **Stories:**
    - What narratives are told about safety?
    - Can you give me some examples or stories about safety successes or failures?
    - What do these stories demonstrate about leadership's handling of safety concerns?
- **Consequences:**
    - What happens when someone reports an injury or close call?
    - How do supervisors and managers react to the information?
    - How do leaders use positive reinforcement and feedback to encourage safety?
    - How are unsafe or at-risk acts disciplined?
    - Are negative consequences fair or do they vary because of unclear parameters?

Assessment process

The assessment consists of observations and interviews to gain information about multiple angles of the formal and informal safety systems. **Observations** allow you to see what people do on the job and in meetings. You can compare your observations to what they describe when you interview them. Table 3.1 offers elements to look for when conducting observations.

Table 3.1. Elements of a Safety Observation

What to Observe	Elements to Look for
Leadership team meetings	☐ Safety is first on agendas ☐ Incidents and close calls are reviewed ☐ Weekly safety action plans are developed for each meeting participant
Safety committee meetings and work sessions	☐ Structured written agendas are created and guide the meeting ☐ Agenda includes review of incident reports and safety data ☐ Decisions and action items are recorded in meeting notes ☐ Items from the last meeting are reviewed ☐ Improvement plans are developed, reviewed, and implemented
Weekly or monthly safety meetings	☐ Meeting includes safety content: hazards in specific areas, how leadership is addressing those issues ☐ Agenda includes information about incidents and close calls ☐ Employees are engaged in discussions ☐ Meeting facilitators and leaders welcome dialogue
Daily toolbox or start-of-work safety meetings	☐ Hazards or exposures associated with a task are discussed ☐ Clear plans to control each exposure are discussed and demonstrated ☐ Employees are engaged in discussions
High-risk areas in the workplace	☐ Employees follow all safety procedures ☐ Area is clean and well organized ☐ Tools and materials are stored properly

Interviews and focus groups allow employees to open up about the strengths and challenges of the job and safety culture. While it's necessary to tailor your questions to your organization, Table 3.2 provides sample questions to consider for interviews and focus groups. Develop an initial list of questions you want to ask, then plan your interviews and group discussions by selecting five to seven questions from that list, depending on the time you have to conduct your interviews. You may spread your longer list across the associates you plan to interview, but be prepared to adjust your discussion as you listen to your associates' comments and concerns. In some cases, you will likely dig into the details on a small number of issues.

Be sure to gain input from all employee groups, not just senior leaders. Frontline workers may experience the culture very differently than managers and executives. Observing and talking with employees reveals subtleties of cultural dynamics that aren't visible in a written mission or values statement. To understand culture—and to improve it—you need to learn about how people behave and interact with one another. Conduct observations and interviews across key groups:

- **Safety committee members**: Observe meetings, review minutes and materials, interview members.
- **Individual associates:** Assess their perception of leadership's priorities and their supervisor's commitment to safety versus production, assess their trust in leadership and willingness to raise issues.
- **Frontline supervisors:** Gather their perspectives on policies in practice, challenges in managing priorities, and how they respond to employees who take or report injuries or close calls.
- **Managers and executives:** Discuss how their behavior is aligned, or not, to safety values and policies; discuss the formal and informal safety systems and their effectiveness.

The goal of observations and interviews is to assess how the social norms of the workplace stack up against the formal systems and leadership's stated values.

Table 3.2. Interviews to Conduct When Assessing Your Safety Culture

Who	Process	Sample Questions
Site manager and/or executives responsible for operations	Individual interviews	• How do you personally support safety? • What is your relationship with your direct reports? How would you rate their trust in you? • How do you track safety work orders? • How are safety considerations part of design reviews on capital and new construction projects? • What safety metrics do you use? • How do you receive information about safety? • How do you send safety messages to employees? • What meetings have safety on the agenda? What kinds of things get discussed? • Do all injuries get reported? Do you know of any on-the-job injuries that were not reported? • How strong is your organization at reporting close calls and what is the process? • What do you do with close call and incident report information? • What pressures do you balance between production and safety? • How much time do you spend in work areas? • How often do you talk with employees about on-the-job safety? • What activities and areas put employees at the greatest risk of a serious incident? What do you do to ensure those jobs are done safely? • Do you review plans for or data from special efforts to prevent serious injuries and fatalities?

Table 3.2. (Continued)

Who	Process	Sample Questions
Safety manager	Individual interview	• Are you involved in approving and tracking safety-related work orders? How quickly are issues resolved? • How are safety considerations part of design reviews on capital and new construction projects? • How do you interact with the leadership team regarding safety? Do you find them supportive of your efforts? • How do you communicate with management about safety? What do those communications consist of? • Are management's expectations for safety and production reasonable? • Do any of management's expectations create safety risks? • How often do you communicate with employees in work areas? • Do all injuries get reported? Do you know of any on-the-job injuries that were not reported? • What safety metrics do you track? • How strong is the organization at identifying and responding to close calls? • Tour location of serious injuries and close calls and ask: "Can you give me a description of the context in which the serious incident occurred?" • What challenges do you see to further improving safety?
Safety committee members	Individual interviews or focus group	• How effective do you think you are as a committee member (and team)? • What projects has your committee initiated in the past year? What was accomplished in those projects? What enabled those successes? Did anything block progress? • Does management review your efforts? • Do you trust leadership to always do the right thing in response to a safety issue? • How often do you communicate with management about safety? What do those communications consist of? • How do you communicate with employees in work areas? How often? • What safety metrics do you use? • How do you report close calls? What is done with the information? Examples? • Do all injuries get reported? Do you know of any on-the-job injuries that were not reported? • Are management's expectations for safety and production reasonable? Do any of management's expectations create safety risks? • Is there a peer observation and feedback process? Who conducts observations? How often do observations occur? What happens with observation and feedback data? • How is your committee involved in preventing serious injuries?

Table 3.2. (Continued)

Who	Process	Sample Questions
Operations and maintenance managers	Individual interviews	• Do you have a process for tracking and prioritizing safety-related work orders? How quickly are they addressed? • How do you personally support safety? • How would you describe the relationships and trust between supervisors and employees? • What safety metrics do you use? • How do you receive information about safety? • What meetings have safety on the agenda? What kinds of things get discussed? • Do all injuries get reported? Do you know of any on-the-job injuries that were not reported? • Do you report close calls and how? • Do you know of any disciplinary actions taken in the past year? Were they appropriate and fair? • Are there production pressures that jeopardize safety? • How much time do you spend in work areas? • How often do you talk to employees about on-the-job safety? • What activities in your area put employees at the greatest risk of a serious incident? What do you do to ensure those jobs are done safely?
Frontline supervisors (typically one or two groups per shift, 10%–20% in large organizations, all supervisors in small organizations)	Individual interviews or focus groups	• Have you ever submitted a safety-related work order? What happened with it? • How would you describe the relationships and trust between you and your direct reports? • How would you describe the relationship and trust between you and your manager? • How do you receive information about safety? • What meetings about safety do you participate in? What is your role in those meetings? • What safety metrics do you use? • Do all injuries get reported? Do you know of any on-the-job injuries that were not reported? • Do your employees report close calls and how? • Do you know of any disciplinary actions taken in the past year? Were those appropriate and fair? • Are there production pressures that jeopardize safety? • How much time do you spend in work areas? • How often do you talk with employees about on-the-job safety? • What activities in your area put employees at the greatest risk of a serious incident? What do you do to ensure those jobs are done safely?

Table 3.2. (Continued)

Who	Process	Sample Questions

Sample of employees (5%–10% of population)	Individual interviews or focus group	• How do you report safety concerns? Do they get addressed? How quickly?
		• Do you participate in safety improvement efforts? Tell me about it.
		• How would you assess your relationship and the trust between you and your supervisor?
		• If you observed another employee doing something that caused a safety concern, would you approach them and discuss it?
		• How do you receive information about safety?
		• What meetings about safety do you participate in? What is your role in those meetings?
		• Do all injuries get reported? Do you know of any on-the-job injuries that were not reported?
		• Do you report close calls and how?
		• Do you know of any disciplinary actions taken in the past year? If so, were they appropriate and fair?
		• Are there production pressures that jeopardize safety?
		• How often are you observed doing your job?
		• Do you receive positive feedback for correct safety actions? How do observers handle corrective feedback?
		• What activities in your area put you and your peers at the greatest risk of a serious incident? What do you see leadership doing while these tasks are being performed?
		• Tour worksites/areas with serious injuries or close calls and ask employees these questions:
		  ◦ Could you describe what happened during the serious incident?
		  ◦ What gets in the way of improving safety?
		  ◦ How do leaders make high-risk tasks safe?

Review safety documents. Take the time to review all safety documents, including incident reports and close-call data (if available). Use incident report data to plan which site visits to prioritize. Injury reports provide the basis for collecting stories and descriptions of the context surrounding the event.

Some of the data you collect can be quantified. For example, you can determine the percentage of associates at each level of the organization who believe that all injuries get reported. This metric often reveals very different perceptions across executives, managers, and employees. Quantifying the qualitative data allows you to summarize it for leadership, giving them a snapshot of employees' perceptions and how they relate to the perceptions of managers and supervisors. Later, as you develop and implement improvement plans, these data provide useful baseline measures to assess the effectiveness of your improvements.

Reporting assessment findings. After you finish the assessment, you want to summarize your findings into a report that leaders can digest and that captures the current state of the safety culture. It should have an analysis of cultural strengths and gaps—for instance, a discrepancy between a formally documented policy and employees' behavior on the job.

Present your findings to leadership and open the discussion about the elements impacting safety culture in your organization. The assessment report is just the beginning of updating leadership and reinforcing their efforts to drive change forward. While the leadership team may take on the work on some of the issues, they more typically create a separate safety leadership team to take the assessment findings, establish priorities, and develop action plans. They focus on identifying areas where safety leadership can improve and where the culture can become more safety oriented. The team then collaborates to design targeted initiatives that bolster safety leadership skills, including training workshops for managers and interactive sessions that emphasize the importance of safety in leadership roles (see Chapter 4). To foster a strong safety culture, they may implement programs that reward safe behavior, create communication campaigns to highlight the organization's value for safety, and organize events that encourage active employee participation in safety initiatives. The team sets clear, achievable objectives and assigns specific responsibilities to ensure effective execution of these initiatives. They involve both leaders and employees in this endeavor, promoting a sense of shared responsibility and commitment to safety. The team should regularly review progress and gather feedback, adapting their strategies as necessary, ensuring continuous improvement in safety culture and leadership.

Conducting periodic safety culture assessments is important for continuous improvement. These types of assessments bring insights from across the organization, so safety and leadership teams can prioritize their change activities to better address the organizational elements that have the greatest impact on safety culture through all levels of the organization.

3.8 Steps Toward the Shared Vision

In your assessment, you have discovered whether your company does or does not have established, relevant versions of the above-the-line items of purpose, mission, or vision statement, and set of values. Or perhaps those elements do exist, but the company treats safety the way Great Plains Railroad did.

If the company does not have these elements established, they need to be created. In other cases, these elements may need to be improved. Not only will these elements support every employee and leader—how they conduct their work, make decisions, and select new business ventures—but they are critical for teams responsible for the design and implementation of safety programs. If the company already has these elements outlined, but they are outdated or irrelevant, they should be rewritten or reintroduced. The approach described in Chapter 10 can be adapted to developing or improving statements to clarify a company's purpose, mission, vision, and value statements.

Purpose, mission, vision, and values should not be created in silos, but with the help and input of many members of the organization. The goal is for everyone to understand how their daily activities contribute to the company's objectives and align with its purpose, mission, vision, and values.

Typically, organizations form a working group or committee to draft their statements. Your working group may divide these tasks among participants to avoid overloading one person, while still getting input from everyone. Begin the process by reading examples from other companies. This will give you a flavor for how elements fit with one another, and you'll notice features you like and dislike. Then hold conversations with the working group, draft statements, revise them, test them with employees, and revise them again. There are numerous resources on how to produce such elements, but this set of questions can help facilitate the conversation:

Purpose statement

A purpose statement outlines the fundamental reasons why an organization exists and how it benefits society.

Questions to consider:
- Why do we exist?
- What would the world be like if we didn't do the work we do?
- What value do we bring to our customers, employees, and the community?

Mission statement

A mission statement is a tactical declaration of an organization's activities and intentions. It defines the audience for and scope of the organization's products and services. Mission statements are more concrete than purpose statements. It answers this question: *What does the organization do, for whom, and how?*

Questions to consider:
- What do we do?
- Why do we do it?
- How do we do it?
- Whom do we serve?
- Why does what we do matter to the people we serve?
- What image do we wish to convey to our audience?
- What kinds of relationships do we have with our customers and employees?

Vision statement

A vision statement expresses the long-term aspirations of the company. It's the statement that keeps employees engaged in working toward something bigger than their daily activities and annual goals.

Questions to consider:
- Where are we headed?
- Where do we want to be in 3–5 years?
- How might the world—within our area of focus—look different if we were to achieve our aspirations?

Values statement

A values statement defines the set of principles that a company uses to shape how people will get work done and how they will conduct themselves while doing the work. Values provide ground rules or standards for how individuals interact with their work and their colleagues.

Questions to consider:
- What is important to us as a group?
- What is unique about how we work together?
- Think about people and organizations we admire. What do they do in their work and when making decisions that makes them admirable?
- Write down words, phrases, and examples that employees add when you brainstorm about values. Look for overlap and pare down the list to three to seven values.

The development or improvement of a company's purpose, mission, vision, and values is not just a procedural task, it's a fundamental step toward aligning the organization's culture with its operational and safety goals. Whether these elements already exist and need updating or are absent and need to be created, they play a crucial role in guiding behavior and decision-making. Involving diverse members across the organization in this process ensures these elements resonate with and are relevant to everyone. This inclusive approach, facilitated by a working group or committee, helps create a shared vision where every employee understands and contributes to the company's objectives. By aligning daily activities with the company's foundational elements, organizations foster a stronger, more cohesive culture and lay the groundwork for effective safety programs and sustainable business success.

3.9 Final Thoughts

To foster a robust safety culture, organizations must align their formal systems, such as safety policies and procedures, with their informal culture, including leadership behaviors and social norms. This alignment ensures that safety values are lived experiences within the organization, not just documents. The chapter uses the fictional example of Great Plains Railroad to illustrate the pitfalls of a dysfunctional culture that prioritizes efficiency over safety. In such cultures, employees often face dilemmas between adhering to safety procedures and meeting productivity targets that lead to unsafe practices. The chapter concludes with recommendations for assessing and improving safety culture. A thorough assessment involves examining formal systems and informal behaviors, with the ultimate goal of aligning the organization's stated values with actual practices. These include understanding the current culture; developing missing elements, such as a clear purpose or values; and deciding to implement a VBS process. Following these recommendations not only enhances safety outcomes but also contributes to the overall health and well-being of employees, fostering a more productive and sustainable workplace.

CHAPTER 4

Safety Culture, Part 2: Safety Leadership

A thriving safety culture requires strong leadership. In fact, you can judge the strength of a company's safety culture by looking at what leaders say and do. Even though leaders say and do slightly different things, depending on the size, location, and industry of their organization, the core principles of effective leadership are nearly the same across the board. If an organization is to implement and sustain a Values-Based Safety (VBS) process, strengthening leadership's role in safety is the first step.

In this chapter, we will look at the influence leaders at every level—executives, managers, and supervisors—have on their company and its safety culture. We will define safety-critical behaviors, along with high-leverage practices that enhance the implementation and maintenance of safety improvement efforts.

4.1 Leaders, Managers, and Supervisors: Is There a Difference?

Claire Hughes Johnson, former chief operating officer of technology company Stripe, distinguished between leaders and managers in her book, *Scaling People* (2023). "Great leaders put forth a vision and set lofty goals," while "great managers run teams and do the actual building" (p. 44). Hughes Johnson's explanations boil down to the differences in daily activities between leaders and managers. These descriptions apply to safety: Executives set forth a vision and the intended outcomes for their safety programs, while managers and supervisors are responsible for executing on that promise.

In this chapter, we separate leadership into three roles:

- **Executive** is a title reserved for leaders at the top of the organization: CEO, CFO, managing director, or a leader of a product area (people who set forth the product vision). Executives set the overarching strategy and objectives for the organization. They carry ultimate responsibility for ensuring the purpose, mission, vision, and values are realized. If there's a problem with company culture, organizations must train, coach, or, in a worst-case scenario, replace executives or managers who reinforce that culture. In promoting a safe workplace, executive leadership ensures that every leader is equipped with the tools, coaching, and time to implement and sustain a safety improvement effort such as VBS.

- **Manager** refers to middle management, or the people who bridge the gap between senior leaders and frontline employees. These individuals may carry the titles of department head or regional manager. They take high-level strategies from executives and put them into practice for their teams. Managers ensure that their teams complete certain activities so that their progress will roll into results for the company. In safety programs, managers are responsible for ensuring their teams understand and share the company's value for safety and look out for the well-being of their coworkers. Managers work with supervisors to evaluate task performance and look for factors that contribute to serious injuries. They have a clear understanding of how they support safety improvement efforts. Every day, managers ensure that safety observations and feedback sessions take place, that problems are reported to executives, and that executives are visible to employees.

- **Supervisor** is the role that coordinates and oversees daily work. The individuals ensure tasks are completed, goals are met, and problems are solved. Supervisors need adequate time to be *on the floor* observing and coaching employees. Executives and managers turn to supervisors for their insights on what they observe in the field, since they are closest to the work as it's happening. They also turn to supervisors when safety practices drift.

Recall the Great Plains Railroad scenario from Chapter 3. The manager and supervisor (Andy and Keith) were the ones who directly spoke and acted in a way that dismissed safety, but that tone was set by senior leaders. Top executives emphasized certain priorities and values for the organization and reinforced what managers and supervisors did that aligned with those priorities. For instance, Keith was praised for "record low" safety delays, even though he accomplished that by discounting safety and discouraging reporting.

We use the term "safety leadership" to describe a set of behaviors that leaders at every level of the organization must demonstrate. When executives, managers, and supervisors engage in these behaviors consistently, a safety culture can flourish. Leaders should involve themselves in safety on a weekly basis. In fact, Cooper (2006) found that employees who see their leaders take at least one safety action every week are more likely to create a safety culture that supports safety improvement efforts with resulting injury reductions.

4.2 MasterBuild: The Culture You Want

As a counterexample to Great Plains Railroad, let's look at a positive safety culture created by executives, managers, and supervisors at MasterBuild, a hypothetical construction company in the Midwest.

MasterBuild's leadership wanted to be first-rate in safety. And to get there, they needed to do things differently from the organizations they had worked at previously.

Initially, MasterBuild had all the "right" mechanisms in place: an incident reporting system, federal and state-mandated safety training, guidelines on how to conduct the job safely, and a zero-tolerance policy for not following those guidelines. But they didn't stop there. Executives completed self-assessments to identify how they were contributing to or hindering the VBS process. And behavioral coaches were brought in to help leaders improve their feedback delivery and other safety-critical behaviors.

Every week, MasterBuild's executives, managers, and supervisors were found in safety meetings asking good questions: "How did you handle that situation?" "How can we make this task easier and safer?" "Does that piece of equipment need to be replaced?" Leaders visited worksites and participated in observation and feedback sessions. When employees voiced safety concerns, leaders listened, thanked the employees, and followed up with safety work orders, when appropriate, then updated the employees on the status of actions taken to address their concerns.

Monthly, executives hosted a virtual town hall to update employees on the safety programs. Between town halls, executives and managers sent out communications to employees: celebrations, reminders, and notifications about emergencies.

Executives empowered managers to visit jobsites, observe work, and talk about safety with employees. If a manager found an issue with the safety process, a piece of equipment, or a worksite condition, they were to address it immediately. Regardless of schedule impact, if equipment malfunctioned, it was to be inspected and cleared before operating again.

Executives emphasized the importance of the safety process to managers and required that they meet with supervisors and remove barriers that prohibited them from conducting regular field-safety observations. Managers requested additional resources when supervisors couldn't keep the workplace safe, and funds were almost always granted. Managers and supervisors always conducted a field-safety review of any task that exposed workers to the risk of a serious incident. They routinely observed fall protection efforts on jobs involving scaffolding. They checked for proper permits and compliance with vessel entry requirements for jobs that required workers to enter confined spaces. They were adamant about 100% compliance on such jobs and constantly emphasized the criticality of compliance with safety requirements in protecting lives.

The VBS steering committee worked with executives, managers, and supervisors to improve the overall process, feedback and reward systems, implementation plans, and most importantly, human relationships.

MasterBuild created the culture of their dreams. Employees easily approached managers to ask questions and propose solutions to new problems. Managers even had time to find new business opportunities. Employees referred their friends for job openings. And when they weren't at work, employees shared their enthusiasm about their jobs with anyone who would listen.

Culture and leadership. MasterBuild exemplifies a culture aligned with a shared purpose, mission, vision, and set of values. Its leadership emphasized safety in all parts of their jobs.

In cultures like MasterBuild, leadership demonstrates that they value safety in these ways:
- attending meetings and visiting worksites
- talking about safety every day
- embedding safety into conversations on other topics (e.g., operations, finance)

- considering safety in every decision: process changes, new opportunities, hiring, promotions, and employee performance reviews
- aligning safety with all other goals: productivity, sales, and financial
- seeking solutions instead of blame
- humanizing employees

Leadership interacts with their employees in ways that foster positive relationships, such as:

- holding conversations with different employee groups and asking positive questions
- following up and following through after conversations
- observing work firsthand to see the consequences of their decisions (e.g., equipment selection, processes, expectations)
- reinforcing safe behaviors and correcting unsafe or at-risk behaviors
- removing barriers for design team and steering committee members
- communicating that safety is part of the job, not an addition to it
- soliciting feedback from direct reports and the larger work environment

Leadership that puts resources and energy into safety initiatives does the following:

- invests in initial and ongoing training and coaching
- adds people resources to ensure sufficient observation and feedback occurs
- defends the design team and steering committee's efforts
- removes barriers that block committee progress

Self-Awareness. Reflect on the lists of leadership behaviors provided and consider these questions:

- How many of those behaviors do you demonstrate *consistently*?
- Do other executives, managers, and supervisors do the same?
- What barriers prohibit you and your colleagues from engaging in those behaviors?

Complete this reflection yourself, then do it with your colleagues. It can open a conversation about what's working, what's not, and what needs to change.

4.3 Barriers to Safety

MasterBuild's leadership and the list of sample leadership behaviors provided exemplify ideal actions of executives, managers, and supervisors who promote a safe workplace. In our experience, a few issues impede that ideal state:

Measurement systems. Organizations collect measures on production, cost, and quality of work. Sometimes, leadership overemphasizes these measures and sacrifices measures related to safety. For instance, many organizations track production on an hour-by-hour basis. Managers and supervisors watch these figures carefully across the workday. When data aren't headed in the right direction, they make a change. But that change may put employees at risk.

Meanwhile, measures of safety are frequently reported as incident rates: slips, trips, falls; electric, fire, and explosions; or close calls. These are measures of safety *outcomes*, not safe *behavior* and *decision-making*. It's important to have these measures in place, but if incidents rarely occur, leadership's attention will lean toward measures that change frequently (production, quality), not those that rarely change (safety). When leaders fixate on incident rate data, it sends the message that outcomes are more important than employee safety and well-being. Effective leaders balance their attention to incident rates and safe, at-risk, and unsafe behavior.

Accountability systems. Measurement is linked to accountability. When leaders de-emphasize behavioral measures of safety and hold employees accountable for other metrics (productivity, cost), safety often plummets. After all, if you're praised and rewarded for meeting certain measures but not others, which ones will you focus on? It's the responsibility of executives to change this dynamic.

Manage by exception. Managers and supervisors who are hands-off in daily operations, except when something deviates from the norm, *manage by exception*. In safety, this describes the manager who only focuses on serious safety issues: major equipment malfunctions, injuries, or fatalities. The rest of the time, their attention is somewhere other than supervising employees' work.

Management by exception is a reactive tactic and doesn't foster a safety culture. Many manage-by-exception leaders would never dream of leading other areas of the business the same way (production, quality). If a manager's attention drifted from the quality of a product, the product could fail.

Inadequate monitoring and follow-up. A closely related barrier to management by exception is simply not spending sufficient time monitoring safety practices and systems. Managers either fail to observe work at all or go out to jobsites and spend time discussing topics other than safety. When monitoring drops off, so too does safe behavior and employees' faith in leadership. Over time, conditions may worsen and injuries may occur. This issue also occurs when leaders fail to carefully review safety reports and meeting notes.

Manage with fear. Managers who motivate employees to work safely by using threats and fear tactics often produce negative outcomes. Rather than improve safe behavior, employees learn when to act safely (e.g., a manager watching) and when they can relax (e.g., during the night shift). Managers who use threats and fear should consider this: *If employees aren't already working safely to avoid personal injury, why would adding fear help?*

4.4 Promoting Safety Through Organizational Alignment

In our experience, there are five categories of leadership behaviors that improve safety outcomes and demonstrate a value for safety (see Figures 4.1, 4.3–4.6).

Safety is everyone's job and should be incorporated into every level of the organization. To reach alignment across the organization, three elements must work

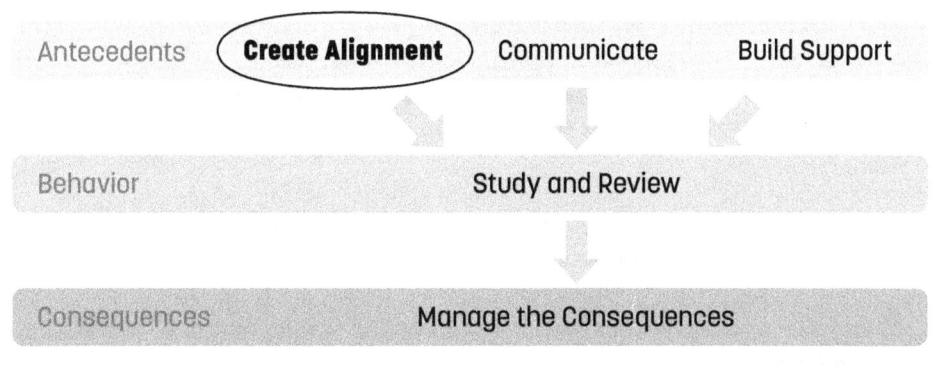

Figure 4.1. *Leadership practices that improve the alignment of values, behaviors, and systems often have the biggest impact on improving safety culture and outcomes.*

together: a leader's personal commitment to safety, their demonstration of certain leadership behaviors, and an organizational system that allows for safety practices to occur. Personal practices include wearing proper protective equipment when visiting sites or driving without distractions. Leadership behaviors may include regularly reviewing safety data with teams or considering the impact of resourcing and hiring decisions on the safety process. Systems alignment means ensuring that policies, procedures, and incentives work cohesively to promote safety, rather than create conflicting demands. Performing the following actions will help achieve organizational alignment:

- Model safe behaviors in daily work.
- Hold weekly safety reviews with direct reports.
- Evaluate all decisions against the impact they have on safety.
- Learn the organization's safety processes.
- Include safety expectations in performance reviews.
- Ensure management systems facilitate (do not impede) safety.

Establish a values statement for safety. Employees want their coworkers to go home safely. This is an unspoken truth in organizations. Creating a formal values statement with that sentiment helps align everyone in the organization. (One approach that could be adapted for this purpose is described in Chapter 10.) The leadership team or safety committee can draft the values statement. Once defined, leadership should discuss the statement, reflect on it, and determine how their current behavior does or does not communicate that message. Using cascading meetings (discussed later in this chapter) ensures leaders' behaviors are aligned with and demonstrate support for the organization's safety values.

Improve say-do correspondence. Your clear, ongoing messages about the importance of safety should indicate what executives, managers, supervisors, and employees will ***do*** to create a safe workplace. When people do what they say they're going to do, it builds say-do correspondence and trust. The strength of say-do correspondence is a major predictor of how successful a safety program will be. Some examples:

At a town hall, the CEO proclaims, "We're going to ensure every vehicle in the fleet is winterized before it goes out on the road this December" (say). After servicing 50 of the 200 fleet vehicles, managers are shocked at the cost of winterizing, so they decide to skip most of those steps for the remaining vehicles and just check fluid levels instead (do).

- Leadership's *say* and *do* were not aligned. This kind of misalignment promotes distrust and frustration among employees.

A supervisor observing an employee doing an unsafe act on the job says, "Hey, we need to have you retrained on that piece of equipment before you operate it again" (say). The supervisor immediately arranges for training and the employee completes it on their next shift (do).

- The supervisor's *say* and *do* are aligned. This interaction builds trust between employees and leaders. It sends the message that what is said gets done and is enforced.

Actions speak louder than words. This adage applies to safety culture, especially in companies where leaders have historically said one thing and done another. Table 4.1 lists what leaders might say (talk about) and do (act on) to strengthen their safety culture.

Table 4.1. Examples of Safety Talk and Safety Actions

Say/Talk	Do/Act
• Always start meetings with safety items	• Ensure safety work orders get addressed
• Ask direct reports what has been done or planned to improve safety	• Provide recognition to those who champion safety
• Ask about the VBS process often: level of participation, number of observations, steering committee action plans	• Arrange and participate in celebrations for safety achievements
	• Model safe personal actions
• Provide feedback on safety practices	• Conduct safety observations
• Include safety requirements when communicating job assignments	• Monitor safety processes
• Ask a balanced number of questions about safety actions and results	• Ensure incident investigations are conducted
	• Ensure employees have time to participate in safety improvement efforts
	• Conduct regular facility audits to identify and address conditions
	• Review VBS process data

For some leaders, this list of say-do items is already part of their daily habits, while others need support in making it a reality. Table 4.2 is a decision-making tool that helps with deciding what support executives, managers, or supervisors might need to start, stop, or continue certain safety-related behaviors.

Table 4.2. How to Address Different Types of Say/Do Combinations

		The person **behaves** (do) in ways that promote safety	
		Yes	No
The person **talks** (say) about safety	Yes	• Recognize • Reward • Promote	• Train and coach
	No	• Train and coach	• Train • Coach • Ultimately terminate • Improve hiring and selection process

Here are examples of using the matrix to make a decision about a leader's performance:

Jonathan, a frontline supervisor, talks about safety at every team meeting. When a safety issue arises, he addresses it immediately and communicates when the issue has been resolved. He allocates time on the shop floor to coach employees.

- Jonathan talks about safety (say: yes) and acts safely (do: yes). Our recommendation for responding to his behavior is to recognize, reward, or promote Jonathan. He is a supervisor we hope other supervisors will imitate.

Carmen, a regional manager, visits worksites regularly, but most of her conversations are about productivity, human resources, and growth plans. When not at the worksite, she responds quickly to supervisors who request investigations into safety incidents.

- While Carmen doesn't talk about safety (say: no) at jobsites, she shows some safety-related behaviors (do: yes). We recommend that Carmen receive coaching to improve her safety-related interactions on-site. She is engaged in other aspects of the business, but her engagement in safety is lacking, which could lead to a detrimental outcome.

Marcus, head of production, is hyper-focused on warehouse expansion across the United States. He's focused on meeting deadlines and moving at an aggressive pace. Each expansion project has brought challenges: fires, broken equipment, several injuries, and one fatality (so far). Project managers have voiced their safety concerns and shared the discontent of employees. Marcus ignored all of the complaints but acknowledged the fatality.

- Marcus pushes results and outcomes over safety. He *manages by exception*, meaning he only addresses the most serious incidents. Marcus is neither talking about safety nor acting safely. We recommend that Marcus receive training and coaching, and if that doesn't work, he should be terminated. In the end, an organization can narrowly tolerate missteps in safety. Terminating an employee might be the only solution.

Properly resource safety. When starting a behavioral safety program, leaders commit resources to get it started and keep it running. A common mistake is underestimating how much time and money are required to build and maintain the program. Some believe training employees is the biggest safety resource. Safety is not a one-time activity. It requires attention all day, every day. Success only happens when leaders commit resources to safety for the long haul.

Expand new hire orientation to include on-the-job safety. New hire orientation must demonstrate the organization's value for safety. During orientations, new hires often spend more time reviewing HR benefits and completing paperwork than learning and practicing safety-critical behaviors for the job. In some companies, supervisors are asked to brief new team members on proper lifting or cutting techniques before they start their jobs. But this approach leads to variation in training: Some employees will have a better experience than others and master safety practices, while others will barely learn them at all. We recommend that leadership do the following regarding new hires:

- Create a new employee orientation checklist that includes safety-related items.
- Standardize training materials (delivered online or in person using scripts or facilitation guides) to ensure every new hire has the same experience.
- Require new hires to complete performance checkouts to demonstrate skill mastery.
- Update the orientation to align with changes in process, work conditions, or business.

Create and use a safety leadership checklist. Like a safety checklist used to monitor an employee at work, a leadership checklist includes critical behaviors the leader should do to improve the alignment of leadership practices and the organization's value for safety. Managers and supervisors can develop a checklist of safety-critical behaviors to demonstrate their support for safety on a weekly basis. Figure 4.2 is an example of what a safety checklist might look like.

Safety Leadership Checklist

Name: _____ Date: _____

Behavior	Yes	No	N/A
1. Conducted a behavioral safety observation			
2. Reviewed observation data in safety meeting			
3. Encouraged at least one employee to do safety observation			
4. Corrected an unsafe condition			
5. Conducted one informal area safety review this week			
6. Held celebration when group met goal			
7. Gave positive feedback related to safety at least once			
8. Provided feedback to employees on safety behaviors			
9. Completed new employee orientation			
10. Completed checklist and returned to safety team by Friday			

Figure 4.2. *Example of a self-observation checklist for leadership.*

As with other safety observations, completed forms should be summarized, reported, and reviewed regularly. Leaders also need feedback, recognition, and reinforcement for their safety-related behaviors. (The section on cascading that comes later in this chapter provides an example of a slightly different kind of checklist to support safety leadership practices.)

4.5 Communicate the Importance of Safety

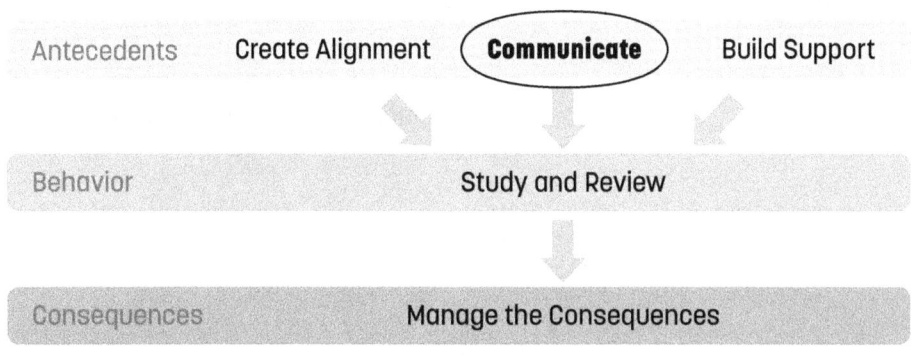

Figure 4.3. Communication practices should reflect a value for openness and honesty. Listening, soliciting input, communicating values, and sharing plans along with the rationale for changes all help align expectations throughout the organization.

When leaders have a chance to talk about safety, they should! Communicating the importance of safety through formal presentations and informal interactions keeps leadership and employees on the same page. These communications include sharing personal stories with an underlying safety message or making safety a standing agenda item at meetings. The goal is to influence hearts and minds by conveying the moral imperative and the business purpose of safety. Leadership can perform the following communication practices to help employees see the importance of safety:

- Discuss safety in meetings and presentations.
- Relate safety to organizational and personal values.
- Highlight safety as a priority in conversations.
- Ask employees for safety improvement ideas.
- Share personal experiences that have shaped safety perspectives.
- Recognize safe behaviors publicly.

Send a clear message. For leadership to build trust with employees and gain their buy-in for safety improvement efforts, managers and supervisors must be visible in the organization. Their actions demonstrate the importance of safety in an ongoing fashion. Written or spoken communications are one way to send a clear message about safety. Another way is to establish formal systems around safety: safety procedures, audits, checklists of leadership actions and critical worker behaviors, and regulatory compliance. Formal systems are the bedrock of everything a leader says and does.

Create a safety alert system. Sometimes urgent issues require immediate attention between scheduled safety meetings. A safety alert system gets out an urgent message to leadership. It allows leaders to quickly learn about a problem and act to resolve it. Employees should never wait to inform leaders of urgent safety issues.

4.6 Build Participation and Support

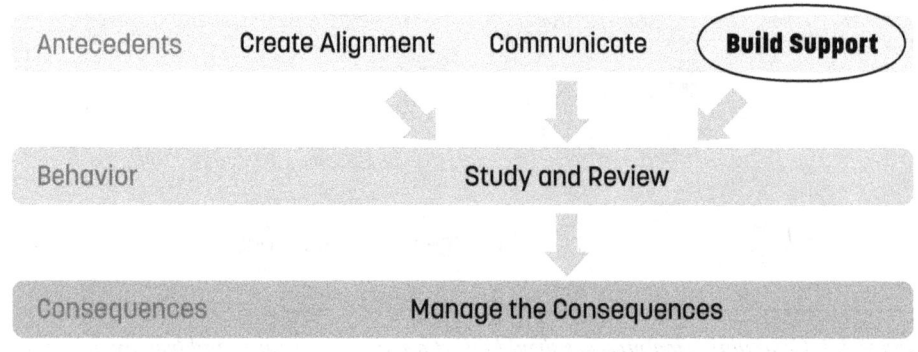

Figure 4.4. *Building support involves getting help and input from shareholders. The best way to create ownership is through involvement in planning.*

To sustain a safety program, leaders must motivate and support employee participation. In early stages of implementation, this means communicating the need for improved safety, providing resources for implementation, and reviewing progress. Later, leadership transitions to supporting safety committees, recognizing safe behaviors, and removing barriers to participation. Leadership teams committed to sustaining a safety program are usually involved in the following actions:

- allocating resources for safety committees and celebrations
- thanking employees for their participation in safety initiatives
- attending safety events and meetings
- requesting progress reports for safety initiatives
- providing assistance when barriers to participation arise
- sharing success stories publicly

Select a Safety Point of Contact. It's beneficial to have a behavioral safety advocate, safety ambassador, or employee safety representative as a Safety Point of Contact on every team or in every work group. Regardless of what they are called, this person—ideally a volunteer—is the point of contact for two-way communication on safety issues and improvement efforts. The crew or team goes to this person to ask questions and the Safety Point of Contact promotes safety through what they say and do. They might also be charged with:

- training new observers to conduct safety observations and feedback
- conducting frequent behavioral safety observations and modeling how the process works for other employees
- ensuring behavioral safety observation forms are completed and submitted to the appropriate location
- reviewing injuries, close calls, and safety data in safety meetings with their team
- posting and updating safety improvement graphs
- arranging recognition and celebration events with supervisors and the safety committee

The Safety Points of Contact become informal leaders that do not have the responsibilities or authority of managers and supervisors. In smaller companies, they may serve on the safety committee, but in larger organizations Safety Points of Contact are not typically formal members of the safety committee.

To make a Safety Point of Contact program productive, the steering committee should be in contact at least monthly with the point of contact to:

- listen to what's happening in the field
- readjust or reemphasize priorities and action plans
- encourage the Safety Point of Contact to reinforce communications sent by leadership
- gain feedback about the process and incorporate it into continuous improvement plans

4.7 Review and Study Safety in the Workplace

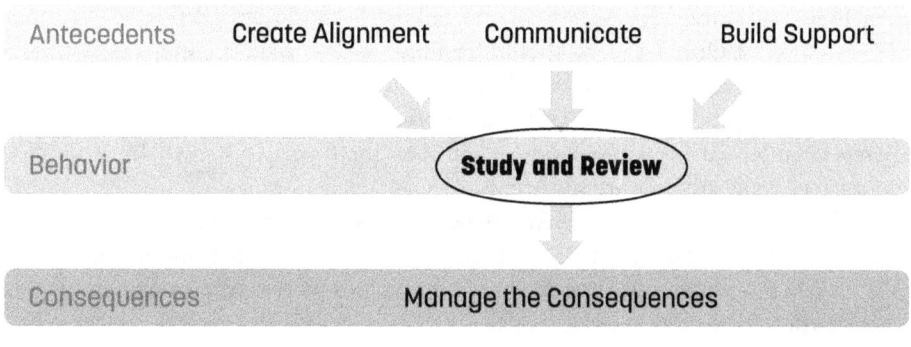

Figure 4.5. Studying and reviewing practices ensures that leaders become students of their business. They review and assess the effectiveness of their efforts to improve safety and to find new ways to achieve continuous improvement.

As you implement safety programs, the amount of data you can access increases. Those data are only useful if leaders can interpret and review them to help improve safety programs. Reviews should prompt leaders to recognize successes, resolve gaps, and shape the future of safety programs. Leaders who continuously review safety data demonstrate their sustained commitment to safety, which contradicts the perception that safety is a short-term priority. The following actions send the message that safety is a long-term endeavor:

- Analyze safety performance metrics regularly.
- Conduct focus groups to gather employee perspectives.
- Review how safety outcomes were achieved.
- Meet with safety teams to discuss improvement plans.
- Inquire about employees' participation in safety initiatives.

Conduct safety observations. Every leader is responsible for conducting safety observations and feedback sessions. If a manager or executive walks by an employee working at height without fall protection and does not intervene, they send tacit approval of the action and communicate that safety is not important.

The safety industry largely agrees that watching people do their work and providing them feedback on it is essential to a safety effort. But whether managers and supervisors should participate in conducting behavioral observations has been an area of debate. Safety success is usually correlated with the amount of time leaders—especially managers and supervisors—spend in the work area.

Observing work is the single most important activity that distinguishes effective leaders from mediocre ones. Behavioral research shows that managers who observe, evaluate, and coach employees on their performance have a greater impact on the consistency and quality of processes being implemented (Komaki, 1998). That usually happens in two ways:

Walking around. Effective leaders *manage by walking around*, meaning they get out of their office, tour the operation, and talk with employees (Peters & Waterman, 1982; Komaki, 1998). Leaders should conduct safety walk-arounds, regardless of whether they are included in the VBS process or not. Some organizations have a formal field verification process whereby leaders observe all jobs with serious incident potential (see Chapter 20 for a discussion of options for formal systems). In other cases, simple safety walk-arounds are sufficient.

To maximize the productivity of safety walk-arounds, leaders should enter an observation with a clear objective, for example, finding areas that present the greatest risk of injury to employees. After the observation, leaders should take necessary action to resolve those risks.

While talking with employees, leaders ask questions about the safety process. They might ask employees to describe how they approached a specific situation. Good questions open a dialogue that helps to keep the conversation casual. It's best to start with broad questions before drilling down to specifics. During walk-arounds, leadership can ask employees if they have any concerns about safety. This question will help bring issues to the surface that have not been addressed previously. For example, an employee might express concern that keeping the production line moving always seems more urgent than stopping to inspect a crane.

Conducting safety walk-arounds and engaging employees in casual conversations are types of informal monitoring that help ensure identification and communication regarding safety issues and concerns. By providing follow-up discussion on concerns, leaders can help ensure that safety committees establish deadlines that get safety problems addressed before a serious incident occurs.

Asking effective questions. When a manager or supervisor walks around, they should ask about employee performance, not just discuss incidents. When leaders monitor work and ask ineffective questions, monitoring becomes a formality. No real safety issues are addressed. Ineffective questions also put employees on the spot, like in an interrogation. Asking effective questions, on the other hand, can generate productive conversations about safety between leadership and employees.

Ineffective questions usually begin with "why":

- *Why does your team have more incidents than other teams?*
- *Why do you not have time to do safety observations?*
- *Why is your team ignoring safety guidelines?*
- *Why do you lift with your back? Where did you learn that?*

"Why" questions try to uncover the root cause of a problem, but they do so by putting employees on the defensive. Trying to escape blame, employees defend their actions instead of providing useful information.

Effective questions promote openness and honesty and nurture relationships between leaders and employees.

Effective questions usually open with "what" or "how":

- *How could leadership support you in lowering the number of incidents on your team?*
- *What obstacles are getting in the way of you conducting observations?*
- *How could we get employees to consistently lift with their legs and not their backs?*

This style of questioning encourages participants to generate solutions that will improve behavior or the outcome of their work. Employees feel that their leader is inviting them into a conversation and that they are part of the improvement. Table 4.3 on the following page provides sample questions for each level of leadership to ask of other leaders and employees.

The questions in Table 4.3 are intended to do the following:

- start the conversation broad before drilling down
- invite honest dialogue
- gain insights about the process
- signal to employees that leadership cares about their safety

Table 4.3. Sample Questions to Ask About Safety

Who Will Ask the Questions	Who Will Answer the Questions	Possible Questions
Executives	Managers	• What kind of tasks in your area expose our people to a potential serious incident or fatality? What are you doing to ensure that those risks are minimized and controlled? • What did you do last week to demonstrate your support for safety? • What will you do this week to demonstrate your support for safety?
Managers and steering committee members	Supervisors	• What kind of safety initiatives do you have in place? How are they working so far? What is working well? What are the challenges? • What percentage of employees are conducting observations? • How many observations have been done in the past week or month? • Who has been active in supporting the process? • What can leadership do to help?
Managers and supervisors	Employees who conduct observations	• What kinds of safety practices are people performing well on? • What kind of safety concerns are you seeing? • How are employees responding to the observations? • Tell me about your daily toolbox meetings. How do you address safety in those discussions?
Supervisors	Frontline employees	• What happened yesterday that went different from what we planned? What new risks were created by that change? How did you control the risk? • What are you scheduled to do today that exposes you to risk of injury? • What can you do to minimize your risk of injury?

When talking with employees, pose the question then pause to allow the person to think and answer. Don't interrupt them or finish their sentence. Once they respond, avoid defending, explaining, or rationalizing your position.

Using effective questions with a struggling employee. When talking with someone who struggles to follow safety protocols, continue to use positive, effective questions. Start by asking, "What have you tried so far?" This question allows you to strategize *with* the person and use their knowledge of the problem. It also helps demonstration care for them, rather than being a way to dole out corrections.

Once you discuss the problem, what has been tried, and what might work, ask, "What are you planning to do next?" This question solidifies ownership for how the person plans to address the issue. Effective questions quickly shift from what happened in the past to what can be achieved in the future.

Participate in formal reviews. So far, our recommendations are focused on how to monitor the safety process through informal means—walking around, talking to people, modeling safe behavior, and so forth. Leaders also play a critical role in formal reviews: assessments, audits, and incident report reviews.

4.8 Manage the Consequences for Safety Practices

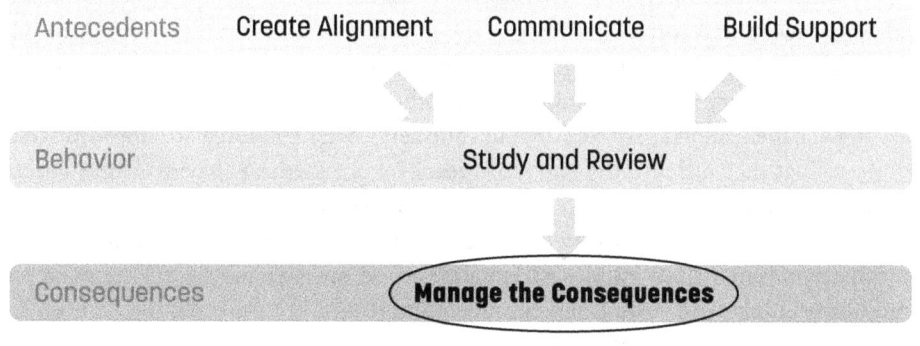

Figure 4.6. *Effective leaders manage the consequences. They use their feedback and comments to verbally recognize and reinforce success. They coach improvement to ensure all employees are consistently meeting safety requirements. They are also fair and consistent in their efforts to enforce their organization's disciplinary policies.*

Every interaction with an employee is an opportunity to shape and recognize safe behaviors no matter how small. Recognize safe actions through praise, tangible rewards, and celebrations. Leaders who exemplify good safety citizenship motivate others to adopt those practices at work and advance the organization's safety culture. To shape and reinforce safety practices, leaders should do the following:

- Recognize safe practice improvements publicly.
- Request employee success stories for recognition.
- Deliver constructive feedback regarding safety behaviors.
- Participate visibly in local safety celebrations.
- Provide resources for small-scale safety recognitions.
- Thank individual employees for their safety contributions.

Recognize and reward safety committee members. Never forget to recognize and reward safety committee members. We emphasize the importance of celebrating employees' adherence to the VBS process, but the people behind those efforts must also be rewarded.

One way to recognize steering committee members is by finding professional development opportunities for them. If a steering committee member is trying their best to create budgets, but they don't have the skills, find them a mentor, online course, or conference to attend that will help them gain those skills. Invest in your steering committee members and anyone else who supports safety.

Just as leadership recognizes and rewards steering committee members, they need to do the same with ambassadors. Many Safety Points of Contact will champion an imperfect process with many hiccups along the way. Our recommendations for designing and implementing celebration plans (see Chapter 13) apply to Safety Points of Contact as well.

Focus on behavior, not discipline. An observation and feedback process allows leaders to reward and correct behavior in the moment, which reduces the need for discipline. If discipline issues are high, more observation is needed. Effective observation prevents disciplinary issues and stops work conditions from deteriorating.

Managers and supervisors should routinely coach employees to improve safety practices. That means delivering corrective feedback for at-risk behaviors. After coaching, if an employee does not work safely, disciplinary policies should be administered in a consistent and fair way. Every employee needs to perform safety-critical behaviors fluently to prevent serious injuries and fatalities. And every employee has the same obligation to comply with established safety requirements.

4.9 An Implementation Plan to Improve Safety Leadership

The strategies introduced in this chapter require varying levels of effort to implement. A positive first step to improving safety is to improve foundational leadership skills and accountability by setting up cascading meetings with teams across the organization.

Action 1. Prepare leaders to take on their safety roles.

Executives, managers, and supervisors must have a strong grasp of safety concepts to lead the organization forward. Provide training to leadership at the start of a safety improvement project and implement ongoing safety training to keep leadership up to date on skills. After training sessions, provide accountability and support for implementing the newly learned skills.

Action 2. Establish a system of cascading meetings.

Start with a meeting for the topmost leadership to discuss safety priorities, then carry (cascade) that information all the way down to frontline employees. Tips to get started:

- **Assign meeting groups.** Create meeting groups based on reporting structures. Executives meet with the managers who report to them; those managers meet with their supervisors; and supervisors meet with their employees.
- **Schedule meeting times.** As much as possible, use meetings already on the calendar to discuss safety topics. Figure 4.4 gives recommendations on how frequently to conduct meetings and what to include on the agendas.
- **Make safety the first item on the agenda.** At your first meeting, explain why the schedule of meetings and the topics of those meetings are changing. You want everyone to understand that the changes reflect the organization's value for safety and its employees.
- **Report out and update.** Start leadership meetings with a review of recent incidents and close calls and follow the review with every leader sharing an example of how they have promoted safety since the previous meeting.
- **Develop action plans.** As the meeting continues, people will be assigned action items and commit to specific safety-related behaviors. Document these in the agenda and review them at subsequent meetings. Some of the actions leaders select to work on may come from the examples we have provided in this chapter.
- **Standardize agenda templates.** A template can help every leader run high-quality meetings. It should include a place to note recurring and new tasks, prompt good questions, and track improvement actions. At the top of the agenda, print the company's values to remind people of the reason for meeting and taking action.

These steps apply to every cascading meeting. For supervisor-employee meetings, the cadence varies depending on the industry and safety risks presented. For example, daily tailgate meetings for high-risk construction or maintenance work, weekly safety meetings for manufacturing, and monthly meetings for process and pharmaceutical industries.

Supervisor-employee meetings should focus on identifying potential areas of injury and hazard exposure that arise on the job. Supervisors should use these meetings to prioritize activities that will minimize risk and control exposures.

Action 3. Continuously evaluate and adapt.

Safety improvement efforts require continuous evaluation to determine their success and define areas for improvement. One improvement might include adjusting the frequency of meetings.

Cascading safety leadership meetings enhance task completion, drive progress, and fortify a safety-centric culture. Meetings are the foundation for a systematic safety process. During meetings, messages and policies are disseminated and employees are made aware of how their behavior contributes to the organization's safety priorities and responsibilities. See Table 4.4 on the following page for a summary of these recommendations.

Table 4.4. Summary of Recommendations for Meeting Frequency and Agenda Items Based on the Level of Leadership

Leadership Level	Typical Frequency	Considerations and Typical Agenda Items

Executive with managers	Quarterly or monthly	• CEO, president, or site managers lead these meetings and prioritize safety as the first agenda item
		• Discuss close calls and incidents
		• Meeting participants share:
		  ○ What they did during the last week to support safety
		  ○ What they plan to do in the next week to support safety

Managers with supervisors	Monthly or weekly	• Report and discuss close calls and incidents • Managers discuss supervisors' plans for daily or weekly tailgate safety meetings • These meetings cover job safety analysis and hazard mitigation strategies, with special attention given to activities with the potential for a serious incident
Supervisor with employees	Monthly, weekly, or daily (depending on risk level)	• Discussions focus on safety issues specific to the work • Discuss the most significant risks in the current work schedule and how those risks will be controlled

4.10 Final Thoughts

Active and visible support from executives, managers, and supervisors is critical for the longevity of safety improvement efforts.

Leaders should focus on two roles when building their organization's safety culture:

- Show a personal commitment to safety through what they say and do.
- Pay careful attention to safety improvement efforts without taking ownership away from employees.

Leaders can achieve both roles by continuously monitoring their own behavior and the behavior of others. Leaders who lack the skills described in this chapter will need training, practice, and feedback to gain those skills. Established leaders also benefit from continuous training, practice, and feedback to sharpen their skills. When employees see their leadership in professional development activities, it reinforces the company's commitment to safety. Employees become collaborative and involved, which leads to better outcomes for the business. The major differences between effective and mediocre leaders that were discussed in this chapter are summarized in Table 4.5.

Table 4.5. Summary of Activities Often Seen in Effective Versus Mediocre Safety Leaders

Effective Leaders	Mediocre Leaders
Conduct safety observations in work areas	Do not regularly conduct safety observations
Monitor: • activities in their areas • steering committee plans • safety observation and outcome data	Do not pay attention to their process Manage by exception Only pay attention when employees do something wrong
Lead by: • example • effective questions • input and suggestions	Lead by mandate Respond in anger or frustration when incident is reported
Build for long-term involvement	Push for immediate results

Whatever form your safety improvement efforts take, the success will ultimately come down to what leaders say and do. That is simple in theory, hard in practice, but worth doing for the safety and well-being of everyone.

CHAPTER 5

Leadership Safety Improvement Projects[1]

Witnessing a catastrophic event or experiencing the consequences of such an incident can make a lifelong impression. The impact can be even more profound if a catastrophe resulting in fatalities or other serious consequences occurs in an operation for which you are responsible.

This was the case for a division manager attending a meeting of a major chemical facility's safety committee prior to his retirement. Even though the vapor cloud explosion that resulted in three fatalities in the manager's division had occurred nearly 2 decades earlier, its impact on the manager was still evident. In his final comments to the safety committee, the manager recognized the importance of continuing to drive down the facility's OSHA-recordable case rate. However, his primary message was a challenge to the organization not to lose sight of its critical responsibilities for preventing serious, high-consequence events that forever change lives. The incident had clearly changed this manager's perspective permanently, and he hoped others would continue to diligently apply those lessons of the past to prevent serious incidents from occurring in the future.

Too often, the lessons learned from such events are short lived. With the passage of time, organizations find that the actions critical to maintaining safe operation are once again being ignored. Because serious-incident prevention is the most important leadership safety improvement project, organizations need a systematic management approach to ensure that actions critical to preventing serious incidents are accurately identified and diligently executed over the long term.

Performance management is a process that incorporates (1) employee involvement, (2) measurement of upstream performance indicators, (3) performance feedback, and (4) reinforcement contingent upon performance. It has provided a framework for significant improvements in key performance areas, including product quality, productivity, customer satisfaction, and safety. As described in other chapters of this book, such processes have formed the basis for successful behavior-based safety (BBS) leading to breakthrough levels of improvement in injury reduction for many companies. Performance management is the foundation for the proven management approach described in this chapter. Leadership safety improvement projects have proven effective for achieving and sustaining serious-incident-free operations.

---

1 This chapter was written by T. E. Burns, based on his book *Serious Incident Prevention* (Burns, 2002). It has been updated slightly for this edition.

These techniques have been successfully implemented to achieve major reductions in incidents such as serious injuries and fatalities, accidental releases of chemicals, hazardous material transportation incidents, regulatory agency violations, and security breaches. To illustrate, Figures 5.1 through 5.3 summarize the results of the improvements achieved in one division of a major petrochemical company through the implementation of the eight-element leadership safety improvement project described in the pages that follow. Each figure compares the average level of performance for the 3 years immediately prior to implementing the leadership safety improvement project with the breakthrough levels of performance achieved during the 3 years immediately following the implementation of the improved prevention process.

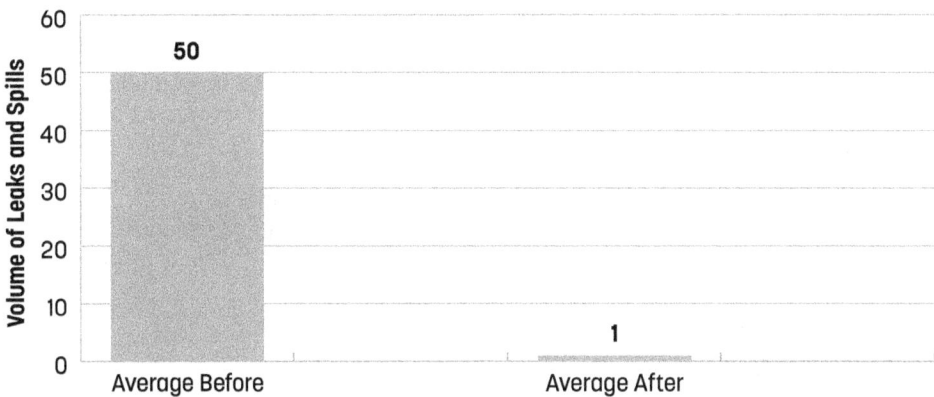

Figure 5.1. Average volume of leaks and spills at a chemical tank farm operation for 3 years before and after implementation of a leadership safety project.

Success in preventing serious incidents over the long term is firmly linked to an organization's capabilities for identifying the tasks critical to success, then successfully managing the many details involved in properly executing these tasks.

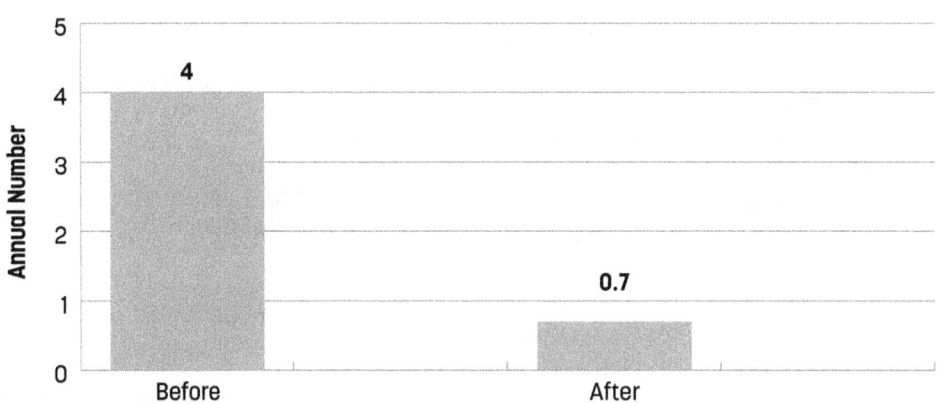

Figure 5.2. Annual number of non-accident tank car releases for 3 years before and after implementation of a leadership safety improvement project.

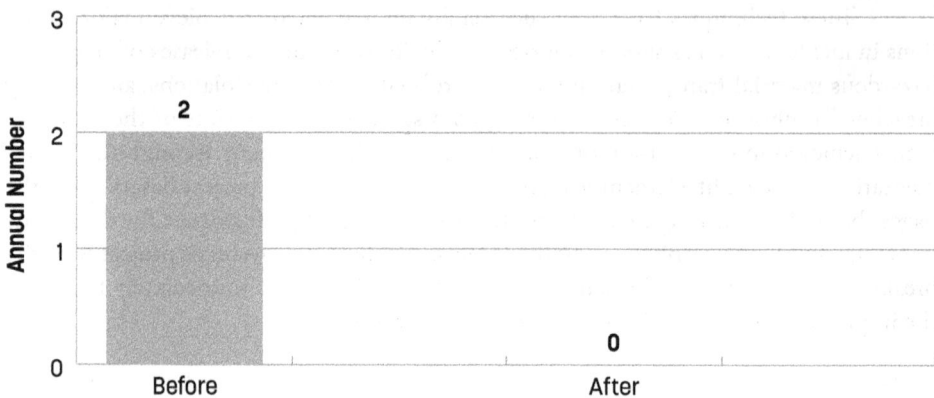

Figure 5.3. Annual number of regulatory agency violations in a pipeline operation for 3 years before and after implementation of a leadership safety improvement project.

Success can best be achieved through application of a process model that merges proven performance management techniques with sound risk management practices. Experience indicates that the eight process elements in Figure 5.4 are essential for effectively maintaining workplace conditions and practices necessary to sustain incident-free operations.

5.1 Element 1: Build Management Commitment and Leadership

Implementing a leadership safety improvement project is generally a management-driven improvement effort. Management commitment and leadership are critical to overcoming barriers to success and for maintaining recognition of the leadership safety improvement project as a top priority throughout the organization. However, even the lack of a clear upper management mandate to implement an improved leadership safety improvement project should not be considered an insurmountable barrier for the individual manager or supervisor who identifies an opportunity for improvement.

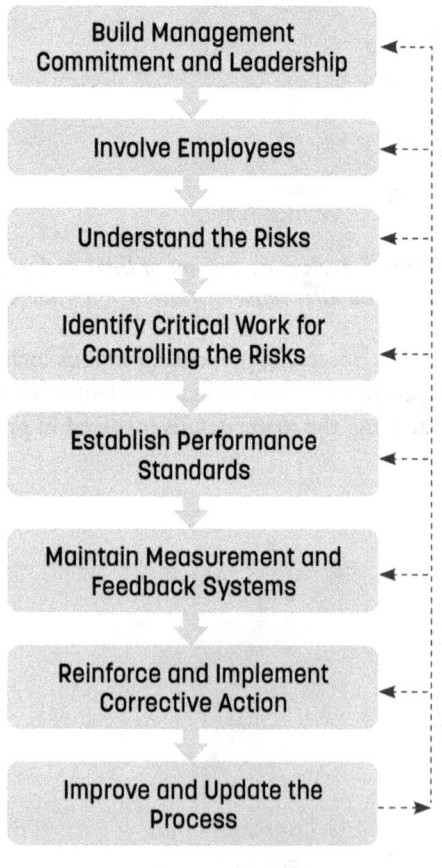

Figure 5.4. Flowchart of a typical leadership safety improvement project.

Once a manager or management team decides to pursue an improvement project such as increasing efforts to prevent serious incidents, they need to educate themselves on this overall approach so that they understand each of the steps outlined below. Supervisors and managers at each level of the organization need to recognize that they are considered "top management" by their subordinates and that each level of management is capable of assuming a strong leadership role. In many organizations, self-directed managers who have a strong desire to make a true difference seek out, work out, and require the procedures needed to improve workplace safety. Such perceptive managers do not wait for a tragedy to occur before taking needed actions. They understand that the organization must be proactive in taking steps to prevent serious incidents.

5.2 Element 2: Involve Employees

Full employee involvement is essential to leveraging the organization's limited resources, harnessing employee knowledge, and facilitating employee ownership of the safety process. Parents typically show polite interest in other people's babies, but they reserve real sacrifice and passion for their own. The development of employees' passion for workplace safety improvement requires comparable active involvement and ownership. The full benefits of employee involvement can be achieved when, instead of simply participating, employees assume leadership roles in developing, implementing, maintaining, and improving the leadership safety improvement project.

5.3 Element 3: Understand the Risks

Success in any endeavor requires knowledge of potential risks. Without a thorough understanding of the risks, safety concerns and the need for risk prevention are, unfortunately, often recognized only after a serious incident has occurred.

In view of the nonroutine nature of serious incidents, the focus must be on *what can happen* rather than on *what has happened* in the past. The argument that a unit has been operating for many years without problems is often offered as rationalization for a lack of concern. However, such a misguided point of view must be granted only limited consideration in evaluating the potential for a future incident. A systematic process involving all levels of the organization must be in place for identifying the risks that can lead to incidents that bring serious consequences for the organization.

5.4 Element 4: Identify Critical Work for Controlling the Risks

Successfully managing serious safety risks involves proactive identification and execution of tasks that are critical to controlling risks. In many operations, these tasks are extensive. Hence an effective system must be established to ensure that all of the proper conditions and work practices are in place and maintained for supporting the diligent execution of this work over the long term. The specific list of critical tasks required for safety success will vary depending upon each organization and the types of risks that must be addressed. Typical examples of these tasks include training, inspections, observation and feedback, equipment testing, emergency drills, and preventive maintenance. The safety improvement model includes the identification of the critical tasks that an organization must focus on to successfully control major safety risks.

5.5 Element 5: Establish Performance Standards

Once the tasks critical to incident-free operations are identified, standards of performance are required to establish expectations for satisfactorily executing them. Performance standards must be based on careful research to provide detailed guidance while avoiding excessive requirements that will increase costs without delivering corresponding benefits in safety performance.

Questions often arise within an organization on the proper frequency for performing tasks. For example, how often inspections, audits, hazard reviews, and training should be conducted. Additional questions may arise regarding the appropriate qualifications and training for employees who perform equipment testing, conduct inspections, or train others. Standards that do not require employees to perform safety tasks frequently enough or that allow unqualified employees to perform critical tasks fail to provide an adequate margin of operational safety. The leadership safety improvement model emphasizes the need to establish standards that are effective in both preventing incidents and fully utilizing resources.

5.6 Element 6: Maintain Measurement and Feedback Systems

Success in any endeavor, including improvement projects like serious-incident prevention, requires more than knowing what to do and when to do it. Unless the tasks critical to safety success are executed as planned, the organization's efforts will simply become another initiative with "good intentions" that failed, rather than a successful one providing an outstanding long-term return on the investment of time and resources. Performance measurement systems will be required to effectively monitor how well the actions necessary to implement the leadership safety improvement project have been performed. Further, effective feedback systems must be established to communicate progress on key initiatives to the employees responsible for performing the work critical to success.

Too often, after an incident, managers find that critical work practices have been inappropriately altered or terminated. The effective measures of upstream performance indicators established by the leadership safety improvement project help ensure that critical actions are sustained for the long term. Establishing an effective feedback system allows time for proactive actions to be taken before an incident occurs, rather than reactive actions being carried out after damage has been done.

5.7 Element 7: Reinforce and Implement Corrective Actions

People tend to sustain activities when they receive positive reinforcement for their efforts. Unfortunately, positive reinforcement in the workplace for employees who execute the tasks necessary for serious-incident prevention is all too rare. In fact, completing tasks required to maintain safe operations may at times seem "punishing" to those responsible for performing them by slowing them down in their efforts to achieve results in areas where the real "glory" may lie (e.g., increased production, productivity, or cost savings). Managers who depend on employees to execute tasks in a timely and thorough manner that are critical to the prevention of serious incidents must ensure that a process is in place to positively reinforce responsible employees for taking and maintaining proper safety actions. Such positive reinforcement is especially critical in shaping new work habits required to achieve a safer workplace.

The leadership safety improvement model utilizes measurement and feedback systems as the basis for identifying appropriate reinforcement milestones and to provide early warning of a need for corrective actions. Adding positive reinforcement actions into the workplace helps ensure that employees feel genuinely appreciated when performance meets or exceeds expectations—a simple but powerful concept. Monitoring upstream performance indicators provides an excellent opportunity to initiate preventive actions before serious incidents occur, rather than after the fact, as is so often the case when employees have no reliable indication of upstream performance indicators.

It is an old adage that "what gets measured, gets done." Perhaps a more accurate statement is that "what gets measured and reinforced, gets done." The reinforcement and feedback elements of the leadership safety improvement project help ensure that outstanding performance is recognized, and early intervention is initiated when indicated. This is never more important than in serious-incident prevention.

5.8 Element 8: Improve and Update the Process

Most workplaces are ever-changing. Changes in equipment, facilities, personnel, and materials, among other factors continually impact most organizations and the specific actions required to sustain safe operations.

The leadership safety improvement model recognizes the importance of ongoing changes within organizations and the need for a systematic approach to ensure that actions required for incident-free operations remain effective. As illustrated by Figure 5.4, the eight elements of the process functioning together provide the framework for achieving and sustaining the workplace conditions necessary to operate free from the catastrophic consequences that often result from serious incidents.

5.9 Implementation of a Leadership Safety Project: Pipeline Operations Case Study

History confirms that the potential frequency of incidents involving the transport of hazardous materials in pipelines is inherently low. However, personnel involved in pipeline operations fully understand that, in the event of a pipeline incident, the potential for catastrophic consequences clearly exists. Thus, a challenge for personnel operating pipelines is to maintain diligence and constancy of purpose even when operations seem almost always to go smoothly.

One company's pipeline team, comprised of a first-level supervisor and other personnel responsible for operating and maintaining the pipeline system, established an objective of developing a more effective approach to serious-incident prevention based on the eight-element process model. The team's assessment of risks included evaluating causes of past U.S. pipeline accidents. Department of Transportation (DOT) data (Figure 5.5) identify third-party damage as the most frequent cause of pipeline incidents, followed by defective equipment or repair, external corrosion, internal corrosion, and operator error.

The team's thorough evaluation of potential risks has helped ensure that the appropriate tasks and safe practices are identified for sustaining incident-free operations (Table 5.1). The pipeline team has established appropriate frequencies for performing tasks critical to sustaining incident-free operations and a system to document scheduled completion dates for the critical tasks.

The team monitors the percentage of critical work completed and charts the results on a monthly basis (Figure 5.6). The figure includes each month's performance score, a 12-month moving average helpful in highlighting trends, and an indication of the team's improvement goal. To reinforce excellent performance, pinpoint improvement needs, provide feedback, and callout corrective actions, handwritten notes are often added to the charts posted in the work area.

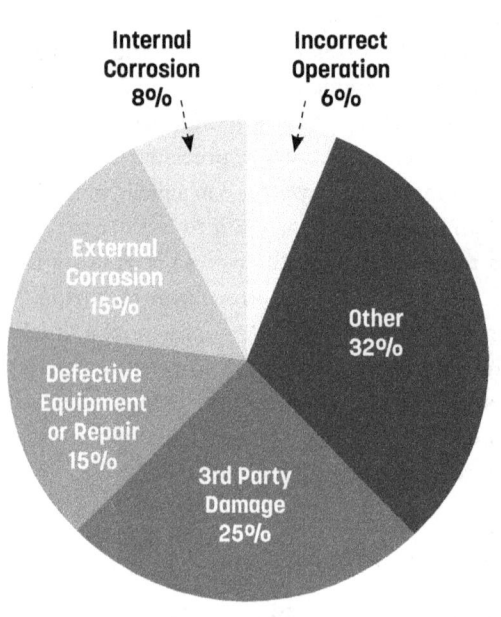

Figure 5.5. Causes of U.S. hazardous liquid pipeline accidents (based on year 2000 reports to DOT).

The company's pipeline operations are subject to an annual regulatory agency audit to determine compliance with DOT requirements. Before implementing the improved management process, the team routinely received violation notices following these audits. Since implementing the improved management process, diligent execution of safety tasks identified as critical by the pipeline team has eliminated post-audit violation notices. Specifically, after implementing the improved process, the team completed 5 consecutive years with *zero* regulatory violations, despite the continuation of thorough annual regulatory agency audits. The team's breakthrough improvement is reflected in the measurement system for monitoring the number of violations (Figure 5.7).

The status of each performance measurement is reviewed by the pipeline team each month. Positive reinforcement is triggered when the measurements demonstrate that performance milestones have been achieved. When measurements indicate improvement opportunities, root causes are identified and proactive corrective actions are initiated. The team drives continual development by focusing on improvement opportunities it can control.

Table 5.1. Critical Work for Serious-Incident Prevention

Critical Work	Frequency
Third-Party Damage Prevention	
(a) Investigate each planned excavation near right-of-way	Prior to excavation
(b) On-site monitoring of all excavation work on right-of-way	Each excavation
(c) Fixed-wing aircraft aerial right-of-way patrol	Weekly
(d) Inspection to ensure right-of-way marker signs in place	Monthly
(e) Mowing of right-of-way	Each June and August
(f) Ground-level inspection of entire right-of-way	Annually
(g) Navigable waterway inspections by diver	Every 5 years
Defective Equipment and Repair Prevention	
(a) Audit: • Management-of-change process • Welding certifications for authorized repair personnel • Contractor safety and training programs	Semiannually
External Corrosion Prevention	
(a) Cathodic protection rectifier inspections	Monthly
(b) Interference bond inspections	Monthly
(c) Corrosion grid inspection	Semiannually
(d) Cathodic protection test station survey	Annually
(e) Close interval cathodic protection survey	20% of pipeline each year
Internal Corrosion Prevention	
(a) Monitor rate of corrosion inhibitor injection	Daily
(b) Corrosion coupon inspections	Quarterly
(c) Piping grid inspection	Semiannually
Prevention of Operator Errors	
(a) Review and update operating manual	Annually
(b) Formal pipeline operator training	Initial training within 1 month of employment; refresher every 3 years and prior to significant changes
(c) Procedure updates for process changes	Prior to implementing each change
(d) Review and update training requirements	Annually
(e) Ergonomic/human factors review of control systems	Annually
(f) High-pressure shutdown checks and instrument calibrations	Semiannually
(g) Audit of anti-drug and alcohol misuse program	Annually

Table 5.1. (Continued)

Critical Work	Frequency
Emergency Preparedness	
(a) Test remote valve operation	Monthly
(b) Test low-pressure valve shutdowns	Monthly
(c) Exercise and inspect manual valves	Semiannually
(d) Visit public emergency response agencies	Annually
(e) Conduct emergency drill	Annually
(f) Test combustible gas analyzers at pump stations	Quarterly
(g) Inspect fire extinguishers	Quarterly
(h) Inspect and test uninterruptible power supply units	Quarterly
(i) Inspect and test relief valves	Per documented schedule
Other	
(a) Investigate all close calls	Each close-call incident
(b) Audit safety permit system compliance	Semiannually
(c) Conduct safety review meeting with contractors	Semiannually
(d) Process hazards analysis	Every 3 years
(e) Confirm pipeline integrity with pressure test or smart pig	Every 10 years
(f) Review and update risk assessment process	Annually

The pipeline team's reinforcement plan (Table 5.2) includes primarily intangible reinforcement, such as notes of appreciation and verbal recognition. Reinforcement milestones have been established for achieving results and for improvement actions. Celebrations are included in the reinforcement plan and have proven to be an effective form of reinforcement for recognizing the achievement of major milestones.

The pipeline team also promotes the timely reporting of close calls and the investigation of other possible early warning signals of potential pipeline problems.

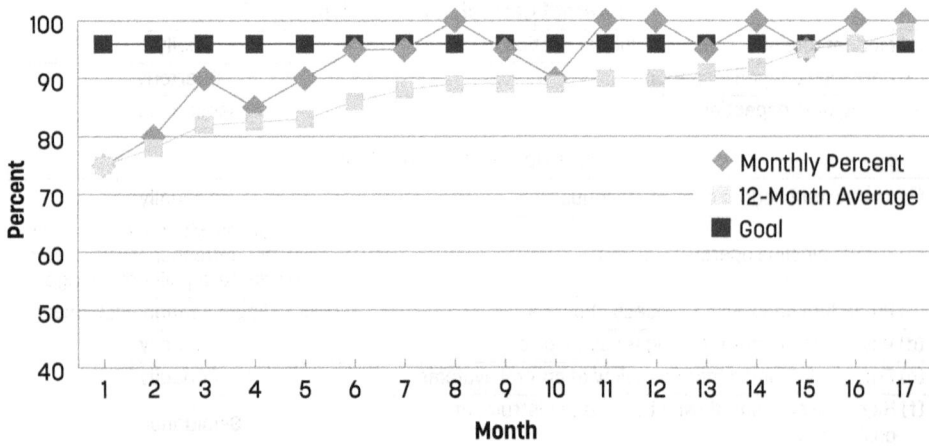

Figure 5.6. Critical work completed on pipeline operations over a 17-month period.

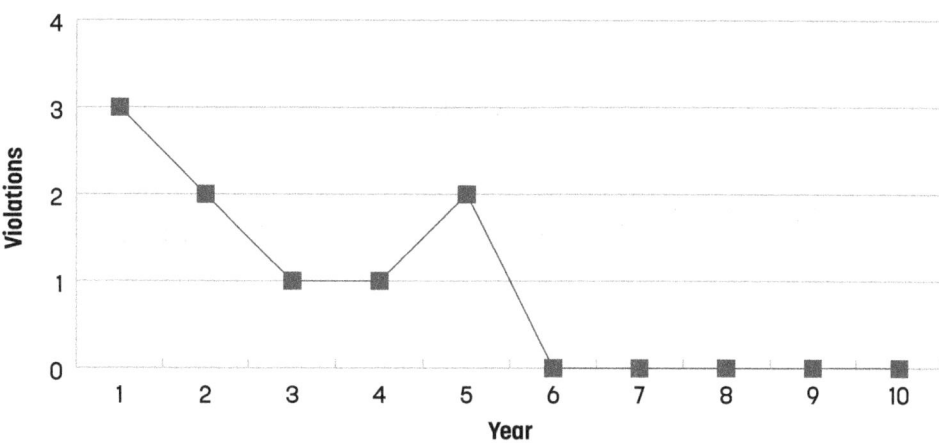

Figure 5.7. Pipeline regulatory agency violations over a 10-year period.

Red-flag conditions, such as the prospect of future construction near a pipeline right-of-way or instrumentation not providing accurate readings, are proactively identified and investigated. Emphasis is placed on taking action in the early stages to prevent the progressive development of more significant problems.

The team understands the importance of continually improving the process and is active in gathering and analyzing new information that has potential impact on pipeline serious-incident prevention. The process is periodically reviewed and updated. The team is proud of its achievements and remains fully committed to its critical objective of maintaining incident-free operations. Leadership safety improvement projects have provided major benefits for all stakeholders: employees and their families, managers, shareholders, customers, suppliers, regulatory agencies, and members of the public who live and work along the pipeline rights-of-way.

Table 5.2. Reinforcement Plan for Pipeline Operations Serious-Incident Prevention

Result or Action to Reinforce	Who Receives Reinforcement?	Who Delivers?
Serious-incident prevention process fully developed	Pipeline team	First-level supervisor and department head
Performance measure fully implemented for 1 month	Process steward and other team members	First-level supervisor
100% completion of critical work achieved for 1 month	Pipeline team	First-level supervisor
Completion of 12 months without a regulatory agency violation	Pipeline team	Chemical-handling department team
Action taken to identify and arrange for correction of red-flag condition	Individual or team taking the action	Chemical-handling department team (in form of red-flag note of appreciation)
Moving average above goal for 3 consecutive months and new goal established	Pipeline team	Chemical-handling department team

CHAPTER 6

The Values-Based Safety Process

Safety culture and safety leadership play pivotal roles in securing safety outcomes and fostering a safe work environment. Prioritizing safety leadership and design enables some companies to operate without harming employees or the environment. Conversely, certain organizations' work practices may increase the risk of injury among employees. Particularly in sectors like heavy industry, construction, mining, and maintenance services, employee actions significantly influence their exposure to inherent hazards. Such organizations benefit from implementing Values-Based Safety (VBS) to cultivate a culture of mutual care and open communication about injury risks. Additionally, various organizations adopt VBS to enhance employee participation in safety initiatives or to fast-track safety culture transformations (see the safety culture changes resulting from behavior-based safety documented in Figure 1.13). The rest of this book is for those companies interested in adopting VBS.

The figure on the previous page provides an overview of the stages of the implementation process. The first stage is discussed in Chapter 7, and subsequent chapters discuss later stages.

6.1 Values-Based Safety

As discussed in the Introduction, we call our approach to behavioral safety the Values-Based Safety (VBS) process. While this book can undoubtedly be an effective guide to implementing a behavior-based safety (BBS) process without consideration of values, discussing your personal and company values will help you ensure a more successful process. Talk about how you treat each other and what your behavior says about your values. Plan a process that demonstrates alignment with your values, and you will likely get a better response from your associates when you begin implementation.

6.2 What's in a Name?

As you will design a process that meets the needs of your organization, your team may want to find a name that fits your organization's new process. Companies have called their safety improvement efforts the employee safety process, the safe acts process, the positive safety process, the continuous incident prevention process, etc. (See the discussion in Chapter 23 for suggestions on involving employees in selecting a name for the VBS process.) A new name is most appropriate when you want to indicate that the new safety process is different from what was done in the past. However, you may choose not to give your VBS process a name. If you are refining an existing process, you may want to emphasize just the enhancements. Consider that giving your process a name may increase the chance that employees within your organization will react negatively to a change in direction and what they perceive as yet another new program.

6.3 Team-Based Process

The key to a successful VBS process is getting the right teams together to plan the implementation. Figure 6.1 shows a typical team structure for the design and implementation phases of the VBS process. Table 6.1 clarifies who participates in each of these teams and some of their responsibilities.

The success of this effort is based on creating a VBS process in three successive iterations, each addressing a different level of detail, with guidance from a management team or a health and safety committee:

1. During the initial assessment of safety factors, the design team (or teams) develops its preliminary plans for the key elements of the process. These plans are simply a general framework for implementation, without all the logistical details that will come later.

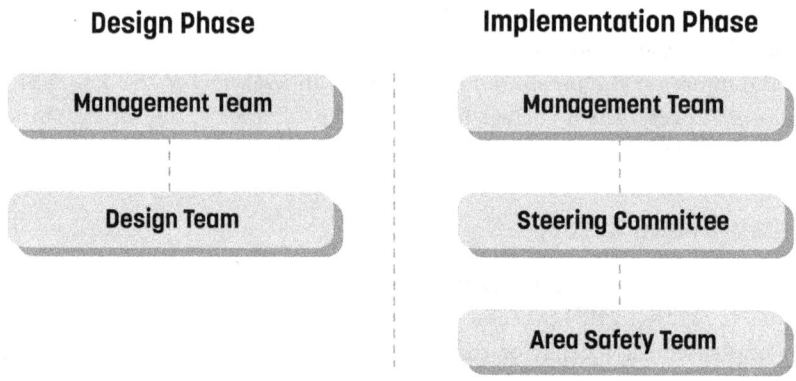

Figure 6.1. The team structure varies for the design and implementation phases.

Table 6.1. Teams Typically Involved in Implementing a VBS Process

Group	Who Participates	Deliverables
Management team	• Senior management (sometimes union leadership)	• Initial charter for design team • Approval and input into design team's plans • Active participation in support activities defined by the design team
Design team(s)	• 8–12 representative employees, a safety professional, a representative from engineering, and a representative from management • May need multiple design teams for large sites	• Assessment of organization • Preliminary presentation to management • Implementation plans that include procedures, forms, and training materials • Assessment of process trail and revised procedures, forms, and training materials
Steering committee(s)	• Typically same membership as design team • May change membership to improve representation • May add steering committees to support areas, shifts, or departments	• Conduct and publish statistical analysis of observation data • Problem-solve and ensure maintenance of VBS process • Set improvement goals • Develop and carry out action plans
Area safety team(s)	• Supervisor, employee safety representative, and employees who normally meet for safety meetings	• Participate in observations • Set improvement goals • Implement action plans appropriate for their areas

2. During the design phase, the design team uses the preliminary plans to develop a detailed implementation plan, complete with forms, procedures, and training materials.
3. During implementation, the steering committee (or committees) may tailor the basic design to the needs of their respective areas or locations.

As a rule, a single design team takes responsibility for the assessment and implementation planning. Sometimes during the assessment, the design team will identify areas that are not represented and add team members to represent those areas. Steering committees have primary responsibility for implementation. The management team periodically reviews and provides guidance throughout both the design and implementation phases of the process. Most organizations already have a health and safety committee structure with the equivalent of a management team and steering committees.

If such teams already exist, then the design team may define the responsibilities of existing teams for the implementation and maintenance of the VBS process.

The terminology used to identify different teams involved in the VBS process varies from organization to organization. For clarity, the terms presented in Figure 6.1 will be used throughout this book. As noted above, in some organizations a management team or central health and safety committee will provide the guidance for the process. For our purposes, we will refer only to the management team. If you work in a large site or you have smaller locations that are geographically dispersed, you may decide to have multiple design teams and steering committees (group[s] of employees that have the final responsibility for implementation), but we will refer to a single design team and single steering committee as we discuss the process. Depending on the size and complexity of the organization, you may also have some combination of these.

6.4 Programs Versus Process

A popular management bandwagon is to create a *process*, not a *program*. A process is said to be never-ending, while a program has a discrete beginning and an end. However, it is important to create a *safety process* that is ongoing and relatively stable. The key elements of the VBS process are regular observations, data review and problem-solving, safety meetings, and safety recognition and celebrations.

In this book, creating a basic, ongoing observation and coaching procedure to support a safety process is discussed at length. However, we also need safety programs. In an organization with a VBS process, the steering committee implements safety programs to address areas of concern that are identified through the observation data. Such programs may include campaigns that provide novelty to keep safety fresh. They help keep employees interested in different aspects of safety. Companies use ever-changing processes for marketing their products and they develop advertising programs that run for fixed periods of time. In the same way, an organization may use an ever-changing and evolving series of programs that support the company's basic process for managing safety.

The safety process provides ongoing measurement and evaluation. Under the umbrella of this ongoing safety process, you may want to initiate a series of programs that uses a set of basic concepts in new ways. The idea is to continually prompt consideration of safety factors. Constantly changing the programs helps maintain interest in your safety efforts by providing reviews of safety requirements in a variety of ways.

For example, you may run a program on back safety for 3 months or conduct a seatbelt campaign for employees and their families. The campaigns can include behavioral interventions, such as training on proper lifting techniques, and efforts to address facilities issues that contribute to at-risk behaviors, such as reengineering lifting devices to make them easier to use. Safety campaigns and promotions are valuable but should not be continued until they become stale and lose their effectiveness. Rather, plan a fixed life cycle for each program. At the end of that life cycle, begin the next program or promotion. The key is to use the observation data to select targets and measure success. Chapter 23 provides an overview of a variety of other process elements and programs that may be important in supporting your improvement efforts.

CHAPTER 7

Safety Assessment

7.1 What Is a Safety Assessment?

A safety assessment is a formal study of your organization's current level of safety performance and the practices that impact safety. It is not the same as a safety audit. A safety assessment examines the process the organization uses to manage safety.

A typical safety audit, on the other hand, examines the extent to which employees are in or out of compliance with established safety procedures and environmental conditions are in or out of compliance with established requirements. Table 7.1 contrasts the safety assessment and the traditional safety audit.

7.2 Why Conduct a Safety Assessment?

Although you may be thoroughly familiar with your organization's safety improvement efforts, you should generally still conduct a formal safety assessment. Conducting the assessment serves two purposes:

1. An accurate and complete understanding of the organization's current safety efforts will result in better recommendations.
2. The interviews, presentations, and discussions resulting from the assessment will help you build support for initiating improvement efforts.

Table 7.1. Key Differences Between Safety Assessments and Traditional Safety Audits

Feature	Safety Assessment	Traditional Safety Audit
1. Observation of unsafe acts (behavioral sampling)	Yes	Yes
2. Observation of unsafe conditions	Sometimes	Yes
3. Summary of historical performance	Yes	No
4. Assessment of employees' knowledge of area safety procedures	Yes	No
5. Assessment of management practices affecting safety	Yes	No
6. Review of existing safety efforts (audits, safety meetings, awards, and special programs)	Yes	No
7. Final report identifies conditions that need to be corrected	Sometimes	Yes
8. Final report identifies unsafe behavior	Sometimes	Yes
9. Report includes recommendations for enhancing safety efforts	Yes	No

Conducting a safety assessment involves a team of employees engaging in systematic data collection and careful analysis that should result in a common understanding of your organization's safety efforts. The assessment provides an opportunity to check your understanding of safety improvement efforts in your organization through direct observation and independent verification. The assessment may prove or disprove your beliefs about the safety efforts in different areas. It also helps ensure that your perspective is not biased by experience with an unrepresentative part of the organization. It allows you to check the accuracy of your beliefs before you present your observations and recommendations to management.

For example, you may suspect that personnel are not conducting safety meetings on the back shift, but you may not know that for a fact. When two independent sources tell you that is the case or you show up at the scheduled meeting and find no one there, you will have a basis for your suspicion.

Using the assessment as a "reality check" will help ensure that your suggestions do not lose credibility because of inaccurate or unrepresentative information about the organization. Accurate observations regarding current efforts will give everyone greater confidence in your recommendations. If your audience agrees that you have described their current efforts accurately, they will be more likely to support your recommendations.

The assessment process also builds support for safety improvement efforts in other ways. Talking with employees about their involvement in safety efforts provides them with an opportunity for input. The discussions will increase everyone's awareness and understanding of your company's current safety practices and thereby provide a starting point for additional employee involvement.

7.3 Who Should Conduct the Assessment?

You will need to decide who should be involved in the initial assessment and planning. The assessment can be either a team or an individual effort. Using a team requires greater coordination but will usually result in a better implementation plan and broader support for that plan. You should also consider the use of outside consultants to either conduct the assessment or guide your assessment efforts. Outside experts are often useful in building management support for such efforts. Table 7.2 outlines the options for who might be involved, the roles they may play, and possible advantages or disadvantages of each.

Table 7.3 provides guidelines for selecting an outside resource to support your assessment, design, and implementation efforts. Be sure to ask the questions given in the figure about the specific consultant who will be working with your organization, not just about the firm. As indicated in Table 7.3, the ideal consultant should have 10 years of hands-on experience implementing behavioral safety programs, not including other types of safety experience. Consultants with less than 10 years' experience should generally work with a project manager who has the appropriate level of experience.

Table 7.2. Considerations for Deciding Who Should Participate in Assessment Efforts

Possible Participants	Potential Roles	Considerations
Individual manager or staff member	Conducts assessment and develops preliminary implementation plan	• Simple logistics • Time to conduct assessment • Real or perceived biases can influence outcome • Depending on experience, individual may need extensive training or guidance
Design team	Team conducts assessment	• Builds broader support • Better final product than individual alone • Coordination is more complex • May take longer to complete • Team members often need extensive training or guidance • May need support from outside consultant
Design team	Team reviews interim assessment findings and final results	• Builds broader support • Better final product • May take longer
Outside consultant	Conducts independent assessment	• Adds objectivity • Adds to short-term costs • Often useful in building management support • Consultant must have appropriate experience
Outside consultant	Provides assistance to design team or individual	• Consultant can provide needed training and support • Adds objectivity • Adds to short-term costs • Often useful in building management support • Consultant must have appropriate experience

7.4 Objectives of the Assessment

The assessment has several objectives:

- identify existing efforts and develop a plan that builds on these efforts
- incorporate input from key personnel
- identify high-risk areas and activities
- identify training needs
- identify potential design team members
- build management support for implementation

Table 7.3. Considerations for Selecting a Consultant to Support the Design and Implementation of a VBS Process

Questions to Ask	Ideal Candidates Will Have
1. What is the consultant's experience in implementing behavioral safety improvement efforts?	• 10 years of experience implementing behavioral safety improvement efforts • Several customers that you can visit and talk with about their experience
2. What is the consultant's background in behavioral psychology?	• Formal training in a program that specializes in behavior analysis • Membership in the Association for Behavior Analysis International (ABAI) • Membership in the state chapter of ABAI (some state associations maintain a registry)
3. What industries does the consultant have experience with?	• Experience with either your industry or a closely related industry that shares some of your problems and concerns
4. Will this consultant be available to maintain a relationship with your organization for the long term?	• Consultant or project manager should have track record of long-term customer relationships
5. What level of on-site support should you expect?	• Consultant should work as a member of your design team through all phases of the project, sharing responsibility for implementation • Cost for this level of support should be clearly identified in the proposal
6. What travel costs will be involved?	• Include an estimate of all travel costs when comparing proposals

Not all organizations want the same output from an assessment. Sometimes the objective is simply to assess the readiness of the organization for a VBS process and establish a team method for beginning one. For some organizations, a planning assessment is necessary for both management and the design team to have a preliminary plan for how the safety process will work. For other organizations, management needs to know what it must do to build a foundation that will support an effective VBS process.

The scope and depth of the assessment will vary extensively depending on the objectives. Some assessments are very formal and involved, requiring 6–8 weeks for implementation and the preparation of a formal report, while others may require only a few days and a 2-hour presentation to management. This chapter describes a full behavioral safety planning assessment. However, many organizations will not require such an extensive assessment.

In some cases, organizations need more specialized assessments. An assessment of basic safety systems would check to ensure that an organization's basic safety management system is complete and functioning effectively. Other specialized assessments might examine organizational culture or leadership practices.

Identify existing efforts and develop a plan that builds on these efforts. Before developing your recommendations, you should identify the key elements of (1) your organization's current safety efforts, (2) what was done in the past, and (3) related improvement efforts. This history will enable you to develop and position your plan to build on existing and past efforts instead of creating an impression of a "new program of the month." During the assessment, you should also identify major initiatives to ensure that your safety improvement efforts align with them, especially those that have broad support. To maximize support for your VBS process, you do not want to create an improvement effort that is at odds with other initiatives. For example, you will often need to coordinate safety and quality improvement efforts. A new safety process can easily be complementary to quality initiatives by exemplifying the philosophy of continuous improvement, using a team approach, analyzing data, and providing recognition.

Incorporate input from key personnel. As part of the assessment process, you should talk with people in each area of your organization. Such interchanges will provide them with an opportunity to have input into your plans. As mentioned, these discussions also begin to model the involvement that will continue later in the implementation phase.

Identify high-risk areas and activities. Another objective is to identify the high-risk areas and activities within your organization. You can do so via interviews and a review of your organization's incident records. As you interview employees, you should ask them what they consider the most dangerous tasks in the area. This question will provide data on the work areas that employees perceive to be the most dangerous. Then compare this information with incident statistics to identify which work areas have the greatest risk and which jobs and tasks within those areas are highest risk. You can use this information to identify work areas that will be high priority and jobs and tasks that will receive special attention. It may also suggest the areas where you will want to pilot the VBS process and identify practices you will want to include in your observation checklists.

Identify training needs. During your assessment observations, you may also identify skill deficits that are likely to have an impact on the success of your safety efforts. In the initial stages, the focus of your assessment will be on management and supervisory personnel rather than the employees. You should thereby learn how well supervisors conduct their safety meetings and how well they know the safety requirements in their areas. Later you will have to plan to address the deficiencies in these areas through training and coaching.

Identify potential design team members. One of the primary objectives of an assessment is often to determine who should participate on the design team. The best way to identify design team members is to take nominations from employees. Generally, the design team will be made up of 8 to 10 representative employees, a safety professional, one person from the engineering department, and a representative from management. During interviews, employees can provide the names of coworkers they would recommend for the design team. Ideal candidates are employees who have demonstrated an interest in safety, are well respected by their coworkers, and are assertive about asking questions and stating their opinions. The employees in each area who have the most nominations should be invited to participate on the design team.

Build management support for implementation. Finally, the most important objective of the assessment is to create management understanding of and support for your implementation plan. Once you have completed your assessment, you should prepare a final report and schedule a presentation to give to management. Your report should summarize your findings and recommend a plan for enhancing your organization's safety efforts. The assessment report and presentation will provide you with an opportunity to ensure that (1) management understands what you are attempting to do and (2) it is willing to support the recommended improvements. This presentation is generally a decision point. If management agrees with your assessment and is willing to participate and support your recommendations, it will give approval to move ahead with your implementation steps.

7.5 Outcome of the Assessment

The primary outcome of the assessment may be a presentation or a formal report. Both would typically include the following:

- a summary of observations and findings
- the recommended team implementation process
- suggested design team participants
- preliminary plans for each stage of the project
- a detailed schedule and cost estimate

In your assessment report, you should include a summary of your observations and findings so that management understands the existing safety situation. The remainder of this chapter will guide your data collection and provide research-based standards for evaluating your organization's safety efforts. Your final report will then be primarily a matter of describing those safety efforts and making recommendations on how to implement changes that will move your organization closer to aligning with the standards suggested by the current research.

The remainder of your final report should describe the implementation plan. During implementation, one of your goals is to ensure that you have broad ownership for the enhancements you are recommending. The only way to create such ownership is through involving others in the final design and implementation process. Therefore, as you conduct your assessment, you will plan a team structure to finalize and initiate the implementation plans. If the organization has an existing safety team structure, you will usually plan a team process that utilizes existing safety teams.

If your company does not already have a safety team, the assessment team will need to plan a safety team structure to ensure effective implementation and maintenance of the new safety process. Such team structures usually include two levels, one that provides management review and another that functions to develop detailed implementation plans based on the assessment report. The plan in the assessment report thus provides a preliminary design that the design team members use as a starting point for developing their detailed recommendations. The design team will generally develop additional details and implement the VBS process, then move into a steering committee role once implementation is underway (see Figure 6.1 and Table 6.1). During the assessment, you should identify a team structure and a preliminary list of participants for both the design and implementation phases of the process.

The assessment report is the design document for implementation. The recommendations in the report serve as a preliminary design and provide a starting point for the design team. The design team can study the recommendations and decide whether to support, change, or discard the recommendations. Most often, they will revise the recommendations based on their experience and knowledge of the organization. They can then develop the additional procedural details required for implementation.

Finally, the assessment report may contain an estimate of cost and a preliminary implementation schedule. By including these items, you can give management a clearer picture of exactly how your organization might implement your recommendations and the potential costs involved.

7.6 Safety Assessment Process

An assessment is somewhat analogous to completing a puzzle. First, you gather all the pieces. Then you complete the picture of (1) the organization's current safety performance and (2) what people within the organization are doing to achieve this level of safety. The assessment involves more than simply gathering data. It also involves analyzing the information on your current safety efforts, developing recommendations on potential improvements, and building support for those improvements.

How Do You Conduct a Safety Assessment?

The assessment generally consists of five steps, as presented in Table 7.4. Although these steps are presented in sequence for simplicity, in reality the first four steps often occur at the same time. For example, while you are conducting interviews, you may identify and arrange to visit a safety meeting before completing the interviews.

Table 7.4. Steps in Conducting a Safety Assessment

Step Number	Activity
1	Review safety data
2	Conduct interviews
3	Observe safety meetings, safety audits, and safety practices in work areas
4	Analyze information and develop an improvement plan
5	Make the final report and presentation

Step 1: Review Safety Data

The first step is to review your organization's safety data, both the statistics and the actual incident reports. The incident data will help you understand whether the company has a significant safety problem and will be useful in planning how you will sell the importance of the proposed improvement efforts. Find out whether your organization is above or below the industry average. If the safety department does not have data about your industry, OSHA, the National Labor Relations Board, or industry associations can usually provide such data.

If your organization's rate of incidents is higher than the industry average, you should have no trouble building support for improvement efforts. Management will usually support a well-developed plan to move your organization to a leadership position in safety within your industry. If your organization's rate of injuries is greater than the norm for your industry, safety improvements will produce significant dollar savings in insurance, workers' compensation, and liability costs. Such savings will more than offset the cost of improvement efforts. If your organization's safety rates are better than the industry average, you have a somewhat greater challenge because management's motivation for improvement may not be as strong.

The safety data should also help you identify groups with the highest and lowest incidents rates. Conduct the bulk of your interviews and observations with these groups to learn what factors account for their current levels of safety performance. Also be sure to review individual incident reports to determine special hazards within the at-risk areas. What equipment and activities place employees at risk? When you begin your interviews, ask people to identify areas and tasks with the greatest risk and what employees can do to avoid incidents when working in these areas. Table 7.5 provides a guide for completing the review of safety data. At this stage, you do not need to identify the behaviors that will prevent injuries. The design team should complete that task in developing the checklist, as described in Chapter 11.

Table 7.5. Suggested Activities for Conducting a Data Review

Activity	Look for	So You Can
1. Review safety reports that summarize incident data	(a) The rate of recordable injuries for the site or organization (b) Areas with high injury rates	(a) Compare with industry average to assess relative safety performance (b) Interview personnel in high-risk areas
2. Review individual accident reports	Tasks and equipment involved in injuries	(a) Prepare questions to ask about high-risk jobs during interviews (b) Begin identifying specific tasks to include in the observation process
3. Collect data on compensation costs and, if possible, costs of property damage from accidents	Calculate an average cost per incident	Estimate cost savings that may result from reduced accident rates

Step 2: Conduct Interviews

In your assessment, try to conduct interviews with people from a "diagonal slice" of the organization.

During interviews with managers, assess their interest in supporting additional enhancements to existing safety efforts. As mentioned, getting their support should be easy if safety has been a problem for the organization. If their areas have a good safety record, you may have a greater challenge. You may want to discuss how confident they are about how they achieved their current level of safety performance: Were they just lucky or do they really know what people are doing in their area to ensure safety? If managers have safety goals or objectives that specify improved numerical targets, they may be interested in developing a concrete plan for how they will achieve those objectives.

In conducting your discussion, be sure to get very precise answers. Any time an answer is not clear or specific, ask for more information or an example. You are looking for concrete observations, what people have directly seen or heard. When possible, you want to get concrete facts, not opinions, hearsay, or feelings about things. Try to validate information learned in the interviews through either corroboration in other interviews or direct observation in the next step.

As you are conducting your assessment, you need a standard of comparison to evaluate the information you collect. The checklist in Table 7.6 includes some of the questions you should try to answer through your interviews and observations. It also provides a recommended standard of comparison based on the research studies cited previously. This standard of comparison will give you a starting point for planning possible enhancements to current safety efforts.

Table 7.6. Safety Assessment Checklist

Questions to Ask	Standard of Comparison
1. Does the area have regular safety meetings? How often? How meaningful are they?	Managers or employees conduct short, weekly meetings that include relevant discussions of safety data, emergency procedures, close-call incidents, etc.
2. Do supervisors and managers regularly talk to employees about safety? How often?	Besides safety meetings, supervisors talk with each employee about safety on the job at least once a week.
3. Does the work area have a formal process of safety audits or observations? How often? Who participates?	Supervisors and managers conduct daily or weekly observations and formally collect data on safety. Employees also conduct regular safety observations.
4. Do the observations focus on behavior or the environment? Do they identify problems or what people are doing right? What kinds of data come out of the process?	The observations focus on behavior and what people in the work area are doing right. The data yield the percentage of safe behaviors or a safety index.
5. Are the data graphed and reviewed with people in the work area?	Observation data are plotted on a graph that is posted in the area. Graphs and observation data summaries are discussed during safety meetings.

Table 7.6. (Continued)

Questions to Ask	Standard of Comparison
6. How are supervisors evaluated on their involvement with the system?	Supervisors are evaluated on how regularly safety observations are conducted in their areas. The evaluation includes how well they manage discussions in safety meetings and team reviews of safety data.
7. What kinds of safety goals are set in each work area?	The goals focus on process rather than incident reduction. Supervisors and employees set improvement targets for their work areas based on the safety observations or other data.
8. How does the area identify and respond to close calls?	The area has an active program to encourage employees to identify close-call incidents. These are discussed in safety meetings and communicated to other shifts and areas. Employees may use such events as the basis for videos, slide shows, or other training materials.
9. What kind of safety training is provided?	Formal safety training is provided to new employees when they begin work in an area. The training includes a formal checklist for on-the-job orientation activities conducted by the supervisor. In addition, operators annually recertify in their units and go through a refresher course, as necessary. Special training is scheduled in safety meetings to address issues identified in observations or by close calls. New supervisors, managers, and employees receive formal training on how to participate in the observation process.
10. What kind of safety awards program is in place?	The safety awards process provides recognition and celebrations of participation and success within the safety process. Awards are provided to teams that meet established goals and to individuals who report close calls and conduct all scheduled safety observations within the area, for example. Awards are not merely based on going some period of time without an incident.
11. How do managers and supervisors communicate the importance of safety as compared with production and cost?	Managers and supervisors make clear statements communicating the importance of safety. These statements are consistent across group and individual meetings, regardless of the situation. Safety is the first agenda in every meeting. It is also a primary consideration in all personnel decisions (again, emphasizing the process of managing safety, not the incident statistics).
12. How can employees identify safety problems in the area? What is done about problems so identified?	(a) The area maintains a safety suggestion system and employees are encouraged to identify safety concerns either through suggestions or in safety meetings. Suggestions may be signed or anonymous. The safety committee responds on area bulletin boards to all concerns. Signed safety suggestions are also one basis for safety awards and recognition. (b) Safety teams have a formal problem-solving process with clear, easy-to-use guidelines for assessing cultural issues and analyzing observation data, close calls, and incidents. In addition, they track significant issues to resolution and maintain a list of concerns and their status on the bulletin boards. Management works with maintenance to ensure timely responses to safety-related maintenance items.

Supplement the questions from the safety assessment checklist with additional questions you identify as you review the safety data and conduct the interviews. In addition to the items on the safety assessment checklist, here are some other questions that may be appropriate:
- What are the most hazardous tasks in the area?
- How quickly do safety problems get corrected?
- What are your current safety programs? What have you tried in the past? What other improvements or team efforts are currently underway?
- Do managers or supervisors directly or indirectly emphasize production over safety?
- What kinds of training have you received?
- Is equipment well maintained and safe to use?
- Who should participate in designing the safety improvement effort?
- Who should I talk with to learn more?

If you are assessing a large organization, you may also want to conduct a survey of safety management practices. A survey allows you to get input from a large number of employees without the time required to conduct interviews. Perhaps more importantly, a survey can help you identify groups or pockets of employees for further study. By using survey data in combination with safety performance data, you can use interviews to gather information on safety management and leadership practices in exemplary areas and areas that need improvement.

If you use a survey, you may want to conduct a small initial round of interviews to broaden your understanding of the kinds of issues you should investigate through a written survey. Then, after you have analyzed the survey results, conduct more extensive interviews to gain additional understanding of the information that you learned from the survey.

Constructing a well-designed survey requires experience or training in survey construction. You must carefully plan the kind of information you want and what you will do with that information. Generally, items should ask about specific practices rather than attitudes or opinions. Consider developing categories of items that reflect your values and the practices that support or detract from those values. Obviously, such items must be written in an appropriate manner for everyone taking the survey. Table 7.7 presents examples of possible survey categories and the kinds of practices that might be examined through a written survey.

Step 3: Observe Safety Meetings, Safety Audits, and Safety Practices in Work Areas

Try to visit several safety meetings and observe several typical safety audits in different areas. Some organizations will have different types of safety meetings and you should attend a sample of each. They may have a large monthly meeting and smaller, daily or weekly "toolbox" meetings. As you observe the safety meetings, attempt to answer the following questions:
- Are the meetings well run (is the agenda prepared in advance, do they stick to the agenda, is the discussion controlled, etc.)?
- Do employees participate in exercises or discussion?

Table 7.7. Sample Safety Culture Survey Categories and Practices for Written Surveys

Part I—Safety Leadership

Function	Practices
Direction	• Area safety teams have clearly defined responsibilities • Employees discuss task hazards prior to starting work
Guidance	• Area safety team receives feedback on adequacy of its efforts • Leaders provide feedback to associates on safe practices • Leaders provide feedback to associates on unsafe practices
Motivation	• Area safety teams receive recognition for their efforts • Employees receive recognition for their on-the-job safety • Employees are disciplined for unsafe practices

Part II—Alignment of Values and Practices

Values	Practices
Mutual Support	• Employees and supervisors provide assistance to other employees when appropriate • Supervisors provide time for employees to participate in the safety process • Supervisors are evaluated on their support of the safety process • Management provides resources to support the safety process
Shared Participation	• Employees are able to contribute their ideas and suggestions for safety improvements • Employees participate in discussions during safety meetings • All employees participate in the safety process
Trust and Respect	• Employees respond non-defensively to feedback on safety • During safety team meetings, team members talk about others only in ways appropriate to their presence • Observers and supervisors ask for reasons when they observe employees working unsafely • Observers act as if they expect others to do their best • Supervisors discuss suggestions or concerns without being critical

- Does the meeting include a review of current safety data, incident rates, or safety process measures?
- Does the agenda include discussion of close-call incidents?

Besides sitting in on safety meetings, try to observe typical safety observations or audits. Safety staff, management, or other personnel often conduct these activities. A common problem is that they focus primarily on environmental conditions rather than on what people are doing in the area. As you observe the existing audit/observation process, try to confirm the information you learned during interviews regarding items 3 and 4 from the safety assessment checklist (Table 7.6). Also, identify how observers respond to employees who are engaging in unsafe practices and how they respond to employees who are performing their jobs safely.

You may also wish to tour work areas and observe on-the-job safety. Use your experience to evaluate employees' use of personal protective equipment, housekeeping, and general safety. If you are unfamiliar with the work area, you may want to tour the area with an experienced employee or supervisor and ask them to identify practices that are safe or unsafe and where injuries have occurred in the past. Table 7.8 provides a guide for completing the observations during the assessment.

Table 7.8. Suggested Activities for Observations During Assessments

Activity	Look for	So You Can
1. Attend safety meetings	(a) Does the content of the meeting reflect the agenda? (b) Do employees participate in exercises or discussion? (c) Does the meeting include a review of current safety data or incidence rates? (d) Does the agenda include discussion of close-call incidents?	(a) Identify additional questions for interviews (b) Develop plans for improving the safety meetings
2. Observe existing audit or observation process	(a) Who conducts audits or observations and how? (b) What occurs when an employee is observed being unsafe? (c) What is done with the audit or observation data?	(a) Prepare questions to ask about high-risk jobs during interviews (b) Begin identifying specific tasks to include in the observation process
3. Observe safety practices in work areas	Safe and unsafe work practices	Use as examples in draft safety checklists and training materials

Step 4: Analyze Information and Develop an Improvement Plan

Once you have completed data gathering, analyze your information and develop an implementation plan. Analyze your information by comparing your organization's current safety management practices with those proven to be effective in the research studies described in the first chapter. Then develop a plan for implementing changes to your safety process that move your organization toward the model suggested by current research. The standards of comparison in the safety assessment checklist may provide additional suggestions for enhancing your organization's safety efforts. The outcome of this step is an outline for the final report and presentation, which you will be preparing in the next step. You might prepare an outline that includes a single summary statement about a particular topic, like the following examples:

- Significant observations of the organization's current safety efforts: "The area has one safety audit every year conducted by the safety department."
- Recommendations on how those efforts might be enhanced: "Create a process of weekly observations for collecting data on the area's compliance with safety procedures."
- Implementation steps: "Establish a design team comprised of frontline supervisors and representative employees to develop the observation checklist and procedures."

In developing your plan, decide who should participate in the design team that will be responsible for the final design and implementation process. Before deciding on design team members, make a preliminary decision about what areas are going to be involved. As stated previously, while some research suggests that all employees participate in conducting observations, current research suggests that the ideal number of participants should be roughly equivalent to 8%–10% of your total employee headcount. See the section in Chapter 11 on how observers will be identified, and discuss how you will determine who should conduct observations.

Usually, before deciding who should be involved, you will have to decide what work areas will participate. If you work in a large organization or at a large site, consider whether to pilot your behavioral process. A pilot is a good idea if your organization is likely to be particularly resistant to the idea. Most employees should view the pilot areas as representative of the organization, and those pilot areas should usually have

- a high rate of incidents and
- management personnel willing to support the VBS process.

You will also need to recommend whether observations should be conducted by managers and supervisors, or employees, or both. Many organizations are moving to a philosophy of greater employee involvement and self-managed teams. In organizations with a well-developed team process, employees should conduct safety observations. However, in some organizations, safety remains primarily a responsibility of management and supervision. In such cases, the observation process should be part of the supervisor's job. Once the supervisors have a good understanding of the observation process, they then can begin to involve employees in the observations, often with the ultimate goal of involving all employees.

Once you have a preliminary idea of who should be responsible for the observations, you will have a better idea of who to involve in the design team. As a rule, you need to involve the people who will initially do the observations.

Additional details on different options for addressing each element of the VBS process and how to implement the process will be discussed in subsequent chapters of this book. Remember that your recommendations are preliminary plans and that the design team will ultimately make changes and work out the many logistical details.

Step 5: Make the Final Report and Presentation

One of the primary goals of the assessment is to create management support. At the end of your assessment, your task is to explain to management how the organization can enhance its current safety efforts. Generally, you will want to prepare a short report that summarizes your observations and recommendations. However, do not assume that management will read your report; they may not. Your best strategy is to schedule a short presentation and discussion that allows you to summarize your assessment and discuss the recommendations. This approach will ensure that management has a basic understanding of what you are trying to do. For simplicity, your report and presentation should follow the same outline. Figure 7.1 presents one possible outline for such a report and presentation.

Remember: This is a sales presentation. You are trying to sell your management on the value of implementing your recommendations. Before talking about the details of your recommendations, stress the realistic benefits that will result from a systematic implementation of the VBS process:

- employees who better understand safety procedures
- greater compliance with safety procedures
- exemplary injury rates
- sustainable processes

This presentation also provides an opportunity to get input from management team members so that you can incorporate their ideas as you move ahead.

You may want to schedule several individual meetings with key leaders before or after your group presentation. Use the individual meetings to explain your efforts and enlist support on an individual basis.

During your presentation, explain the kind of support and involvement required from management to make this effort successful. The VBS process will usually require several forms of management support:

- participation in design review meetings and training
- participation in weekly observations
- a review of safety data in existing meetings
- allowing employees time to participate

The goal of these discussions with management is to get a "go-ahead" decision. This decision should include an agreement to actively participate and support the design team's improvement efforts.

Assessment Report Outline

I. **Introduction and Executive Summary**

II. **Assessment Methodology**

III. **Our Current Process:**
   (use checklist items to determine relevant headings)
   A. Safety meetings
   B. Safety audits or observations
   C. Safety awards
   D. Management practices
   E. Data analysis

IV. **Recommendations**
   A. Team process
   B. Implementation steps
      1. Pinpointing safe acts
      2. Creating the safety observation process
      3. Feedback and involvement
      4. Safety awards
      5. Problem-solving and continuous improvement

Figure 7.1. Suggested outline for assessment report and presentation.

CHAPTER 8

Management Overview and Design Team Workshop

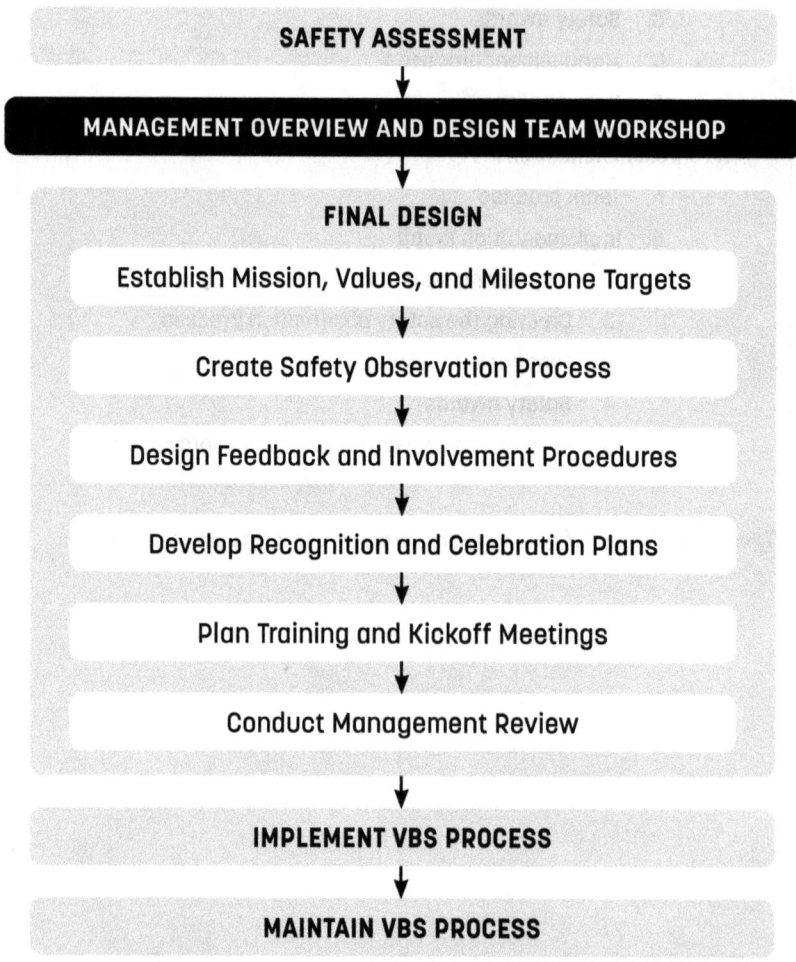

To ensure success, you should initiate your process in a carefully planned and well-organized manner that ensures a high level of understanding of the changes you propose. You will have at least three groups to consider: managers and supervisors, those who will be participating in the design team, and other employees. You will need a strategy that combines communication and training. In the management overview, you provide managers and supervisors with an outline of your plans for enhancing their current efforts. The overview will tell them what the design team will be doing and what they can expect as the process develops. By providing a behavioral safety workshop, you will give design team members an understanding of their tasks and the basic set of skills they will need for planning activities. You will also establish a group of knowledgeable employees in the work area who can provide information to others about the Values-Based Safety (VBS) process. Later, the design team will have to plan additional communication and kickoff meetings with employees.

8.1 What Is the Management Overview?

A management overview is an orientation for management and supervisory personnel that introduces the enhancements you plan to make to the organization's safety improvement efforts. You should generally invite management personnel who were not present at your assessment presentation, especially those from the work areas targeted for initial implementation. This meeting may have the same basic agenda as the final presentation of the assessment results except that you are now explaining plans that have management approval.

Despite management's approval, you still need to sell the value of your recommendations. In particular, you should ensure that your audience understands the basic elements of the VBS process and how they can have input into its final design. The goal is to ensure that managers and supervisors in the area know about the proposed changes. This understanding will remove fear of the unknown and help build their support for the new process. Their support will help you overcome resistance to the changes required in a new safety improvement effort. You should also let them know how the process will evolve and when they can expect to learn more about the design team's plans.

If your organization involves shift work, you will probably need to hold several such meetings to ensure the participation of supervisory personnel from all shifts. Depending on the size of your organization, you may want to provide a series of kickoff meetings for all employees, instead of just managers. These may be short overviews presented as part of regular safety meetings or a separate series of meetings. The purpose of the meetings is basically the same as that of the management overview described above.

8.2 What Are the Objectives of the Management Overview?

These meetings have several objectives:
- to provide an overview of the elements of the VBS process and why it is being implemented
- to ensure that line management knows how to support the implementation process at this stage
- to let people know how to influence the process

8.3 What Is the Design Team Workshop?

The initial workshop is similar to the management overview except that it usually includes formal training for those who will participate in the design team (refer to Figure 6.1 and Table 6.1 for the typical team process). If your design team involves primarily supervisory personnel, you may only need one meeting. This initial workshop will generally include all of the people who will be participating in the design meetings. You may want to include a variety of other personnel. For example, you might include volunteers from each shift and area involved in the implementation. You may choose to include union leadership or people from work areas that may develop a similar effort in the future. In particular, you should consider including informal leaders who will help support your effort later if they understand what you are trying to do. Again, one of your goals is to let people know how they can have input in the design process and where to go if they have questions.

8.4 What Are the Objectives of the Design Team Workshop?

This workshop has several objectives:
- to provide the necessary skills to those who will participate in the design process
- to build better understanding and support from key managers and employees
- to get initial input from participants as a basis for later development

8.5 What Is the Agenda?

The behavioral safety workshop is typically 3 days long, depending on the level of skill you want to provide to the design team and the amount of detail you want to provide to other participants. Figure 8.1 provides a typical agenda for a behavioral safety workshop. Formal exercises or small group discussions follow each agenda item. These exercises help ensure that the participants understand what they will do in the implementation process. The agenda parallels the organization of this book, which might be used as a supplement to the workshop. The workshop might also include a module on developing values and identifying practices aligned with those values along with additional exercises on each of the key elements of the VBS process.

This meeting should serve as the kickoff meeting for the design team. You may want to establish ground rules for later meetings and conduct an exercise that enables team members to develop a preliminary purpose statement, in preparation for your first design team meeting.

Design Team Workshop

Part 1: Basics
- Safety basics
- Analysis of traditional safety programs
- Pinpointing behavior
- Our values

Part 2: Implementation Overview
- Pinpoint safe acts
- Safety observations
- Feedback and involvement
- Recognition programs
- Maintaining the behavioral process

Part 3: Behavior Analysis
- ABC analysis of safety
- Behavioral incident investigation

Figure 8.1. A typical agenda for a VBS process design team workshop.

CHAPTER 9

Final Design

Here you will be working with the design team to carry out the next phase of your recommendations: the development of a detailed implementation plan for the new safety process within your organization. If a team conducted your assessment, some of the assessment team may also be participating with you on the design team.

The recommendations from your assessment along with initial ideas captured during the design team workshop will serve as a preliminary design and provide a starting point for the design team's efforts. This way you will not walk into a design team meeting and begin to brainstorm what the team members think needs to be done. Rather, you will start by presenting the assessment recommendations and the rationale for those recommendations along with the team's input from the design team workshop. After this presentation, you will change hats and become a participant in the meeting. As a participant, you will work with the other team members to finalize the implementation plans.

Design team members may occasionally decide to proceed in a different way than you recommended on the basis of the assessment. As a team member, you have input into the team's decision, but you cannot force your views. If the team wants to do something that differs significantly from the plan originally approved by management, you will need to go back to the management team and reach agreement on the team's purpose. Otherwise, trust the team process. If you do not agree with a course of action, say so and try to find a mutually agreeable course of action. You will often be able to support a team member's ideas while you continue to champion progress on the assessment recommendations.

Over the long term, the safety process should be responsive to data and experience. The group should ensure an observation process that gets modified on the basis of incidents and close calls. The important thing is to create an adaptive system that responds to experience in ways that will help employees prevent future incidents and injuries.

9.1 What Are the Objectives of This Phase?

In this phase, your goal is to work with the design team to complete detailed plans for enhancing your organization's process for managing safety in the work areas. Completion of the implementation plans usually means developing additional details for carrying out the assessment recommendations. The specific objectives include creating or enhancing the following:

- a safety observation process that provides a regular measure of on-the-job safety
- feedback procedures for communicating and reviewing observation data
- safety awards tied to on-the-job safety improvement
- an involvement process that ensures an appropriate number of observers

A design and implementation process to be followed as though you are initiating a completely new safety initiative will also be discussed in this book. You should be able to adapt these basic procedures if you are simply refining your existing efforts.

9.2 Design Team Process

A key element of the design team's job is to clarify the responsibilities of steering committees both during and after implementation. You will need to establish such safety teams if they do not already exist. In large organizations, the design team's plans should clarify the responsibilities of local steering committees. These committees may be site safety teams, if your organization has relatively small locations, and they may report to a divisional or centralized company safety team. They may be area or unit safety teams within a larger plant and report to a site steering committee or central safety team (see Figure 6.1 and Table 6.1). The design team(s) will also need to plan the responsibilities of management for supporting the new process. The design team should operationally define the responsibilities of these groups for both their initial participation and their long-term support of the safety process. The design team may also need to plan its own responsibilities during a pilot process and its responsibilities as a steering committee, if it plans to continue in this capacity after implementation.

The details of your implementation plan will vary depending on the size and complexity of your organization. Table 9.1 provides guidelines for planning the implementation structure and process. For large organizations or organizations that are spread out geographically, you will usually want to conduct day-long planning meetings in order to complete your planning prior to beginning implementation. We have found that 2-day planning meetings are most effective. You will need to plan a logical implementation sequence, bring steering committee members to a central location for the first phase, and provide a single workshop that covers all elements of the process. Next, you should provide similar implementation workshops at central locations for the steering committees in the later phases.

Table 9.1. Guidelines for Planning Implementation Structure and Process

If Your Organization Is	Then
Small (300 people or less) and at a single location	The design team and steering committee will be the same, often using periodic planning meetings
Spread across multiple locations	The design team should conduct 2-day marathon planning meetings to plan the process and develop materials, then implement through steering committees
At a large, single location	The design team may use either marathon or periodic planning meetings, then implement through steering committees

You should evaluate training and implementation efforts at each stage so that you can refine the process throughout implementation.

If your organization is resistant to change, you should consider doing a pilot in work areas where you are confident you can achieve success. The ideal pilot areas should

- be viewed as representative of the other work areas of the organization
- have managers and personnel who are likely to be supportive of the process
- need improvement as indicated, for example, by incidence rates

The implementation process described in this book assumes you have a design team that will complete multiple 2-day marathon planning meetings, then implement the process through steering committees. The same process can be adapted for simple organizations where the design team will become the steering committee. The periodic planning meetings are discussed at each of the primary stages when the process differs from the 2-day planning process.

The time required for implementation will be a function of the size of your organization and whether your planning and implementation are concurrent or sequential. As a general rule, conducting several day-long planning meetings is preferred for larger organizations because it reduces the length of time required to complete the planning and implementation process. Table 9.2 provides an overview of these options along with guidelines on the time required for implementation in a relatively simple organization or a single component of a more complex organization.

Whether you choose a periodic or a marathon planning process, more complex organizations, organizations that are resistant to change, and organizations that lack strong and active management support are more likely to need outside assistance. An experienced outside consultant can help you avoid mistakes and build the credibility of your improvement efforts. Such an outside resource is more important in the marathon planning process because the schedules are usually more compressed.

Table 9.2. Considerations for Selecting Periodic or Marathon Planning Meetings

Design Team Meeting Options	Considerations
Periodic planning meetings (2-hour weekly or biweekly meetings)	• Allows implementation of observation process before planning other elements of the process, often as soon as 2 months after beginning planning • Takes longer for implementation, usually 8-12 months for planning and implementation in a small- to medium-size facility
Marathon planning meetings (2-day, off-site meetings)	• Minimizes length of time required for planning and implementation, usually 4-8 months for initial implementation • Facilitates design team participation from multiple sites with minimal travel costs

9.3 Role of the Management Team

The management team has several functions during this phase. Its first responsibility is one of project management, especially if the design team is using a periodic planning process. It should provide the design team with an initial goal or purpose statement, then ensure that the design team develops its own initial goal or purpose statement in a manner that is consistent with the management team's intent.

If the design team uses periodic planning meetings, the management team should also review the design team's schedule and agree on the milestone reviews. One of the difficult aspects of implementing this kind of change effort is establishing a sense of urgency. A schedule will assist the design team's leader in maintaining progress. The design team leader should generally provide regular updates to the management team on the design team's progress.

The management team is also responsible for changing organizational policies and procedures to better support the VBS process. In particular, it should deal with issues that are beyond the span of control of the design team. These might include making changes to company incentive programs, performance appraisals, and compensation systems in ways that support the new safety process. The management team may also work closely with the design team on defining management's role, to ensure maintenance of the safety process. The assessment should identify and include recommendations for addressing these issues.

Finally, the management team will be responsible for approving and sanctioning the design team's recommendations. Once the management team approves the design team's plan, the design team proceeds with implementation. The management team's approval should involve commitment of resources, including management participation and funding for various elements of the process, such as time for meetings, money for training, travel costs, safety celebrations, and related activities.

What Are the Steps in This Phase?

Generally, design and implementation efforts will follow the six-step process given in Table 9.3.

Table 9.3. Typical Steps in Designing a VBS

Step Number	Activity
1	Establish a mission statement, values, and milestone schedule
2	Create the safety observation process
3	Develop feedback and involvement procedures
4	Develop recognition and celebration plans
5	Plan training and kickoff meetings
6	Conduct a management review

For simplicity, these steps will be presented as a sequential process. Although this description may not always apply, it captures the critical tasks and serves as a guide for your design efforts. If your design team is conducting periodic planning, some of these steps may occur almost at the same time or in a different order. For example, you may conduct the area kickoff meeting (step 5) and initiate the observation process before addressing the planning involved in steps 3 and 4. If this is your approach, be sure to review each element with management prior to its implementation.

Also, especially in periodic planning meetings, individual group members will frequently champion one or more special programs (see the discussion on providing for a variety of ongoing support programs in Chapter 23) while you are planning elements of other steps. The team members should encourage this involvement by supporting such initiatives. Seeing their ideas come to life is the natural consequence of participation in safety teams and committees. The resulting changes will help maintain participants' interest in working on the safety teams and make recruiting future participants easier.

CHAPTER 10

Step 1: Establishing Mission, Values, and Milestone Targets

Before finalizing the design of the safety process, work with the design team to develop a goal or purpose statement. In some cases, you may have a charter of the initial statement of purpose from the management team or a draft produced by participants in the design team workshop. If you do not already have one, draft a preliminary purpose statement before the first design team meeting. Or you may choose to develop the mission or purpose statement as a group exercise during the meeting (review discussion of mission statements in Chapter 3). Also, prepare a sample schedule, based on your best guess, about the activities and the amount of time required for each. Then in the first meeting, allow the team to discuss, modify, and approve both the purpose statement and the schedule for presentation to the management team. Figure 10.1 presents a sample goal or purpose statement.

To: Implement improvements to our process of managing safety on the job

In a way that:

provides regular observations and feedback for safety practices in our work areas,

establishes increased employee involvement in observations and safety meetings, and

provides safety awards for achieving high levels of compliance with our safety practices

So that:

We achieve a safer workplace as measured by our safety observations and our rate of OSHA recordable incidents

---

Figure 10.1. A sample purpose statement for a design team.

10.1 Clarifying Values: A Structured Approach

After 5 years of using an unstructured approach to assist organizations with the task of defining their values, we developed a more structured process using common themes that kept recurring as we worked with different organizations. Outlined below, this structured approach requires less time and provides a set of value statements and corresponding practices found to be just as effective in guiding the development and assessment of the new VBS process.

An unstructured approach may still be appropriate for organizations that want to develop a very personalized set of value statements with corresponding practices.

The design team that will be planning the new process for the organization typically undertakes this exercise. If the design team is large, breaking it down into smaller groups may best accomplish the first three of the steps shown in Table 10.1 and assist your organization in creating a values-based safety improvement process.

Table 10.1. Typical Steps in Defining Organizational Values

Step Number	Activity
1	Brainstorm actions likely to impact the process
2	Pinpoint those practices
3	Sort these practices into "value" categories
4	Use values in designing your safety process
5	Discuss values during kickoff meetings and training
6	Use values as criteria for evaluation

10.2 Step 1: Brainstorm Actions Likely to Impact the Process

Brainstorm a list of positive and negative actions that would either support or damage your efforts to implement a new safety improvement initiative. This needs to be a true brainstorming effort. Simply capture everyone's ideas on a flip chart. Write them all down on the chart without editing what they say. Do not try to make the items more specific or identify pinpointed behaviors. At this stage, you will typically get very general statements, such as "need visible management support" on the positive list and "lack of communication" on the negative list.

10.3 Step 2: Pinpoint Those Practices

Pinpoint all the items on your lists. (For more detailed instructions on pinpointing, refer to Chapter 21.) Restate each of the positive items on your list to describe a specific activity or behavior. Also restate each of the negative items in the positive. In other words, restate items that would damage safety efforts as statements of action that will have a positive impact on the process. To use the examples given above: "Need visible management support" might be restated as "Get upper management to introduce the safety process and explain why it is important." "Lack of communication" might first be stated in the positive as "Develop good communication," then further developed into "Keep employees informed about planning and the implementation progress." Each point should be a description of a specific behavior that demonstrates support for the process. In addition, each point should be worded in language that is meaningful to the employees who will see them.

10.4 Step 3: Sort These Practices Into "Value" Categories

Most design teams identify activities that can be readily categorized into the following value categories:
- concern for the well-being of others
- open and honest communication
- personal leadership
- teamwork and employee involvement
- continuous improvement

Have each group sort their pinpointed practices into the value categories. If you have activities or practices that do not correspond to one of these values, you can modify the categories or insert one or two additional value statements.

After listing all the group's responses, review each list to ensure that each practice is recorded under the value that it best supports. Also look for closely related practices that might be combined. The ideal number is between three and seven practices for each value. More than seven makes the list of values and associated practices too long and complex to provide practical guidance to managers and employees.

At this stage you should combine the lists produced by each of the small groups. Revise and combine similar items. Once you have condensed the list as much as possible, have each group select the three to five practices they consider most important in each category. Next, create a master list of values and practices by combining the lists prepared by each group. Again, as a group, condense and combine items as much as possible, then again select the three to five practices in each value category that will be most important to the success of your process. Continue this process until you have achieved a consensus on the three to five practices that are most critical to the success of the process in representing each value. Once you have identified your initial set of values and related practices, go back over the list to see if you can identify any other practices that relate to each value statement that should be considered.

After getting an appropriate number of practices for each value statement, do a final edit to ensure the specificity and clarity of your practices. Also try to ensure that your practices are mutually exclusive. If two of your practices are similar or potentially overlapping, either combine them or rewrite them to make them more distinct.

Table 10.2 presents examples of critical practices related to the value statements identified above.

10.5 Step 4: Use Values in Designing Your Safety Process

These values and critical practices should guide you in the many decisions that you will need to make in designing your process as outlined in the sections that follow. For example, some of your critical practices will specify roles and responsibilities for those who will be involved in the process, including observers, steering committee members, supervisors, managers, and support staff. These practices may include roles that you want to define formally as procedures or responsibilities within your behavioral process. Other critical practices may specify behaviors that you want to use to provide guidelines on how people interact with one another within your new process.

Table 10.2. Examples of Value Statements and Corresponding Critical Practices

Value Statements	Critical Practices
Concern for fellow employees	• Provides feedback to others to help them • Identifies potential risks and actions needed to eliminate or reduce them
Continuous improvement	• Identifies and documents problems and opportunities for improvement • Ensures that improvements are properly executed • Promotes improvements to the VBS process
Personal leadership	• Trains/coaches others in safety processes • Sets examples for others • Makes time for participation in safety activities • Provides recognition for safety practices and accomplishments
Open and honest communication	• Listens well and responds appropriately to others • Follows through on verbal commitments • Communicates safety-related information promptly
Teamwork and employee empowerment	• Participates and contributes to team effectiveness • Solicits ideas and suggestions from others • Strives for consensus

10.6 Step 5: Discuss Values During Kickoff Meetings and Training

Be sure to discuss your values and critical practices when you introduce your VBS process to employees. Kickoff meetings are ideal times to communicate your expectations about how employees are to participate in your new safety process. Discussing your values at these meetings will communicate your expectations from the start as to who will participate and why. When discussing "open and honest communication," for example, you can talk about the importance of (1) having an open and honest discussion about what is observed and (2) recording accurate information on the observation forms.

The purpose of these discussions is to clarify the organization's expectations and sharpen the employees' understanding of each value statement. You will usually not have to conduct extensive skill development exercises because most employees will already have an intuitive understanding of what these statements mean. The purpose of the training is to clarify situations that are appropriate for applying their existing skills and knowledge. In some cases, you may need to provide additional training to help employees develop or refine the communication and leadership skills necessary for a successful safety process. Other approaches to this training might utilize case studies for analysis and discussion. The goal of these exercises is to get participants to consider how they will respond when faced with situations that they are likely to encounter as you implement your VBS process.

10.7 Step 6: Use Values as Criteria for Evaluation

In your safety process, values have two additional uses:
1. They provide a basis for safety teams to evaluate the quality of the new safety process once it is up and running.
2. They provide a basis for evaluating individual performance within an organization's performance appraisal process.

When your employees complete their initial observer training, your organization's newly established values should serve as ground rules for their interactions with one another. The statements of values and practices provide a basis for reciprocal feedback and for evaluating actions and potential actions. The question "Did this particular practice support our values?" should be a standard part of evaluating past actions, and the question "Does this decision support our values?" should be a standard part of decisions regarding future actions. In short, the values can serve as guidelines for the kinds of behavior expected within the organization and thereby clarify behavior that members of the organization will support.

Your steering committee can use these values and practices as a basis for evaluating the quality and integrity of its safety improvement efforts. Chapter 17, which focuses on maintaining the VBS process, presents additional details on using values as part of the assessment process.

10.8 Establish a Milestone Schedule

Your team will also need to develop a milestone schedule for completing each stage of planning and implementation, especially if you are conducting periodic planning meetings. If you are using the 2-day planning meetings, you may simply schedule a presentation to your management team during your final meeting. Otherwise, the schedule should include milestones that indicate when the team expects to review its plans for each implementation step with the management team. These design reviews provide management the opportunity to have input into your plans and ensure that management is informed and willing to support those plans. At a minimum, the design team should plan to meet with the management team to review the completed plans for the following:

- observation process
- feedback and involvement procedures
- safety incentive program
- kickoff meetings and observer training

After implementing the basic elements of the VBS process, the design team may need to schedule additional steering committee presentations to seek approval and support for various special programs (described in Chapter 23).

You should schedule the equivalent of 6 full days for planning the implementation of the VBS process. If your team is conducting 2-day planning meetings off-site, schedule three 2-day meetings to complete your detailed planning. Your team may complete its tasks more quickly, but this is a rough guideline for your initial planning. As stated above, with the 2-day planning meetings, you will probably only need a single meeting with the management team to review your final plans for implementation. If your team is conducting periodic planning meetings, then you may want to schedule management presentations after critical milestones. That way your team can implement each component as it begins to plan the other elements of the process. Regardless of your approach, you will need to coordinate your schedule with management to ensure that they are available to participate in the design review(s).

CHAPTER 11

Step 2: Creating the Safety Observation Process[2]

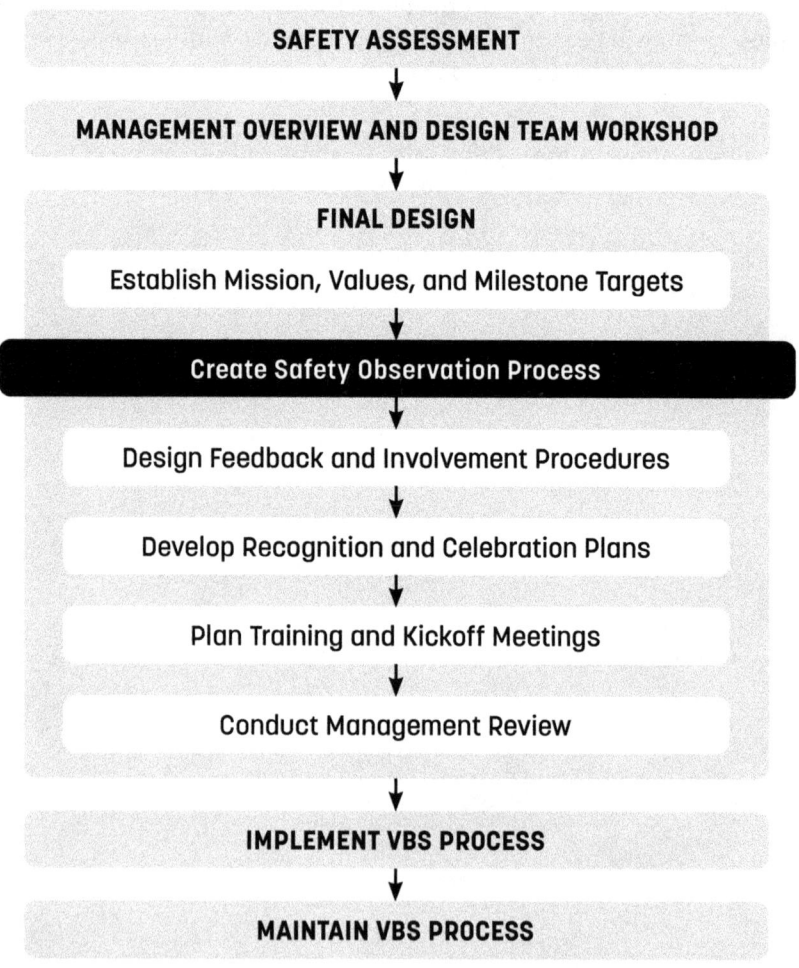

---

[2] The approach discussed in this chapter is based on Fellner and Sulzer-Azaroff (1984). We encourage you to read the original article, which includes an excellent example of a well-designed safety observation checklist from a paper mill.

The foundation for maximizing the effectiveness of your safety process is the regular observation of safe practices. Early studies suggested that monitoring work activities was the single most important activity a manager could engage in to ensure good performance (Chhokar & Wallin, 1984; Fellner & Sulzer-Azaroff, 1984; Komaki, 1986; Komaki et al., 1986, 1989). More recent studies show how important observations are in improving the safety performance of observers (see Chapter 27). An effective observation process offers the following advantages:

- improves the safety practices of observers
- results in better hazards recognition
- provides feedback on the effectiveness of the safety process
- establishes a baseline for setting improvement targets
- provides practice in observing and discussing safety
- adds social consequences for safe work practices
- provides a basis for forms of employee recognition

As discussed previously, one of the benefits of an observation process is that employees who conduct observations learn to work more safely (see the discussion of the observer effect in Chapter 27). Observers begin to perform the behaviors on the checklist much more consistently, even when they have not been observed or received feedback on their own safety practices. In addition, by conducting safety observations, employees learn to identify hazards in their work areas, which may, at least in part, explain why they begin to work more safely.

The observation process also provides a measure of the success of your safety management process. By collecting data on safe practices, you have an *in-process* measure of safety. This use of observation data contrasts with the traditional use of incidence rate data, which is an outcome measure of safety. An observation process provides an opportunity to work proactively with employees on their work practices before someone gets hurt. It also enables you to evaluate the effectiveness of specific safety improvement efforts. If you conduct a campaign on back safety, for example, the observation process can provide data about whether employees are lifting safely. In addition, an observation process can identify possible problem areas regarding work activities. In this case, the observation data might indicate that you needed a program on back safety before a worker injured their back.

This approach to safety parallels the quality improvement efforts of many organizations. One of the key features of such efforts is a focus on the process rather than simply on outcomes. In safety, paying attention to the process means paying attention to safe practices.

The observation process directs attention to and arranges feedback on how employees are doing their job. Several studies suggest the importance of verbal feedback in establishing and maintaining safe practices on the job (e.g., Komaki et al., 1980). The observation process arranges for regular opportunities for such feedback and helps ensure that it occurs.

The observation process also provides a source of data for employees to use in identifying practices that need improvement. In several of the studies discussed earlier, employees used observation data as the basis for setting improvement targets (Sulzer-Azaroff et al., 1990). The data enable employees to set improvement goals based on what they have been doing and what they think they can do better. The employees could then develop action plans to achieve those goals.

One reason for establishing a Values-Based Safety (VBS) process is to help employees within the organization get into the habit of talking to one another about safety. Our ideal organization establishes a culture in which employees look after each other. Operationally, this practice might mean that everyone is paying attention to how coworkers are doing their jobs and regularly talking with them about the safety of their work practices. In reality, using the typical informal approach, it is difficult to get supervisors and managers to consistently attend to safety compliance. A VBS process ensures that everyone, managers and employees alike, knows how to observe and provide feedback on safety. It then ensures that everyone practices observing and talking to one another about on-the-job safety.

To summarize, the observation and feedback process is probably the most important element of the VBS process. The design team must design a realistic observation process, complete with appropriate forms and guidelines, on the logistics of conducting observations within the organization.

11.1 How Do You Create the Observation Process?

The steps in the implementation of the observation process are outlined in Table 11.1.

Table 11.1. Implementation of Observation Process

Task Number	Activity
1	Analyze past incidents and injuries
2	Develop a list of critical safe practices
3	Identify safe practices that prevent serious injuries
4	Draft and revise checklists
5	Develop the observation procedure
6	Trial run the observation checklist and process

11.2 Analyze Past Incidents and Injuries

The first task in developing an observation procedure is to analyze the incidents and injuries within your organization. Typically, you will want to review every incident that has occurred within the last 3–5 years, then determine the practices that would

have prevented the injuries from occurring. During this analysis you have five objectives that will be important as you develop your observation process:
1. Identify critical behaviors for observation checklist(s) based on both the frequency of their occurrence and their potential severity.
2. Identify whether severe injuries most likely occur during routine or nonroutine operations.
3. Identify department-specific behaviors for use on department-specific checklists (optional, depending on assessment results).
4. Identify specific examples to include in definitions.
5. Identify the time of day and days of the week that injuries are most likely to occur.

Your design team members should review past incidents and close-call records to identify unsafe practices that caused or nearly caused incidents in the past. These incidents should be fundamental in constructing your list. Prior to beginning your analysis, you should sort the incidents by department and separate the lost-workday injuries from medical treatment cases. Then use the worksheet shown in Figure 11.1 to assist in identifying the behaviors that are the common thread in the injuries experienced in your facility. This worksheet will also help you identify the practices that occur most frequently. Use the extra space in each category for other behaviors that may contribute to injuries.

You should also do an analysis of when employees are most likely to experience an injury, in terms of both the time of day and the day of the week. This information will be critical in designing your process, as explained below. You may also want to collect data on the extent to which behavior contributes to injuries so you can create a pie chart, such as the one shown in Chapter 1, Figure 1.7. Later, in your kickoff meeting or during observer training, you can include the chart to help explain why you are implementing this new approach to safety.

11.3 Develop a List of Critical Safe Practices

The next step is to prepare a list of safety practices that will be needed to create your checklists. Use the information you gathered in the previous step to sort the categories and behaviors in the order of their contribution to injuries. Organize the remaining categories in order of their contribution to injuries, with the category that contributes most at the top of your list. In other words, place the worksheet category that makes the largest contribution to injuries (usually "body position and ergonomics") at the top of your list. Then sort the behaviors within each category to reflect this same order of contribution to past injuries. This will relegate the behaviors that have historically contributed to the most injuries at the top of each category and those that have contributed the least at the bottom of each category.

Your next step is to compare the lists developed for each department to determine whether they share a common set of critical practices, or if each department is unique enough to warrant a separate checklist.

Incident Analysis Worksheet

Department/Area: _____

1. Body Position and Ergonomics	No. of Incidents	Examples/Tasks (Use reference no. on additional sheets)
1.1 Proper body mechanics when lifting or carrying		
1.2 Proper body mechanics when reaching or pulling		
1.3 Clear of "line of fire"		
1.4 Eyes on path		
1.5 Eyes on work		
1.6 Appropriate pace		
1.7 Clear of pinch points		
1.8 Clear of sharp edges		
1.9 Clear of hot surfaces or materials		
1.10 Maintains three points of contact (when ascending or descending stairs, steps, or fixed ladders)		
1.11 Ergonomics/repetitive motion		
1.12 Stays on paths and walkways		
1.13		

2. Tools and Equipment	No. of Incidents	Examples/Tasks (Use reference no. on additional sheets)
2.1 Use of scaffolding and portable ladders		
2.2 Selection of tools and equipment		
2.3 Proper use of tools and equipment		
2.4 Condition of tools and equipment		
2.5 Location or storage of tools and equipment		
2.6 Use of vehicles and mobile equipment		
2.7 Guards in place		
2.8		

Figure 11.1. Worksheet for analyzing past injuries and incidents.

In general, you should start with the assumption that you will need different checklists for different areas. In other words, you should assume that production, maintenance, the laboratory, and the warehouse will each need a separate checklist. In some cases, you may be able to justify having a single checklist. Often, the ideal will be to

Incident Analysis Worksheet

(Continued)

3. Work Conditions/Housekeeping	No. of Incidents	Examples/Tasks (Use reference no. on additional sheets)
3.1 Use of tags and locks		
3.2 Equipment de-energized		
3.3 Proper permits		
3.4 Work areas free of slip and trip hazards		
3.5 Electrical cords and hoses rolled and stored properly		
3.6 Signs		
3.7 Barricading of hazardous conditions		
3.8 Fire and emergency equipment		
3.9 Adequate lighting		
3.10 Chemicals and materials stored and labeled properly		
3.11		
3.12		

4. Personal Protective Equipment	No. of Incidents	Examples/Tasks (Use reference no. on additional sheets)
4.1 Proper use of respirator/breath apparatus		
4.2 Fall protection		
4.3 Eye/face protection		
4.4 Proper work gloves or hand or arm protection		
4.5 Hard hat		
4.6 Hearing protection		
4.7 Protective clothing		
4.8		
4.9		

Figure 11.1. (Continued)

have a checklist that is roughly 75% generic, with a separate section that is specific to each department. Figures 11.2 and 11.3 show examples of the front and back of a generic checklist that might be appropriate for a location, while Figure 11.4 shows a checklist with generic and department-specific items.

Safety Observation Checklist

Observers: _____ Date: _____ Time: _____

Team: _____ Location: _____

Instructions: For each safety practice you observe, record a tally mark in the appropriate column to indicate each safe practice that causes you to be concerned about the potential for injury. Keep a running tally by recording these marks in the appropriate space. Describe each significant safety practice and concern in the "Comments" section. Record "Job-specific safe practices" in the appropriate space.

	No. of Safe Practices	No. of Concerns	Comments (Do not use names)
1. Body Position			
1.1 Body mechanics when lifting, reaching, or pulling			
1.2 Eyes on path or work			
1.3 Clear of pinch points, sharp edges, and hot surfaces			
1.4 Clear of "line of fire"			
2. Work Conditions			
2.1 Proper permits			
2.2 Equipment locked out and de-energized			
2.3 Work areas clean and free of slip or trip hazards			
2.4 Storage of materials			
2.5 Signs and barricading			

Figure 11.2. Recommended format for a generic safe-behavior observation checklist.

While the design team is conducting this analysis, you may want to conduct several brainstorming sessions with employees to identify items they consider important to include on the checklist. (Before you begin, you may wish to look ahead to the section on pinpointing in Chapter 21.)

3. Tools and Equipment

3.1 Use of tools and equipment			
3.2 Use of vehicles and mobile equipment			
3.3 Location of tools			
3.4 Condition of tools and equipment			

4. Personal Protective Equipment

4.1 Fall protection			
4.2 Respiratory protection			
4.3 Job-specific eye and face protection			
4.4 Job-specific hand and arm protection			
4.5 Hearing protection			
4.6 Protective cloting			

Job-Specific Safety Practices

TOTAL			

Figure 11.2 (Continued)

When brainstorming, record both behaviors and conditions. Do not be concerned about labels or abstractions at this stage; simply record the employees' ideas. After completing the list, go back over each suggestion to ensure that it identifies a pinpointed behavior or condition. Often this exercise will fit well within an existing safety meeting. You may also want to review your initial list of safe practices with other appropriate employees and managers to get their input and suggestions on what practices or conditions should be added to the list.

Definitions

Body Position	
Body mechanics when lifting, reaching, or pushing	Body positioned close to load, maintaining natural curve in low back, using mechanical lifting devices when possible, getting help when not sure of load or with heavy or bulky load. Squared up to task (not twisting at waist). Also consider risk of repetitive-motion injury and discuss "body breaks" when appropriate.
Eyes on path or work	Face and head generally pointed in the direction of travel (looks when stepping down or backward). Observing path prior to tracing lines. Watching hands engaged in tasks.
Clear of pinch points and sharp edges	Body parts kept from places where they might be mashed, pinched, cut, or burned (as when freeing jammed equipment or frozen bolts); fingers kept clear of doors, lids, and covers.
Clear of "line of fire"	Not working or standing in the path of equipment or materials that might shift, relieve pressure, move, or fall (e.g., never working in front of a pressure-relief valve).
Work Conditions	
Proper permits	Compliance with all steps required in the organization's safety rules and regulations; also welding/burning permits, tagging and flagging, confined-space entry, lockout/tagout, blinding, excavations.
Equipment locked out and de-energized	Equipment locked out when possible and de-energized of all types of power (electrical, hydraulic, pressure, and mechanical).
Work areas clean and free of clutter	Walkways and buildings kept clean and free of spills and clutter that might contribute to slips or falls (e.g., hoses and cords routed to avoid crossing walkways when possible and coiled and stored when not in use).
Storage of materials	Chemicals (paints, solvents, lubricants) labeled properly and stored in proper containers and location. Parts and supplies stored properly (e.g., spray cans capped).
Signs and barricading	Slippery surfaces and hazardous work areas surrounded by barricades, tape, or signs. Comply with signs and barricades.
Tools and Equipment	
Use of tools and equipment	The right tool used in the manner intended. Tools not substituted for others (e.g., not using a file for a pry bar or a screwdriver for a chisel). Guards in place. Tools/equipment de-energized for maintenance (as when changing a saw blade or drill bit). Pneumatic and electrical tools, impacts, grinders, drill masts, jack stands, chain falls, hoists, chokers, overhead cranes, and other lifting devices used only for applicable tasks. Ladder used appropriately (i.e., properly sloped; not standing on top step; tied off when necessary; etc.). (See mobile equipment category for stationary welding and cutting equipment.)

Figure 11.3. Samples of operational definitions that would be on the back of the previous checklist.

Tools and Equipment (Continued)	
Use of vehicles and mobile equipment	The right equipment used for tasks. Go-devils, forklifts, winch trucks, aerial lifts, and other mobile equipment used in a safe manner (e.g., no loads carried on booms, terminals guarded on welding machines, proper caps on cutting rigs, gas turned off for unattended cutting rigs, fire extinguishers available, etc.).
Location of tools and equipment	Tools positioned so as not to create a hazard and stored properly when not in use.
Condition of tools and equipment	Tools and equipment maintained in good working order. Guards in place. (Electrical cords free of fraying, wooden handles free of cracks, hammer heads in good shape, welding hoses or leads properly maintained, etc.)

Personal Protective Equipment	
Fall protection	Proper use of handrails, scaffolds, harnesses, lifelines, and retrieval systems, and three points of contact maintained at all times.
All other items in this category	Selection, condition, and use of personal protective equipment, as described in the organization's safety rules and regulations. Additional protection used for specific tasks when required, such as goggles when working with corrosive chemicals or grinders or a faceplate when welding. Appropriate gloves used when handling solvents and other chemicals, welding, and electrical work.

Job Specific Practices
Use this section to document job-specific practices or procedures that are not included above.

Figure 11.3. (Continued)

Finally, go back over the list and change each item to describe the safe behavior rather than the unsafe behavior. Again, you may wish to refer to the section on pinpointing in Chapter 21. You must define the desired safety practices in precise detail so that different observers can agree on how to score a given situation.

Coaching Checklist

Observer: _____ Day: _____ Date: _____ Time: _____

Instructions: Record the number of times you observe each safety practice and the number of times you have had a concern. Check the important positive practices you plan to recognize and significant concerns you plan to discuss, if any. ***Do not*** record names of associates.

Circle one: VBS   Serious-Incident Prevention (use back)

Safety Practice	No. Safe	No. of Concerns	Comments (No Names!)
Manual Lifting (41) — Bends knees, keeps back straight, holds load or crane close to body, pivots feet rather than twisting body when manually lifting. Grasps load securely before moving. Only lifts balanced and steady loads. Asks for help or uses lifting equipment for loads > 50 lb.			
Eyes on Path (32) — Focuses eyes in direction of travel to avoid bumping into, tripping over, or slipping on objects or liquids (e.g., when walking, using air crane, or carrying slip sheet). Has a clear line of vision to floor when carrying or pushing an object. Looks at steps, platforms, etc., before stepping up to ensure secure footing. Ties shoelaces. Walks instead of runs.			
Eyes on Task (29) — Focuses eyes on task in which hands are involved. Avoids pinch points (i.e., keeps hands out of equipment during runs, while changing rollers or signatures). Keeps hands out of the line of fire.			
Housekeeping (20) — Picks up and stores or disposes of any unnecessary item on floor and wipes up spilled liquids as soon as observed. Uses absorbent matting. Dries decks of spray mist. Wipes up drips from carrying racks. Keeps walkways free of obstructions. Puts tools and materials away when finished.			

Figure 11.4. Example of format for a department-specific safety observation checklist that includes the operational definitions with the generic safety practice. The numbers in parentheses reflect the number of injuries that occurred during the previous 3 years that could have been prevented by this safety practice. See Figure 11.5 for the backside of the checklist, Serious-Incident Prevention Observations.

Bindery Pinpoints

Safety Practice	No. Safe	No. of Concerns	Comments (No Names!)
Safe Cutting — Cuts away from body and keeps other hand out of blade direction. Has a firm grip on tools (e.g., wrenches) before applying force.			
Right Tool — Uses tools designated for task.			
Guards in Place — Puts guards in place before operating equipment (e.g., protective covers on trimmer knives).			
Eye Protection — Wears glasses with side shields (e.g., when working on trimmer). Wears face shield when grinding.			
Comments or suggestions:			

Figure 11.4. (Continued)

On your checklist you want to include safe practices, not unsafe practices. The rationale is twofold. First, you must be very clear about desired safety practices in order to facilitate communication to everyone in the area. Second, you want to increase the attention being paid to safe behavior and what employees are doing right. A large part of the acceptance of this safety program comes from taking a positive approach versus the more traditional but negative approach of looking for unsafe practices.

As you identify safe behaviors for your checklist, you should also try to eliminate redundant items and items that can be logically combined. For example, your initial list of pinpointed safe practices might include such behaviors as "wearing hard hats," "wearing safety glasses in designated areas," and "wearing hearing protection in high-noise areas." Your design team might combine these behaviors into a broader practice, such as "wearing appropriate protective equipment." Or you may sometimes want to leave such items separate to emphasize the importance of each to the safety of your workplace.

You generally want the items to be mutually exclusive so that your observers are less likely to make errors when recording their observations on checklists. For instance, you may not want checklist items to include both "wearing appropriate protective equipment" and "wearing safety glasses in designated areas." This would create confusion for observers and would make observation data less reliable.

 Rule of Thumb:
Develop a list of safety practices for each department or area. Then see how that can be simplified and combined.

11.4 Identify Safe Practices That Prevent Serious Incidents

Before drafting your checklists, you should go through a separate planning process to address the risk of serious incidents and fatalities. You must plan the process, including whether and how it will be integrated with the everyday VBS process. As with that process, you will need to identify the behaviors critical to preventing serious incidents and make preliminary plans for how the observations will be conducted.

Consideration 1: Identify critical behaviors and tasks that create exposure to serious incidents. The VBS must include safety practices that prevent serious incidents and fatalities. These may include practices that might impact the facilities or the environment. Because serious incidents are generally rare events, design teams often have difficulty finding critical behaviors for preventing serious incidents from a review of injury reports. Therefore, you must identify these behaviors through input from subject matter experts, such as safety professionals or process engineers. The analysis of exposure to a potential for serious incidents must also identify the most common tasks that put employees at risk for serious incidents. Observers must plan observations during these tasks to minimize the risk of such incidents. See Table 11.2 to clarify the two types of analyses for identifying critical safety behaviors to include on a VBS observation checklist.

Krause (2012) and Krause and Murray (2012) emphasize that behaviors leading to serious incidents usually correspond to high-risk activities. These behaviors frequently find codification in a company's safety rules. Companies may label this set of rules as their "safety absolutes" or another term signifying that they are the guidelines preventing serious harm and death. Safety absolutes generally encompass practices such as fall protection, lockout/tagout, and permit use. The behaviors outlined in safety absolutes must be included on VBS observation checklists. Listing those behaviors helps ensure that the VBS process identifies contexts in which employees are exposed to the risk of serious incidents. Preventing serious incidents requires that observers observe tasks with exposure to high-risk hazards. As indicated in Table 11.2 you should clearly define which tasks should be the focus of serious-incident prevention observations.

This approach applies to other aspects of process safety as well. Process safety hinges on critical behaviors such as maintaining accurate logs of process upsets in logbooks, conveying process events at shift changes, communicating leadership decisions, and keeping precise process and instrumentation diagrams. These behavioral matters influence the probability of catastrophic events and remain subject to evaluation through behavioral observations.

Table 11.2. Comparison of Design Considerations for VBS Targeting Reduction in Injury Frequency Versus Prevention of Serious Injuries and Fatalities

To Reduce and Prevent	Source of Critical Behaviors	Observations
OSHA-recordable incidents	Identified through analysis of 3–5 years of data	Conducted at random
Serious incidents and fatalities	Hazard analysis by subject matter experts	Conducted during high-risk tasks

Consideration 2: Plan your approach to serious-incident prevention. Many organizations set up a serious incident prevention process separate from their VBS process. Typically, they create a checklist based on their critical safety practices. Figure 11.5 is an example of one organization's checklist for serious-incident prevention.

Serious-Incident Prevention Observations

Observe for **serious-incident prevention activity potential**. Mark observations as safe (S), concerns (C), and requiring feedback (FB). Discuss potential impact and alternate behavior for any concerns.

☐ **Electrical**   Concern Comments

S C FB   1. Is the electrical work area barricaded or taped off?
S C FB   2. Is the system energized? Or de-energized and locked out?
S C FB   3. Are electrical insulated gloves used?
S C FB   4. Is Arc protective clothing used?
S C FB   5. Are insulated tools being used?
S C FB   6. Was a job safety analysis (JSA) or work permit completed?

☐ **Maintenance/Lockout/Machine Guarding**   Concern Comments

S C FB   1. Is equipment shut down?
S C FB   2. Is equipment locked out?
S C FB   3. Has each person installed their lock?
S C FB   4. Are pinch points avoided?
S C FB   5. Are sharp edges protected?
S C FB   6. Are correct tools being used?
S C FB   7. Are corded electrical tools protected by ground-fault circuit interrupter (GFCI)?

Figure 11.5. Sample serious-incident prevention observation checklist, which might stand alone or be on the back of the previous sheet, Figure 11.4.

☐ **Forklifts and Industrial Trucks**	Concern Comments
S C FB 1. Is the driver wearing a seatbelt?	
S C FB 2. Is the driver sounding the horn at intersections and when near pedestrians?	
S C FB 3. Is the driver operating at appropriate speeds?	
S C FB 4. Does the driver have a clear view in the direction of travel?	
S C FB 5. Are pedestrian and equipment travel lanes separated to protect pedestrians?	
S C FB 6. Does the driver use 3-point contact while getting on and off the vehicle?	
☐ **Hoisting and Rigging**	Concern Comments
S C FB 1. Are colleagues clear and not under the load while lifting?	
S C FB 2. Are taglines and/or push-pull poles used to maintain safe distances?	
S C FB 3. Do colleagues avoid pinch points and close clearances between the load and stationary objects?	
S C FB 4. Is the rigging equipment in good condition?	
☐ **Working at Heights**	Concern Comments
S C FB 1. Is fall protection being used?	
S C FB 2. Is it appropriate?	
S C FB 3. Will it protect the person in a fall?	
S C FB 4. Are hands free of objects while climbing ladders?	
☐ **Rail**	Concern Comments
S C FB 1. Are repeat commands used for movements?	
S C FB 2. Does the driver sound the horn before moving, and/or is the track alarm system activated?	
S C FB 3. Does the brakeman or driver have a clear view in the direction of movement?	
S C FB 4. Are people clear of rail movement?	
S C FB 5. Are rail movement speeds appropriate?	
S C FB 6. Are crossings guarded by the brakeman?	
☐ **Confined Space**	Concern Comments
S C FB 1. Are all energy hazards controlled through lockout?	
S C FB 2. Are all entrants logged on the entry permit?	
S C FB 3. Is the atmosphere in the space being continuously monitored?	
S C FB 4. Is the watch in communication with the entrants?	
S C FB 5. Can the watch immediately call for help without leaving their post?	

Figure 11.5. (Continued)

Serious-incident prevention can be integrated with VBS in several ways. Some organizations may decide to simply include serious-incident prevention items on their normal VBS observation checklist. So, "fall protection" may be an item in one section of the checklist, without any special designation beyond perhaps placing it first in its checklist category to signal its importance (see Figure 11.2). Other organizations might have a separate category for behaviors critical to reducing the risk of serious incidents (e.g., fall protection, lockout/tagout, confined space, etc.).

One of our past clients had what we consider to be the most robust approach to integrating serious incident prevention into their VBS process. They took the checklist present in Figure 11.5 and put it on the back of their VBS checklist. On the front, their checklist had a box to check indicating whether the observer was doing a VBS observation or a serious-incident prevention observation. Also, a best practice is to add definitions to the front of the sheet. Adding definitions often requires reducing the number of checklist items. Typically, you can reduce potential redundancy by removing serious-incident prevention items from the front, as they are now included on the back. Notice that the serious-incident prevention checklist in Figure 11.5 has details specifically pinpointing the requirements for each hazard exposure. If the observer saw coworkers doing a task that could result in a serious incident, the VBS observation became a serious-incident prevention observation and focused on the relevant section of the serious-incident prevention checklist. All serious-incident prevention observations were given special treatment by the steering committee, as described in Chapter 20.

Another approach to serious incident prevention is to focus on regular observations of high-hazard tasks by leadership. Often this approach has a checklist unique to each of the organization's serious-incident prevention exposures. Figure 11.6 on the following page shows an example of a checklist that reflects the controls expected for employees working at heights above 6 feet. In this approach, supervisors are expected to complete the appropriate checklist for all high-hazard work being performed in their area of responsibility. These observations are often conducted on nonroutine tasks that create exposure to high-risk hazards.

11.5 Draft and Revise Checklists

Once you have developed the list of pinpointed safety practices, begin the process of designing the actual checklists. The first step is probably to shorten your list of pinpointed items. To do so, consider the following criteria:
- importance to safety (based on incident records and design team members' opinions)
- frequency of occurrence
- observability
- overlap with other items on the list

Do not eliminate any safety practices that you identified on the basis of serious incidents. If possible, every unsafe act that has caused an incident during the last several years should be addressed by a safe work practice reflected on your final list, although it may be combined with other behaviors under a common safety practice. You should

Working at Height

Name: _____ Date: _____

Location (circle): Warehouse   Staging   Production   Packaging/Palletizing

Behavior	Safe	Concern	Tasks/Comments
1. Is associate wearing a safety harness tied to anchor point above head?			
2. Does the harness have a current inspection tag?			
3. Controls in place to prevent dropped tools and objects?			
4. Associates tied off when working above 6 ft?			
5. Associates stand on appropriate steps and platforms (not rails or pipes)?			
6. Area below protected with appropriate barricades?			
7. Associates on scaffolding tied off to approved anchor points?			
8. Ladders used properly (associate holding extension ladder or tied off, 75° angle)?			

Figure 11.6. Example of a supervisor's field verification checklist for employees working above 6 feet.

also consider eliminating pinpointed checklist items that (1) have a relatively low risk of minor injury *and* (2) would not have a major impact on performance.

 Rule of Thumb:
Keep your observation checklists short, no more than one side of one sheet of paper.

This book outlines the checklist's inception as a paper-based tool, highlighting its foundational role in organizational workflows. Beginning with paper formats allows easy modifications during initial trials, smoothing the adaptation process. Transitioning to digital tools, such as apps and software, later enhances observation tracking and data analysis, significantly boosting efficiency. Implementing tablet-based systems or smartphone apps cuts down on manual data entry needs, whether by observers or intermediaries, streamlining data collection. Software solutions not only improve problem-solving abilities through robust data analysis tools but also generate detailed reports that clarify which observers are conducting their observations. Such software packages and online services also provide data summaries that support the steering committee in creating action plans that target safety improvements identified from the safety observation data.

Note that this discussion has been about developing multiple checklists, not a single checklist. You want the observation data to reflect the responsibilities of a single group or area. Each checklist will be more meaningful for discussion in safety meetings if those participating in the meetings are clearly responsible for the data on it. This usually requires that each checklist reflect a single functional unit from the organizational structure.

Depending on the size and complexity of your organization, you may need several different checklists. Safety practices are different in the laboratory, in the warehouse, on the plant floor, and for maintenance. At the same time, keep the number of checklists as small as practicable. If your organization is not large and complex, you may be able to get by with one or two checklists.

You will need to designate what data must be collected in the checklist headings. You will also typically want to record the name of the employee conducting the observation; the employee's department, where the observation is being conducted; and the date and time. Other information to be collected as designated by the headings at the top of your form might include the shift, the crew, whether the worker observed was an employee or a contractor, and the number of people observed (if more than one). Be sure to include a brief set of instructions for completing the form. You may also want to allow space, typically at the bottom of the checklist, for additional comments.

Generally, you should not identify the specific work task that is being observed in the header information as that is better included in the observer's comments. If you use a database to analyze your observation data, you will be able to identify what was being done when a specific concern occurred if observers record the task as part of their comments. Including the task as part of the heading makes this type of analysis more difficult when using most commercially available databases.

Figures 11.2 through 11.6 show several alternative approaches to checklist design. At this point you must find the right compromise between ease of use, completeness, and level of accuracy.

The checklist seen in Figure 11.2 shows several key features typical of a checklist design that are important to consider. Under "Comments" notice the statement "Do not use names!" to remind observers not to include the names of the employees they observe. Also, in the column headings, notice the wording "No. of Concerns" rather than "No. of Unsafe Practices." The rationale for this wording is to remove the stigma attached to the word *unsafe*, which implies that an employee is breaking a safety rule or doing something wrong. Most employees are uncomfortable about telling their peers they are doing something wrong, but they are more comfortable expressing personal concern for their coworkers' safety and well-being. This language is also consistent with the values identified by the design team. And it helps demonstrate the alignment of the process with those values, in that the number of concerns is consistent with a stated value of "concern for fellow employees." Further, this language supports the terms that should be used in discussing the observations (feedback discussions are covered later in this chapter). Other organizations use terms like "at risk" to communicate that an observer considers a coworker to be engaging in a practice that places them at risk of injury.

Also note the length of the checklist in Figure 11.2. This is probably close to the upper limit on the number of safe practices to include on your checklist. In fact, you should probably try to limit the number of critical practices to 12 to 15 or less, if possible. As an alternative to having several checklists, you may choose to have a section in which observers add pinpointed safety practices appropriate to the tasks they plan to observe, as shown in the final section of Figure 11.2, entitled "Job-Specific Safety Practices." This section is open-ended, and observers simply fill in specific safety practices applicable to the tasks they observe or plan to observe. Observers may refer to written job procedures, task hazard evaluations, material safety data sheets, or other employees to help define the specific safety practices appropriate for the tasks being performed during their scheduled observations.

Figure 11.3 shows the back of the checklist in Figure 11.2. You must provide the observers with clear operational definitions of the safety practices that you are targeting on your checklist. Your definitions should include a pinpointed description of the practices on the front of your checklist (see the section on pinpointing in Chapter 21). The pinpointed definitions should include examples, and whenever possible, examples should come from incident investigations. Such definitions will ensure that the behaviors that have caused problems in the past are clearly addressed in the observation process. You can later add additional examples should other incidents or close calls occur. You may want to place your examples in parentheses throughout this page. Including actual examples is another way in which observers come to see that the checklists as relevant to your organization.

In addition, including the definitions on the back of the checklist ensures that they are available to observers for easy reference. Some organizations laminate the definitions onto clipboards that the observers use when conducting observations.

Having a multipage list of definitions separate from the checklist is not a good idea, as they will not be available for easy reference. Some organizations have kept them separate with the rationale that it forces observers to learn the definitions. However, observers learn more from conducting the observation, and having the definitions readily available for easy reference contributes to more reliable data collection. Further, some observers will simply make their best guess about where to score a particular practice, seldom taking the time to look elsewhere for the applicable definition.

Figure 11.4 shows an example of a department-specific checklist that combines a sitewide section with a department-specific section. Notice that this organization elected not to use the standard categories given in the incident analysis worksheet seen in Figure 11.1. Its checklist is organized simply into two categories: sitewide pinpoints and bindery pinpoints (which are the items specific to the bindery department).

The checklist in Figure 11.4 illustrates another strategy worth considering in the construction of your checklists. It includes the number of injuries (in parentheses) that could have been prevented through each safety practice, which helps employees realize that these items are important to safety. Generally, including the actual number of injuries is more effective than using percentages. Because percentages are often fairly small when spread across all the practices on your checklists, they inadvertently trivialize the contribution that each practice makes to safety.

The checklist in Figure 11.7 illustrates yet another option in how you may choose to format your checklist. The advantage of this format is that it more clearly communicates the expectation that observers will find three practices, one positive and one or two of concern, to comment on during their observations.

Safety Observation Checklist

Observer: _____ Date: _____ Time: _____
Observer's Dept: _____ Location: _____

Instructions: For each safety practice you observe, record a short vertical line "I" in the appropriate column to indicate each safe practice and to indicate each practice that causes you to be concerned about the potential for injury. Keep a tally in the appropriate space. Describe each significant safe practice and concern in the "Comments" section.

1. Body Position	No. Safe	No. of Concerns	3. Tools and Equipment	No. Safe	No. of Concerns
1.1 Body mechanics when lifting, reaching, or pulling			3.1 Use of tools and equipment		
1.2 Eyes on path or work			3.2 Use of vehicles and mobile equipment		
1.3 Clear of pinch points, sharp edges, and hot surfaces			3.3 Location of tools		
1.4 Clear of "line of fire"			3.4 Condition of tools and equipment		

2. Work Conditions			4. Personal Protective Equipment		
2.1 Proper permits			4.1 Fall protection		
2.2 Equipment locked out and de-energized			4.2 Respiratory protection		
2.3 Work areas clean and free of slip/trip hazards			4.3 Job-specific eye and face protection		
2.4 Storage of materials			4.4 Job-specific hand and arm protection		
2.5 Signs of barricading			4.5 Hearing protection		

	Behavior*	Comments
Safe Practice	__-__	Description: _____ Potential impact: _____ Contributing factor(s): _____
Concern	__-__	Description: _____ Potential impact: _____ Contributing factor(s): _____
Concern	__-__	Description: _____ Potential impact: _____ Contributing factor(s): _____

*Fill in code corresponding to behavior in top portion, or write "Other."

Figure 11.7. Alternative format for a generic safe-behavior observation checklist.

Figure 11.8 shows a checklist that uses a point system to weight the importance of the different safety practices. This checklist is designed to reflect that not all the practices will be relevant during a single observation. Because of this, only what is observed will be converted into a percentage using the equation at the bottom of the figure. If all the practices on the checklist will be observed each time an observer conducts an observation, then a simpler approach would be to create the weighting by allocating 100 points across the practices on the checklist. Observers can then simply add the points at the end of their observation to calculate an overall percent. This approach is not appropriate for most organizations that do not require an overall percent safe for every observation.

You may choose to count the occurrence of safe practices and concerns while scoring the physical condition of different work areas as safe or unsafe for other items. An empirical study by Sulzer-Azaroff et al. (1990) used an observation sheet that combined these approaches. On the upper half of their observation sheet, they counted the frequency of safe behaviors related to compliance with procedure and the use of safety equipment. On the lower half of the sheet, they scored the condition of various zones of their facility as either safe or unsafe based on the presence or absence of several pinpointed safety hazards. They included a simple layout so that observers could mark the location of hazards and space to describe the hazard.

Do not be concerned about designing a perfect checklist. Developing a good checklist is an empirical process that you will learn more about as your experience increases. Your best strategy is to experiment for several weeks, then design your best observation checklist and use it for 3–6 months. Remember that the checklist is a dynamic tool. It should change to meet the changing needs of your work environment, yet it should remain stable for periods long enough to document goal achievement, generally from 6 months to a year.

Table 11.3 summarizes considerations for constructing your observation checklists.

Table 11.3. Questions That Need to Be Answered When Constructing an Observation Checklist

Question	Yes	No
1. Is the checklist no longer than one page?		
2. Are all items clear and specific?		
3. Are all items mutually exclusive of other items?		
4. Are the instructions clear and concise?		
5. Is a space provided for the observer's name?		
6. Is a space provided to record the date and time of observations?		
7. Are operation definitions available for each item?		
8. Do your definitions include examples from your incident investigations?		
9. Does your checklist address practices that prevent serious incidents and fatalities?		

Safety Observation Checklist

Location: _____ Date: _____ Time: _____
Task(s): _____

Instructions: For each specific safety practice below, record the number of points possible if all employees you observe are 100% safe on that practice. Then record the actual number of points earned on the basis of your observations. Make comments on safe practices and practices that create a risk of injury.

Excavations and Trenching	Wt.	Possible Points	Points Earned	Comments (Do not use names)
Soil placed at least 2 ft from edge	20			
Properly sloped or shored (5 ft or deeper)	10			
Ladder exit within 25 ft (4 ft or deeper)	10			
Vehicles and equipment at least 5 ft from edge	10			

Aerial Basket Operations

	Wt.			
Maintaining safe distance from AC power	20			
Using voltage tester prior to tasks	20			
Both feet on bottom of basket	5			
Vehicle's rear tires chocked	5			

General Safety

	Wt.			
Rescue or fall protection used	10			
Correct body position	10			
Proper use of tools	5			
Proper use of heavy equipment	5			
Worksite protected with signs, cones, barricades, etc.	5			

Personal Protective Equipment

	Wt.			
Hard hats	5			
Job-specific eye/face protection	5			
Job-specific gloves	5			
Hearing protection	5			
Company-approved footwear	5			
Total				

$$\frac{\text{_____ No. Points Earned}}{\text{_____ No. Possible Points}} \times 100 = \text{_____} \% \text{ Safe}$$

Figure 11.8. Alternative Format for a Safe-Behavior Observation Checklist Using a Point System

11.6 Develop the Observation Procedure

Your design team should develop formal guidelines for conducting observations. You may wish to consider flowcharting the procedure to ensure that you have a logical sequence of events everyone can understand. Here are some questions your design team should consider:

- Who will conduct the observations?
- Is being an observer voluntary?
- Is being observed voluntary?
- Should the observer announce the observation?
- How often will observers conduct observations?
- When will observations be conducted?
- Will observations occur across or only within departments?
- Will employees observe an area, a single employee, or specific tasks?
- How will you handle contract personnel?
- Where do observers get observation checklists and how do they submit completed observations?
- What happens in a VBS observation when an observer sees the potential for a serious incident?
- What tasks will be observed that have the potential for serious incidents?

The remainder of this section will discuss some design options and considerations for answering each of these questions. After your design team has resolved them, you should draft a written procedure with step-by-step instructions for each of these components.

Who will conduct the observations? In developing the observation procedure, the first question to address is who will conduct the observations. Most organizations plan to involve employees in conducting observations. Some organizations may strive to involve all employees in conducting regular observations. For other organizations, getting managers and supervisors involved in conducting safety observations, at least as an initial step, is often an appropriate start. Table 11.4 summarizes considerations for deciding who should conduct observations.

Having a dedicated small group of observers appears to be the most efficient and effective strategy for most organizations, with the goal of involving all employees through rotation. Current data (Spigener et al., 2022) suggest that a relatively small number of observers is most effective in reducing incidents. The data suggest that for most organizations the ideal number of observers equals 8%–12% of the total number of employees. In fact, for some organizations, the steering committee members may be the only observers.

If employees are to conduct the observations, steering committee members may initially conduct observations with employees who have volunteered and have been trained to conduct them. Remember, participation in the design team is based on who will be taking on the responsibility of conducting observations. If observations will be a management responsibility, your design team members should primarily be managers and supervisors. If observations are to be an employee responsibility, the design team should involve representative employees.

Is being an observer voluntary? For most organizations that implement VBS, participation as an observer is voluntary for employees, but this is a decision that should be made by the design team. In some organizations, conducting observations is voluntary for employees but is required of managers, supervisors, and steering committee members.

Some organizations implement programs in which conducting observations is a job requirement. The problem with this approach is that it can increase the number of forms that are completed as a paperwork exercise without actual observations. See considerations for deciding who should conduct observations in Table 11.4 on the following page.

The steering committee must then address this problem by developing plans to encourage quality observations, and tracking the quality of observations is difficult. On the other hand, if conducting observations is voluntary, the steering committee has only to develop action plans that encourage employees to conduct them. While this is a challenge, measuring participation is much easier than measuring the quality of the observations.

If the process is voluntary, the organization has a way of measuring complacency. When employees begin to get complacent about safety, they stop conducting observations. These organizations must then take action to promote safety awareness and get employees involved in safety improvement efforts. When observations are mandatory, the organization will often continue to get observation forms and be unaware of a growing complacency toward safety.

For these reasons, a voluntary process is most appropriate for the employees of most organizations. However, because participation by managers, supervisors, and steering committee members is highly important, most organizations should make their participation a requirement.

Is being observed voluntary? Being observed should generally be considered a job expectation in most organizations that implement VBS. In the early days of VBS, observers in some organizations asked permission of coworkers before conducting the observation. The problem with this approach is that it effectively allowed employees to opt out of participation in the company's safety improvement efforts. When this question is formally asked, employees elect not to allow the observation. Still, this is an option that the design team should consider, and it may be appropriate for organizations with very low levels of trust between employees and management. Often, in organizations with low trust, a better option is to make being observed a job expectation but to allow employees to opt out of a particular observation. Thus, an employee has the right to refuse a particular observation but not to refuse to allow observations altogether. This gives employees the freedom to choose when observations occur and allows them to opt out if they have a personality conflict with a particular observer, if they are in a hurry and do not want to take the time to discuss the observation, or

Table 11.4. Considerations for Deciding Who Should Conduct Observations

If Your Organization Is	Then	Considerations
Typical of most organizations	A number equaling 8%–12% of the total employees should conduct observations	• Observers should be coached by steering committee to ensure quality
Aggressively trying to actively engage employees	Strive to maximize the number of employees participating as observers	• Ensures a high level of understanding of safety requirements • Requires ongoing steering committee effort to maintain observations • Use reinforcement to support voluntary observations • Do not use quotas
Seeking sustainability and lowest maintenance costs	Steering committee members should be primary observers	• Focus on high-quality observations • Often employees may volunteer for training and participate in observations • Steering committee members should rotate through the position on a staggered schedule
Still working on the design and implementation of a VBS process	Design team members should conduct observations	• Ensures a realistic process • Provides a base for training others
A traditional chain of command with management that has not routinely shown a commitment to safety	Managers and supervisors should conduct routine safety observations	• Supervisors develop a good understanding of the process • Employees will not get the benefit that comes from being observers • Often easier to maintain • Works well for weekly or monthly observations • Often important in building readiness
A traditional chain of command with evolving involvement in safety or quality team process	Start with management, supervision, and representative employees, then begin involving all employees	• Important to have both employees and managers participate on the design team
A traditional chain of command with evolving involvement in safety or quality team process, but low trust	Employees should conduct observations without involvement of management in the behavioral process	• Managers and supervisors should continue to perform routine audits and observations but outside of the formal behavioral process • Not ideal as it tends to support an "us versus them" mentality • Typically, should be a step toward full involvement

perhaps if they think an observation at another time would have more value. Providing this option often helps overcome resistance to the observation process and is therefore appropriate for some organizations.

Should the observer announce the observation? You also need to consider whether observers should announce when observations are going to be conducted. For most organizations, announcing safety observations is an important practice in support of the values of openness and respect for employees. An observer can easily announce the observation when he or she enters the work area, often by simply making eye contact with the coworker to be observed, then holding up a clipboard (or tablet or smartphone) and pointing at it prior to starting the observation. Or the observer can schedule the observations of coworkers during a Monday toolbox safety meeting, for instance, or at the start of work. The observer might simply mention something like this: "I'll be coming out to visit your job site sometime later this morning to conduct a safety observation" or "We'll probably do an observation of the maintenance shops on Thursday afternoon."

Obviously, the disadvantage of this approach is that observers may not observe a work sample typical of normal practices. Social psychology studies have revealed that people act differently when they know they are under observation. This is not really as large a problem as it may seem. If employees work more safely during observations, observers have the opportunity to reinforce safety practices that are more likely to be performed in the future. Also, when the observation is announced, concerns that are noted will be more important issues for discussion because the employee is not aware of these issues. Thus, such concerns are more likely to be true training problems when employees do not know what they should be doing to protect themselves from injury. Some organizations may, however, choose unannounced observations to ensure truly representative data on compliance with safety procedures. You may want to announce observations initially and then, when employees understand and trust the process, begin performing unannounced observations.

How often will observers conduct observations? The frequency of observations is important. The risk associated with your business should determine whether observations are made daily, weekly, or monthly. If you are in a high-risk business with many employees, you should probably conduct daily observations. Most manufacturing and construction organizations will want observers to conduct observations every week. Current data suggest observers should conduct two observations per week (Spigener et al., 2022). You may also choose a different frequency of observations for different work areas or levels. You might require supervisors to conduct weekly observations of their work areas, for example, while upper-level managers and staff members conduct monthly observations. Table 11.5 on the following page summarizes these considerations.

When will observations be conducted? The observers themselves should generally decide when to conduct observations. Accordingly, you might ask supervisors to conduct their observations during the week without specifying when they should do so. However, it is important to vary the time and day that observations are conducted. You do not want employees to be able to predict when observations will occur.

Table 11.5. Guidelines for Deciding on Appropriate Frequency of Observations

If Employees in Your Organization	Consider Conducting Observations	Considerations
Are at moderate to high risk of an injury incident	Each observer should conduct two observations each week	• Current data suggest that a low number of observers is most effective
Are at low to moderate risk of an injury incident	Weekly or biweekly	• This is a good frequency for observations conducted by managers and supervisors • Most empirical studies use weekly observations
Have very low risk of an injury incident (e.g., office workers)	Monthly or periodic, if at all	• May need greater frequency to ensure consistency of process • Can be useful to develop an understanding of ergonomic issues in an office environment

You may want to schedule the observations for times when incidents are more likely to occur. Data on when incidents are most likely, gathered from your analysis of incidents and injuries, should provide guidelines on when observations will have the most value. You may also want to create a separate observation process for special events, such as plant turnarounds or new construction within the work area.

Will observations occur across or within departments? Employees will usually be most comfortable observing jobs they are familiar with, so many organizations start by encouraging observations within observers' departments. Data show that having observers conduct observations in their own areas is the most effective strategy (Spigener et al., 2022). If observers need to conduct an observation in an area they are not familiar with, especially in the case of particularly high-risk work areas, observers should find a steering committee member, supervisor, or someone else who is familiar with the work to accompany them when they first enter the unfamiliar area. This approach has a couple of advantages. The employee being observed has someone who can ensure the safety of the observer as well as someone who can discuss issues that the observer has questions about. This approach also makes observers more comfortable when they begin doing observations outside of their own work areas.

Will employees observe an area, a single employee, or specific tasks? The best answer to this question will depend on the nature of your organization and the kind of incidents that your organization has experienced. For manufacturing observations that have many employees working in an area, conducting an area observation will often be most effective wherein observers can observe and provide feedback to several employees in a single observation using a single checklist. For many process plants, on the other hand, observers have to "go where the action is" and thus leave the control room or another vantage point to observe coworkers who are performing work activities somewhere within their unit. Also, the information collected when you analyzed past incidents may have indicated that injuries are particularly likely when employees are performing specific tasks, in which case the observation process needs to ensure that employees observe those tasks. Your analysis should also have told you whether incidents are more likely during routine operations or during upset conditions. Obviously, you need to plan your observations accordingly because you want employees to do observations when incidents are most likely to occur.

Sometimes you will want to address this question based on the nature of the activities identified on the observation checklist. You will often have a combination of different types of observations on the same observation sheet. If "forklift boom in proper position" is on a warehouse observation form, then you would want to try to stay in an area until you observed forklift operations. Depending on the level of activity, the observer might wait a few minutes to observe this task or simply score this item as "not applicable." You might establish a simple guideline, like this: "Try to observe the occurrence of a checklist activity (or a completed task sequence) if you can do so in less than 5 minutes."

How will you handle contract personnel? Many of today's companies make ongoing use of contract personnel. If your organization uses contractors, your design team should consider whether to involve them in safety observations. Options for doing so include the following:

- Work with contractors to establish an observation process unique to them.
- Involve contractors in the design team and in making observations.
- Observe the contractors' activities but do not involve them in conducting observations.

As a rule, if you have contract personnel on-site on an ongoing basis, you should find a way to involve them in safety observations at an appropriate level. Probably your best option would be to observe them, then provide feedback as you would for any other employee. In some cases, you may want to be more aggressive with contract personnel than with your own employees. For example, you might be less likely to announce observations in advance or give them the right to opt out of observations. In certain instances, you may want to share the observation feedback with the contractors' supervisor.

Where do observers get observation checklists and how do they submit completed observations? You will also need to plan the administrative aspects of supporting observations. For example, where employees will obtain blank observation checklists and how they will submit the completed checklists to the steering committee. As part of the data feedback process described in the next chapter, you may want to establish a safety bulletin board in each area. This board can display the blank checklist, and it is a good area in which to locate drop boxes for submitting completed observations. In some cases, employees can submit completed observations through interoffice mail. In other case, the observers can enter their observation data into a database.

What happens in a VBS observation when an observer sees the potential for a serious incident? When this occurs during an observation, typically the focus of the observation changes to ensure that the behaviors and barriers that will prevent a serious incident from occurring are present. Depending on your design, these may be incorporated into your normal checklist or placed on the back. The design team has to be clear about the procedure so that it can be integrated into the observer training.

What tasks will be observed that have the potential for serious incidents? Typically, your design team will have identified the normal tasks that create exposure to the risks of serious incidents. You may identify these tasks on the checklist (as in Figure 11.5, which shows the back of the serious-incident prevention checklist). Oftentimes, supervisors direct observers to those tasks with hazardous injury prevention. Regardless of the process, the design team will generally develop the procedure that ensures observers are able to conduct observations any time associates are working on a task that exposes them to the risk of hazardous injury or fatality.

11.7 Feedback on Observations

As a general rule, you should plan a process in which observers routinely provide immediate feedback as part of their observations. Some practitioners have suggested that the data collection (observation) process and intervention (feedback) process should be separate. The problem with this approach is that encouraging sufficient feedback is difficult if it is not an integral part of the observation process. Sometimes the two are separated, when in a less formal observation process employees carry a data collection card in a shirt pocket for use any time they observe other employees. In addition to a difficulty in prompting feedback, this approach to data collection often results in an undue focus on unsafe acts, as it is often just such an act that prompts an employee to record what is observed. Once a focus on the negative begins to characterize the process, however, employees begin to view observations as a "safety-police-like" strategy of catching people putting themselves or others in danger of injury.

For these reasons, observations and feedback should generally be integrated. Observers should provide feedback almost every time they complete an observation. Exceptions to this rule include situations in which providing immediate feedback produces risk. For example, any time that stopping to discuss an observation would create a hazard, any time an observation is conducted in a high-noise environment, or during special situations such as when both employee and observer are wearing a breathing apparatus that would make a discussion difficult. In these cases, the feedback should be given as soon as it is practical to do so. Other than in situations like these, observations and feedback should go hand in hand.

How should observers provide feedback on their observations? The discussion of the observation should be a dialogue between the observer and the employee(s) observed. This feedback procedure should be an important element of the training provided to all observers. The observer should summarize the significant safety practices that were observed then communicate the one or two practices that caused the greatest concern. Generally, the observer begins by listing one or two of the things that the employee was doing right: "Here are some ways that you are minimizing your risk of injury ... (lists the relevant safe practices)." Or the observer might use a variation such as this: "Some practices that I thought contributed to your safety are ... (lists the relevant safe practices)." Our observer next goes on to summarize the unsafe practices: "Here are some things I am concerned about ... (lists relevant unsafe practices)." Or you could use a tandem variation, such as this: "These are a few practices that are placing people at risk ... (lists unsafe practices)" followed by "How would it work if ... (make a request for the safe practice)."

When giving feedback, a *three-step* feedback process works equally well for both positive and corrective feedback:

1. Describe the behavior that was observed.
2. Discuss the potential impact on the employee and their coworkers.
3. *Listen to what the employee has to say.* Then, for corrective feedback, make a specific suggestion that pinpoints what he or she should be doing differently.

Using this model to discuss a safe practice, the observer might say something like "I noticed you used proper lifting techniques by lifting with your legs while keeping your back straight. Lifting like that will help you keep your back healthy." Then, pause and listen to any response from the employee. Similarly, when discussing an area of concern, the observer might say, "I was concerned about the fact that you were not wearing a harness or any other form of fall protection. At 6 feet off the floor, you're high enough to suffer a serious incident if you were to fall." Then listen to the employee's response.

An employee who has a reason for an at-risk behavior is likely to tell the observer at this point. In the above example, the employee might respond, "Yeah, I stopped by the storeroom, but they didn't have a harness available, and I needed to get this job done." When employees have a reason for their action, the observer should record it on the observation form as it will be important in helping the steering committee develop action plans to address that concern.

While getting such information is important, observers should be taught not to interrogate the employees that they observe. The discussion should be a two-way, problem-solving discussion that is educational for both parties. In particular, observers should avoid two kinds of problems caused by (1) asking rhetorical questions and (2) asking questions that start with "why." The problem with rhetorical questions is simply that they tend to make employees angry. This is the problem with the *two-question method* often taught to observers in DuPont's Safety Training Observation Process (STOP). In this procedure observers ask two questions. First they ask, "What could happen?" This prompts the employee to identify the risk in the situation and thus respond to the same aspects of the situation the observer is inquiring about. Next they ask, "How could the risk be avoided?" This prompts the employee to identify the appropriate safe practice or corrective action. Recent research on leadership suggests that such questions tend to generate anger rather than the hoped-for educational impact.

Asking why an employee is doing something also has a negative impact in that it tends to make the employee defensive rather than setting the occasion for a constructive problem-solving discussion. The same information can always be gathered by asking questions that start with "what" or "how," which does not seem to create the same defensiveness. Asking a question such as "What are the barriers that prevent you from using a harness?" creates much less defensiveness than "Why aren't you wearing fall protection?"

If your observers will be conducting observations of small groups of employees, they might provide feedback to the group using basically the same technique. If the group is working on a common task, the observer can usually give feedback to the group. If group members are working on different tasks but in the same general area, the observer should usually give individual feedback. Once the observer has completed the observation, the observer might approach the group, review the things that the group was doing well, then discuss problem areas by saying, "Here are some things I have concerns about ..." before reviewing the unsafe practices they observed. Notice that the observation checklist in Figure 11.2 has columns for the number of safe practices and number of concerns followed by a column for comments. The form then prompts the kind of discussion planned by the design team consistent with one of the stated values: "concern for fellow employees."

In addition, you should provide guidelines on how to handle disagreement about a safety practice. If a disagreement arises, the observer should always try to reach a consensus with the employees who were observed. If that fails, the question should be referred to the steering committee for resolution.

Some common configurations. Organizations need to design their VBS processes to meet their unique needs. Many issues, including factors such as the size and complexity of and organization and the history of involvement of employees in safety improvement efforts, affect the final design. Table 11.6 presents some common configurations for VBS processes.

11.8 Trial Run the Observation Checklist and Process

At this point, your design team is ready to do a trial run of your observation process. This trial run has three objectives:

1. fine-tune the checklist and observation procedure to ensure ease of use
2. ensure the reliability of the observation procedure
3. develop baseline data for each checklist (i.e., for each separate area or function that will be observed)

You should walk through the entire observation process and debug each step. Be prepared to go through several revisions of each checklist and procedure.

At this stage, you should also work on developing a reliable observation procedure. Have two observers go through the steps side by side. They should first go through the observation procedure, collaborating on how to complete the checklist. After this *calibration training*, at their next observation session they should again score the work areas simultaneously, this time without discussion. Then their checklists should be compared, and a reliability coefficient should be calculated using the following formula:

$$\text{Reliability coefficient (\% agreement)} = \frac{\text{number of items in agreement}}{\left(\begin{array}{c} \text{number of items in agreement} \\ + \\ \text{number of items in disagreement} \end{array} \right)}$$

Table 11.6. Common Configurations of VBS Processes

	Current Best Practice	Organizations Targeting Involvement	Employee Based	Empirical Studies	Management Based	Staff Based
Observers	Dedicated small group of observers	All employees who wish to participate (including supervisors and managers)	Employees only (either all employees or a dedicated group of observers)	Independent (often from outside organization)	Managers and/or supervisors	Staff personnel (usually safety staff but senior maintenance person may observe conditions)
Frequency	Twice each week	Weekly	Daily or weekly	Weekly	Weekly	Weekly or monthly
Feedback	• Behavioral feedback during observations • Data reviewed in safety meetings	• Behavioral feedback during observations • Data reviewed in safety meetings	• Behavioral feedback during observations • Data reviewed in safety meetings	• Data summaries to manager • Data reviewed in safety meetings	• Behavioral feedback during observations • Data reviewed in safety meetings	• Data summaries to manager • Data reviewed in safety meetings
Observations Announced?	Usually (at least in early stages)	Usually (at least in early stages)	Usually (at least in early stages)	No	For some programs	No
Role of Management	• Approve plan • Participate in kickoff meetings • Review data shared by steering committee • Ensure actions taken to address hazards identified by steering committee	• Approve plan • Participate in kickoff meetings • Review observation data • Conduct observations • Approve and participate in safety recognition and celebrations	• Approve plan • Participate in kickoff meetings • Review observation data • Approve and participate in safety recognition and celebrations	• Approve plan	• Approve plan • Participate in kickoff meetings • Review completion of observations • Approve and participate in safety recognition and celebrations	• Approve plan • Participate in kickoff meetings • Review completion of observations • Approve and participate in safety recognition and celebrations

For this kind of application, you should strive for a reliability coefficient of 80% or better. The better your reliability at this stage, the easier it will later be to train observers. If you have a very clear and simple checklist with well-pinpointed items, new observers will be able to conduct their observations with very little observer training.

Save the data you collect during this phase, especially as you finalize your checklist. It will provide a baseline for evaluating future efforts. It may also provide a basis for setting improvement goals and problem-solving in later stages of implementation.

Before the management review, the design team should review its procedure or flowchart, brainstorm what could go wrong at each step, and discuss how to refine the process to minimize the likelihood of each potential problem.

Table 11.7 provides clarification on the next steps:

Table 11.7. The Next Steps

If Your Design Team Is Conducting	Then You May Choose to
Marathon planning meetings	• Skip the section on management review and go on to Step 3 of the VBS process: ○ develop feedback and involvement procedures
Periodic planning meetings	• Conduct a review with management as described, then proceed to Step 5 of the VBS process: ○ conduct training and kickoff meetings in each area

11.9 Conduct Management Review

Once you have completed your trial run and made final revisions to both your checklist and procedure, the design team should present the observation process to management. This step should be one of the milestones on your initial schedule. Use this meeting as an opportunity for

- management to provide input to the safety process
- safety team members to be recognized for their participation
- the design team to obtain approval to implement the observation process

All design team members who want to participate should be involved in this presentation. The recognition from management should reinforce their participation in the safety process.

Getting management's input and suggestions on your observation system during this presentation helps ensure it will support your implementation efforts. This meeting also provides an opportunity for ensuring that management understands each component of the VBS process at each stage of its implementation. Figure 11.9 presents a typical agenda for such a meeting.

Purpose: Obtain management approval to implement observation system
- Background on how the design team came into being
- Objectives of the observation system
- Process for developing the observation system
    - List of initial pinpoints
    - Final checklist
- Observation procedure
- Plans for addressing tasks with serious incident potential
- Management's role
- Next steps
    - Kickoff meetings with employees
    - Developing feedback and involvement process
- Discussion and management input

Figure 11.9. Typical agenda for presenting observation system to management.

CHAPTER 12

Step 3: Designing Feedback and Involvement Procedures

Creating an effective feedback and involvement process includes the implementation tasks shown in Table 12.1.

Table 12.1. Tasks to Implement an Effective Feedback and Involvement Process

Task Number	Activity
1	Develop guidelines for using graphs
2	Plan reviews of safety process data: • in safety meetings (observation data) • in management meetings (data on the percent of observations completed)
3	Develop guidelines for setting improvement goals
4	Establish guidelines to rotate observers

12.1 Develop Guidelines for Using Graphs

Your design team should develop guidelines for using graphs to provide feedback. Numerous studies have shown that posting performance graphs has a significant positive impact on employee performance (Andrasik, 1980), and most research studies investigating behavioral safety programs have included graphs of the observation data. Graphing safety observation data is a good way to communicate the data to employees. In addition, graphs help employees identify trends and set improvement targets. In contrast, some companies have had bad experiences with poorly planned efforts to graph quality data. Such companies may want to avoid the negative associations that some of their employees have with posted graphs. Table 12.2 provides guidelines for using graphs.

Table 12.2. Considerations for the Use of Graphs

If	Then	And
Your employees have experience using data to self-manage their work areas and have a good relationship with management	Post graphs in work areas	Review the graphs in weekly safety meetings
Your employees have had a bad past experience with graphs – or – Your employees have a poor relationship with supervision or management	Don't post graphs	Steering committee should review graphs during their meetings and introduce those graphs to employee safety meetings only after employees are comfortable with the observation process

In developing guidelines for using graphs, you should consider making suggestions on what to graph, provide sample forms for graphs, and provide suggestions on their use. Your design team should consider recommending two graphs for each area, one showing "percent safe" observation data and the other showing the percentage of observations completed each week, as in Figures 12.1 and 12.2, respectively. The graph of percent safe can either be across all observations or track a single behavior that the area is targeting for improvement. Sometimes, the steering committee may decide to post a bar graph that shows the percent safe on each practice on the checklist. This graph would be appropriate, for example, when the steering committee wants to share the data with area employees so that everyone knows the basis for the priorities and action plans being developed by the steering committee. The steering committee may create the graphs by hand or use computers. The most important requirement is that all graphs be simple and easy to understand.

Rule of thumb for a posted graph:
The graph should be easy to understand, enough that an employee can glance at it when walking by and interpret it without breaking stride.

Note that the graph for recording the observation data also has space for recording when the observation was conducted and by whom. Each steering committee should have a separate graph for observation data from its own area, meaning that you may have several graphs on the same scoreboard depending on how you have designed the observation process. For example, you may want each shift to have a separate graph of weekly safety observations specific to that shift.

Initially, depending on the technical sophistication of your workforce, asking observers to update the graphs manually is preferable to generating them by computer. Requiring that observers record the data on the graphs ensures that they understand the data being presented.

Entering the data into a database or spreadsheet does have some advantages, however. It enables you to easily generate summary reports for distribution, which is particularly important for tracking the percentage of observations conducted in a large organization. Computers can also easily generate monthly or weekly reports on the percentage of observations completed in each area for review in steering committee meetings.

If you recommend that your organization post safety graphs in the work areas, be sure you provide guidelines to all managers and supervisors on how to use such graphs effectively.

First rule of thumb on using data:
All managers and supervisors should be instructed not to respond in any way to a low percent safe or safety index on graphs. Managers must not put pressure on employees to improve these numbers. They may problem-solve the observation data with employees within the context of appropriate safety meetings but should refrain from any negative or critical comments.

Second rule of thumb on using data:
All managers and supervisors should be encouraged to make positive comments on good percent safe or safety index scores or improvements evidenced on such graphs. They should also make positive and appreciative comments to appropriate employees during the workday and during meetings.

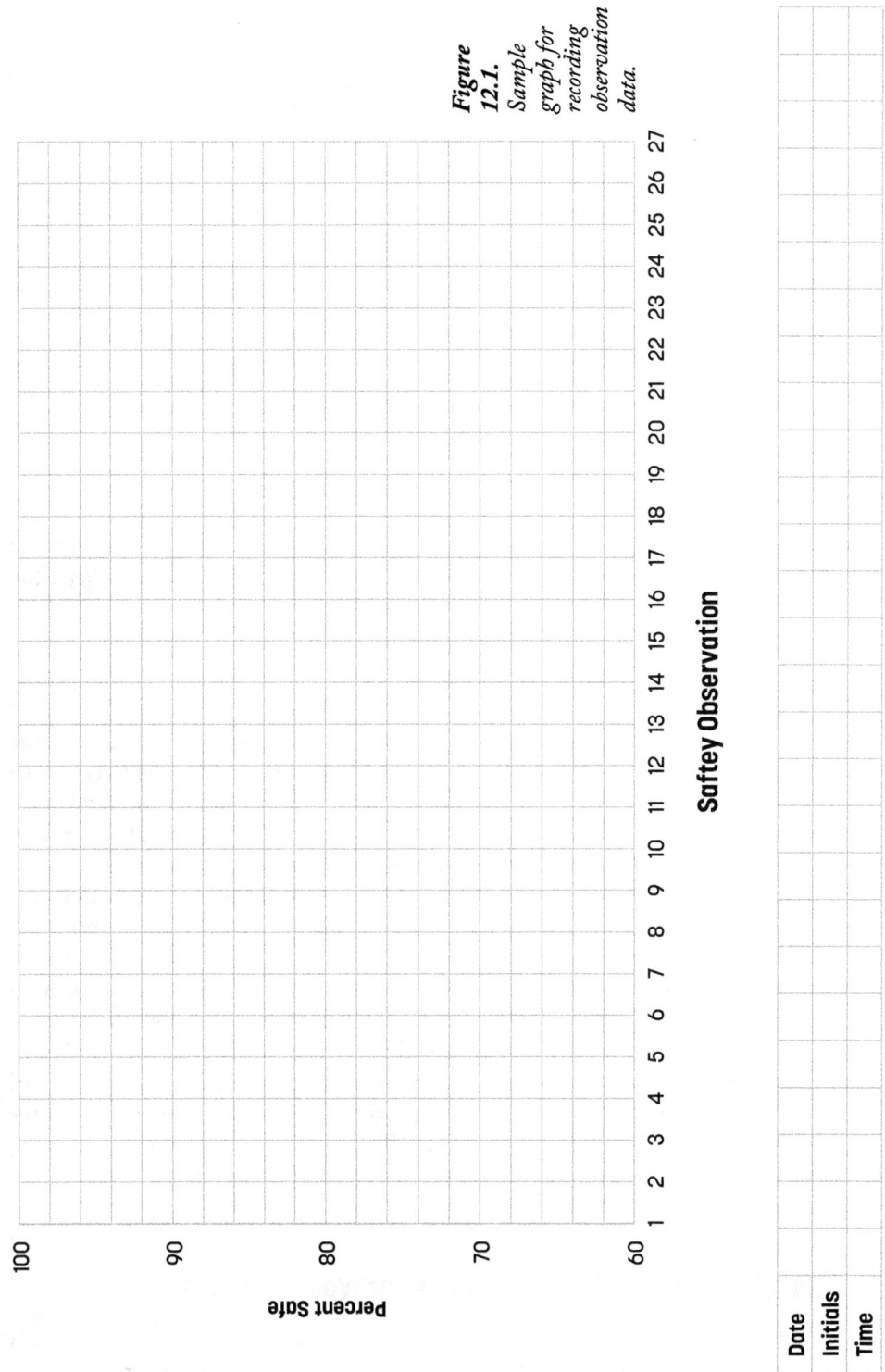

Figure 12.1. Sample graph for recording observation data.

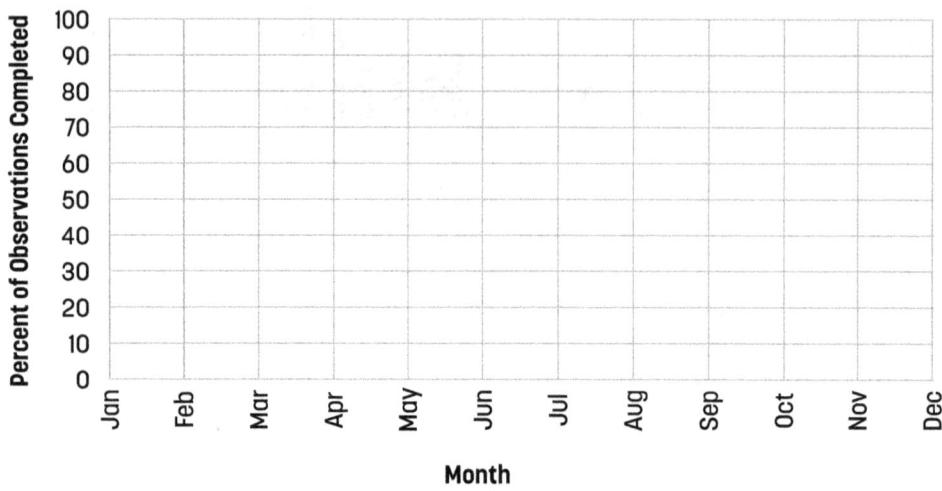

Figure 12.2. Sample graph for data on completed observations.

In planning to use graphs, you must emphasize safety on the job, not numbers on graphs. The risk in using graphs is placing too much emphasis on the numbers. The result is that you influence reporting, not performance.

12.2 Plan Review of Safety Process Data

To get the maximum benefit from the observation process, you must ensure that the organization makes use of the data. In other words, the data must be reviewed and employees must respond to it. The best way to ensure that people look at the observation data is to build a review of the data into existing meetings. Ideally, the graphs and observation sheets will be reviewed as one of the first agenda items in weekly safety meetings.

Data on the percentage of observations completed should be reviewed both by the steering committee and in management meetings. Management should focus on managing the safety process, not the results of the process. If management attempts to manage the results of the observation process, it will ruin the integrity of the system. Such pressure from management will eventually bias the observation process and destroy the value of the data.

This is not to suggest that managers and supervisors should forego attention to safety on the job. The observation data are a measure of the extent to which employees work safely. Managers and supervisors must provide daily feedback to employees for on-the-job safety to ensure the success of the VBS process. However, they should emphasize safety on the job and maintaining scheduled observations, not the percent safe resulting from completed observations.

12.3 Develop Guidelines for Setting Improvement Goals

The design team should provide guidelines for establishing improvement goals based on the observation data. Ideally, as part of the data review process in safety meetings, employees will establish improvement targets for their area's percent safe. These improvement targets should be based on the existing level of safety practices, as indicated by the observations. The goal should be for some fixed time period, such as the next 1–3 months. The goal is best set for some fairly short period of time, not for the entire year, so that the steering committee can make frequent corrections to the process and have regular opportunities to celebrate success. Once the target is agreed upon, each steering committee should draw a goal line on its safety graph with a colored marker so that all employees can tell where they stand relative to the target. Then the employees should identify which safety practices they are going to work on to reach their target.

An alternative goal-setting strategy is to establish *process goals* that focus on improving specific safety practices. In other words, rather than setting a specific percent safe, the employees might target achieving 100% for the coming week on a specific safety practice or set of practices identified as needing improvement on the basis of observations completed during the previous week.

To ensure that the goals get set, the design team should ensure that responsibility for setting the improvement target is clearly assigned and communicated. In most cases, the steering committee should set safety improvement targets or goals. This procedure would be appropriate if the observation process combined several shifts or work areas that each had separate safety meetings. For other organizations, the person responsible for leading the safety meetings should take responsibility for ensuring that each team of employees sets a safety goal. While employee participation in goal setting is consistent with the philosophy of an employee-driven process, current data do not show a significant advantage for employee participation in goal setting versus goals assigned by management, although employees do like to participate in setting goals (Fellner & Sulzer-Azaroff, 1985). Thus, for other organizations, the design team might plan for management to take responsibility for reviewing the data and setting improvement targets. Table 12.3 on the following page summarizes the options and considerations for goal setting. Obviously, many organizations will have some combination of these.

Establishing this improvement goal is important for several reasons. Progress toward an explicit goal provides a positive source of motivation and helps build pride in the area's safety efforts. In addition, goal setting helps reduce competition by providing a noncompetitive standard of comparison. An effective goal or performance target gives the area team a standard for evaluating its performance. Members can compare their performance with their own goal rather than where they stand relative to other groups. Downplaying competition is particularly important because different work areas may have very different risks and safety requirements. Leading a group of employees toward a common goal is a far better process for building teamwork and cooperation. Chapter 22 outlines the steering committee's responsibilities in this area in more detail.

12.4 Establish Guidelines to Expand Involvement in Observations

Once the steering committee has successfully established the observation process, the next objective is to sustain the desired number of competent observers. Rather

Table 12.3. Considerations and Options for Setting Improvement Targets

Targets Set by	Would Typically Include	Considerations

Natural work groups (groups of employees that typically meet together for safety meetings)	• Safety targets:
	  ◦ Top 1–2 concerns (improving % safe on that behavior)
	• Process targets:
	  ◦ # of observations
	  ◦ % participation in conducting observations
		• Most appropriate when many important issues are behavioral or are conditions that can be addressed at the local level

Management team	• Safety targets:
	  ◦ Top 1–2 concerns (improving % safe on that behavior)
	• Process targets:
	  ◦ # of observations by managers and supervisors
	  ◦ Participation by managers and supervisors
		• Most appropriate for addressing facility issues and ensuring visible management support
		• May be the best option when steering committee meeting time is limited

Steering committee	• Safety targets:
	  ◦ Top 1–2 concerns (improving % safe on that behavior)
	• Process targets:
	  ◦ # of observations
	  ◦ % participation in conducting observations
		• Best overall for most organizations—integrates action plans to address target behaviors and facilities related to those behaviors
		• Adds to the time required for steering committee meetings

than significantly expanding participation, the focus remains on ensuring the continuous availability of trained observers to maintain optimal safety conditions.

This expanded participation could initially manifest as joint observations, where new observers learn alongside supervisors or seasoned observers. Every quarter, a fresh set of observers should be brought into the rotation, with each observer typically serving a 12-month term. This strategy ensures all employees can participate as observers while maintaining consistency in the observation process.

Above all, remember to offer thorough training and orientation for new observers, as detailed in the previous section (also refer to Chapter 14). Members of the steering committee should typically provide training and coaching for new observers, ensuring they are proficient in both conducting the observations and delivering feedback to their fellow employees. This approach empowers employees, enhances safety awareness, and fosters a collaborative environment.

12.5 Checklist for Planning Feedback and Involvement

Figure 12.3 is a checklist to use in planning feedback and involvement.

Does Your Design Team's Plan Include Recommendations on	Yes	No
1. Posting graphs and copies of the last completed observation data sheet in work areas?		
2. Graphs and observation data to be reviewed in weekly safety meetings?		
3. The review of data on the "percent of observations complete" in area safety meetings and regular management meetings?		
4. A process for setting area improvement targets based on observation data?		
5. Rotating observers in the observation process?		

Figure 12.3. Checklist for planning feedback and involvement.

CHAPTER 13

Step 4: Developing Recognition and Celebration Plans

As discussed in Chapter 1, traditional safety awards programs often reward people who take chances or encourage employees not to report incidents accurately. Too many people simply roll the dice. The chance of injury is usually low enough that they do not get hurt even though they take chances. In awards programs based on going a fixed time period without an incident, such employees usually get the same award as employees who always comply with safety procedures. Furthermore, if the award is significant, and particularly if the award is significant to a group of employees, such programs tend to discourage the honest reporting of minor incidents by most employees.

To avoid such shortcomings, safety awards and incentives should be based primarily on behaviors that promote safety, such as conducting observations, leading safety meetings, and other activities that directly or indirectly contribute to the safety and well-being of coworkers. In addition, small awards can be provided for maintaining a safe workplace, as measured by observation data, perhaps in combination with no lost-workday cases. The safety awards process provides a way of celebrating successes and expressing appreciation for employees who work safely and those who make special contributions.

Safety awards—first rule of thumb:
Provide safety awards for safe behavior on the job and for activities related to maintaining the safety process (e.g., observations, conducting safety meetings, setting safety goals).

Safety awards—second rule of thumb:
Keep safety awards and incentives small. Your awards should be significant enough to support compliance but not significant enough to generate false reporting of safety data.

The second rule is especially critical, as illustrated by the court decision mentioned in Chapter 1 in which an employee in Texas won a workers' compensation case against an employer whose safety bingo program discouraged employees from accurately reporting incidents (*Paragon Hotel Corp. v. Ramirez*, 1990). Depending on other aspects of a company's loss prevention efforts, any incentive that encourages employees not to report incidents may increase a company's liability should an incident occur. Such an incentive increases an employee's ability to successfully file a compensation claim well after the typical time periods established for such a claim.

Regardless of the kind of awards system you design, you will have to create an internal marketing campaign to promote your safety effort with employees. You will want to consider posters, announcements in safety meetings, articles in newsletters, and other methods of promoting and communicating the new process. Whether you choose to announce the awards program is a separate question. As discussed below, sometimes you may be better off not to "dangle the carrot" by kicking off your awards program with a great deal of hoopla.

In planning a safety awards and recognition program, be aware that many people have had negative experiences with traditional awards programs. Employees may have had experience with awards that were not meaningful or were a product of favoritism, programs that did not fairly recognize their efforts, or awards that were determined by chance rather than performance. Such experiences often create resistance to well-designed awards and recognition programs. Employees who resist awards programs, however, are normally receptive to team celebrations of success and recognition for individual efforts and contributions.

The administration of recognition and celebrations is as important, perhaps even more important, than the initial planning. Chapter 22 will provide additional details related to using recognition and celebrations as effective positive consequences.

There are three basic options in designing effective safety incentives:

1. Create a safety awards process.
2. Support the safety process through an existing compensation and promotion process.
3. Provide incentive compensation based on the safety process.

13.1 Overview of Safety Awards and Incentives

Safety awards programs are usually fairly easy to create, but an effective incentive program is relatively complex and involved. Safety awards programs are most effective if they are administered locally and with a high level of involvement by the safety teams and line management. Incentive programs, on the other hand, usually require a higher level of approval and are often administered organization wide.

Table 13.1 shows various options for safety awards. Obviously, you may choose to combine several of the options. For example, you might combine a concurrent safety awards program, a recognition process, and one of the compensation options. Your design team can create a recognition and concurrent safety awards process for your steering committee to implement at the local level, but changes to compensation will usually require working with executive management.

13.2 Safety Recognition

The least formal safety awards process tries to maximize use of personal recognition, often in the form of appreciative feedback. Such recognition may be provided in safety meetings, as part of other group meetings or activities, or privately to individual employees. With this approach, your design team might recommend that the steering committee and management put recognition on the agenda at the beginning of every meeting and allow time for participants to pass along their thanks to others in the organization who have done something worthy of recognition. You might also promote the use of handwritten thank-you notes, perhaps using copies on bulletin boards to publicize both the appreciation and the specific contribution. This approach is usually more successful when it is supported through a training process that helps everyone understand the rationale for the approach and how to provide effective personal recognition. Often, this can be part of the observer training provided to all employees, supervisors, and managers.

Table 13.1. Design Options for Safety Awards, Celebrations, and Incentives

	Safety Recognition	Simple or Concurrent Safety Awards	Tiered Safety Awards	Professional Development Opportunities	Career Path Opportunities	Safety Integrated With Traditional Compensation	Safety Incentives
Recognition or Awards	Social recognition, often a formal agenda item in meetings and handwritten thank-you notes	Fixed awards for everyone – or – Menu of items or events	Multiple tiers with menu of recognition items or events appropriate to each tier	Opportunity to participate in safety conferences and workshops	Promotion from hourly employee to supervisor	Merit increase or annual performance bonus	Incentive bonus or time off provided upon meeting criteria
Criteria*	Usually not established in advance	Specified in advance for each separate program	Provide guidelines on behaviors or results appropriate for each tier	Active participation in steering committee meetings and observations	Effective at safety observations and feedback	• Number of observations • Lost-workday injury rates • Workers' compensation cost	• Recordable injury rates • Lost-workday injury rates • Workers' compensation cost
Participants	Individuals and teams	Individuals and teams	Individuals and teams	Steering committee members and observers	Individual observers	Usually, management personnel	Individuals and teams
Considerations	Often difficult to ensure that all levels and functions are included equally	• Simple programs must be constantly varied to maintain novelty and keep awards meaningful • Multiple, concurrent awards provide better distribution and variety of awards and increase the probability of an employee receiving an award	• Provide good variety and wide distribution of awards • Increases the probability of awards for those who champion safety	• Helps ensure ongoing steering committee participation • Helps encourage others to volunteer	• Provides effective motivation to be a good observer • Limited number available in any given year	Requires that those who evaluate personnel know the applicable safety activities	• Usually requires management or staff observations of safety activities in their work areas • Gainsharing often funded by savings in workers' compensation

*Ideally, awards are based on behavioral criteria, not on a fixed period of time without an incident.

You should encourage the steering committee to arrange for some form of recognition and appreciative feedback for your observers. In particular, observers who are conscientious about completing their observations should receive meaningful recognition from their supervisors and managers. This recognition might come as a simple, personal expression of appreciation during safety meetings or via thank-you notes or letters of commendation. Ultimately, providing some form of recognition for completing observations will be important to maintaining the observation process.

Appreciative feedback is a very important element of the safety awards options discussed below. All awards should include a clear, pinpointed statement of what was done to earn the award and a suitable statement of appreciation.

13.3 Simple and Concurrent Safety Awards

The easiest option for creating a simple safety awards program is to identify the criteria and arrange an awards or recognition event, or perhaps a menu of awards and recognition events appropriate to the criteria. The idea is to strive for planned, yet spontaneous recognition. It is planned in that you know what pinpointed behavior or accomplishment you plan to reward, but it is spontaneous in that you do not know when the criteria will be met. These awards programs resemble traditional safety awards except that employees earn the awards based on specific actions that promote safety, not by going a fixed period of time without an incident.

In contrast to most traditional safety awards, simple awards can support on-the-job safety when provided to employees for simply going without an incident. To be effective, the awards must be small enough to avoid impacting reporting and be based on avoidance of injuries for a relatively short period of time (e.g., one month).

Typically, the design team creates a simple awards program and suggests several possible criteria and potential awards. It then allows the steering committee to modify the plans to best support the behavioral process once employees begin doing observations.

If the safety awards are unchanging and are the same for everyone (e.g., jackets, caps, coffee cups, or the like), the steering committee should realize that they are usually creating an awards *program*, not a process that can continue on indefinitely. As such, it should have a planned life cycle. The steering committee should maintain such a program for a fixed period (e.g., 6 months) then design and initiate a new awards program to take its place. By varying the awards and criteria, the steering committee keeps the awards novel and helps keep employees interested and thinking about safety.

To create a longer-lasting recognition *process*, your design team may suggest that the steering committee create a flexible awards process based on a menu of awards rather than a simple fixed award. By using a menu of awards, your steering committee can select an award that can be more meaningful to a given individual or team. Some of the more elaborate procedures described in the following section on tiered awards may be useful in developing a menu of reinforcers for safety awards.

In addition, your design team may choose to encourage the steering committee to start with a simple awards process and add concurrent awards later.

This approach eventually leads to a more complex, concurrent safety awards process. For example, the initial safety awards program might provide a catered meal for a group of employees who achieve their percent safe target for proper lifting in their area.

Another example of a concurrent safety awards process would involve the creation of one plan for recognizing individual contributions and another plan for celebrating team successes. Table 13.2 presents an example of such a concurrent awards process.

Table 13.2. Example of Concurrent Safety Awards Processes Providing Individual Recognition and Team Celebrations

	Individual Safety Recognition	Team Safety Celebrations
Administrated by	Steering committee	Steering committee

Criteria	• Completing scheduled observations
	• Conducting quality safety meeting
	• Specific contribution or level of support
	• Identifying a significant unsafe practice or condition
	• Close-call reporting
	• Off-the-job or home safety
		• Targets set by steering committee (monthly or quarterly)
		• Suggested criteria:
		  ◦ Number or percent of observations
		• Other criteria (usually downplayed):
		  ◦ Percent safe
		  ◦ Percent safe over time
		  ◦ Number of unsafe acts reported

Awards or Celebration	• Social recognition in safety meeting • Positive feedback from "next-level" leader • Recognition article in company newsletter	• Barbeque prepared by area manager • Breakfast • Chicken lunch • Cookouts • Dinner • Donuts • Ice cream social • Pizza • Watermelon break
Other Elements	• Employees may earn recognition for activities and contributions not on initial list of criteria • Recognition usually provided as part of a meeting, often in conjunction with team celebration	• Not announced in advance • May be used as opportunity to provide individual recognition

13.4 Tiered Safety Awards

The best safety awards programs have various awards that are appropriate for different kinds and levels of performance. They are similar to frequent-flyer awards: You get the awards no matter when or where you fly, and the more you fly, the greater the value of the awards. Multiple tiers establish different levels of contribution and their corresponding awards. Such an approach often builds on or incorporates simple awards programs and the use of personal recognition. It may expand simple or concurrent awards processes by combining them into a single awards process in which the concurrent awards are placed within the appropriate tier. The safety recognition process may become the lowest tier of the process, often with additional guidelines regarding the types of behaviors that would justify recognition. The idea is to recognize a large variety of individual and group contributions.

The design of a model tiered safety awards process often requires completion of several tasks, as shown in Table 13.3.

Table 13.3. Tasks That Must Be Completed in the Design of a Tiered Safety Awards Process

Task Number	Activity
1	Develop the criteria for different levels of performance
2	Identify potential awards and forms of recognition
3	Survey area personnel regarding their preferences
4	Finalize a menu of celebrations and awards for each level of performance
5	Plan the awards delivery process
6	Present the safety awards plan to management

Develop the criteria for different levels of performance. Figure 13.1 provides a worksheet for designing the tiers for this type of safety awards process. One of the key elements is that the guidelines or criteria for awards are clearly established, although they may be adjusted if a safety-related behavior occurs that deserves recognition. The idea is to create a flexible system with guidelines that assure consistency. Plan to establish three to five levels of recognition for individual contributions (e.g., submitting a high level of implemented safety suggestions) and team successes (e.g., achieving a safety goal).

As your first task, identify the kinds of activities and accomplishments you wish to recognize. You may want to brainstorm an initial list of criteria, then ask several design team members to use this list to develop a more complete list of safety contributions you might want to recognize and sort them into different levels.

Figure 13.2 provides examples of criteria that could represent five levels of recognition.

Identify potential awards and forms of recognition. Your next task is to develop a list of possible recognition and awards ideas. Before establishing the awards system, you should find out how much money is available for the steering committee to spend on safety awards. Once the awards system is established, awards should be a standard item in the annual budget.

You should keep each award relatively small, generally $10–$25, although rare awards in your highest level might be as much as $250. The idea of an awards program

Recognition Worksheet

Level	Criteria	Menu of Recognition Activities and Celebrations
1		
2		
3		
4		
5		

Figure 13.1. Example worksheet for planning a tiered safety awards process.

Recognition Worksheet

Level	Criteria	Menu of Recognition Activities and Celebrations
1	• Individual submits safety suggestion that is approved for implementation • Individual leads safety meeting • Individual participates on steering committee	
2	• Individual reports a close call or identifies a significant uncontrolled hazard • Individual with most valuable safety suggestion in a given month • Safety team achieves milestones	
3	• Area achieves new high on safety index (from observations) • Observer completes all scheduled observations for a quarter • Area meets its safety target for a month	
4	• Area meets its safety target for a quarter	
5	• Area maintains safety observation process for a year and betters industry average for injuries • Observers complete high number of observations for the year • Individual makes year's best safety suggestion	

Figure 13.2. Example recognition worksheet showing possible criteria.

is for the company to express its appreciation in a way that is meaningful to the employee(s), but it is not supposed to be compensation. Also, you do not want to place too significant an award on safety because of the danger of damaging the integrity of the reporting and observation processes. If the awards are overly valuable, they can negatively influence these processes.

Again, you may simply brainstorm recognition awards and events with the design team. Figure 13.3 presents a list of possible safety awards items and events that your team may want to consider. You may also want to solicit additional ideas from employees outside the design team (e.g., using the form in Figure 13.4 during the kickoff meeting to get such input).

Social	• Letter from supervision	
	• Letter from upper management	
	• Name of individual or team on bulletin board at plant entrance	
	• Recognition memo from managers from other areas	
	• Write-up in plant publication	
	• Letter to spouse or family	
Work Related	• Plant tour	
	• Special assignments	
	• Opportunity to participate on steering committee	
	• Training for different job within area	
	• Other training courses	
	• Time to discuss issues with supervisor	
	• Assignment to preferred duties	
	• Area discussion with plant manager	
	• Opportunity to participate in management presentation	
	• Opportunity to participate in safety conferences and workshops	
Tangible	$25 - $50:	• Dinner
		• Gift card
		• Pizza for team
	$50 - $100:	• Tablet computer
		• Television streaming device
		• Headphones
	$100 - $200:	• Camping equipment
		• Television
		• Video doorbell

Figure 13.3 Example list of possible safety recognition activities, celebrations, and awards.

Area Safety Awards Survey

Your steering committee is working on a team management process to enhance our safety efforts. As part of this process, we want to create celebrations of our safety successes that are fun for everyone involved.

Please assist us by responding to the following survey items. We are looking for awards and activities to recognize individuals and teams. Your input into our safety recognition activities will help us develop a more effective program!

For each of the following approximate dollar amounts, what are some awards you or your team would enjoy?

$200 (for example, TV): _____

_____

_____

$100 (for example, tablet computer): _____

_____

_____

$50 (for example, dinner for two): _____

_____

_____

$25 (for example, gift card): _____

_____

_____

What suggestions do you have for creating a fun safety awards process? Use the space below and on the back of this sheet (if you need additional space) to make your comments and suggestions. _____

_____

_____

_____

_____

Figure 13.4. Sample initial survey to get ideas for recognition menu.

Survey area personnel regarding their preferences.[3] Establishing an awards menu enables you to select an award or form of recognition that is meaningful to the recipient. You will therefore find it useful to have some idea of how significant the awards are to employees. You could work with the design team to rank the items on your list of potential recognition items and events, or you could use a survey. Figure 13.5 shows an example survey that you might construct, based on your initial list of awards ideas, to help determine how significant those awards are to employees. You may choose to survey other design team members or a broader sample of employees.

Safety Recognition Survey

Name (optional): _____

Please help the steering committee by giving us your input. Circle the choice that indicates how important each of these forms of recognition is to you.

1. Social

    1.1 Letter from supervisor

Low importance	Somewhat important	High importance

    1.2 Letter from upper management

Low importance	Somewhat important	High importance

    1.3 Name of individual or team on board at plant entrance

Low importance	Somewhat important	High importance

    1.4 Recognition memo from other department managers

Low importance	Somewhat important	High importance

    1.5 Write-up and picture in plant publication

Low importance	Somewhat important	High importance

    1.6 Letter to spouse or family on safety achievement

Low importance	Somewhat important	High importance

Figure 13.5. Example survey to help rank value of items for recognition menu.

---

3   This approach is based on Andrasik (1991).

When you get the surveys back, summarize the data and develop a prioritized list based on the survey responses. Figure 13.6 presents an example of a prioritized list of recognition items showing the average scores based on survey responses. Notice how the list is divided into five categories based on logical breaks in the preference scores. At the end of this task, you should have a list of individual and group awards and recognition ideas ranked in tiers that correspond to the number of criteria levels you identified earlier.

Form of Recognition	Preference Score*
Dinner at restaurant of your choice	4.8
Catered barbeque	4.6
Assignment to preferred duties	4.3
Time off	4.3
Gift card	4.3
Cafeteria lunch certificate	4.0
Time to discuss issues with supervision	3.9
Opportunity to participate in steering committee	3.7
Area discussion with plant manager	3.7
Letter from upper management	3.4
Training to do a different job within area	3.2
Donuts and coffee	3.2
Longer break	3.2
Special assignment	3.1
Name of individual or team on board at plant entrance	3.0
Write-up and picture in plant newsletter	3.0
Pizza party	3.0
Barbeque cooked by supervisor or management	3.0
Letter from supervisor	2.8
Breakfast cooked by supervisor	2.8
Breakfast cooked by manager	2.8
Letter to spouse or family on safety achievement	2.6
Recognition memo from managers from other areas	2.6
Opportunity to participate in management presentation	2.6
Items with company logo	2.6
Plant tour	2.3
Plaques	2.3

* The preference score is the average of all survey responses scored as 1, 3, or 5, with 5 being the "High importance" response.

Figure 13.6. Sample data on employee preferences, ranked and grouped into tiers based on recognition survey.

Finalize a menu of celebrations and awards for each level of performance. The remaining task in designing your safety awards process is to match the performance criteria and the award levels. When that has been accomplished, you will have a complete model for the steering committee to use in developing a safety awards and recognition process. Figure 13.7 presents a completed safety awards planning worksheet that lists criteria for individuals and teams and the awards appropriate for both at each level.

Recognition Worksheet

Level	Criteria	Menu of Recognition Activities and Celebrations
1	• Individual submits safety suggestion that is approved for implementation • Individual leads safety meeting • Individual participates on steering committee	• Letter to spouse or family about safety contribution • Opportunity to participate in management presentation
2	• Individual reports a close call or identifies a significant uncontrolled hazard • Individual with most valuable safety suggestion in a given month • Safety team achieves milestones	• Breakfast cooked by supervisor or manager • Letter from supervisor • Barbeque cooked by supervisor or management • Pizza party • Write-up in plant newsletter
3	• Area achieves new high on safety index (from observations) • Observer completes all scheduled observations for a quarter • Area meets its safety target for a month	• Special assignment • Longer break • Donuts and coffee • Opportunity for additional training • Letter from upper management
4	• Area meets its safety target for a quarter	• Area discussion with plant manager • Opportunity to participate on steering committee • Time to discuss issues with supervisor • Cafeteria lunch certificates
5	• Area maintains safety observation process for a year and betters industry average for injuries • Observers complete high number of observations for the year • Individual makes year's best safety suggestion	• Gift card • Time off • Assignment to preferred duties • Catered barbeque • Dinner for two at restaurant of choice

Figure 13.7. Example of a completed recognition planning worksheet that provides criteria and menu of possible forms of recognition.

Plan the awards delivery process. The delivery of the safety awards is critically important to the overall success of your awards process. Your goal is to create a process that is fun for everyone in the area and a true celebration of safety achievements.

The delivery process will vary for each level of award, and individual recognition will often differ from group celebrations. Generally, group celebrations are good opportunities for recognizing individual contributions. By giving recognition this way, everyone wins—the employees enjoy the group celebration, and individuals get attention for their contributions.

The important task here is not planning all of the details in advance for each award on your menu but rather suggesting an awards process that the steering committee can administer and criteria that will trigger awards and a celebration. You will probably want the steering committee to oversee the process and establish a regular cycle of review to identify who has earned a recognition or safety awards. Planning safety recognition and celebrations should be a regular item on the steering committee's agenda.

Ideally, your procedure will be flexible enough so that each award is selected and planned in a way that is significant to the person or group that earned it. As stated earlier, the reason for a menu is to allow you to select something meaningful for significant safety contributions. You will usually want to ensure management's involvement in delivering awards and a level of management appropriate to the level of the awards. Such personal involvement by management helps ensure the credibility of the awards process.

In addition, the menu of celebrations and awards should only serve as a guide. Your steering committee should be encouraged to identify meaningful awards and celebrations that are not on the menu but are in approximately the same category as recognition items or events appropriate to a particular contribution. As you select new safety awards, add them to the menu so that they can be considered in the future.

Although lotteries and contests can be a fun and positive way to provide additional awards, they sometimes create problems because of the competition and danger of hurt feelings. Certain contests can be effective, however, especially in some of the support programs discussed in Chapter 23. Table 13.4 on the following page compares the features of contests, recognition programs, and incentive compensation plans.

Lotteries can also be used to deliver safety awards effectively and increase the value of the more significant awards. The key is to make delivery a fun celebration for everyone and to have many small awards in addition to a main prize so that you have many "winners." Lotteries can be especially effective as part of the celebration during a safety awareness day (see Chapter 23).

Lotteries are also effective in conjunction with token systems in which observers dispense tokens to employees as part of the observation process. Typically, the token is a "thank you for being safe" card that is also a lottery ticket. Such tickets are handed out, for example, when an area scores 100% safe on an observation checklist. Employees can continue to collect the lottery tickets up to a deadline date, perhaps the safety awareness day cited above. The more tokens an employee has, the greater that employee's chances of winning. Employees might earn tokens in other ways too, such as by submitting safety suggestions or participating in a slogan contest. (Note, however, that a lost-workday case

Table 13.4. Comparison of Contests, Recognition, and Incentives

Contests	Recognition Programs	Incentive Plans
Announced	May be either announced or unannounced	Announced
Based on behavior and/or results	Based on behavior and/or results	Based primarily on results
Criteria are typically competitive	Criteria are flexible and may include improvement	Criteria are fixed
Provide motivation only to top performers	Provide motivation to all employees	Provide motivation to all participating employees
Design is very easy	Design is fairly easy	Design is more difficult

during this time will prevent the area's participation in the lottery or may end the lottery altogether. No one wants to celebrate if someone has been injured.)

The advantage of token systems is the immediate, tangible presentation of items that provide direct support for on-the-job safety compliance. The tokens provide both positive feedback and a positive source of motivation for compliance and participation. Again, using an award that is very significant or has great monetary value creates problems because of the disappointment and hard feelings created by those who do not win the lottery. Done correctly, token systems can be fun and help build pride in an organization's safety efforts.

Your records of safety awards should include the names of employees who earned awards, the level of the awards, and the event that celebrated their achievement. Such records will enable you to check what was done in the past and prevent the possible embarrassment of giving the same award to the same individual or group.

Present the safety awards plan to management. If you are using periodic planning meetings, completing your safety awards plan is another of the milestones in your project plan. Before initiating the awards process, you should get management's input on and approval of your criteria, awards, plans for delivering the awards, and, perhaps most importantly, the budget that you will need to support the planned process. Generally, you will have to make some assumptions about how many individuals will earn recognition and how many teams will earn celebrations so that you can estimate the likely costs of your process. At this stage, you are better off slightly overestimating how much you will need to fund this part of your process rather than risk having to ask for more money later or, worse, having coworkers earn awards that you cannot provide because you have exceeded your budget. Certainly, when you present your budget for approval, you will want to outline the assumptions you made so that management understands the basis for your request. As mentioned earlier, you should also carefully outline management's role in the delivery of safety awards, especially for awards that require managers to write commendation letters—or cook breakfast on third shift! Also, you will usually need to prepare a budget for your recognition plan. Once management approves this budget, the steering committee must administer its recognition and celebration plans within the constraints of the budget.

13.5 Opportunities for Professional Development

An engaged steering committee is a vital element in any Values-Based Safety (VBS) process. It parallels the importance of an active safety committee in organizations that do not utilize a behavior-based safety (BBS) process. The steering committee serves as the guiding force behind the implementation and ongoing success of the VBS process, making it crucial that its members are motivated and committed to their roles.

To build such commitment and ensure continuous participation, organizations must find ways to express appreciation for the contributions of steering committee members. This reinforcement could be in the form of acknowledging their volunteer efforts, commending their active involvement in observations, or recognizing their sustained participation as observers and steering committee members. By doing so, you create an environment of encouragement and recognition, boosting morale and fostering active commitment to safety.

The most effective method to bolster participation and enrich expertise is to provide opportunities for further professional development. Exemplary organizations often arrange for steering committee members to travel to and participate in safety conferences. These conferences can offer invaluable insights into the latest safety practices, trends, and innovations in the field, broadening the knowledge base of committee members and providing a platform for networking with safety professionals from different organizations.

By actively participating in these conferences, steering committee members gain fresh perspectives and ideas, which they can integrate into VBS and action planning efforts. Ultimately, their attendance at such events benefits the individual members in their professional growth and significantly enhances the overall effectiveness and adaptability of VBS within the organization.

13.6 Support Through Promotions and Traditional Compensation

The ability to recognize hazards and provide constructive feedback that safety observers cultivate is essential for frontline supervisors. Given the significance of these abilities, organizations should consider the effectiveness of supervisors as potential safety observers when making selection decisions. The evaluation should encompass their ability to identify workplace hazards and provide feedback as well as their peers' reaction to their observations. The quality of feedback is influenced by the relationship between the observer and their colleagues. Therefore, the observation process aids organizations in assessing safety observation and feedback skills and the observer's relationship skills outside of the observation process. Most organizations should consider making the observation process a formal part of the supervisor development process.

Compensation can serve as a pivotal factor in upholding an efficient safety management process. Often, this strategy applies exclusively to managers and supervisors who bear the responsibility for preserving the safety of their respective areas. The method of tying safety to salary increments is contingent upon the protocols for such increases within the organization. It could involve listing safety as a distinct aspect on the performance appraisal form or establishing a procedure that enables managers to set annual safety maintenance goals, such as completing a certain percentage of observations each month. Similar to safety awards, the focus should be on sustaining the safety system. Compensation decisions frequently encompass an evaluation of the area's safety performance, which includes the safety processes and the resulting incident rates. The assessment process should provide a balanced evaluation of procedural and outcome metrics.

13.7 Safety Incentive Compensation

As with other forms of tangible rewards, the challenge is to support the observation and feedback processes without generating false reporting. In general, the use of bonuses tied to safety is not recommended, except when safety is included as part of an overall management scorecard.

Effective safety incentive compensation typically includes three elements:

1. financial incentives based on measured safety outcomes that reflect economically on the company's success
2. recognition and feedback that support maintaining the VBS process and employees' compliance with safety procedures
3. severe penalties, including loss of employment, for falsely reporting incident or observation data

When setting up a cash incentive for safety, the two rules of thumb from the beginning of the chapter still apply: The award should be relatively small, and it should be based primarily on maintaining the observation system and its components.

Cash awards and paid time off are both such significant awards and may be considered forms of compensation. You must use them carefully to ensure that they support your safety process and do not encourage false reporting.

If you plan on developing an incentive compensation plan, it should be based on outcome measures, such as total workers' compensation claims, recordable injuries, or lost-workday cases.

Total workers' compensation claims. The total dollars spent on compensating injured workers would seem to be an ideal basis for an incentive bonus. This measure has several advantages and avoids the disadvantages of incentives based on working a fixed period without injury. On the plus side, it is easy for both the managers and the employees to understand. It is also an important cost that directly impacts a company's profitability. Because it affects profits, it is often easy to sell to upper management. Documented savings in compensation costs could be used to fund the safety portion of the incentive bonus. This approach is particularly good for companies looking for ways to partner with employees to share the risks and potential savings associated with safety. A complete implementation of the VBS process allows companies to make employees responsible for the safety process and share the economic benefits of good safety performance. If the safety efforts do not produce savings in workers' compensation costs, the incentive system will not have money to fund bonuses. The savings may also fund a separate bonus pool for managers and employees.

Using total dollars spent on compensating injured workers is an appropriate incentive criterion for two reasons. First, it does not directly discourage reporting incidents. The managers and employees have very little incentive to hide minor incidents because such incidents add very little to the total compensation costs. Second, it encourages managers to be proactive in managing an injured employee's return to work. The sooner an employee gets back to work, the less it costs the company.

However, this measure has several significant problems: It is often not readily available or is only available several months after the fact; the most significant costs often accrue over a long period of time and may not be evident in the initial months following the incident. These problems make using a 12-month moving average a good basis for bonus calculations, but even 12 months can be too short a period to assess the total costs associated with a serious incident.

OSHA-recordable cases. Generally, OSHA recordables should not be used as a stand-alone basis for incentive bonuses. The problem, as we have talked about before, is the difficulty of ensuring the integrity of reporting these injuries. While OSHA-recordable incidents or incident rates are not a good stand-alone basis for an incentive bonus, they may be part of the criteria, as discussed in the next paragraph.

Safety index and scorecard approach. The best approach for creating a safety bonus is probably to use an index that combines and weights several measures. Lost-workday injuries or compensation costs might be weighted heavily, while recordable injuries and even process measures can be included and weighted less. The advantage of this approach is that it balances the emphasis on process and outcomes, and recordable injuries can be included but given a small enough weight that the integrity of reporting is easier to maintain.

13.8 General Guidelines on Supporting Safety Motivation

As a review of the options for using recognition, awards, and incentives, Table 13.5 on the following page summarizes the methods of providing motivational support for safety.

13.9 Checklist for Ensuring the Effectiveness of Recognition and Celebrations

The steering committee is responsible for ensuring that VBS remains a positive process. This means that employees participate because they want to, not because they have to. Positive reinforcement, primarily in the form of individual recognition and team celebrations, will be the primary tool to ensure a positive process. Earlier in this chapter we talked about designing an effective recognition and celebration process.

Table 13.5. Considerations for Supporting Appropriate Motivation for the VBS

Rules for Effective Safety Motivation	Considerations
Provide recognition for employees who appropriately complete their observations.	Such recognition is important to maintaining the observations.
Make recognition personal and meaningful to recipients.	The steering committee and managers should plan to make the recognition meaningful.
Do not use data from employee observations as the basis for salary evaluations or disciplinary action against employees.	Managers and supervisors should use documented observations made outside of the VBS process as the basis for decisions regarding salary and disciplinary actions.
Evaluate supervisors on their support for the observation process and use of observation data in their work areas.	Use this as one indicator to ensure the process is maintained. Be careful that supervisors do not pressure employees to participate.
Evaluate supervisors on the basis of management observations conducted in each work area.	Such observations should include discussions with employees about how the supervisors are managing the VBS process.
Do not evaluate supervisors on the basis of the percent safe or safety index from their work areas.	The impact of such evaluations would potentially distort the observation data.

The following guidelines will help the steering committee administer those processes effectively:

- Effective recognition and celebrations are based on achieving a goal or meeting a criterion, not on the passage of time. Once-a-month parties, employee-of-the-month selections, and periods of time without an injury are examples of time- instead of performance-contingent recognition and celebration programs.

- Recognition and celebrations may occur frequently or infrequently, depending on when the established goal or criterion has been met.

- Recognition is earned by performing desired behaviors to meet a specified criterion (e.g., completing 10 observations). Celebrations are earned by achieving specified goals (e.g., 100% proper lifting). Both are determined objectively, not judged subjectively.

- Recognition and celebrations are win-win propositions. Everyone can earn recognition by meeting the specified criterion, and everyone in the group can celebrate when a goal is achieved. Recognition is not awarded only to the employee or group that was first or best but to anyone who meets the criterion and any group that achieves the goal. Whether an employee earns the recognition or a group earns the celebration is independent of whether another employee or group earns it.

- Recognitions and celebrations may be unannounced or "planned spontaneous." That is, the steering committee decides in advance what will be recognized during a specified reporting period and looks for opportunities to reinforce such individual performances as conducting an observation, completing a quality observation, doing more observations than those scheduled, observing a specific department or task, and the like.
- Both individual recognition and organization celebrations can be formal or informal. Formal recognition might include placing letters of commendation in an employee's personnel file; making positive comments on a performance appraisal; increasing compensation by means of a bonus or raise; arranging choice assignments to certain locations, on projects, or in departments; or even granting a promotion. Informal recognition might include individual thanks and commendation in private, public acknowledgment, a letter to the employee's family, or posters on bulletin boards that recognize an employee or employees. Formal celebrations might be company dinners while informal celebrations might be free barbecue in the lunchroom.
- Social or personal (i.e., nonmaterial) recognition is best for avoiding common employee concerns, such as these:
  - An awarded material item is less valuable than awards given to others.
  - The value of an awarded item is not equal to the value of the performance.
  - Some employees have received more recognition than they deserve while others have received less.
  - Some employees perform the desired behavior only to receive material items.
  - An awarded item is not meaningful to the individual.

If symbols or tokens of recognition are used, choose those that are free or almost so. Money is best saved for celebrations. Tokens do have one advantage: They can facilitate interaction between the employee giving and the employee receiving the recognition. Such interaction is often especially important early in the process, when giving and receiving recognition may be new to many employees.

- Celebrations are most effective when:
  - They bring everyone together in one place at one time for food and refreshments.
  - They pinpoint the reason for the celebration.
  - They include a discussion of the goal and how it was met, followed by setting the next goal.
  - They recognize individuals during the celebration who contributed to meeting the goal.
  - They involve others who are significant to the person you want to recognize, such as respected leaders who make the awards meaningful by offering sincere comments of recognition, well-liked employees who tell

their story of involvement in the safety process, or family members who describe the value of a safe practice.
    - Everyone is invited to a celebration, not only those who contributed to achieving the goal. Inviting everyone helps encourage all employees to participate in achieving the next goal.
- Customize recognition to the employee receiving it by asking these questions:
    - Would this employee prefer to receive recognition from a steering committee member, teammate or colleague, supervisor or manager, organization manager, safety professional, or someone completely different?
    - Would this employee prefer private or public recognition?
    - What small token might signify recognition and remind this employee (and others) of the recognized behavior?

CHAPTER 14

Step 5: Planning Training and Kickoff Meetings

Once you have planned recognition and celebrations to support your safety process, you are ready to plan how you will introduce the process to employees, how you will train observers, and how you will implement other training that is important to the success of your process. One of the decisions that you will have to make is whether you will need to have a kickoff meeting (or meetings) to introduce your process. Generally, you will need one unless you have a small site and can get all employees through observer training in a fairly short time. You will have to train observers before you can really get the process started. Also, this is a good place to acknowledge that elements of observer training, and even the kickoff meeting, may be offered online. Whether online or in person, new observers should begin with coaching from steering committee members, or other experienced observers.

14.1 Observer Training

For most organizations, a recent study suggests that having a relatively small number of volunteer observers is most effective at reducing injuries (Spigener et al., 2022). The general guideline is to train roughly 10%–20% of your employees to conduct observations. Ideally, you should strive to have an observer in each area, or one on each crew of 10 employees.

The previous recommendation, provided before the guideline described above, was to require all employees to complete observer training, regardless of their willingness to volunteer. This recommendation aimed to enhance the effectiveness of the behavior-based safety process. The rationale was that observer training provides a much higher level of understanding of the process compared to what can be achieved in a kickoff meeting. By undergoing the training, employees gain increased understanding, which leads to greater acceptance and support, even among those who do not volunteer to conduct observations. Furthermore, requiring all employees to complete the training helps ensure that employees are making informed decisions regarding what they are signing up for or opting out of. Some organizations might still adopt this approach if they plan to maximize employee participation in conducting observations.

The observer-training workshop will usually require 8 hours. Figure 14.1 presents a typical agenda for observer training. During the first hour of the workshop, employees learn the rationale for the behavioral approach and how the checklists were created. The remainder of the day is spent learning how to pinpoint behavior (see Chapter 21), how to conduct observations, and how to discuss their observations with associates. When learning to conduct observations, employees need to practice conducting observations and discussing what they observe. To aid in this practice, you should film several short work samples that instructors can use to train workshop participants in how to use the observation checklists. Work samples that have not been staged work best for this purpose because they offer realistic opportunities for practice observations.

After the practice observations and a discussion of how to complete the checklists, participants should break into pairs and role-play how they would provide feedback to the employee they just observed in the video. After the first role-playing exercise, participants should switch roles so that both can practice the feedback discussion. If you can arrange it, after completing several exercises of this type, you should allow the employees to go into the workplace and conduct an observation, then return to the classroom to discuss their experience. In this way, the observers get significant

> **Three objectives:**
> - Understand and support the process
> - Be able to use the checklist
> - Be able to discuss observations effectively
>
> **Overview and introduction:**
> - The design team
> - Why a behavioral approach?
> - What is VBS?
>
> **Observation skills and practice**
>
> **Feedback skills and practice**

Figure 14.1. Typical agenda for the observer-training workshop.

practice conducting observations, which will ensure they have the skills to participate in the process.

14.2 Plan Kickoff Meeting(s)

If you are not able to train all employees in your facility in a fairly short time, you will need to conduct kickoff meetings with employees to introduce VBS. The design team should provide a suggested meeting agenda and make general recommendations for the meetings, which will usually be conducted by the steering committee. Covering all work areas and shifts will generally require several meetings. Small groups of 8 to 10 individuals are ideal as they provide participants with a better opportunity for questions and discussion than do larger groups. Often the agenda will look very much like the presentation to management described in the next chapter.

Depending on the size of your organization, design team members should participate in as many kickoff meetings as possible to enable employees to ask questions of those who designed the process. You may also want to suggest a role for management in the kickoff meetings. For example, you might suggest that the steering committee invite either a representative of upper management or the area manager to comment on management's support for the safety improvement efforts.

Figure 14.2 presents a typical agenda for a kickoff meeting. As with the other elements of the process, if your design team is developing a process that will be initiated by the steering committee, the design team should provide a suggested agenda. It will enable each steering committee to develop its own kickoff meeting agenda based on the model provided by the design team.

> **Purpose:** Introduce VBS to employees
> - Background on how team came into being
> - Objectives of the observation system
> - Process for developing observation system
>   - List of initial pinpoints
>   - Final checklist(s)
> - Observation procedure
> - Management's role
> - Next steps
>   - Observations begin
> - Questions and discussion

Figure 14.2. Typical agenda for kickoff meetings to introduce the observation system to employees.

14.3 Plan Training Needed to Support the Process

As you consider implementing the observation and feedback processes, you will need to consider the existing skills and training needs of the participants. For the VBS to be successful, employees will need skills in the four areas given in Table 14.1.

If your design team is planning VBS to be initiated by the steering committee, you will need to ensure a well-developed formal training process for steering committee members. The primary objective of this training is to teach steering committee members to implement and support VBS. Implementation training for the steering committee is often the most complex training involved in the process (other than training for the design team). Steering committee members will need to know how to take the guidelines developed by the design team, tailor those plans for their respective work areas, and initiate and maintain each element of the process. Such training usually requires a formal workshop that resembles the initial training provided for the design team.

Steering committee members who will be implementing VBS will also benefit from an understanding of the rationale or basic theory underlying VBS, including the observation and feedback procedures. They will provide better and more consistent support for the elements of VBS when they understand the reasons for those elements.

In addition to identifying the training needed to make implementation successful, your design team should decide on the most effective way to deliver each type of training. You want a training process that balances effectiveness with minimal cost and disruption to the workplace. The training options include the following:

- individual coaching (tell, show, observe, and provide feedback)
- mentors
- seminars or workshops
- videos or slides

Table 14.1. Skills Needed to Support VBS

Who	Description	Specific Skills
Management	How to support the implementation and maintenance efforts of the steering committee	• How to participate and follow up on implementation efforts • How to use data on completed observations to evaluate the process • Observation and feedback skills described above (so that they can model the process)

Steering committee members	How to implement and maintain VBS	• How to use the guidelines provided by the design team to:
		  ◦ refine observation checklists
		  ◦ conduct the area kickoff meeting
		  ◦ initiate observations and provide feedback
		  ◦ train others to conduct observations and provide feedback
		  ◦ initiate a recognition program to support process
		• How to evaluate and problem-solve the process

Observers	Observation and feedback skills	• How to use the observation checklist • How to provide feedback on observations
Steering committee members and observers	Leading safety meetings	• How to discuss data • How to set improvement targets
Employees who conduct the specific job tasks	Job-specific safety skills	• Specific practices identified from the safety observation checklist

While you will usually want to provide a detailed workshop for the steering committee and line management, you may consider individual coaching and mentors for training new observers. Such an on-the-job training process is a less disruptive process than providing workshops or seminars. The steering committee may later arrange additional training to provide an understanding of the rationale for VBS as part of ongoing safety meetings.

To address job-specific skills, consider allowing employees to make training videos or a slide show. A video of actual work is an excellent tool for training observers in how to use the observation checklist and can also be used to illustrate the use of the checklist during area kickoff meetings. Employees might also develop training materials showing close-call incidents or past incidents. Such a strategy provides an effective training tool that creates a high level of involvement. (See Chapter 16 for an additional discussion of such training and involvement efforts.)

CHAPTER 15

Step 6: Conducting Management Review

Once you have completed your planning efforts, the design team should present the Values-Based Safety (VBS) process to management for its input and review. This step should be a critical milestone on your initial schedule. This meeting is an opportunity for management to

- provide input to the safety process
- approve implementation of the new process
- commit to personal involvement in the process
- approve the budget for recognition and celebrations
- provide recognition of the efforts of the design team

Getting management's input and suggestions for your observation system will help ensure that management will support your implementation efforts. This will also provide an opportunity for ensuring that management understands each component of the VBS process at each stage of implementation. Figure 15.1 presents a typical agenda for such a meeting. As stated before, this agenda is appropriate for management review if a process was designed quickly and used 2-day planning meetings. A longer planning process in which the design team meets for 2 hours every other week should have a milestone review at the completion of each significant stage of planning.

Purpose: Get management's input and approval for the design team's plans

- Introduce design team members
- Overview of the design process
- Team's mission and values
- Overview of the observation process
    - Observation checklist
    - Steps in conducting an observation
    - Feedback discussions
- Observation checklist and procedure
- Data collection and analysis
- Rollout plans
    - Kickoff meetings
    - Observer training
- Individual recognition and team celebrations
- Conclusions and requests for support

Figure 15.1. Typical agenda for the management presentation.

All design team members should participate in the presentation. Each design team member should take responsibility for presenting one agenda item, with all members participating in a question-and-answer session at the end. Managers will usually be particularly interested in the observation checklist and how it is constructed. They will often have questions and may have additions that your team should consider. You should also pay special attention to the discussion of recognition and celebrations. In the presentation, you will have to explain the assumptions that you made in creating the budget and explain how you calculated your anticipated costs. Also, be clear about your requests for funds and other forms of support you want from management.

Design team members will be nervous about this kind of presentation. For many it may well be the first time they have given a formal presentation of this type to management. Consider having a dry run so team members can practice their presentation and use of visual aids. Generally, they should have slides or other visual aids to support their message. Pay special attention to the transition from one team member to the next. In the end, the presentation does not have to be a polished professional presentation that you might expect from consultants or experienced managers. The team's enthusiasm and sincerity will make the presentation work. Management will be able to tell that the team members are "speaking from the heart" and *that* will make the presentation effective.

Management's role should be to understand the process and support design team members in their participation in planning the VBS process. They should ask questions, being careful to be positive and supportive of the team's efforts. Obviously, managers need to voice any concerns they have, but they should keep the overall tone of the meeting positive and support the design team's enthusiasm.

CHAPTER 16

Implementing the Values-Based Safety Process

The implementation of a Values-Based Safety (VBS) process will usually be the responsibility of your steering committee. The implementation process outlined in Table 16.1 provides the team with the opportunity to change the checklist to meet particular needs of each area or site. Such additional input will not be necessary if your design team and safety team are the same group.

Table 16.1. Implementation of a VBS Process

If	Then
Your design team conducts periodic planning meetings and is implementing the VBS process concurrently with their planning efforts.	Read this chapter as it relates to the implementation of the particular element on which you are currently working.
Your design team is implementing in a pilot area.	Continue with this chapter to clarify the responsibilities of the steering committee and management for implementing the VBS process within the pilot areas.
Your design team planned the VBS process and will become the steering committee and take responsibility for implementation.	As you read this chapter, substitute *design team* for *steering committee*. Continue with this chapter to review the respective responsibilities of the design team and management for implementing the VBS process.
Your design team planned the VBS process, but the steering committee will be responsible for implementation.	Continue with this chapter to clarify the respective responsibilities of safety teams and management for implementing the VBS process throughout the organization.

16.1 Conduct Training for the Steering Committee

If your steering committee includes employees who were not on the design team, the first step in initiating the VBS process is to train new steering committee members. This training typically requires a 2- or 3-day course created by the design team. If you have planned management participation as part of your effort, ensure that all levels of management participate and learn how to conduct observations and deliver feedback so they can model the process when they visit the work areas. The training should clarify the roles outlined in this chapter for the process owner, the steering committee, and management. The steering committee's role is discussed in greater detail in Chapters 20 and 22.

16.2 Establish a Process Owner

As you move into implementation, one member of the steering committee should be appointed as the local *process owner*, or coordinator, for your new safety process. This person may be a staff member, supervisor, or hourly employee who will serve as the employee safety coordinator. If the position is assigned to an hourly employee, you may want to rotate it annually.

The behavioral safety coordinator has primary responsibility for ensuring that the steering committee implements and maintains the VBS process. The duties include working with management to develop agendas for steering committee meetings, scheduling observations, reviewing completed observation checklists, and all other tasks not explicitly assigned to other team members. These coordinators become the formal champions of the new safety process and are responsible for working with the steering committee to ensure the integrity of the process.

In addition to the behavioral safety coordinator, you will often want to identify an *employee safety coordinator* in each natural work team. This employee should serve to champion the process and be the point of contact for the steering committee in areas that do not have steering committee representation.

16.3 Steering Committee's Responsibilities

The steering committee has the primary responsibility for implementing the design team's plans (see Table 16.2).

When you implement the VBS process, get the observations started as soon as possible because they are the foundation of the process. Your steering committee can then take the time to develop a consensus and get input from area employees on the vision and values created during the design team's planning efforts. As during the design phase, you may choose to place these activities in a different order. You will often work on activities in different phases at the same time. Your steering committee, for example, may be reviewing safety data and identifying safety practices that need additional effort at the same time it is working on a written statement of the area's vision and values.

Table 16.2. Responsibilities of Steering Committee

Phase Number	Activity
1	Begin safety observations
2	Ensure employees are trained to conduct observations
3	Use observation data to drive improvement
4	Develop plans for individual recognition and group celebrations
5	Administer and deliver safety awards

Begin safety observations. Table 16.3 summarizes the steps involved in starting observations:

Table 16.3. Steps to Begin Observations

Step Number	Task
1	Revise safety observation checklist to meet area needs
2	Plan kickoff meeting
3	Conduct kickoff meeting
4	Begin conducting observations and providing feedback

If the steering committee was not part of the design process, your implementation process should be flexible enough to allow it to modify the observation checklist to suit the needs of a particular work area. At the same time, the steering committee should be encouraged not to delete safe practices that were identified on the basis of past incidents.

Once the observation checklist is finalized, the steering committee should plan and conduct the area kickoff meetings. Generally, their agenda will look much like the one recommended by the design team (see Chapter 14, Figure 14.1). The steering committee will need to decide which team members will take responsibility for each agenda item. In addition, the teams will often modify the agenda to meet the needs of their work areas. Encourage the steering committee to schedule adequate time for the kickoff meetings. While it is possible to introduce the process in an hour, an ideal agenda probably requires 2 hours, to allow sufficient time for employees to ask questions and discuss the process.

Here are some additional agenda items that the steering committee might want to include in the kickoff meetings:

- Role-play an observation, including the feedback discussion of the safety checklist.
- Show a video of work in progress and allow employees to complete the safety checklist based on what they observe.
- Include participation by management and design team members.

Make every effort to ensure that all employees have the opportunity to participate in the kickoff meetings. Employees who only hear about the process secondhand are more likely to misunderstand it and have a negative reaction to your efforts. Give special consideration to communicating with employees on back shifts and those who may be on vacation or special assignments.

Ensure that employees are trained to conduct observations. A primary goal of the steering committee is to recruit observers from each area and ensure that they complete the observer-training workshop as quickly as possible so they can begin their observations. Often steering committee members are responsible for conducting this training. Certainly, the steering committee needs to track this training and ensure that an adequate number of trained observers are available in all areas of the facility. The steering committee will have to work with management and supervision of each area to ensure that employees are available for training. The steering committee may wish to graph the percentage of employees who have completed the training as a tool to assist in setting improvement goals and getting management support for this task.

Use observation data to drive improvement. Table 16.4 summarizes the typical steps involved for using the data to drive continuous improvement of safety:

Table 16.4. Steps for Using Data

Step Number	Task
1	Post graphs of safety data
2	Begin reviewing observation data in safety meetings
3	Set improvement goals
4	Develop and implement action plans

(Review the design team's responsibilities for developing guidelines for each of these steps in Chapter 12.)

If consistent with the design team's guidelines on the use of graphs, the steering committees should post graphs showing the observation data in work areas and locations where employees are likely to see them. A good practice is to establish a bulletin board for safety in each area. You can then readily display observation forms, safety graphs, and other safety-related information.

The steering committee should try to find a location where employees will see the bulletin board. The best locations are work areas, the cafeteria, the break room, and other high-traffic areas. Try to place one bulletin board in each area. If possible, avoid multiple bulletin boards that present the same information because of the time and effort required for observers to update graphs and reports on bulletin boards in different locations.

Develop plans for individual recognition and group celebrations. While the design team will usually be able to provide guidelines for individual recognition and group celebrations, the steering committee will need to plan these activities and prepare to initiate them once employees in the area begin meeting the criteria. As with the other elements of the behavioral process, the design team's plan should serve as a model for the steering committee. The steering committee may take the model process and use it as is or modify it extensively to suit employees in a specific work area.

Recognition is too important to be dropped or forgotten. Because many employees have had bad experiences with poorly designed awards programs, some participants may try to eliminate this element of the plan. The design team should establish and communicate firm boundaries that support both individual recognition and team celebrations of success while allowing the steering committee to develop plans that meet the needs of a particular work area. For example, the steering committee should review the criteria established by the design team and tailor them to an area's needs. They should then review the recognition, awards, and celebration plans and decide how to make these elements meaningful to employees in an area. The ideal recognition process should provide recognition of individual contributions as part of an overall celebration of the area's achievements.

In some cases, responsibility for recognition will remain centralized with site management or the site's safety and health committee. In other cases, a separate safety awards committee may take responsibility for recognition and celebrations.

Administer and deliver safety awards. A successful awards program requires that the awards be both significant and delivered in a meaningful way. The awards menu should serve as a guide, but it is based on the group's responses and may or may not reflect the preferences of a given individual. The steering committee should work with the management team to ensure that the menu remains only a guide and that each employee who meets the criteria receives an award that is meaningful and significant.

In the same way, the criteria should serve as guides. The steering committee can thus provide deserved recognition to employees who have made safety contributions not yet included on the existing list of criteria. The existing criteria should serve as a standard of comparison for considering the value of a given contribution. The delivery is often as important as the award itself. Ensure that the person delivering the award is specific about what the employee (or team) did to earn the recognition and expresses sincere appreciation for the contribution of the employee (or team).

Delivery is important for tokens as well. If an area achieves 100% safety compliance and area employees earn thank-you cards (as described in Chapter 23), the supervisor or observer who distributes the tokens should personally hand each employee in the area a token, explaining why they are receiving the token and expressing appreciation. All supervisors and observers should use their imaginations to create novel ways of adding "hoopla" to such events and make the whole process fun for all involved. Hand shaking, backslapping, picture taking, and providing food and beverage are all appropriate additions to a standard process.

Pay special attention to the design team's suggestions on delivering recognition. An effective delivery will make recognition successful; a poor delivery will make the recognition seem insincere and will therefore be ineffective. Again, ensure that the person delivering the award expresses sincere appreciation for the employee's (or team's) contribution and is specific about what the employee (or team) did to earn recognition. The more personal your recognition and celebrations are, the more meaningful they will be. Such items of appreciation as mugs, baseball caps, belt buckles, jackets, and the like can likewise be effective if they are handed out to individual employees with a handshake and appreciative comment. If you simply place a box of such items in the area and tell employees to help themselves, your recognition efforts will not be meaningful to many employees.

16.4 Management's Responsibilities

Management should carry out the following responsibilities to support the implementation efforts of the steering committee:

1. Discuss its vision of safety within the organization.
2. Discuss its expectations for implementing the VBS process.
3. Participate in training on the observation process.
4. Model observation and feedback practices.

Discuss its vision of safety within the organization. Management should discuss its vision of safety with employees within the organization. Managers may discuss a formal vision or mission statement if they have developed one, or they may simply discuss their personal commitment to safety and the priority of safety compared to other areas of performance. The goal is to communicate the personal commitment of individual members of management and to create a better understanding of the formal safety vision or mission statements among all employees.

Discuss its expectations for implementing the VBS process. In addition to discussing its vision, management should clearly communicate its expectation that all managers and supervisors will ensure the successful initiation of the VBS process. It should also clearly communicate when it expects the process to be initiated, the personal involvement expected of line management, and any other expectations regarding the VBS process or how it will be initiated within the organization. There should be two-way discussions in which the managers and employees ask questions. The discussions should include a review of the implementation plans, the progress of training area management, and participation in steering committee meetings.

Participate in training on the observation process. Management should participate in VBS process training. Such participation will demonstrate management's commitment to the process and help ensure that all managers also acquire the skills to conduct observations and support the process.

Model observation and feedback practices. Finally, if the design team has created a process that involves managers in the observation process, upper management should serve as model participants in the VBS process. As they visit work sites within their organization, they should conduct safety observations along with managers from the work area. As part of the observations, they should provide feedback in the same way as local-level observers. Management should take special care to emphasize safe practices observed along with observations of practices and conditions that cause concern.

CHAPTER 17

Maintaining the Values-Based Safety Process

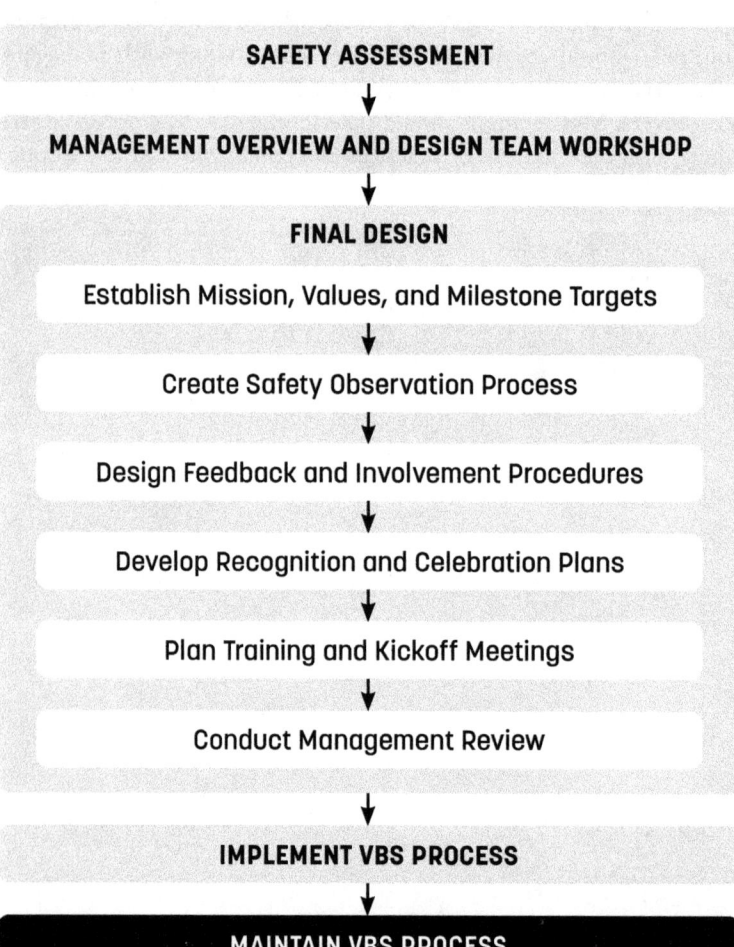

17.1 Steering Committee Members' Responsibilities

The primary objective of the steering committee is to ensure the integrity of the VBS process. Because the primary component of this process is conducting observations, the steering committee should pay special attention to ensuring that the observation process is functioning properly. The employee safety coordinator and the steering committee must work continuously to ensure an adequate rate of observations. Steering committee members are the informal leaders of the VBS process and thus have a part in safety leadership.

Daily responsibilities. Ideally, all steering committee members will champion the VBS process. They should model practices that are aligned with the stated values and be supportive of the process, including the following:

- Listen to and understand the concerns of others regarding the safety process.
- Solicit suggestions for improving the process.
- Answer questions about the VBS process.
- Provide feedback to other team members and employees on:
    ○ conducting observations,
    ○ safety practices,
    ○ alignment of behavior with values.

In their daily interactions with other employees, steering committee members must listen attentively to the concerns expressed by employees, carefully noting both the content and emotions expressed in such discussions. Employees may express anger, discomfort, or other negative emotions that stem from distrust and other bad experiences. Such responses are especially likely from employees who were unable to participate in the kickoff meetings. All that you and other team members can do at this point is ensure that you accurately understand their concerns, ensure that they fully understand the process, and solicit suggestions for addressing their concerns. Often, many of their concerns will disappear as they gain experience with the VBS process.

You and your steering committee members must also be models for the kind of behavior expected of all employees, such as providing feedback to others on both daily work practices and participation in the safety observation process. Such modeling is particularly important because you want employees to understand that they should be using their feedback and observation skills all the time, not just during scheduled safety observations. Thus, whenever employees see an unsafe work practice or condition, they should try to correct the situation in the same way they would if they observed that situation during a formal observation. Getting employees to consistently interact in this manner requires that area management and safety team members consistently model such feedback and observation practices and provide feedback to employees on those practices.

In addition to such day-to-day interactions, the steering committee needs to pay special attention to the observation process, including reminding people to conduct their observations and, in particular, providing appreciative feedback to employees who have completed their observations. Strive to make such feedback a normal part of informal daily interactions. A simple "thanks for completing your observations this week" will let employees know you noticed their efforts.

Weekly responsibilities. The steering committee has two basic weekly responsibilities: the observation process and weekly safety meetings. To fulfill these responsibilities, they must complete the following tasks:

- Develop a schedule for observers.
- Conduct observations.
- Plan discussions for safety meetings:
  (a) Review the past week's observation sheets.
  (b) Identify the week's strengths and areas of concern.
  (c) Calculate and graph the percentage of target safe behaviors.
  (d) Graph the number of observations and percentage of employees participating in observations.
- Conduct weekly safety meetings
  (a) Discuss the previous week's observation data (strengths and concerns).
  (b) Recognize individual contributions.
  (c) Create celebrations of an area's successes.
  (d) Establish improvement targets with employees.

The steering committee ensures that the observers are conducting observations in a way that aligns with the design team's implementation plan. Most organizations will have a small, dedicated group of observers. The steering committee must ensure that observers maintain their target number of observations (typically, two per week). The steering committee must also ensure that observers receive enough support to maintain their weekly observations. This may be through positive feedback, individual recognition, and/or feedback on how the data are being used.

If all employees are being trained as observers, the steering committee may need to develop a schedule for observers for a month, or even a quarter, with a simple rotation of all trained observers. During observer training, until a significant number of employees volunteer to do observations, the steering committee will probably want all observers to do at least one observation every week.

During training, the steering committee will need to complete the following tasks:

- Encourage newly trained employees to conduct observations.
- Schedule new observers, then perform the following duties:
  (a) Explain how to complete observation forms and deliver feedback.
  (b) Conduct a joint observation, showing the observation and feedback process.
  (c) Conduct a joint observation, observing and coaching the employee's observations and feedback.

Steering committee meetings. Try to conduct a steering committee meeting once each month. During these meetings, the steering committee should formally evaluate how well the VBS process is working. In evaluating the process, review the percentage of observations completed on schedule. The team should also assess the accuracy of reporting, how often all employees are observed, the effectiveness of recognition efforts, and how well the feedback practices are functioning.

Your team should also provide an ongoing evaluation of the quality and integrity of its safety improvement efforts. Figure 17.1 presents a sample of self-evaluation questions for this purpose. The evaluation process might be fairly informal, based on the team members' opinions, or it might be a formal assessment conducted on a regular basis (e.g., annually). Formal evaluations might include interviews or written surveys with employees throughout the organization. In addition, the safety team should evaluate the interactions of its own members during team meetings to ensure that the team process remains one of openness, shared participation, and trust.

1. Are we completing the observations as we planned?
2. Have we consistently emphasized the positive (i.e., safe practices) in our discussions with employees?
3. When discussing unsafe acts and conditions, have we done so in a way that communicates our personal concern for their individual safety?
4. When discussing unsafe acts and conditions, have we done so in a way that does not embarrass or humiliate any individual?
5. Are our data from the observations meaningful?
6. Are we using the data effectively in safety meetings?
7. Are we recognizing individuals for their contributions?
8. Are we celebrating our successes as a team?
9. Have we provided observers with enough time to conduct their observations?

Figure 17.1. *Sample questions to consider when evaluating a Values-Based Safety process.*

Summary of steering committee responsibilities. Table 17.1 summarizes the ongoing responsibilities of the steering committee. The employee safety coordinator (or other designated process owner) is responsible for ensuring that the team is actively addressing these responsibilities.

Table 17.1. Steering Committee's Ongoing Responsibilities

When	Responsibility
Daily	1. Listen and ensure the understanding of concerns of others regarding safety, then address concerns constructively 2. Answer questions about the VBS process 3. Provide feedback to other team members and other employees on: • Conducting observations • Safety practices • Alignment of behavior with values
Weekly	1. Schedule observers and observations 2. Conduct observations 3. Plan discussion for safety meetings • Review past week's observation sheets • Identify week's strengths and areas of concern • Calculate percent safe to determine trend • Graph number of observations or percent safe • Plan discussion
At weekly safety meetings	1. Conduct discussion of previous week's observation data 2. Recognize individual contributions 3. Create celebrations of area's successes 4. Establish improvement targets with employees
During steering committee meetings	1. Evaluate and problem-solve observations and other elements of VBS 2. Assess alignment of the steering committee meeting with the team's values
When planned by steering committee	1. Plan how you will involve other employees in observation process; manage rotation of observers 2. Schedule new observers, then: • Explain how to complete observation forms and deliver feedback • Conduct joint observation, showing observation and feedback process • Conduct joint observation; observe and coach employee's observations and feedback

17.2 Common Situations

Table 17.2 presents five typical situations that steering committees may discover as they assess the VBS process and possible responses to these situations.

17.3 Steering Committee's Responsibilities

After completing the design and implementation, the design team may evolve into an ongoing team of employees with responsibility for ensuring the maintenance and continued refinement of the VBS process. The design team may then assume the name of *steering committee*, to reflect its new role of maintaining the safety process in conjunction with the management team (see Chapter 6, Figure 6.1). The steering committee may have different membership from the design team. Rotating new employees onto the steering committee broadens employee participation in the process. The steering committee participants are usually employee safety representatives, often the VBS process "owners" from within different areas of the site or organization. The steering committee has four primary responsibilities that may be assigned to subcommittees:

- analyze and problem-solve safety data
- communicate relevant safety information
- address employee concerns
- coordinate recognition

Table 17.2. Common Problems Found During Evaluation and Suggested Solutions

If	Then the Steering Committee Should
Number or percent of observations is below target	1. Ensure that supervisors and observers are trained in the observation process and what is expected 2. Enhance feedback and recognition for completing observations 3. Ensure that supervisors are evaluated on observations completed in their work areas
Observation data suggest safety is decreasing (downward trend in percent safe)	1. Ensure effectiveness of problem-solving discussion in area safety meeting 2. Ensure discussion results in commitment to improve specific safety practice or practices 3. Consider changes in observation process to increase effectiveness of observations (e.g., more observations, more employees involved, and other steps)
Observation data suggest safety is increasing (upward trend in percent safe)	1. Arrange recognition or celebration of improvement in area safety meeting
A few employees are negative about the VBS process	1. Ensure that the negative employees have participated in orientation and training 2. Involve those employees in observations and in the steering committee
Most employees are negative about the safety process	1. Ensure that observers are stressing positive factors when providing feedback on observations 2. Ensure accuracy of observation data 3. Increase use of safety awards and recognition based on observation process

Analyze and problem-solve safety data. The steering committee analyzes safety data to find meaningful information. The analysis should include identification of trends and Pareto analysis of both the observation data and the data on injury rates.

A Pareto diagram ranks issues from most to least frequent, serving as an essential tool for prioritizing safety concerns. It enables the steering committee to visually identify and focus on the most prevalent safety issues within a specific area. By highlighting the frequency of at-risk behaviors, the diagram allows for an assessment of the severity of risks posed. For example, Figure 17.2, based on the data in Table 17.3, reveals that the most common problem is body mechanics issues related to improper lifting and pulling. However, the Steering Committee may choose to address the less frequent, yet more hazardous, failures to lockout and de-energize equipment, due to the greater risk of serious incidents. Thus, the Pareto diagram facilitates critical discussions on safety observations, guiding the steering committee in effective, data-based decision-making.

These data may identify areas where employees are not maintaining the observations or suggest safety practices that need additional training or attention. Often the steering committee will publish company-wide data comparing the data from observation categories with the causes of incidents that resulted in injury. Depending on the size of your organization, such data will frequently show a clear correlation between the practices with a low percentage of safe practices (or high percentage of unsafe practices) and the causes of injury incidents. Table 17.3 shows an example of a comparison of data on unsafe practices with causes of injury incidents. The steering committee may also work with other steering committees to ensure that the process is working effectively and to address problems such as those discussed in the previous section.

Table 17.3. Sample Statistics Comparing Observation Data With Causes of Incidents

Category	Safety Practice	Percent At-Risk	Percent of Incidents
Body position	Steps to avoid burns	16	15
	Proper pulling and lifting	24	11
	Avoids pinch points	8	7
	Repetitive motion	4	4
	Eyes on path	0	4
	TOTAL	52	48
Tools and equipment	De-energize	8	4
	Proper use of tool	12	4
	Other	8	7
	TOTAL	28	15

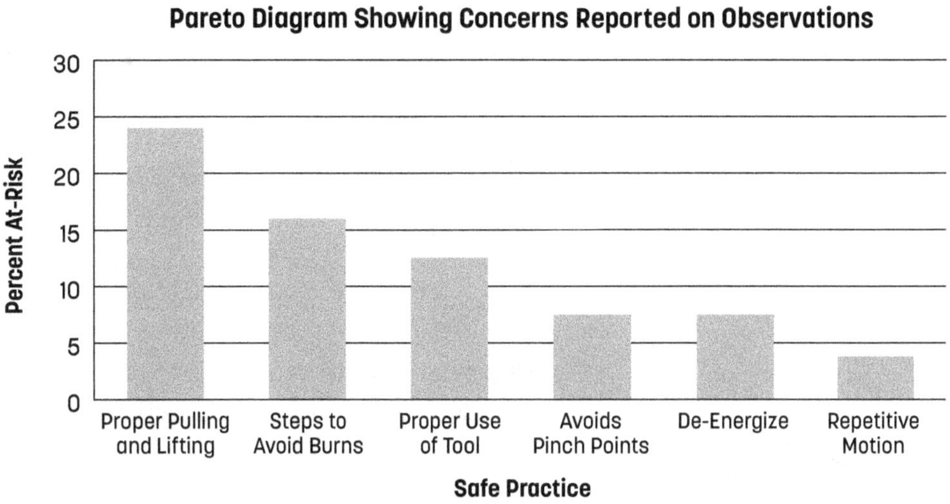

Pareto Diagram Showing Concerns Reported on Observations

Figure 17.2. An example of a Pareto diagram using the percent at-risk data presented in Table 17.3.

Communicate relevant safety information. The steering committee also communicates relevant safety information to employees throughout the company, often using a newsletter or area bulletin boards. Usually this includes publishing the results of the steering committee's statistical analysis in tabular and graphical form. It may also include additional information that supports the VBS process, such as discussion topics or training materials for safety meetings.

Address employee concerns. Another steering committee responsibility is evaluating and responding to employee concerns about the VBS process and other safety-related issues. Often observers will note employee concerns during observations or identify safety concerns or questions about safety that go beyond the responsibility of the area. Employees may also raise such concerns during safety meetings. The employee safety coordinator should ensure that such concerns are passed along to the steering committee for a response.

Coordinate recognition. The steering committee may also be responsible for planning and coordinating individual recognition and area celebrations. The steering committee may, for example, nominate individuals for recognition on the basis of a particular contribution to area safety. The steering committee may evaluate such nominations for sitewide recognition, determine whether such recognition is justified, then plan recognition that is appropriate for the contribution. This role helps ensure that recognition is consistent across the organization.

17.4 Management's Responsibilities

Maintaining the observation process and other elements of the VBS process requires an ongoing effort from management and the steering committee.

Implementation is not like walking into a room and flipping on a light switch. Keeping the process alive requires sustained attention to the observations, use of the data, and recognition. Table 17.4 provides guidelines on management's responsibilities to ensure effective maintenance of the VBS process.

Table 17.4. Management's Responsibilities for Maintaining a Values-Based Safety Process

When	Responsibilities
During visits to work areas	1. Conduct observations and provide feedback using area's observation sheet (model emphasis on positive feedback) 2. Review and provide feedback on completion of observations 3. Discuss process with steering committee members 4. Provide appreciative feedback to: • Steering committee members who champion the process • Employees who complete observations • Area management and all employees for improvement, goal attainment, and other area successes
At management meetings	1. Review and provide feedback on percent of completed observations in each area (not the percent safe resulting from observations) 2. Discuss plans for further process improvement 3. Identify individual contributions worthy of recognition
During performance reviews with managers and supervisors	1. Assess level of support of and participation in VBS process (percent of completed observations, not the percent safe resulting from observations)

CHAPTER 18

Some Final Suggestions on Implementation

Here are seven suggestions to improve your chances of having a successful VBS process.

Suggestion 1: Don't use a cookbook approach.

Although this book provides some guidelines, your success depends on your ability to apply these guidelines in the context of your organization's culture. This suggestion pertains not only to the approach described in this book but also to comparable approaches from consulting organizations around the country. Do not simply buy a package. Make sure you use the key elements of the approach to develop a system that meets the needs of your organization. In addition, do not be too quick to discard key elements just because they are difficult to implement or maintain in your organization.

Suggestion 2: Plan and clearly define management's role.

The observation process requires time and a great deal of effort. It will require active support from all levels of management. Pay special attention to suggestions for involving management and defining management's role in the process. Management's role will be the critical factor in both the long-term success of your observation process and the day-to-day elements of your safety improvement process.

Suggestion 3: Maximize participation in the final design.

The only way to create ownership is through meaningful involvement in the design process. This process requires a high level of participation and provides several options for ways to involve people. Do not make the mistake of designing a safety process in a vacuum then trying to implement the program by mandate. Involve people in the design at each stage. Then have those who assist with the design take it back to their work areas and get input and suggestions from their colleagues.

Suggestion 4: Create a different checklist for each area.

The research studies used checklists of specific safe behaviors that were job and area specific. Unless you are in a small facility, do not try to develop a generic checklist that works for all work areas. Maintenance has different safety requirements than a laboratory, for example, and their respective checklists need to be different. To maximize the value of the checklists, they should be explicit enough to address the specific safe practices of different job functions.

Suggestion 5: Don't create a bureaucracy around the data.

The value of this process is in getting everyone to pay attention to on-the-job safety but creating a lot of red tape will hinder the process. Instead of bureaucracy and red tape, build informal systems of accountability based on the observable parts of the system. Do not create an elaborate system of reports. Do pay attention to the safety process during informal contact with individuals in the work areas and during formal meetings at each level of the organization.

Suggestion 6: Use classroom training only when needed.

Place emphasis on designing a training process that satisfies your needs, not on putting all employees through extensive classroom training. Provide enough training to develop the level of understanding people need to support the process. Also, do not think of training as strictly a classroom activity. When training observers, for example, giving them an opportunity to actually conduct an observation is often more effective than classroom training alone. Use training only when appropriate and select a suitable process for delivering the necessary training.

Suggestion 7: Persevere. Don't quit—ever!

False starts typically characterize the implementation of any significant new process. Implementation is often two steps forward and one step back. The key to success is continuous improvement. Learn from each step so that you can do it better the next time. Just keep fine-tuning your process until you achieve zero incidents. Then strive to maintain that level of safety excellence.

CHAPTER 19

Special Topics: The Self-Observation Process[4]

A Values-Based Safety (VBS) process based on self-observations may be more appropriate for some companies. A self-observation process is particularly appropriate when:

1. their employees work in isolation or on small crews of two or three (e.g., loggers, electrical lineworker, or truck drivers).

2. their employees are extremely resistant to the idea of peer observations. In these situations, a self-observation process has been shown to improve safety practices and reduce incidents (see Olson and Austin, 2001, and the case studies in Chapter 25).

Implementing a self-observation process is generally easier than implementing a peer observation process. With self-observations, observers do not have to be trained to provide feedback to their coworkers, and they do not need to develop skills in handling resistance to the observation process. In addition, the self-observation forms typically do not include comments related to conditions, and the steering committee usually does not have to do the same level of detailed analysis and problem-solving that are required in a peer observation process.

A self-observation process addresses three primary questions that directly influence safe performance:

1. What must I do to successfully carry out my job?
2. How am I doing?
3. What's in it for me?

A sports analogy illustrates how these three questions apply. Imagine for a moment you play first base in the game of baseball. Is it clear what you need to do to do your job successfully? Yes, it is. The best behaviors and practices you would engage in are straightforward: fielding a specific area, holding runners on base, handling bunts and relays, and so on, in addition to hitting the ball when at bat.

A good deal of feedback that is based on data exists for answering the second question for the team and for individual players. The data also applies to game scores, the team's won-lost record, and statistics regarding the team's performance and the performance of each player.

---

4   Ann Pinney made significant contributions to this chapter.

The answer to the third question—"What's in it for me?"—is also clear in this example. For instance, when a person playing first base executes a double play by catching a line drive and tagging out a runner who left first base, they receive accolades from their team and the fans, not to mention a considerable amount of self-satisfaction. Furthermore, in professional baseball, the players' financial success is closely tied to their performance.

The same three questions are addressed in the self-observation process and correspond to the stages of implementation.

19.1 What Must I Do to Successfully Carry Out My Job?

The individual worker or the crew members list the actions that must be engaged in to do their job safely. This list of actions or behaviors becomes the foundation for a detailed personal index of safe behaviors.

19.2 How Am I Doing?

After the index has been constructed, individuals or crew members identify a sampling method of self-observations they can use to measure their performance against the index daily. The samples are triggered at random times, during which the workers measure themselves with regard to the safety of the actions they are engaged in at that moment. For example, the index in Figure 19.1 was constructed by a crew of loggers for the specific activity of cutting down a tree at a logging site. A faller typically cuts down trees with a falling partner. Although they are working in the same work area, they must be at least two tree lengths apart. They are often able to hear each other's saws, but they do not have visual contact. The two workers typically contact each other every hour or so via mobile radios. About three times a day, a faller will contact their falling partner at a random time and ask him to conduct a self-observation using the index. At the end of the day, all sampling observations are collected without names attached and calculated to create a team score.

When the concept of self-scoring is brought up, a common concern is that some employees may cheat on their score. Though employees might inflate their scores initially, they soon learn that the data will not be used against them and begin to trust the process. They realize that whether they check "yes" or "no" regarding performing safe behaviors, they have to think about what they are doing. They have to lift themselves out of their more or less automatic work behavior long enough to assess their performance. It is through this assessment that they become more conscious of their safety practices and, as a result, can begin to work on improving their safe work habits.

When introducing this index and the self-monitoring process at one of the logging sites, a veteran faller commented, "I've been falling trees for 35 years, and since I still have all my fingers and toes, I don't think this process will help me." After trying it for 2 weeks, he reported with some surprise that at one point he would have had to put himself in danger to get to his axe. Something he never would have believed had he not had to measure himself. That is typical for most of us; we are unconscious of our habits.

Conditions/Behaviors	Yes	No	N/A
1. Boots are in good condition with sharp caulks			
2. Well-marked trail to work site			
3. Saw or axe ready at hand at the tree			
4. Overhead hazards checked			
5. Ground clear of possible hazards or chain reactions			
6. Getaway trail established			
7. Partner is at least two tree lengths away			
8. Clean undercut pertains			
9. Backcut is 2 inches above undercut			
10. Wedge is in backcut			
11. Body position is clear of hazards while bucking			

Yes + No = Total _____

(# Yes ÷ Total) × 100 = % Safe Behaviors

Figure 19.1. Example of a self-observation checklist (safety index) for loggers.

When we are prompted by some external event, such as a safety observation, we realize what we are actually doing.

The main obstacle in the sampling process is not the time it takes to do a self-observation (most take less than 1 minute) but determining how to trigger samplings at remote work sites for isolated workers. Some methods for triggering them are discussed in the sections on index development and sampling later in this chapter.

19.3 What's in It for Me?

Individual crew members need to experience satisfaction and self-mastery as they improve in safety performance. This is actually a natural by-product of workers beginning to conduct self-observations in earnest. Immediate self-correction starts to take place with every sampling. The challenges of using the sampling process are getting employees to try the process in the first place and then keeping the process simple, meaningful, and fun to perform. Focusing on using external forms of acknowledgment along with celebrations for improvement and participation are critical to starting and maintaining the self-observation process. If it is a work situation in which employees rarely see one another, additional creative approaches must also be taken. These are addressed in the section on recognition later in this chapter.

19.4 How to Implement a Self-Observation Process

Select a Safety Representative From Each Work Group

For groups (which may include isolated solitary workers) and crews that work independently, the first step in establishing the self-observation process is to have each group or crew select from their ranks a representative to learn the process in detail.

The safety representative's role is to trigger the samplings of self-observations, calculate and post the daily scores, and deliver individual and team reinforcement for participation and improvements in performance. The following is a list of specific safety representative duties:

1. Calculate the scores as soon as possible after a self-observation sampling has been called for and post the data on a graph.
2. Look for improvements in participation in the self-observation process and improvements in safe behavior, and provide recognition.
3. Manage the recognition budget.
4. Talk informally with workers about how the index process is working for them and note when the index seems to be getting stale and should be changed.
5. Once a week, show the graph and briefly discuss the most recent scores with the group or crew members in a safety meeting. (This interchange may take place with individual solitary workers in person or remotely.)
6. Provide recognition and conduct celebrations when significant improvements in participation and/or safety performance have taken place.
7. Choose an alternate representative to maintain the process for periods when you will not be available.

Create an Index

Each worker or crew member creates a list of desired safety actions he or she needs to engage in to perform the job 100% safely. As with developing peer observation systems, these workers should analyze past safety data on injuries, accidents, and close calls to determine the behavioral content of the initial index. A prototype index can typically be created by a group of performers, such as tree fallers or truck drivers, who do the same job but perform it alone. Once the prototype index has been established for a particular job, the index can be customized to incorporate special safe behaviors that may pertain to the tasks of individual workers. Each individual or group checks to ensure that the listed safe behaviors meet the pinpointing criteria (see the pinpointing guidelines in Chapter 21). An element of pinpointing that can be modified for the self-observation process pertains to listed items that are not normally observable by another person but can be measured by the individual during self-observation. For example, in some operations employees have elected to include on their index items such as "mind on task." Difficult for anyone else to assess, this item definitely helps address a worker's safety concern of having his or her mind wander while operating a dangerous piece of equipment.

After all workers have listed the safe behaviors that they believe will be most valuable for improving their safety, the behaviors are entered into an index of items, each followed by columns for checking "yes," "no," or not applicable "(N/A)." When a sampling self-observation is triggered, the individual checks "yes" if engaged in the listed behavior, "no" if not engaged in the behavior but should have been, and "N/A" if the item is not necessary or pertinent at that moment.

Figure 19.2 provides an example of an index for truckers loading and hauling cut trees from a logging site to an area for unloading and sorting. As you will note, this index includes a variety of safe behaviors for each activity involved in the trucker's daily work duties. When a trucker receives a radio call from the dispatcher to conduct an observation, they may be involved in loading, transit, or off-loading. The trucker simply checks off the behaviors listed in the activity in which they are engaged at that time.

Conditions/Behaviors	Yes	No	N/A
LOADING:			
1. Wait for signal from loader, back in when safe to do so			
2. Drive slowly when backing and pulling out and hooking up reach			
3. Provide feedback to loader on stability of load			
4. Voice signal to second loader during binding up			
5. Check for overheight and overweight			
6. Give horn warning and check for second loader when leaving area			
7. Check load for stability			
IN TRANSIT:			
8. Perform walk-around inspection (pre-trip, load, mechanical, etc.)			
9. Drive to speed limits and road conditions			
10. Be prepared for the unexpected			
11. Frequently check mirrors			
12. Follow correctly (use 3-second rule)			
OFF-LOADING:			
13. Check that personal protective equipment is in good condition			
14. Maintain three-point contact when ascending or descending truck			
15. Ensure no overhead hazards when loading			
TRAILER:			
16. Walk around reload deck to ensure trailer loaded securely			

Yes + No = Total

(# Yes ÷ Total) × 100 = % Safe Behaviors

Figure 19.2. Example of a self-observation checklist for logging truck drivers.

Develop a Sampling Process

Once each worker has developed an index, it is time to begin collecting a baseline. The first data item on a specific self-observation is actually the true baseline when feedback intervention has begun. However, most groups try to collect five or six observations before posting a group baseline. They must first establish some prompt that will trigger the random observation samplings. In work situations that involve cell phones, pagers, radios, or even plant horns, these items can be used to signal that it is time to make self-observations. Some work situations demand more creativity in prompting the process. In a nuclear plant in which self-observations were taken, a small, inexpensive timer triggered sampling with an alarm inserted in each of the work packets prior to each shift. An engineering group for a forestry department used the first sound of a plane flying overhead to trigger filling out the safety indexes.

The key element in the process is triggering the observation at random moments to get the most accurate picture of a worker's safety habits. The more samples taken, the more accurate and complete the picture. The frequency of sampling must be balanced with the flow of work and workers' normal attention spans. The general guidelines offered by most work groups conducting self-observations is three to four samplings a week for the first 2 months of implementation and an average of two samplings a week after the baseline has been posted.

Post the Self-Observation Data

Once the samplings have been triggered and completed, the workers either drop off their indexes at a collection box or hand it in to their safety representative for calculating the group or crew score. Again, the index does not have a name on it, only the identifying group (for individual workers) or crew name (for crew members) and the date. The safety representative adds together the "yes" responses and "no" responses from all of the indexes and divides the number of "yes" responses by the combined total of "yes" and "no" responses to obtain the percentage of safe performance for that day.

What happens in the case of solitary workers who are not members of a group or crew? Employees usually work near their associates sometime during the week and typically belong to a group that can be considered a team. The team collects the data from team-member observations. These teams also have daily or weekly safety huddles and celebrate safety improvement together. The other workers in the group are likely to have the most influence on the daily work habits of their teammates and therefore would be most likely to compliment the improvements of individuals in the group. A sawmill using the self-observation process split its employees into crews that did not perform the same work but worked together at the same time and location. Each crew consisted of several production workers and an individual on-site maintenance employee. Although the safe behaviors on the separate indexes were different, the influence they had on each other remained high, especially in the area of reinforcement.

As for posting the data, many of a company's considerations with peer observation data also pertain to the self-observation process. The data should be posted in the respective group's or crew's work area for review and kept up to date. The applicable safety representative incorporates discussion of trends in the current data, analyzes behaviors that are getting many no responses, and helps determine when changes or new behavior items should be incorporated into the index. If the scores begin to achieve 90%–100% safe for five or six samplings, this usually indicates that the behaviors listed have started reaching a high and steady rate. It would make sense at this point to develop a new index with safe behaviors that address concerns uncovered by the increased awareness of the self-observations. In these instances, the safety representative might want to trigger self-observation sampling using the previous index on occasion, just to make certain that the safety practices established in the early sampling are still strong.

Provide Group and Individual Recognition

Providing positive reinforcement to individual workers for engaging in self-observations and contributing to group improvement in safety scores is delivered primarily by the safety representative. Because conducting self-observations is entirely voluntary, acknowledgment and encouragement for increased levels of sampling participation are critical. In fact, when the safety representative posts the day's score, the percentage of participation for the sampling for that score is also displayed.

Figure 19.3 is an example of a graph of safety index scores from a sorting area within a timber operation. This graph illustrates the percentage of safe performance from 25 workers with entirely different indexes who have completed the self-observation. The sorting area is where fallen trees are hauled, cut, graded, and bundled into what are called booms to be transported to market via waterways. It is typically a tight location in which large equipment must be maneuvered carefully around those who are working with the logs on the ground; thus, it is an area fraught with danger that produces either a very close-knit working group or more commonly a somewhat fractious group of workers who do not always get along. Getting workers to adopt a process that calls for workers to admit to themselves and record when they perform unsafe actions is a major milestone.

As demonstrated by the baseline data, the scores are somewhat inflated. Before posting the baseline data, the workers expressed a great deal of fear that the scores would be used against them. When the safety representative posted the baseline, he explained the scores and thanked the workers for participating. To acknowledge their participation, he went to a dock away from the work area, caught two large fish that he traded in a nearby town for several homemade pies, and took them back to the work area to celebrate the workers' participation during a break. Interestingly, the next sampling reflected a lower safety score but a higher level of participation. The representative interpreted those changes as the workers becoming more honest as they realized the scores would not be used against them. This has been a fairly common occurrence in various newly adopted self-observation systems. That is also why new safety representatives are taught to avoid emphasizing collective graph scores for the first 2 months and instead put their reinforcement efforts toward increasing participation.

The success of the safety representative's reinforcement attempts largely depends on their ability to customize social and tangible reinforcement to the workers. Because the safety reinforcement budget is usually small, representatives must be judicious about the celebrations or small, tangible reinforcements they choose. The perceived value of the acknowledgment is also heavily influenced by the level of informal leadership and respect the safety representative commands within the group or crew. Noting small improvements with positive comments and using innovative and fun ways to celebrate group improvement—as in the fish-pie instance—can make or break the early adoption of the self-observation process on a worksite that is experiencing low morale. Also note that safety representatives are selected by the group or crew members themselves, and once they begin to appreciate the power and value of the self-observation process, they sometimes replace an initial representative who was selected more or less casually or politically with an informal leader of the group or crew.

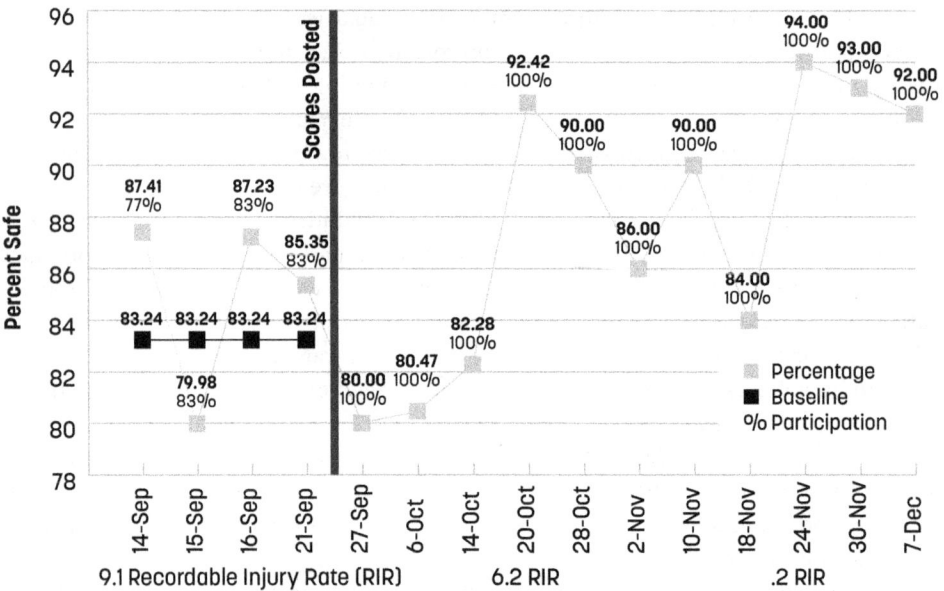

Figure 19.3. Data from a self-observation safety improvement process.

19.5 Final Suggestions on Self-Observations

Implementing a self-observation process is similar in many respects to a typical peer observation VBS process, but much easier in other respects. The role of leadership is equally important in both approaches. While a self-observation approach often does not require the safety representative or a steering committee to do complex problem-solving with the observation data, their use of observation data as the basis for reinforcement is even more critical in this approach. If your organization opts for a self-observation process, these two elements warrant special study and attention.

CHAPTER 20

Special Topics: The Steering Committee[5]

This chapter provides additional details on the creation, training, and specific roles of the steering committee. After discussing formation and training, the chapter describes how the steering committee should manage the process to maintain effective observations. Beyond the observations, the long-term success of a Values-Based Safety (VBS) process requires the steering committee to analyze data and plan projects for improving safe work practices, which is the focus of the latter portion of this chapter and Chapter 22.

20.1 Creating the Steering Committee

In the VBS process, the initial employee-led design team usually becomes the steering committee after all employees have been trained as observers and the process has been kicked off. Steering committees are most effective with five to eight members, although they can be made larger to provide adequate representation. Design teams can be effective with 8 to 12 members. Therefore, some method for decreasing the initial number of team members will be necessary to create an effective steering committee. The effectiveness of these teams begins to decrease significantly as the number of members exceeds 12, and the total number should not exceed 15. Actually, not all design team members will want to continue as members of the steering committee, whose term of office is usually 1 or 2 years, so some members may volunteer to leave. If none do, you might ask some members of the design team to volunteer to serve on the steering committee at a later time.

In a large, task-diverse, or geographically dispersed organization, one central design team may be formed by representatives of each work area that creates a template VBS process for the organization. Following kickoff, each area or group of areas forms its own steering committee. In such cases, these steering committees will need to recruit several additional employees to join the one or two representatives from their area who were on the design team. These steering committees next customize the central template for their specific area. They then manage their VBS process as a separate process. Also, you should ensure that the team members' terms do not end at the same time. Once your process is established, you should set up the schedule so that no more than two new steering committee members start at the same time.

---

5 Grainne Matthews made significant contributions to this chapter.

New steering committee members share the characteristics of the original design team members: nominated for serving on the committee by their peers because they are respected, natural leaders who are interested in safety issues and willing and available to devote several hours per month (often on their own time) to work on the process.

20.2 Training the Steering Committee

In addition to learning how to manage the integrity, outcome, and results of the VBS process, the steering committee members undertake training to learn how to do the following:

1. Identify, encourage, and reinforce safe work behaviors and practices by all employees and management that support the process.
2. Present safety data to other employees in meetings as feedback and lead employees in setting goals and choosing celebrations.
3. Assess whether the process is remaining true to the values identified by the design team and to the behavioral principles on which its success depends and, if it is not, raise their concerns to other committee members.
4. Make effective use of time and resources in committee meetings.

These skills may be taught in an initial 2-day workshop followed by review and feedback during subsequent steering committee meetings. In the case of organizations that have more than one steering committee, meeting together regularly to share best practices and problem-solving techniques can be valuable (see Chapter 23). Many steering committees also receive continuing education (and recognition) by attending safety conferences and seminars.

20.3 Steering Committee Responsibilities

Steering committees play a vital role in the success of the VBS process. They are responsible for managing and improving three aspects of the process:

- outcome data
- observation data
- process data

Managing Outcome Data

If people are working more safely, the organization should experience fewer injuries. The steering committee monitors the VBS process data results to ensure that the process is achieving this ultimate goal. In addition, the steering committee uses this information to improve the process.

1. If an incident occurs, the steering committee pinpoints the safe behavior that could have prevented it or lessened the severity of the incident. (Pinpointing is discussed in more detail in Chapter 21.)
2. If the practice is on the checklist, the steering committee determines if the frequency and severity of incidents related to this practice have been decreasing over time. If they have been, does this incident provide new information that would merit changes in the process?
   (a) If incidents have not been decreasing, the steering committee determines whether the percent safe for this practice has been increasing over time. If it has, does this incident provide new information that would merit changes in the process?
   (b) If the percent safe has not been increasing, the steering committee asks:
      (i) Is the practice being observed often enough (number of observations that include this practice)? Are enough of those observations high quality?
      (ii) If the practice has entailed an active improvement project, is the project based on a thorough and accurate behavioral analysis? Does this incident add any new information to the analysis? Is the project occurring as planned?
3. If the practice that could have prevented or reduced the security of the incident is not on the checklist, does it occur frequently enough or is the risk high enough that it should be added?
4. If the behavior is on the checklist, the steering committee should consider whether the task that was being performed when the incident occurred was one that is routinely observed. If it is not routinely observed, the steering committee needs to develop plans to increase the frequency of observations of this particular task.

Managing Outcome and Observation Data: Serious Incident Prevention

When targeting a typical at-risk behavior from a VBS checklist, the steering committee may plan to simply increase the feedback on that behavior. Such interventions are not appropriate for tasks with the risk of more serious incidents. Ideally, the analysis of those behaviors and hazards should be addressed through engineering the hazards out of the workplace or, when that is not possible, adding additional layers of protection that address the systems issues. For example, in construction, practitioners may not be able to eliminate the task of working at heights, but they might ensure that a safety professional or supervisor participates in the pre-job brief and reviews all the controls (e.g., fall protection, guardrails, and toeboards) at the beginning of the job, throughout the day, and any time the circumstances change.

The steering committee's interventions should ensure a level of control appropriate to the hazard or risk in the workplace. The contexts of serious incidents often justify the capital expenditures associated with robotics or new equipment that eliminate the risk of serious incidents. Lost-workday incidents, the associated hazards that create risk of serious incidents, and behaviors that expose employees to the risk of serious incidents also justify a careful analysis of the work environment. Interventions to address these issues may require guarding or other equipment upgrades that reduce the hazards or help support safe behavior. As a final fail-safe, the leadership team should review the analysis, planning, and implementation of actions taken to address serious incident precursors.

Managing Observation Data

If the process is functioning the way it was designed, employees should be working more safely. The percentage of safe behaviors (i.e., the percentage of times an observed practice is marked as "safe" on the observation checklist by observers) should increase for all practices as a result of increases in observations and feedback. The percent safe on practices targeted by the steering committee in improvement projects should increase even more. Finally, work practices that have reached 95%–100% safe need to remain at that level for an extended period (generally a year) to ensure that the improvement is not the result of natural variations over time.

Accordingly, the steering committee reviews observation data to ensure that the process achieves the desired outcomes:

- What is the percent safe on each checklist practice?
- Is the percent safe on practices targeted by improvement projects increasing?
- Have some of the safe practices remained near 100% for a year or more?

Managing Process Data

The VBS process consists of two major components based on five core principles. Successful VBS processes are true to these principles. The steering committee protects the integrity of these principles.

Component 1: Employee Involvement

Principle 1. Employees who participate as observers improve their safety behaviors as much as or more than those they observe (see Chapter 27). Therefore, the more workers who conduct observations, the better.

Principle 2. The more often employees are observed and receive feedback, the more likely they are to improve their safety behavior. Therefore, the more often observations are made, the better.

Principle 3. Much of the value of the VBS process is in exchanges between the observers and those being observed. Therefore, high-quality observation and feedback sessions are critical.

Component 2: Data Analysis and Improvement Projects

Most of the remaining benefit of the VBS process comes from improvements recommended or implemented by the steering committee, based on its analyses of observation data and related information.

Principle 4. Therefore, the steering committee must conduct high-quality, timely analyses of the data and target behaviors.

Principle 5. Based on this analysis, the committee must also develop and implement action plans targeting improvement.

Steering Committee Functions

The following tasks are necessary for the committee to ensure the integrity of the VBS process. These tasks can be grouped into specific roles or divided among the committee members. Their completion must be monitored to ensure that the steering committee remains on track:

- **Chair:** Sets the agenda, chairs meetings, tracks attendance, and organizes logistics (e.g., meeting location, materials, refreshments).

- **Data Coordinator:** Collects and provides observation checklists, data tables, and graphs; arranges for additional information, if necessary, for analysis. For example, this individual may interview observers to clarify comments on their observation forms or visit work locations to observe tasks discussed on observation forms.

- **Incident[6] Coordinator:** Collects incident documents and arranges for additional information to be collected if necessary for analysis. For example, this person may interview people involved in an incident to clarify information in the documentation or may invite someone involved in the analysis to the steering committee meeting to elaborate.

- **Improvement Project Coordinator:** Tracks action items on improvement projects. The coordinator may assign these items to steering committee members, managers and supervisors, or other employees.

- **Recognition and Celebration Coordinator:** Plans celebrations with management when goals are met and schedules individual employee recognition by steering committee members, supervisors, coworkers, or others, as designated (see the recognition and celebration guidelines in Chapter 22).

- **Scribe:** Records decisions and publishes the minutes.

---

6   *Incident* as used here refers to any incident that has the potential to cause injury or illness. Thus, it includes actual lost-workday injuries and illnesses, non-lost-workday injuries and illnesses, first aid cases, close calls, vehicle incidents, and equipment damage incidents (e.g., forklift collisions with stationary objects, pump failures, spills). Some of these incidents may not be routinely documented in many organizations.

Each member can also function as an area representative for their department or team. Area representatives may do the following:
- post area feedback graphs, tables, and lists on bulletin boards in their area
- personally encourage participation by their fellow employees
- deliver or arrange recognition as planned by the recognition and celebration coordinator
- report on the VBS process to area supervisors and managers
- discuss the process, provide area feedback, and lead fellow employees in setting new goals at area meetings (see the section on setting goals and providing group feedback in Chapter 22)

Should the steering committee decide to create specific roles for committee members, there are several ways to set them up. Some committees assign the roles for the members' entire term of office, which is the simplest method. Other committees rotate the roles, which enables each member to learn about several aspects of the VBS process. In the latter case, longer rotations of perhaps 6 months are generally best because they provide members with enough practice to become proficient at each of the various committee tasks.

Addressing Process Integrity

During its monthly meetings, the steering committee addresses the integrity of the VBS process. It must monitor various measures and trends in each of the basic components. The steering committee should routinely ask the following questions to assess how well they are doing and help identify areas that may need attention:

Component 1: Employee Involvement

(a) Have employees set their own reasonable improvement goals for each involvement measure?

(b) Are employees receiving accurate, timely, and easy-to-understand feedback about progress toward their goals via publicly posted graphs and announcements in meetings?

(c) Are celebrations happening as soon as possible after goals have been met, ideally within the week but no later than 2 weeks?

(d) Are individuals receiving recognition as soon as possible after meeting recognition criteria, ideally within 24 hours but no later than 3 days?

(e) If progress is not being made toward involvement goals, the steering committee conducts a behavioral analysis to determine what antecedent(s) or consequence(s) may need to be strengthened or added:

- Percentage of participation: percentage of all trained observers who are conducting scheduled observations
- Number of observations: total observations
- Percentage of quality observations: percentage of observations containing pinpointed comments for the noted safety concerns and indicating which items and concerns were discussed

Component 2: Data Analysis and Improvement Projects

General:

(a) Is the steering committee meeting at least monthly?

(b) Is there at least 90% attendance at steering committee meetings?

(c) Are steering committee members completing agreed-upon functions between and during meetings (as described above)?

(d) Do steering committee members represent all departments and shifts?

(e) Is the steering committee soliciting input from employees in each department and on each shift?

(f) Is the steering committee analyzing data monthly to address two to three target practices?

(g) Is the steering committee using information from observations, incident reports, experience, and interviews to conduct behavioral analyses of antecedents and consequences for target practices?

(h) Are the steering committee's improvement projects based on missing or weak antecedents or consequences?

(i) Is the steering committee using information from incident reports to do the following?

- improve the checklists (e.g., improve definitions, add examples to definitions, or reorder checklist items)
- guide the process (e.g., encourage observations of tasks at times when injuries have occurred but few or no observations have been made)

Improvement projects on targeted practices:

(a) Are employees setting reasonable, new improvement goals when previous goals have been met?

(b) Are employees receiving accurate, timely, and easy-to-understand feedback about progress toward goals via publicly posted graphs and announcements in meetings?

(c) Are celebrations happening as soon as possible after goals have been met, ideally within the week but no later than 2 weeks?

(d) Are individuals receiving recognition as soon as possible after pertinent behavior, ideally within 24 hours but no later than 3 days?

(e) Are observers focusing on targeted practices with observation and feedback?

(f) Are responsible employees implementing agreed-upon improvement plans?

(g) Are employees receiving recognition when they implement agreed-upon improvement plans?

The steering committee asks these questions at every meeting and makes plans to correct deficits where identified. A VBS process will not achieve its full potential in terms of an increase in people working safely and a decrease in incidents if these components are not implemented as described.

20.4 Responsibility Summary

The steering committee meeting agenda in Figure 20.1 outlines the activities previously described.

Steering Committee Meeting Agenda

Date: _____ Chair: _____ Scribe: _____

Team members present	
Team members absent (and reason)	

Order of Business

1. Review	2. Results/Outcome Measures	3. Behavior Measures	4. Process Measures
• mission • values • meeting ground rules	• incidents related to checklist and targeted practices • severity of injuries (lost workday, recordable, first aid) • injuries *not* related to practices on safety checklists	• Pareto* percent safe • Pareto number of concerns • Pareto percent concerns • trend percent safe on target practices • incident documentation • ABC analysis	• observer participation • number of observations • quality observations • steering committee functioning • improvement projects

Who	Will Do What	By When

* Refers to bar charts on which the bars appear in descending (or varying) order of magnitude, enabling quick identification of the most frequently occurring items.

Figure 20.1. Sample agenda form for the steering committee.

CHAPTER 21

Advanced Topics: Behavioral Basics

We have talked about behavior throughout this book, but what are we talking about? What is behavior? Furthermore, why do people behave the way they do? These are two important questions, particularly for those interested in improving safety.

A basic understanding of the theory that underlies behavioral technology will help you make your efforts successful. Such an understanding will be useful as you:

1. develop your implementation plans
2. problem-solve and refine your efforts
3. analyze incidents to plan preventive measures

The process is straightforward in theory but is often more difficult in practice. First you specify the desired behavior, then you analyze the situational and historical events that support that behavior.

We will start with the first question: What is behavior? Behavior is simply anything someone does or says. Behavior is any activity that a dead person cannot do; any muscular or glandular action or reaction (Malott et al., 2000).

Behavior is not personality, attitude, or intelligence. These are labels or abstractions that we often use to describe someone's behavior in some specific way. For the purposes of this book, we have used the term "behavior" only for observable actions, because observable practices are what concern us at work. Accordingly, we have talked about specific observable acts.

While attitudes may be important, the behavioral approach addresses how people behave on the job. We can only know someone's attitude by our observations of how they behave and what they tell us. If we can change their safety habits, their attitudes about safety will follow, especially as their colleagues also adopt better safety habits. Once we have a group of people with similar habits and attitudes around safety, we can begin to talk about people having a common safety culture. Thus, when we want to talk about changing the culture, we have to talk about changing people's behavior. When behaviors change, changes in attitude and culture will follow.

21.1 Pinpointing

Pinpointing is describing behavior in observable terms, without the use of labels or abstractions. It means being specific in describing exactly what someone does without interpreting or evaluating the observed behavior. Pinpointing means avoiding the use of labels and objectively describing the actual behavior that might lead someone to use a label in normal conversation.

The first step in designing a VBS process is pinpointing a list of behaviors critical to safety without the use of labels or explanations of behavior. Complex safety practices must be broken into components and defined in precise detail.

Sometimes you need to identify the results of behavior rather than the actual behavior. Doing so has an advantage in that the results remain even when the behavior has stopped. For example, you can observe spilled oil without having seen someone spill the oil (or the failure to clean it up). Figure 21.1 presents several examples of common labels, pinpointed behaviors, and results.

Labels	Behaviors	Results
• Aggressive • Angry • Bad attitude • Brownnoser • Dangerous • Good worker • Neat • Unsafe	• Filling out a checklist correctly • Proper lifting (legs bent, back straight) • Putting lockout tags on electrical switches • Wearing safety glasses • Wearing safety harness when working above 6 feet	• Area marked off with safety tape • Electrical wires lying across walkways • Lockout tags in place • Rate of OSHA-recordable incidents

Figure 21.1. Examples of common labels, behaviors, and results of behavior.

Pinpointing is often a two-step process, as described in Table 21.1.

Table 21.1. Pinpointing Steps

Step Number	Activity
1	Pinpoint the problem, undesirable behavior (i.e., an unsafe act), or undesirable result of the behavior (i.e., an unsafe condition)
2	Pinpoint the desired behavior, what you want employees to do (i.e., a safe act), or the desirable result of the behavior (i.e., a safe condition)

The reason for identifying the desired behavior is that it allows you to focus on the positive. Once you identify the desired behavior, you can plan ways to encourage and support the desired behavior. Pinpointing the undesired behavior also enables you to plan ways of discouraging the behavior, but this is the traditional and less effective approach to safety. Establishing a preventive safety initiative requires that you know what behaviors you want to encourage and that you design an environment that provides positive support for those behaviors.

21.2 ABC Analysis

Our basic premise is that behavior is a function of the immediate environment. Once we have pinpointed a specific behavior, we can divide environmental events into two sets of categories: events that precede the behavior and events that follow the behavior. Behavioral psychologists use the term *antecedents* for events that occur before the behavior and *consequences* for events that follow behavior. Figure 21.2 shows a diagram representing these events. Antecedents are events that precede behavior and prompt or cue the occurrence of that behavior. Consequences are events that follow behavior and influence the likelihood that the behavior will occur again under those antecedent conditions in the future. Consequences either strengthen or weaken behavior.

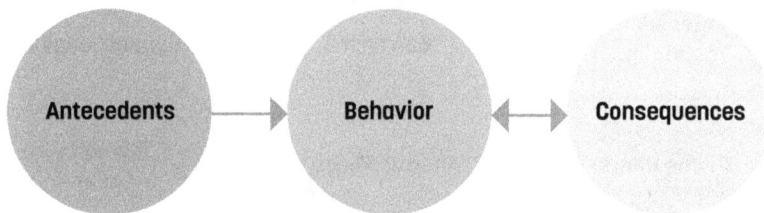

Figure 21.2. Relationship between antecedents, behavior, and consequences (preliminary diagram).

Notice the two-way arrow between consequences and behavior in Figure 21.2. It suggests that consequences affect the likelihood that the behavior will occur again. They may either strengthen or weaken the behavior. Consequences can increase or decrease the likelihood that the behavior will occur again under similar conditions. The relationship between these behavioral events is a contingency relationship (i.e., an if-then relationship). If the antecedent conditions are present, then the behavior will occur. If the behavior occurs, it will be followed by the consequence.

Here are some examples: If you walk into a dark room, the dark room is likely to be an antecedent for what? It will usually prompt you to look for or flip a light switch. The consequence of flipping the light switch is what? When you flip a light switch, the light comes on and you can find your way around the room.

Figure 21.3 on the following page is a contingency diagram that depicts the if-then relationship of the primary behavioral events (Malott, 1992 a, b) in the light switch example. Figure 21.4 presents a similar example.

In each of these examples, what is controlling the behavior? The answer is that both the antecedents and the consequences are controlling the occurrence of the behavior. The antecedent prompts you to respond. In a sense, the antecedent condition determines when the response occurs. Still, you would not continue to flip the switch if the light never came on. Nor would you continue to answer the phone if no one responded. Consequences are important in maintaining the effect of the antecedent

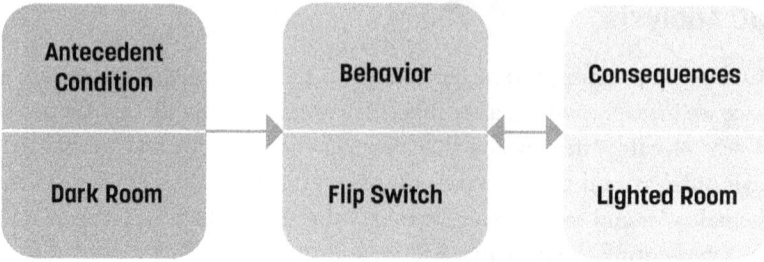

Figure 21.3. Contingency diagram of the environmental events associated with flipping a light switch.

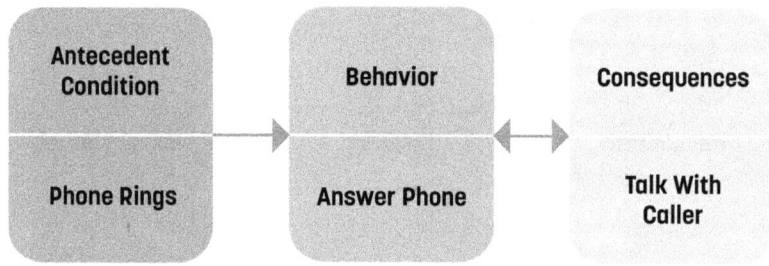

Figure 21.4. Contingency diagram of the environmental events associated with answering the telephone.

condition. In fact, the antecedents are effective in prompting behavior only because of the consequences. Since the antecedent would not be effective without consequences, the consequences are what really control behavior.

But why is the behavior occurring in the first place? The behavior occurs because of a history of experience with the antecedents and consequences. Sometime in the past, we learned about light switches and telephones. We will add "individual learning history" to our diagram after we further discuss consequences and antecedents.

21.3 Consequences

As mentioned, consequences can either increase or decrease the behaviors they follow. The two types of consequences are generally familiar: Reinforcement increases behavior while punishment decreases behavior (see Figure 21.5). In addition, behavior may be followed by a neutral event that neither strengthens nor weakens the behavior. As a rule, safety improvement efforts need to add consequences that support safe behavior on the job. The consequences occurring in the natural work environment simply do not maintain the levels of safety that we strive for in today's workplace. The key to improving safety performance is identifying and arranging consequences that support compliance with safety procedures.

Built-in consequences. The probability of getting hurt because of not following a safety procedure is part of the consequences built into the job itself. Many consequences

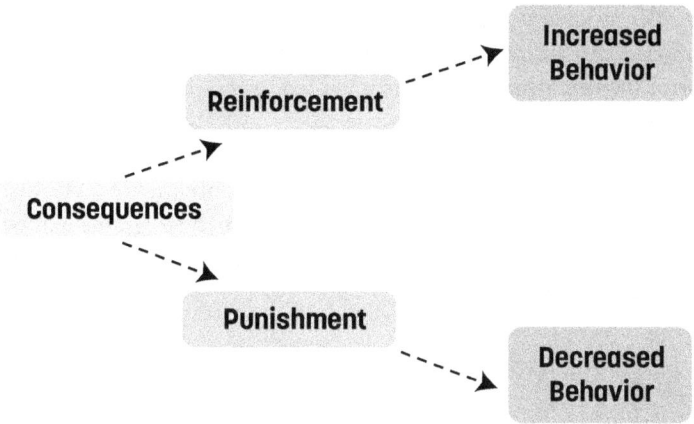

Figure 21.5. Primary types of consequences and their impact on behavior.

involved in safety are natural consequences that occur simply as a result of engaging in the behavior. Discomfort associated with wearing protective equipment on a hot day is built into the act of wearing the equipment and makes the use of that equipment less likely. Following safety procedures often takes more time than shortcutting those procedures. Climbing a structure without a safety harness or making a quick weld without a hot-work permit may result in getting the job done more quickly. Conversely, if a tool is dropped from above, the head is protected by a hard hat. Protection from injury is reinforcement that is built into the act of wearing the hard hat.

Unfortunately, most built-in consequences support unsafe acts rather than compliance with safety procedures. Too often, following safety procedures creates delay, discomfort, or inconvenience that punishes compliance with established safety practices. However, following safety procedures reduces the risk of injury, which is also a built-in consequence. Unfortunately, the likelihood of actually avoiding injury by following the safety procedure is usually too improbable to provide reinforcement significant enough to offset the built-in, punishing consequences.

Added consequences. Because most of the built-in consequences do not support safe practices, we must arrange contrived consequences in the workplace. We use social consequences to provide such support. Social consequences require that another person be present and act immediately following someone's behavior.

In traditional safety management, the most common added consequence is the threat of punishment. It can take the form of corrective feedback, criticism, nagging, or disciplinary action. Employees follow the safety procedures to avoid punishment.

In contrast, the behavioral approach provides added positive consequences for safe behavior. Added consequences that reinforce safe behavior include positive attention from management and peers. Such attention may include simple personal praise and support. Added reinforcement may be provided in the form of publicized comments that employees are making progress toward a goal or have earned recognition or awards. When we create an observation process, the intent is to add social consequences that support safe behavior on the job.

The VBS process also provides corrective feedback from observers. But the observers are more likely to be peers and the corrective feedback does not have the same threat of performance evaluation that is included in the traditional approach to safety.

Delayed outcomes. We often create safety awards programs to encourage employees to behave safely. The awards usually provide additional positive outcomes for not getting hurt but are too delayed to be effective consequences. We discussed problems with such programs in Chapters 1 and 13, yet such programs can be an effective component of a safety process. Figure 21.6 displays a more complete diagram that includes consequences and outcomes.

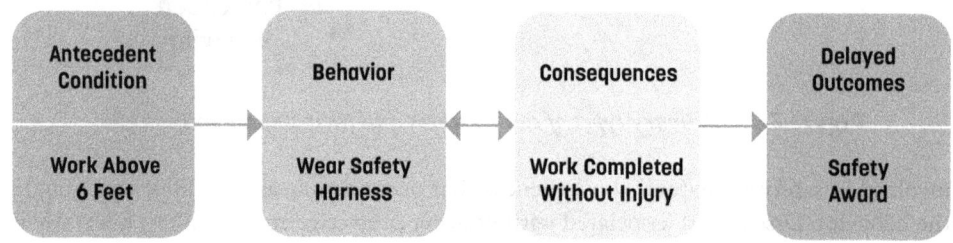

Figure 21.6. Contingency diagram adding delayed outcomes.

Self-provided consequences. The ideal safety program maximizes self-control. The employees know the safety rules and feel good about behaving in ways consistent with those rules, often in spite of built-in consequences. They feel anxiety when they take shortcuts or fail to follow safety rules. People who consistently wear seat belts feel similar discomfort if they ride in an automobile without their seat belt fastened. Such "self-control" is the goal of adding consequences and delayed outcomes, such as safety awards. The "anxiety" results from the potential punishment for breaking safety rules and the potential loss of future safety awards, compensation, and advancement opportunities.

Added consequences and outcomes help create and support self-provided consequences. Seat belt laws provide added consequences that help increase the self-provided consequences that have increased seat belt use. A goal of the behavioral safety observation process is to add social consequences that support self-provided consequences. A complete behavioral process further includes establishing team improvement goals, safety awards programs, and other programs that support self-provided consequences for safe behavior.

Factors influencing effectiveness of consequences. Two factors influence the effectiveness of consequences and delayed outcomes:

- probability of the consequence or outcome
- significance to the individual

As discussed in Chapters 1 and 13, these factors help explain why people do not comply with safety procedures simply to avoid getting hurt, even when they clearly know the correct procedures. The probability of getting hurt from failing to comply with a given safety procedure is generally too small to be effective in maintaining safe practices. Given the incidence rates for most industries, the probability of being hurt on a given job is fairly low, even if an employee fails to comply with safety procedures every time. If the incidence rate is 5 per 200,000 work hours, for example, an employee will have an injury based on chance about once every 20 years. The low probability of injury is part of the problem and the reason we have to add social consequences to better support safe work practices. If the risks were greater, employees would be more likely to comply with safety procedures. Most organizations are safe enough for employees to become complacent. Because of this, the challenge is to provide added consequences that support safe behavior.

21.4 Antecedents

An antecedent must be present immediately before the behavior of interest. When identifying an antecedent, you should identify the stimulus conditions that prompted the behavior to occur. Safety antecedents include verbal instructions, signs, and the situation that prompted action.

Other events not immediately preceding the behavior of interest may include written procedures, safety rules, and safety improvement goals. Because these events do not immediately precede safe behavior, you should consider them part of the person's history rather than an antecedent. Often, an individual's unsafe response to a situation may suggest a problem with the training or instructions the employee has received some time prior to the behavior of interest. These elements will be discussed in greater detail in the next section.

A written procedure may be an antecedent if the employee referenced the procedure immediately before starting the job. Otherwise, the procedure and training on that procedure are part of the employee's individual learning history.

Key point: Antecedents affect behavior because of the consequences. In the contingency diagrams regarding the light switch and the ringing telephone, the antecedents prompted the behavior to occur because of the consequences that usually follow in the presence of those antecedent conditions.

21.5 Individual Learning History

As mentioned, many behavioral events, such as training, role models, and reviewing procedures, occur too far in advance of the behavior of interest to be considered antecedents, yet they are important to how a person responds in a given situation. These factors often establish employees' skills or knowledge of job procedures, both actual on-the-job practices and formal procedures. In formal training programs employees generally learn what they are supposed to do. Then, through on-the-job contact with more experienced employees and their supervisors, they learn how the jobs are actually done. Sometimes the procedures and on-the-job practices are the same. Sometimes there is a difference between the two. Figure 21.7 presents an expanded diagram that includes learning history.

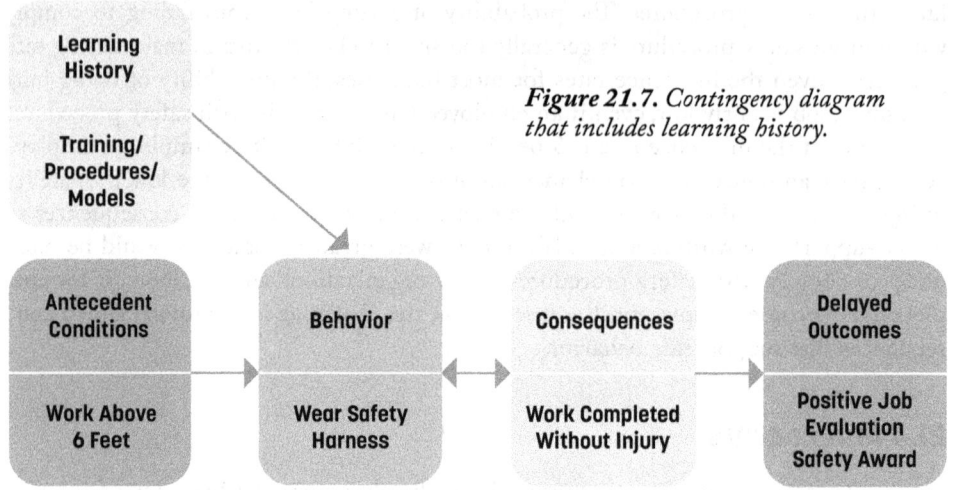

Figure 21.7. Contingency diagram that includes learning history.

This expanded picture of the behavioral environment clarifies all the functions of the VBS process. This safety process supports safe practices on the job by:

- arranging immediate social consequences that support safe practices
- providing training (a learning history) that sharpens the observer's understanding of what is and is not safe under different antecedent conditions
- supplying delayed outcomes (team celebrations and individual recognition) that support safe practices and the observation process

The observation process provides social consequences for safe practices through the feedback that observers provide to those they observe. The positive feedback provided immediately following observations of safe practices should reinforce those practices, while corrective feedback should prompt safe practices and decrease the likelihood of future unsafe practices.

In addition to the consequences, identifying safe and unsafe practices during the observation process trains employees to identify risks in their daily work activities. In many ways, the observation process is analogous to arranging for employees to watch videos and identify safe and unsafe practices and conditions. Employees gain a clearer understanding of what they can do to create a safer work environment. The understanding and new skills help employees ensure a high level of safe practices all the time, not only when they are conducting formal observations.

Finally, the VBS process provides delayed outcomes that support safety. The observation data can be the basis for team celebrations and individual recognition. By participating in a formal observation process, managers and supervisors can more accurately evaluate employee safety performance when making decisions regarding compensation and promotions. Thus, the process helps the normal organizational contingencies support safety more effectively.

In addition, managers and supervisors may be evaluated on how well they implement and maintain the observation and feedback processes. The delayed outcomes (e.g., the manager's annual performance appraisal) then also support the observational feedback process that has a more direct impact on all employees' daily safety practices.

21.6 Behavioral Analysis Worksheet

Analyzing behavioral incidents is a difficult task. Too many safety investigations stop short with a simplistic analysis, such as "failure to follow procedure" or "operator inattention," without doing a thorough analysis of the environmental factors that actually contributed to the behavior. The worksheet in Figure 21.8 on the following page provides an initial overview of factors that may have contributed to an unsafe act. These concepts will be developed more fully in Chapter 22.

21.7 Developing an Action Plan to Address Behavioral Causes

Once you have analyzed the situation by considering the questions in Figure 21.8, use the if-then statements in Table 21.2 as a preliminary guide for developing action plans. This topic will also be developed in more detail in Chapter 22.

Table 21.2. Preliminary Guide to Assist in Developing Action After Analyzing Target Behavior

If	You Might
The job procedure or equipment could be redesigned to eliminate the risk	Redesign the equipment or procedure
The safe practice occurs in specific work areas and signage is nonexistent or weak	Add or improve specificity of signs
The safe practice involves the regular use of a skill or knowledge that the employees do not have	Arrange for job-specific training that provides the needed skills or knowledge
The safe practice involves complex, infrequently used skills or knowledge that the employees do not have	Develop and require use of a checklist for the tasks. Train personnel to complete the tasks using the checklist
The built-in consequences support the desired behavior	Redesign the job so that doing the task safely is more comfortable, easier, and takes less time
The safe practice is not already on the behavioral observation checklist	Add behavior to the observation checklist
This particular safety practice is not explicitly included in the definitions on the back of the observation sheet	Add a pinpointed example to the applicable definition
Employee had not been observed recently because the job function was not routinely included in observations	Revise procedure to ensure all employees are observed
Employee had not been observed recently because scheduled observations are not occurring consistently	Enhance procedure to improve completion of scheduled observations

	Conceptual Questions	Specific Questions
1. Behavior	What was the undesired behavior?	• What was the unsafe act that resulted in an incident?
	What is the desired behavior?	• What was the safe act that could have prevented the incident?
2. Consequences	What built-in consequences support the desired and undesired behavior? (Consider both reinforcement and punishment.)	• Are the employees more comfortable or able to complete the job more quickly or easily by engaging in the unsafe act? • Are employees uncomfortable or less productive if they do the job safely? Is it more work?
	What added social consequences support the desired and undesired behavior? (Consider both reinforcement and punishment.)	• Do supervisors and others routinely provide corrective action for employees who engage in the unsafe act? • Do supervisors and others routinely provide positive feedback for the safe act?
3. Delayed outcomes	What delayed outcomes should support the desired behavior? (Consider both reinforcement and punishment.)	• What safety awards should support the safe act? • What effect does performing the unsafe act have on an employee's compensation or career?
	How significant are the outcomes?	• Are the awards significant to employees?
	How probable are the outcomes?	• Is it likely that an employee will lose a safety award for performing this job unsafely or earn a safety award for performing this job safely? • Is it likely that performing this job safely or unsafely will affect an employee's compensation or career opportunities?
4. Antecedents	What antecedent condition prompted the unsafe act?	• Was the employee encouraged to be in a hurry? • Was the employee instructed to do the job incorrectly?
	What antecedents should have prompted the safe act?	• Did the location of the incident have signs to prompt appropriate procedure? • Were the correct tools and materials present to do the job correctly? • Did the employee have a checklist at hand (should one have been provided or required)?
5. Individual learning history	What other events occurred in the individual's history that may have affected the likelihood of the safe or unsafe behavior?	• Are the procedures correct? • Did the employee know how to do the job correctly (and demonstrate mastery of the procedure during training)? • Do other employees routinely model the correct way to do the job? • Do employees know how engaging in the unsafe act affects their personal safety, their safety awards, and their careers?

Figure 21.8. Preliminary worksheet to assist in analyzing incidents and behaviors.

CHAPTER 22

Advanced Topics: Steering Committee Improvement Projects[7]

This chapter outlines the data that the steering committee analyzes and the steps it takes to select practices for improvement projects. A steering committee is most effective when it focuses on no more than two or three projects at a time. A suggested strategy is to gather baseline data for one reporting period (typically 1 or 2 months), then focus on the one practice that is most important to improve. When this first improvement project has been underway for about 2 months, the second project is selected. The third improvement project might be planned 2 months after that. Approaching projects incrementally has advantages: (a) the steering committee is not overwhelmed yet is taking actions to improve safety that employees can see, and (b) more data are made available for each subsequent analysis.

During each improvement project, the steering committee monitors the implementation of its recommendations and the percent safe on the target behavior. If the percent safe is not improving, the committee refines its recommendations by reviewing and repeating its analysis, perhaps with new or better information. When the goal of 95%–100% safe is met for several consecutive reporting periods (the exact number of periods depends on how frequently the practice targeted for improvement occurs), the committee decreases the amount of attention that it, the observers, and management pay to that practice. Using the same steps, it selects another practice that is causing concern. The committee may decide to delete a targeted practice from the observation checklist when it has achieved 95%–100% safe for a year or more or when revising the checklist.

22.1 Problem-Solving Steps

Step 1

Review the Pareto chart of percent safe on all checklist practices for the last reporting period. Which practices were less than 100% safe?

---

[7] Grainne Matthews made significant contributions to this chapter.

Step 2A

Review the Pareto chart of the number of concerns on practices that were less than 100% safe for the last reporting period. Which of these practices was observed to be unsafe most frequently?

Step 2B

Review the Pareto chart of the percentage of concerns on checklist practices that were less than 100% safe for the last reporting period. Which of these practices was observed as being unsafe a high percentage of the time?

Step 3

Review the trend (line) graph of the checklist practices that result from steps 1 and 2 for the last 12 months. Have these practices been less than 100% safe over time, or is the last reporting period an anomaly?

Step 4

Compare the observation data and injury reports. Of the practices that were observed as being unsafe, which ones have caused injuries since the process began and which ones could cause severe incidents or injuries? In this comparison, you will not select the behavior that is the most frequent concern; you will select an at-risk behavior that has the most potential to cause severe incidents. This is particularly important if you have not specifically addressed behaviors related to serious-incident prevention. Although practices worthy of special attention vary by industry, pay special attention to behaviors associated with fall protection, lockout/tagout, equipment guards, lifting heavy loads, trenching, and confined-space entry.

Step 5

Select the target practice. Combine the information from steps 1–4 to select a behavior to target for improvement based on the probability of injury (based on the number of injuries that have resulted), the severity of potential injury, exposure (the number of times employees perform the practice), consistency (based on the percent safe on a particular concern), and trends in your data.

Step 6A

Gather additional information. Does the steering committee have enough information to complete the ABC analysis? Steering committees often find they do not have enough information to complete a thorough and accurate ABC analysis. In such cases, committees will need to postpone the analysis and gather additional information so they can complete the analysis at the next meeting.

22.2 Methods of Gathering Additional Information

1. Interview the employees who perform the tasks that require this practice.
2. Observe situations where employees perform this practice.
3. Interview employees who have been involved in incidents.
4. Interview employees who have analyzed the incidents.
5. Read policies and procedures, manufacturer's instructions, job safety and job hazard analyses, and other materials that might describe the practice. Talk to experts about the practice.

Step 6B

Conduct an ABC analysis.

1. Pinpoint the safe practice:

    (a) in general, across the department or plant

    (b) for the specific situation described in observations and/or injury reports

If the steering committee decides on (a), identify all the *potential* antecedents and consequences of the practice. If it chooses (b), identify the *actual* antecedents and consequences of the practice in that situation. The steering committee members use their experience and knowledge of the situation, the comments made on the observation checklists, and the descriptions on the injury reports to identify antecedents and consequences. Criteria for a good pinpoint are as follows:

- *Observable:* One could see the action or the result of the action.
- *Specific:* It is specific enough that two people can agree on it. Not a vague label.
- *Objective:* It is a physical description, not a subjective interpretation or judgment.
- *Active:* Describes the desired actions or results. Does not include any negatives, such as *not*. Apply the "dead man rule": If a dead man can do it, it is not behavior.

2. Pinpoint the opposite, unsafe practice and repeat the analysis.
3. Analyze the antecedents and consequences that
   - support the safe practice
   - suppress the safe practice
   - support the unsafe practice
   - suppress the unsafe practice

Ensure that all possible factors that discourage the safe practice and encourage the unsafe practice are covered.

Step 7

Work with management to address facility or procedural issues that contribute to the unsafe act that you are targeting for improvement. If the potential injury is severe or if the exposure is high, look for ways to redesign the job to eliminate or reduce exposure to the risk or hazard. This may involve other groups, such as engineering and maintenance, and typically goes beyond the scope of the steering committee. Your safety professional will be familiar with the concept of hierarchy of controls that should be considered in addressing risk. The point is that while such interventions are usually beyond the scope of your steering committee, you must consider how to best change the work environment to support safe practices. When the risk can be eliminated or designed out of the job in a cost-effective manner, this is the best solution.

Step 8

Plan the behavioral improvement project:

1. List all the missing or weak contingency elements (antecedents and consequences) from the behavioral analysis.
2. Rank them by their influence on the practice.
3. Identify solutions to the two or three most important missing or weak antecedents or consequences.
4. Choose two or three solutions and specify actions to recommend to management or for the steering committee to implement. Include solutions that may be difficult, time consuming, or expensive to implement but might be the most important solutions. Also include several solutions that will be easy, quick, and inexpensive to implement even if they will not have the greatest impact. Achieving some early and visible success will encourage steering committee members, participating employees, and those who implement the improvement projects.
5. Assign steering committee members to implement, arrange for implementation, or recommend implementation to management. If solutions are recommended to management, especially with expensive or time-consuming improvements, prepare documentation of the analysis and the rationale for the choice.
6. Assign steering committee members to track action items and designate review dates or deadlines. Review improvement project action items regularly to recognize those who are supporting the solution.

22.3 Identifying Weak or Missing Contingency Elements

Antecedents

Because weak or missing antecedents can often be addressed with a one-time action, such as training, job aids, or equipment repair, antecedent solutions are easiest to implement. Table 22.1 lists antecedent approaches.

Table 22.1. Common Antecedent Problems and Solutions

Antecedent Problem	Antecedent Solution
SKILLS AND KNOWLEDGE	
Do employees know when and where to use the practice?	Provide education that includes relevant job theory and factors. Consider such job aids as signs, posters, checklists, and other training devices.
Can they perform the practice?	Provide training that includes demonstrations and practice to mastery. Ensure the selection process identifies individuals who are physically capable of performing the task safely.
TOOLS AND EQUIPMENT	
Are tools and equipment available?	Provide tools and equipment.
Are they in good condition?	Replace or repair tools and equipment.
Are they easily and quickly accessible?	Provide additional access or change location.
TIME AND SPACE	
Do the employees have time to perform the practice safely?	Redesign the work process or procedure.
Do they have the kind of workspace needed to perform the practice?	Reengineer the work area or the workflow.

Consequences

Address weak or missing consequences next because these often require ongoing effort, which can be difficult to sustain. Effective consequences are either certain (frequent) or immediate. Ineffective consequences are uncertain (infrequent) or delayed. The most important feature of consequences is their probability (i.e., how certain they are in) of following the practice. Size also matters: Large consequences are more effective than small consequences. Table 22.2 on the following page lists the consequence approach in order of preference.

Providing positive consequences will be most effective for improving your process, that is, for supporting quality observations, participation, and goal achievement (see guidelines for recognition and celebrations in Section 22.4 and in Chapter 13). In fact, consequences for most safety practices are difficult to manipulate. Adding tangible consequences that are soon, certain, and positive for performing a task safely is usually neither desirable nor practical.

If you are unable to redesign the job so that it provides better built-in or natural consequences (e.g., providing eye or hearing protection that is more comfortable), you will often need to increase the frequency of feedback on the targeted behavior through your observation process and site leadership. As you track your success toward achieving your improvement targets, you will need to share data on progress with the employees affecting that improvement, celebrate goal achievement, and recognize individuals who contributed to or assisted with implementation of your action plan.

Table 22.2. Common Problems and Solutions for Addressing Consequences

Consequence Problem	Consequence Solution
1. *Conceptual question:* Are too many negative consequences suppressing the safe practice?	*Conceptual solution:* Remove negative consequences for safe practice.
Practical question: Is performing the job safely uncomfortable, difficult, or slowing down task completion?	*Practical solution:* Redesign the job so that performing the job safely is more comfortable, easier, or quicker.
2. *Conceptual question:* Are there consequences for the unsafe practice?	*Conceptual solution:* Remove positive consequences for unsafe practice.
Practical question: Is the unsafe behavior more comfortable, easier, or quicker?	*Practical solution:* Redesign the job so that performing the job unsafely is less comfortable, requires more effort, or takes longer.
3. *Conceptual question:* Are there enough (certain) positive consequences supporting the safe practice?	*Conceptual solution:* Add frequent positive consequences.
Practical question: Are positive consequences designed into the task? Do observers and supervisors consistently provide positive feedback for the safe practices?	*Practical solution:* Redesign the job so that positive consequences are built into the task. Ensure observers and supervisors are monitoring and providing positive feedback on the safe practice.
4. *Conceptual question:* Are negative consequences for the unsafe practice ineffective?	*Conceptual solution:* (Last resort.) Add negative consequences.
Practical question: Are negative consequences designed into the task? Is coaching certain? Do supervisors understand and consistently enforce disciplinary policies when appropriate?	*Practical solution:* Redesign the job so that negative consequences are built into the task. Ensure observers and supervisors are monitoring and providing corrective feedback on the safe practice. Ensure disciplinary action is taken when appropriate.

Step 9

Use the process to support the intervention:

1. Meet with employees to explain why the steering committee chose the new target practice (show the data) and what the committee plans to do or to recommend be done (show ABC analysis). Ask employees if they have any suggestions.
2. Guide employees in setting a reasonable improvement goal for percent safe on that practice for the next reporting period (see guidelines for setting goals in Section 22.4).
3. Ask employees to choose a celebration for achieving the goal from a list of two or three options.

4. Ask observers to focus on the new target practice with observation and feedback.
5. Post the trend (line) graph of the target practice with the goal marked for the next reporting period. Update the graph as soon as the reporting period is complete. Discuss the data during department or plant meetings.
6. Schedule the celebration as soon as the goal is met. Recognize individuals for working toward the goal even before it is met and especially during the celebration.
7. Recognize individuals who implement recommended interventions (e.g., maintenance staff, engineers, trainers, and managers).

22.4 Guidelines for Setting Goals

Review all safety data at regular steering committee meetings to identify checklist practices to be targeted by improvement projects or process measures to be addressed, such as percentage of participation.

Lead employees in setting goals regarding a targeted practice or other measures during area meetings:

1. Solicit input from employees who are unable to attend area meetings.
2. The smaller the group to which a goal applies, the more effective it is in motivating the group's behavior. The larger the group, the less impact each individual feels his or her behavior will have on achieving the goal. The best practice is therefore to have each area set its own goal. (However, this practice requires separate graphs and data analysis for each area and can be time consuming.)
3. If goals are to be set for the entire organization, the steering committee will need to obtain input from all employees, which can be difficult. The best approach is to hold one large meeting where everyone sees the data and decides the goal. (However, it is usually necessary to obtain the input of each shift, department, or team separately and combine them in some way, such as by using the average suggested goal to set the organization goal.)

Ask employees to select goals by determining current performance relative to the baseline on the trend (line) graph, where they would eventually like to be (the ultimate goal is usually 95%–100%), and reasonable steps to get there:

1. The first goal is best set at the maximum level obtained during baseline.
2. Subsequent goals are set in increments no greater than the current variation from a prior goal. For example, if the maximum variation in percentage of participation is 5%, then a reasonable subsequent goal would be 5% over the current level.
3. New goals are set only when current goals are met. Thus, current goals may be in effect for varying lengths of time.

Once the new goal has been chosen, ask employees to select a celebration from several choices that will be the reward for attaining that goal. If a novel celebration is suggested (i.e., one not on the list of options), the steering committee may offer to explore that as a possibility for a future goal.

Mark the chosen goal and celebration on graphs of the percent safe for that target practice. Provide feedback on progress toward the goal by updating graphs and discussing data in meetings.

22.5 Conclusion

In summary, the data-driven problem-solving process outlined in this chapter provides steering committees with an effective methodology for identifying and addressing key safety practices in need of improvement. By gathering data, conducting root cause analyses, and involving employees in setting improvement goals and selecting celebrations, steering committees can implement targeted interventions that will drive safer behaviors over time. The key is to start small, focus on one or two priority areas, monitor progress regularly, and refine approaches as needed. A thoughtful, collaborative improvement process that engages all stakeholders can transform a safety culture and prevent injuries. With persistence and commitment to continuous learning, steering committees have the potential to lead their organizations to world-class safety performance.

CHAPTER 23

Other Support Programs[8]

The lists below identify other process components and programs that may be useful in supporting your safety improvement efforts. The process components are important, and each is worth considering as a key element of your safety process. The other programs represent a sample of optional activities that may be part of your promotional efforts when kicking off Values-Based Safety (VBS) or that may be useful elements of action plans developed by the steering committee to assist in achieving improvement targets.

23.1 Additional Safety Process Components

- process safety reviews
- close-call program
- involvement in incident investigations
- safety suggestion system
- safety orientation for new employees and contractors

23.2 Supplemental Safety Programs

- contest to name the VBS process
- worker-designed safety slogans and logos
- small group discussions of values
- presentations from process champions
- safety process conference
- safety day celebrations
- safe-behavior pledge cards
- public safety declarations
- verbal feedback support cards

---

8 Author Terry McSween is indebted to Scott Geller (1989) for many of the ideas presented in this chapter. Scott is one of the true gurus of the BBS field.

- tokens for awards or lottery
- "safety share" discussions
- off-the-job safety programs
- presentations or question-and-answer sessions with management representatives
- creation of a VBS process support group

Process safety reviews, involvement in incident investigations, and the safety suggestion system are key elements of the safety process for many organizations. You may wish to consider several of the suggested programs as part of your initial implementation in helping to reduce resistance to your new VBS process. For example, you might decide to have several small group discussions on values prior to your initial kickoff meeting.

In addition, you can arrange a variety of education and training programs covering topics such as standard safety practices both on and off the job. Examples of on-the-job educational programs include courses on lifting and back safety, protective equipment, first aid, and emergency response. Off-the-job safety programs might include courses on yard care safety, common household incidents, gun safety, boating safety, and defensive driving.

23.3 Additional Safety Process Components

Process safety reviews. The real key to safety is designing it into the process. Safety has to be engineered into the design and layout of a site. Use process safety reviews to ensure fail-safe engineering of equipment and controls. Such reviews are technically complex studies that involve careful analysis of "what if" questions about what could go wrong at each step of a process. The reviews need to be a standard step for all new construction and de-bottlenecking efforts. Depending on the nature of your industry, you may also need a group that conducts a regular process safety review in each area.

Close-call program. Close calls are what we used to call "near misses." A close-call program is an important component of a total safety process. Organizations must have a process through which associates can identify situations that could have resulted in injuries or catastrophic process failures. A safety committee should investigate close-call incidents with the objective of preventing actual future occurrences. The key to a successful close-call program is establishing a positive system that encourages honest reporting. Close calls can be the basis for case-study discussions during safety meetings. Employees might develop videos showing close-call situations for use in training and discussion in safety meetings. In developing case studies or videos, be careful not to make the process punishing to employees who have honestly reported such events. This type of process is particularly important in documenting process upsets that could have resulted in catastrophic outcomes.

Involvement in incident investigations. Representative employees should participate in investigating incidents in their work areas. They are often in the best position to help identify and understand the factors that led to the incident. In addition, their involvement helps create ownership and acceptance of the investigation report and resulting recommendations. Their participation in the investigation positions them to help explain what happened so that others in the area can more fully appreciate the report and the rationale for new procedures and preventive measures.

Employee participation in incident investigations can further result in more accurate conclusions from such investigations. In a project involving a bagging operation, several members of a VBS process design team participated with the incident review board to investigate an incident that occurred during the final design and implementation of a new safety process. The design team members were employees who worked in the area where the incident occurred. They were able to verify that the procedure the employee had followed was common practice even though it was not part of the documented procedure. As a result, the incident investigation faulted the system and recommended that supervisors and employees in the area change their work practices to match the formal procedure. Without the input of these employees, however, the review board would have accepted a preliminary finding that the employee was at fault for not following the correct procedure.

Safety suggestion system. For a VBS process to gain credibility, management must be proactive in addressing safety-related maintenance issues. Employees must see such issues being systematically addressed or at least see management's plan for addressing them over a period of time. A safety suggestion system is one way to help get employees involved in identifying such issues.

Employees are often in the best position to identify safety hazards in their work areas. A safety suggestion system is a good way to identify hazards, particularly maintenance items and hazardous conditions, that need correction. Such a system requires a process for reviewing suggestions, assigning priority to those that need to be addressed, tracking their status to completion, and providing feedback to the employee(s) who originated them. Also, the steering committee should provide recognition to employees who make significant safety-related suggestions.

Various studies have documented that the key to making suggestion systems work is providing a clear, immediate response to each suggestion and keeping employees updated on the status of their suggestions. Posting a summary report that lists all active suggestions and their status is often the best way to keep employees informed. Generally, someone on the safety team takes responsibility for tracking the status and resolution of employee suggestions, posting an updated summary for employees, and reporting the status to either the steering committee or management.

Safety orientation for new employees and contractors. The orientation of new employees is a critical element of a safety program, and too often safety gets lost in an orientation filled with human resource issues ranging from company policies to insurance forms. New employees should receive a checklist that includes a list of specific safety items they need to discuss with their supervisor when they enter the work area for the first time. Many organizations need to pay more attention to safety during orientation. The observation process is an ideal method for providing a safety orientation for new employees and contractors. New employees can review the observation checklist with their supervisors and participate in the observation process as part of their own orientation. The observation checklist can also be a formal part of the start-of-work meeting with new contractors or contractor employees. It can help clarify the expectations for contract help and lead to a discussion of the observation process and how follow-up to safety compliance will be provided.

23.4 Supplemental Safety Programs

Contest to name VBS process. While designing the observation process or shortly after implementation, consider holding a contest to name your VBS process. Such a contest is usually coordinated by the design team. The team will have to plan the rules for the contest and the procedure for submitting a name, launch a campaign for promoting the contest to employees, choose the prizes for winners, and determine how entries will be judged. Such a contest is a good way to begin introducing the VBS process to employees.

Worker-designed safety slogans and logos. In another common safety program, the steering committee holds a contest for employee-generated safety slogans and/or logos for the VBS process. The winning slogans and logos can become the basis for signs, electronic message boards, T-shirts, or posters promoting the VBS process within the plant or work area.

Small group discussions of values. After your design team has completed its work on values, you will need a process for communicating the new values to all employees. One of the most effective ways to accomplish this objective is to involve small groups of employees in discussions about practices that support each value statement. Small group discussions can be conducted during normal safety meetings with a spokesperson for each group presenting a summary to the other groups. Before the discussion begins, ask employees to ensure that their practices are concrete and observable (see the discussion on pinpointing in Chapter 21). Consider conducting this type of small group discussion exercise prior to your kickoff meetings.

Presentations from process champions. Either during the kickoff meeting or in special safety meetings held after that meeting, you may want to invite individuals from other parts of the company to discuss their experiences with the VBS process. These guests could be members of the design team, representatives from management, or employees who participated in successful implementation efforts elsewhere in the company. (Note that giving employees an opportunity to visit other locations to talk about an area's successes is a good way to provide recognition for some of that area's participants.) By discussing the similarities and differences between how each site implemented the process, you can learn how to enhance your own efforts and possibly avoid some mistakes made by others.

Safety process conference. Your company might hold a company-wide safety conference. The conference agenda might include a combination of training sessions, a celebration, and social events. The format might include several blocks of concurrent training sessions, presentations or posters from safety teams describing their successful efforts, and a catered luncheon or picnic with an entertaining keynote speaker.

Safety day celebrations. Companies will often sponsor a day-long celebration to kick off special programs or applaud the success of their efforts. Activities could include a company picnic with games and guest speakers, a conference with meetings and seminars, or a combination of events, such as dinners, mixers, and awards ceremonies.

Safe-behavior pledge cards. Safe-behavior pledge cards can be an effective way to initiate a program. They may identify a specific behavior, such as proper lifting or correctly using seat belts, or complex sets of behavior such as compliance with a list of pinpointed safe practices. The idea is to get employees to make a personal commitment to a specific goal, ideally for a fixed period. For example, you might decide to have a seat belt campaign during April and ask everyone to commit to wearing their seat belts 100% during that month.

Public safety declarations. This variation on the safe-behavior cards can take several forms. Again, the purpose is to have employees make a public commitment to achieving a specific compliance goal. It might be in combination with a safety day ceremony on a stage during which employees shake their manager's hand and make a public commitment to comply with safety procedures and perhaps sign a written statement to the same effect that is later posted on the area's safety bulletin board.

Feedback support cards. Written cards can be an effective way to support verbal feedback as part of the observation process in a variety of ways. Observers may distribute thank-you cards to employees who are performing safely on the day they are observed. Alternatively, observers may give the cards to employees to support a specific safe behavior that is being emphasized by a special campaign, such as proper lifting in conjunction with a back safety campaign. Or the observers may give the cards to everyone in an area with 100% safe performance.

Such thank-you cards can also be part of the recognition program. They may be redeemable for a drink in the cafeteria or might be part of a lottery. Another approach is for the company to contribute money to charity based on the number of cards earned by employees. For example, for each thank-you card earned by employees, the company might drop $1 into a collection bowl. Including stickers to place on hard hats on one side of the thank-you cards might be used to provide recognition to employees who are contributing to this process. Figure 23.1 presents an example of a positive-feedback card that might be part of your VBS effort.

THANK YOU FOR WORKING SAFELY

You were observed working safely and are being recognized by management for following company procedures and policies and for protecting yourself, fellow workers, and family.

The company would like to recognize your actions, so please present this card to your foreperson or safety department to receive your recognition.

Figure 23.1. *Sample positive-feedback card.*

Similar cards can be used to facilitate corrective feedback. Cards for this purpose may take several forms. Some companies provide a number of corrective feedback cards to employees to use independently of the observation process, with the idea that they pass them on to employees who are working unsafely. Other cards make personal statements such as these: "Asking me to look the other way is like asking me not to care, and you are much too important" or "Asking me to overlook a simple safety violation would be like asking me to compromise my entire attitude toward the value of your life."

As you may recall, DuPont uses Safety Training Observation Program (STOP) cards as part of its safety process. Employees complete and turn in these cards to document the types of unsafe practices they observe, but they do not include the name of the person or persons performing the unsafe practices. The problem, as mentioned earlier, is that these cards focus almost exclusively on what employees are doing unsafely, rather than what they are doing right.

Tokens for awards or lottery. This support device is similar to the feedback cards except that the employees receive tokens that may entitle them to prizes or special awards. The tokens may be items such as bingo tokens or lottery tickets. They may have a specific value, such points that are used to earn specific awards, or they may allow those who earn them to participate in an award drawing. Safety bingo is one common application. As emphasized throughout this book, such efforts are more effective if they are based on safety compliance rather than simply going without an incident. These approaches can be combined so that bingo tokens are earned based on observations, but the game ends if anyone has an injury.

"Safety share" discussions. Safety-sharing discussions can provide an effective safety meeting agenda. After the meeting gets started, simply go around the room and have all participants share something safety related they have done in the last 24 hours (or 48 hours, or even the past week).

Your steering committee might plan a starting point on such discussions around specific aspects of the observation process. For example, observers might recognize groups of employees who achieved 100% safe or specific individuals for particular safety practices. In addition, observers may want to share specific unsafe activities or conditions they believe other employees should be aware of. As with other aspects of the VBS process, you should take care not to identify specific individuals who were observed engaging in an unsafe practice. These discussions should be kept positive and educational, always avoiding embarrassment or humiliation.

Off-the-job safety programs. Not all of your efforts need to focus on safety in the workplace. You can also create programs focused on safety off the job. These programs might simply consist of a safety meeting in the spring on boat safety or at the beginning of the hunting season on gun safety. Or they may be more complete campaigns targeting seat belt use or preventing off-the-job back injuries.

For example, some plants have initiated seat belt campaigns with posters, training videos shown during safety meetings, and other activities. In some cases, the site management staff has arranged to stand at the entry gate and pass out silver dollars or other tokens to everyone entering (or leaving) the parking lot wearing their seat belt.

(For additional suggestions on increasing seat belt use, see Geller, 1984; Geller and Hahn, 1984; and Geller and Lehman, 1991.)

Presentations or question-and-answer sessions with management representatives. A common complaint from employees is lack of direct contact with management. One way to enhance such interactions and support your VBS process is to arrange for a member of upper management to lead one of your regularly scheduled safety meetings from time to time. You might ask these managers to prepare a brief discussion on their vision or expectations regarding safety and allow time for questions and answers. Your steering committee might develop a list of questions, then arrange for your manager to prepare for and speak to the questions on the list in case the employees do not spontaneously generate many questions.

Creation of a VBS process support group. You may wish to create a VBS support group within your organization. This group could include representatives from several locations who would serve as a sounding board and resource for one another. On a larger scale, you could provide a forum for several groups to share their successes and discuss how they have handled challenges in the VBS process.

23.5 Coordinate Special Programs

The key to maximizing the value of your safety efforts is to coordinate your ongoing safety process and your special programs. Thus, if your plant typically experiences a high rate of incidents during the summer, you might have a special program for the "dog days of summer," for example. You might design a kickoff meeting with a presentation from management, use a safety pledge card for an appropriate time period, conduct a slogan contest related to the dog-days theme, and give every employee one thank-you card for distribution. Ask them to hand the card to another employee during the time period, noting on the card why it was given. At the end of the period, if the area proved successful in not having an incident, you might arrange an *unannounced* special celebration and provide awards to the employees who earned the most thank-you cards.

CHAPTER 24

Long-Term Case Studies

The two case studies that follow show that the Values-Based Safety (VBS) process can be long lasting and help support a sustained level of safety performance for extended periods of time.

24.1 Values-Based Safety in a Refinery[9]

Implementing a VBS process in a large organization with many self-contained areas presents numerous challenges, but the long-term success of this VBS process speaks for itself. A major oil refinery with two large facilities in the United States overcame these obstacles in an effort to improve safety performance. Before behavioral consultation was sought, both plants relied primarily on traditional safety methods to prevent safety incidents, such as focusing on lost-workday incident rates. Despite these safety efforts, there was ample room to improve safety practices.

The initial plant was comprised of six self-contained areas:

1. power thermal
2. central maintenance
3. catalytic cracking unit (CAT)
4. acid-alkylation treatment unit (AAT)
5. oil movement
6. reformer

When the VBS process was initially implemented, this facility had approximately 1,700 employees.

Phase 1: Pilot Area

The power thermal area of the initial plant, with approximately 200 employees, was chosen as the pilot group because it held the most room for improvement. In 1992 alone, this area had five recordable injuries and three lost-workday incidents.

The steering committee for the power thermal area consisted of 10 hourly employees and one manager; the committee leader was always an hourly employee. The committee held weekly, or sometimes biweekly, meetings. Consultants trained the

---

9   Myers et al. (2010).

steering committee members in VBS process methodology in 3 days, then together designed the safety process for each unit within the area in sessions of 2 days a week over 3 weeks, a total of 6 days. The VBS process training of all employees, from the managerial level down, was accomplished by training 20 employees at a time over 8-hour periods.

Conducting safety observations was strongly emphasized, and all employees were required to practice conducting observations using videos of their own work areas. After training, participation as a safety observer was strictly voluntary.

The steering committee recorded three primary measurements from the start of implementation:

1. the number of observations conducted
2. the percentage of participation (defined as conducting two observations a month)
3. types of safety concerns

Figures 24.1 and 24.2 on the following page clearly depict the success of the VBS process implementation. Figure 24.1 demonstrates an inverse relationship between the number of safety observations conducted and the occurrence of accidents. The dramatic decrease in the number of recordable incidents is shown in Figure 24.2. In fact, the single recordable injury in 1994 occurred during the first quarter of the year, prior to implementing the VBS process. The power thermal area had no recordable injuries for 2 years after implementation and no lost-workday incidents 4 years after implementation in the pilot area.

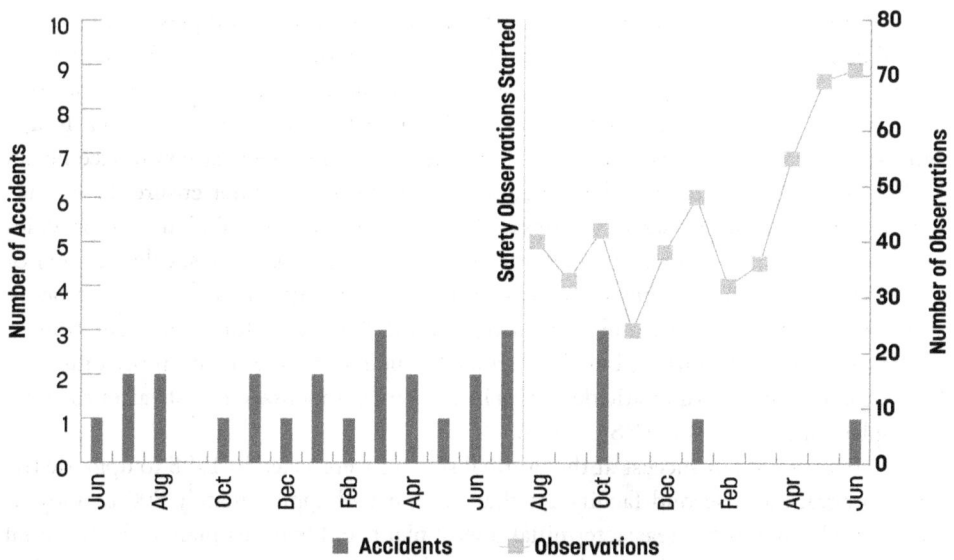

Figure 24.1. Inverse relationship between number of safety observations and number of accidents during the initial implementation.

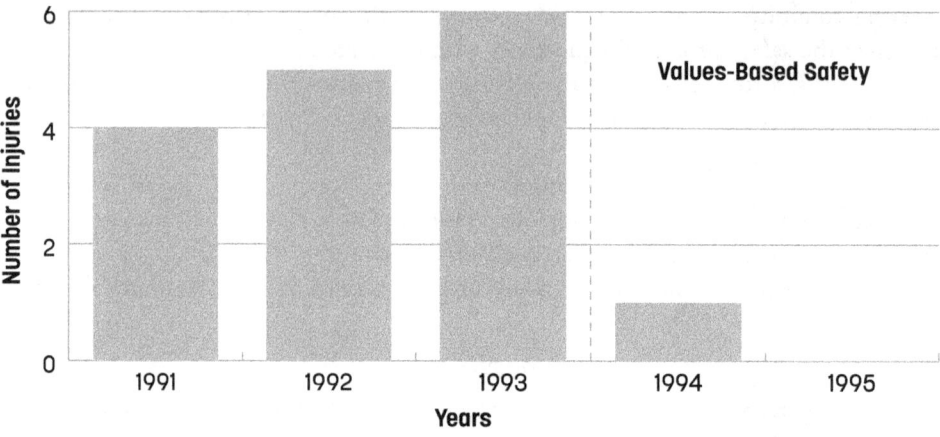

Figure 24.2. *Recordable incident rates for the thermal area before and after VBS process implementation.*

Phase 2: Plant-Wide Implementation

The VBS process helped the site achieve and maintain a low rate of injuries (see Figure 24.3). The five remaining areas followed the same approach outlined above. Central maintenance began implementation in 1994, CAT followed in 1996, AAT commenced in 1997, and the oil movement and reformer areas began in 1998. To overcome the communication barriers that often result from having many self-contained areas, the steering committee designed and utilized several techniques to encourage critical communication. All areas have bulletin boards within each unit solely dedicated to the VBS process. Graphs of the three primary measurements, campaign or contest announcements, and minutes of steering committee meetings are frequently updated and posted within each area. In 2000, the plant-wide steering committee began to distribute a newsletter and developed a safety website to further ensure dissemination of the organization's safety progress. Management at the initial plant also provides funds specifically for the continuous improvement (e.g., recognitions, celebrations) of the VBS process, another key element in the long-term success of its safety process. The benefits of hard work and dedication toward the successful implementation of a VBS process are countless, but the financial benefits are one of the most dramatic. Figure 24.4 shows the dramatic decreases in workers' compensation costs after successful implementation of the VBS process.

Because of our success at the original site, we were asked in 1998 to upgrade the safety program at a second facility. At that time, it had approximately 800 employees and four self-contained areas: a terminal, a west plant, and two east plants. The terminal area was already using behavior-based safety (BBS), but the process was floundering because of infrequent observations, poor recordkeeping, and insufficient communication. For this reason, we began VBS process implementation with the west plant. The

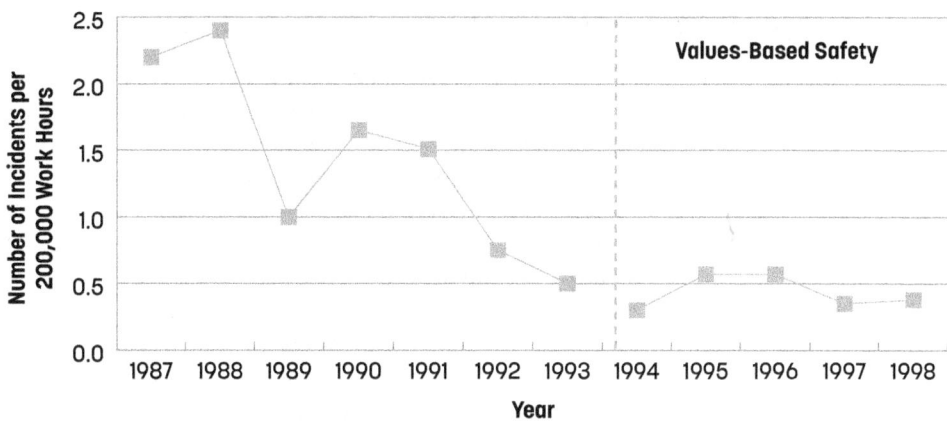

Figure 24.3. Lost-workday case rates for the overall refinery before and after VBS process implementation.

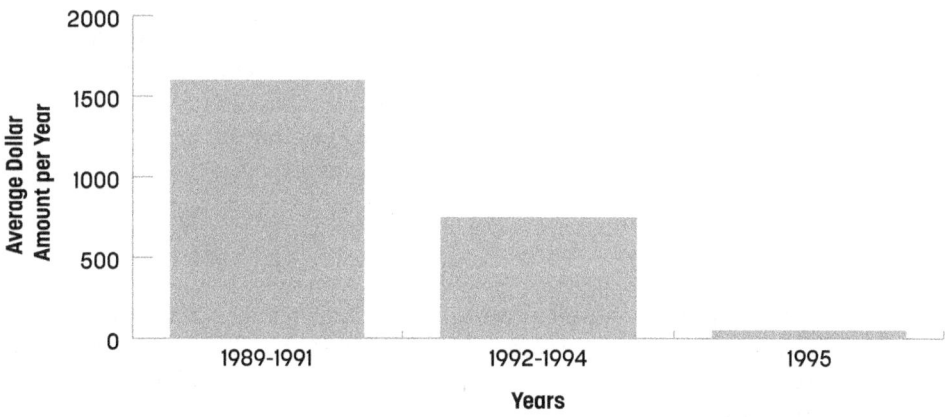

Figure 24.4. Direct costs of injuries for the years before and first year after implementing behavioral safety.

process used was similar to the one described throughout this book, but it was modified to overcome the challenges of an organization with numerous self-contained areas. Terminal area employees attended the observer training provided for the west plant employees and worked to revive their BBS process. In 2001, the VBS process was also implemented in the two east plants.

In recent decades, the corporation, owner of approximately seven businesses worldwide, identified BBS as a best practice and encouraged its implementation throughout the organization. This was a convincing validation of the success of the VBS process described in this book.

24.2 Employee Safety Process at an Ore-Processing Facility[10]

The production of alumina, which is extracted from bauxite ore, is a business with many hazards. Employees work in situations where they are at risk of burns from caustic chemicals, hot liquids, and extremely high heat as well as of injuries resulting from the traditional hazards common to most industrial settings, such as slips and trips. This particular plant, however, had more problems than most. It was built in the early 1940s, and the company had not invested adequately to keep the facility in good mechanical condition. As a result, the plant was in such bad physical condition that workers had to wear acid suits just to walk into the production areas. The organization had cut its injury rates in half the year before we began the project but still experienced a significant number of lost-workday injuries. Both the management and the safety committee were very interested in making further improvements.

Given the serious problems with the physical condition of the plant, we were hesitant to undertake this project. However, employees believed that management was serious about improving safety, and we became convinced that management was serious about safety and would do all it could to maintain and upgrade the facility in conjunction with the behavioral process. These management efforts helped the behavioral process to be successful.

To assist in improving the safety process, we first conducted a safety assessment, as detailed in Chapter 7. A preestablished company safety team became the design team. Most of its 15 members were hourly workers. Quality Safety Edge consultants conducted a 3-day workshop on VBS and then facilitated four 2-day meetings to design a safety process that included the following components:

Training

One goal of the safety process was to have all employees trained in conducting observations. However, given the large number of employees, a novel approach to observation training had to be taken. To accomplish our goal, we held train-the-trainer sessions in which we trained 12 area safety representatives on how to conduct observations, manage safety data, create action plans, and deliver feedback. These safety representatives then trained the other employees in their areas.

Kickoff Event

Following safety representative training, the company scheduled a huge weekend family day to kick off the new safety process. Employees and their families were invited to a park the company had reserved for the event. The plant manager participated, and safety representatives were introduced. The following Monday, three large site meetings were held to explain the process and trained safety representatives conducted small area meetings to discuss questions and details.

---

10 Myers et al. (2010).

Observations

Multiple levels of the organization were involved in the observation process. The goal was to have hourly employees and general forepersons conduct at least one observation per week and managers and department heads conduct at least three observations per week. Conducting observations and being observed were voluntary.

Feedback

Observers gave immediate feedback to the employees observed. Percentage data on concerns and safe acts were then posted on the area safety boards. The crew safety representatives would review the data at monthly safety meetings and send the accumulated observation sheets to the process steering committee for review every 3 months. In addition, safety performance and safety issues were addressed during regular toolbox meetings.

Recognition

Area team celebrations were based on safety process milestones. The process steering committee monitored area team progress and established criteria for recognition. Awards ranged from Starbucks® gift certificates to paid time off from work. As the process has matured, recognition items have changed to such things as T-shirts, coolers, and jackets for participation combined with no lost-workday accidents.

Safety Communication

The company regularly distributed a newsletter that included items and anecdotes regarding the safety process, safety performance levels, and anonymous discussions about the causes and prevention of any injuries that had occurred. The newsletter also provided recognition items and information about improvements initiated as a result of the behavioral process and stressed the importance of safe work practices at all times. Each group's overall safety performance was discussed, and safety improvement strategies were developed during monthly steering committee meetings and shared with work crews in their monthly safety meetings. A steering committee member usually attended each of these monthly departmental meetings.

Although it took several years to train the majority of employees to conduct observations, as of 2003, over 10,000 observations were conducted each year. The graph in Figure 24.5 presents data in the initial phase of implementation. It also shows the critical inverse relationship between the number of observations and the number of injuries. That is, as the number of observations increased, the number of accidents decreased. These data helped management and employees build support for greater participation and an increased frequency of observations.

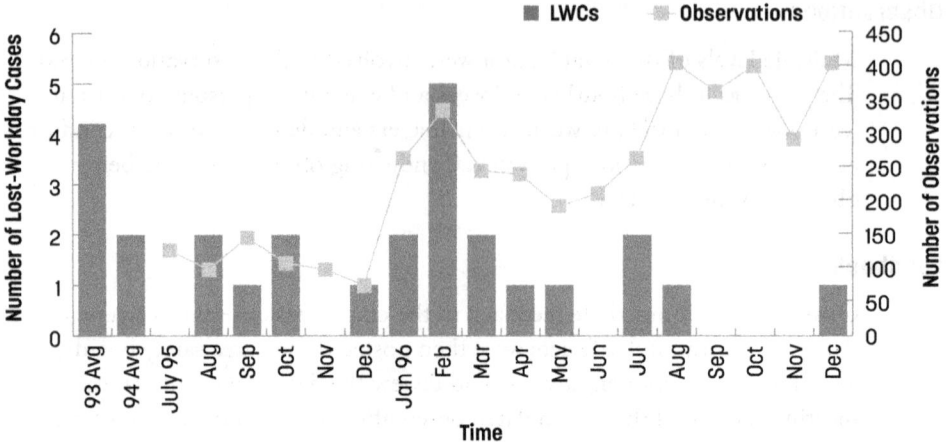

Figure 24.5. *Data showing the inverse relationship between observations and lost-workday cases (LWCs) during implementation at an ore-processing plant.*

As shown in Figure 24.6, since its implementation in 1995, the safety process demonstrated continued success for more than 6 years. Moreover, in the later few years the company twice achieved more than 1 million hours without a lost-workday accident.

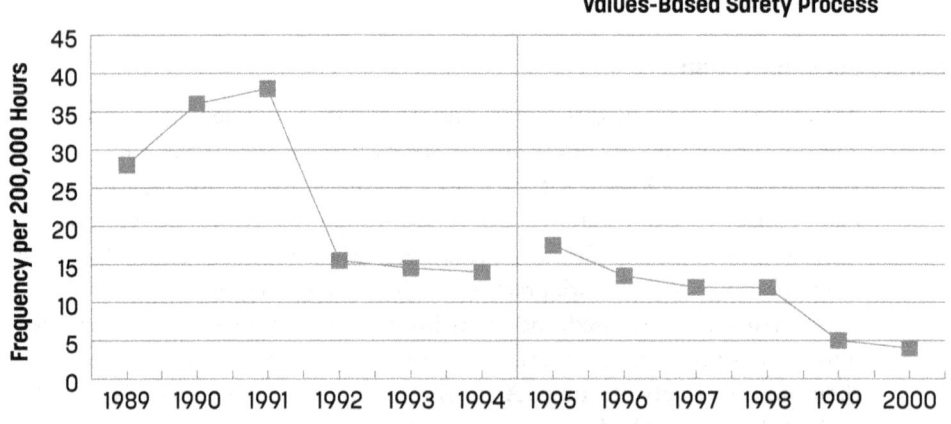

Figure 24.6. *Recordable injury rates before and after implementation of a VBS process (OSHA incident rate).*

The company not only achieved significant reductions in both OSHA-recordable and lost-workday incidents but also had a significant reduction in accident severity. The graph in Figure 24.7 reflects a steady decline in severity and fairly stable results in the last few years displayed.

Another important lesson learned from this project led to this being the last time we used a mentoring approach to train observers. We typically achieved much higher levels of participation when employees participated in formal training led by consultants or internal trainers. Formal workshops not only trained employees in how to conduct observations but also imparted why observations are so important. Although the project was ultimately successful, building support and generating participation in observations took much longer than was typical of our implementation efforts.

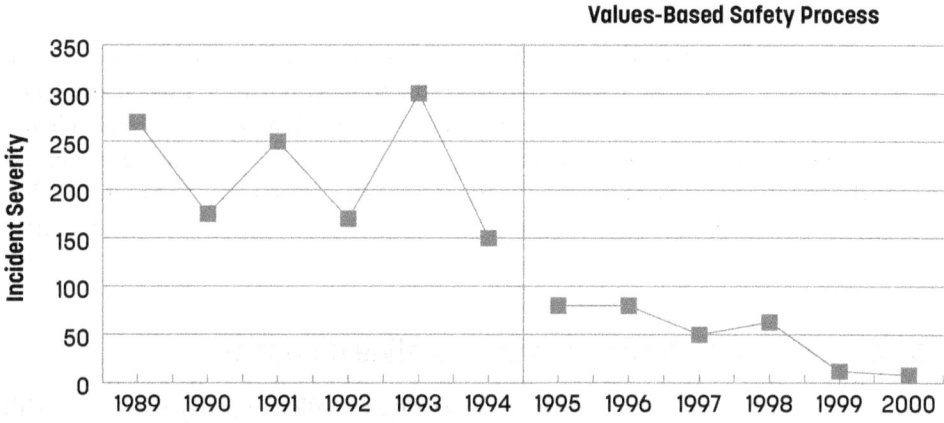

Figure 24.7. Severity rate of injuries before and after implementation of the VBS process.

CHAPTER 25

Self-Observation Case Studies[11]

As we discussed in Chapter 19, a behavior-based safety (BBS) process based on self-observations may be more appropriate for some companies, particularly when applying behavioral safety to employees who work in isolation. One research study has documented that a self-observation-based approach resulted in a significant increase in safe driving practices by bus drivers (Olson & Austin, 2001). The three case studies that follow show that this approach can significantly improve safe behaviors and safety outcome measures.

25.1 Canadian Gas Production and Pipeline Company

Successful safety implementations are often challenging when dealing with lone workers, but sometimes a simple solution and frequent reinforcement are all that is necessary to achieve dramatic results. Such was the case with an organization that collects and processes natural gas. The BBS process we designed for this organization improved overall safety, interaction between employees and management, and employee participation that gave the employees a sense of empowerment.

At the time of consultation, the organization employed 60 workers who worked on wellheads and gas pipes in isolated areas. Safety statistics for the workers themselves were very good before implementation, with most accidents being vehicle related. We therefore designed our implementation to concentrate on two areas: decreasing the number of vehicle accidents and demonstrating the value of the safety process.

Together with a group of volunteer employees we developed a *driving safety index* in 3.5 hours. The index listed eight items related to safe driving—for example, wearing seat belts, not exceeding speed limits, and keeping windows clear. Next to each item were three columns for checking "yes," "no," and not applicable "(N/A)." A safety percentage was calculated by dividing the total number of boxes marked "yes" by the total number of marked boxes and multiplying by 100%. Drivers were contacted via radio to inform them when it was time to conduct a self-observation. Upon receiving the call, drivers pulled off the road and immediately completed the driving safety index. Observations were conducted three times a week during the first 2 months after implementation and two times each week thereafter. As is often the case with self-monitoring, some members of the organization were concerned that

---

[11] Ann Pinney and Alicia M. Alvero made significant contributions to this chapter.

inflated scores would be reported. We did not believe this to be a matter of critical concern because, at the least, the radio call to conduct an observation would prompt the drivers to think about their driving practices one time more than they would have otherwise.

Goals and reinforcement were managed by behavioral safety representatives (safety reps), a group of volunteer employees, but were not announced to the other lineworkers, who were simply told they would be rewarded for increases in safety. The original team safety goal, set by the safety reps, was 85%. When teams achieved this goal, they were given a reward, such as a sausage-and-biscuit breakfast. Deliveries of rewards were not announced in advance and thus served as "surprise" reinforcers, a tactic that encouraged employees to achieve increases in safety as often as possible in order not to miss the opportunity to receive a reinforcer. Although the deliveries were always a surprise, they did occur frequently enough to maintain high levels of safety performance.

Figures 25.1 and 25.2 on the following page show the solid effectiveness of the driving safety index. Figure 25.1 shows the increased average team levels of safe driving performance while Figure 25.2 shows the decrease in vehicle accidents, injuries requiring medical aid, and lost-workday incidents after the behavioral safety intervention. An index was also developed to monitor supervisor behavior. The *supervisor index* listed items related to their role in the safety process, such as these: hold safety meeting, provide feedback to employees on safety behaviors, post data on graph, and the like. Supervisors completed the index each time a driver was radioed to conduct a self-observation.

Because a formal positive reinforcement process was already in place, we were asked to tie that existing process to our new safety process. As a result, in addition to the reinforcer for increases in driving safety, three other reinforcers were set in place: peer-to-peer reinforcement, supervisor-to-employee reinforcement, and employee-to-supervisor reinforcement. In order to monitor these forms of reinforcement, each one was added to the appropriate index. The driving safety index therefore included a row to monitor the receipt of positive reinforcement from peers and supervisors (marked off as "yes" or "no"). Similarly, the supervisor index included a line to monitor the receipt of positive reinforcement from employees. But unlike the driving safety index, the supervisor index included a line for supervisors to monitor their own delivery of recognition to employees. Figure 25.3 shows the increased use of positive reinforcement.

The peer-to-peer reinforcement process also provided an example of employee-delivered reinforcement tied to a tangible personalized reinforcer. Employees were given five special certificates per quarter, each worth five "organizational dollars." The certificates were to be given by one employee to another when the former observed a safety-related task that they thought merited recognition. Receivers could use them toward the purchase of any article they wanted by simply attaching the certificate to the purchase receipt for reimbursement by the organization. Attached to each certificate was a tear-off portion that required the observer to list the specific observed action that resulted in awarding the certificate. These tear-off slips were collected, compiled

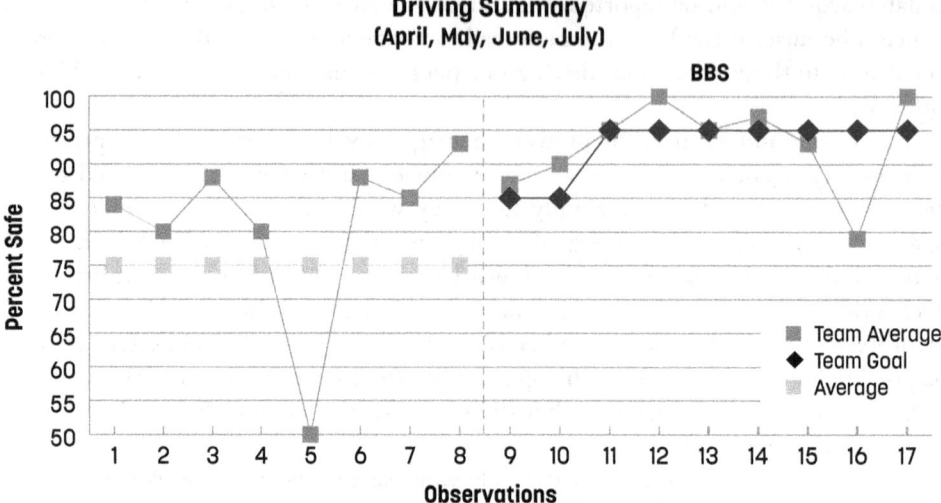

Figure 25.1. *Data on the percent of safe driving practices reported during self-observations by employees working in gas production fields and the plant.*

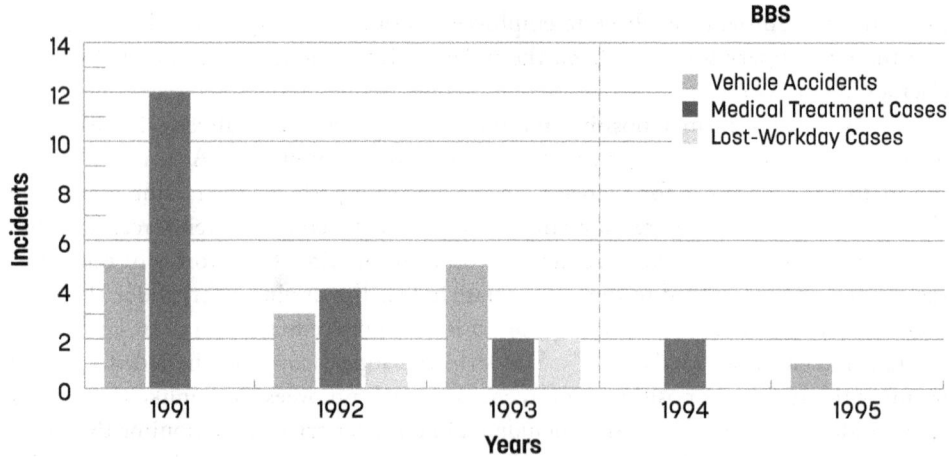

Figure 25.2. *Implementing a self-observation BBS process dramatically cut the rates of vehicle accidents, medical treatment cases, and lost-workday cases for employees at a gas plant.*

into a list, and publicly posted throughout the facility. Though no names were posted, these lists served the purpose of informing everyone about the types of behaviors that resulted in reinforcement. Employees who had not been given certificates used these lists as a valuable information resource. All employees became very judicious about how they awarded their certificates, feeling they needed to be earned instead of merely being given away.

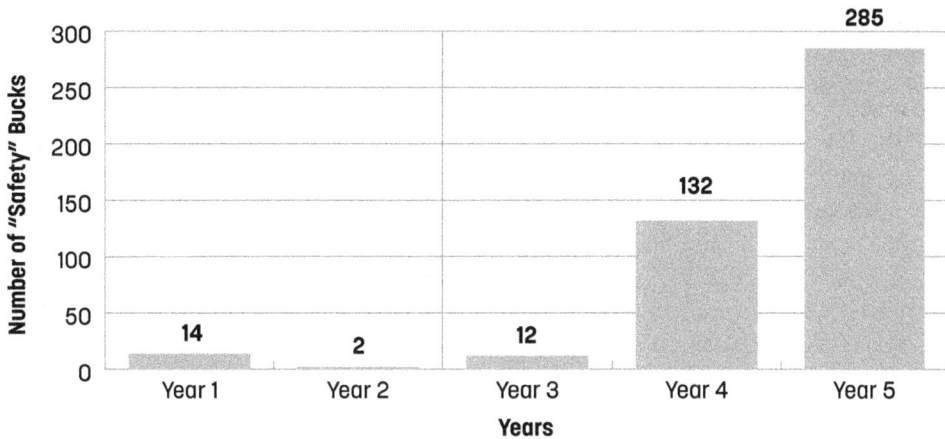

Figure 25.3. *The BBS process helped the organization increase the use of positive reinforcement as represented by the number of "safety bucks" delivered by both peers and supervisors.*

The supervisor-to-employee reinforcement involved the delivery of feedback, praise, and recognition for safety-related accomplishments. Employee-to-supervisor reinforcement also involved the delivery of feedback and recognition as well as gratitude for involvement.

Scorings of calculations and arrangements of surprise reinforcers were done by employee volunteers. All employees provided input regarding their reinforcer preferences, but what was delivered upon goal achievement was a surprise. Employees also provided input concerning the reinforcement budget regarding the monies allocated for the purchase of tangible reinforcers. During a safety meeting, 59 of the 60 employees voted to apply the allocated funds to safety reinforcers instead of traditional safety awards (e.g., employees had previously received prizes such as a television after working 6 months without an injury).

The results of this self-observation process combined with extensive reinforcement were overwhelming. Simply stated, the safety process transformed the organization. There was a dramatic increase in safety awareness, especially among new employees. As a result of employee involvement in developing the driving safety index and managing the reinforcement budget, employees felt an increased sense of empowerment and continued their participation in the process. Evidence of a strong desire to be involved was apparent during the first meeting after implementation. One employee related a concern about being unable to participate: "Sometimes I don't get a radio call to do an observation because of poor reception." The aversive relationship with management previously reported by employees was no longer existent. The safety process substantially increased communication between all members and across all levels of the organization.

One employee put it best: "Not only did safety improve, but every other aspect of our business improved."

25.2 Electric Utility

Organizations with unique occupations and a culture that lacks employee involvement require clever and creative behavioral interventions in order to succeed. Such was the case with a large power and light company that employs numerous lineworkers. These employees perform hazardous work on electrical lines, often in remote locations and always in teams of three. The BBS process created for these employees involved a combination of self- and peer-sampled observations.

Instead of developing a traditional safety checklist, the lineworkers created a *lineworker index* consisting of a list of safe acts necessary to perform each job safely. Each act was assigned a point value. During an observation, each team received a certain number of points for each act based on how safely each was being performed. For example, one act was described as "outrigger down and pads used" and was assigned 10 points. If the team had the outrigger down but did not use pads, they received 5 of the 10 points. The points received were totaled and a percentage was calculated using the following formula: number of points received divided by total number of assigned points multiplied by 100%. These percentages were calculated and graphed on location by the employee immediately after each observation.

Now that a clever intervention had been developed, how could we get it off the ground? We faced two significant challenges. First, how would we establish random sampling of observations? Second, how would we motivate employees to perform the observations? Our solution to both challenges was simple and extremely effective. A fishbowl full of slips of paper was placed near the exit of the lineworkers' station. Written on some slips was a specific time while others were blank. The times shown on the slips indicated when employees should conduct an observation on themselves and their team members. As employees exited the station to head toward a work site, they were asked to take a slip out of the bowl. To motivate participation, they would automatically receive a treat, such as a candy bar, when they did so. The response was extraordinary! Everyone wanted to participate. Employees began to set their wristwatch timers to the time indicated on their slips as a reminder to conduct safety observations, and they offered to pitch in money in order to increase the selection of treats.

Every Friday a group meeting was held to celebrate the safety process. Celebrations were twofold:

1. each team graph was recognized, simply for the time having been taken to conduct observations
2. any increases in safety that occurred throughout the week were recognized and praised

The process was also somewhat dependent on supervisory involvement. The process was more successful for supervisors who were more positive and encouraging. Teams whose supervisors inquired frequently about their safety progress usually experienced the highest levels of participation and safety.

The power and light company experienced substantial safety improvements as a result of our innovative behavioral safety implementation. Figure 25.4 demonstrates the

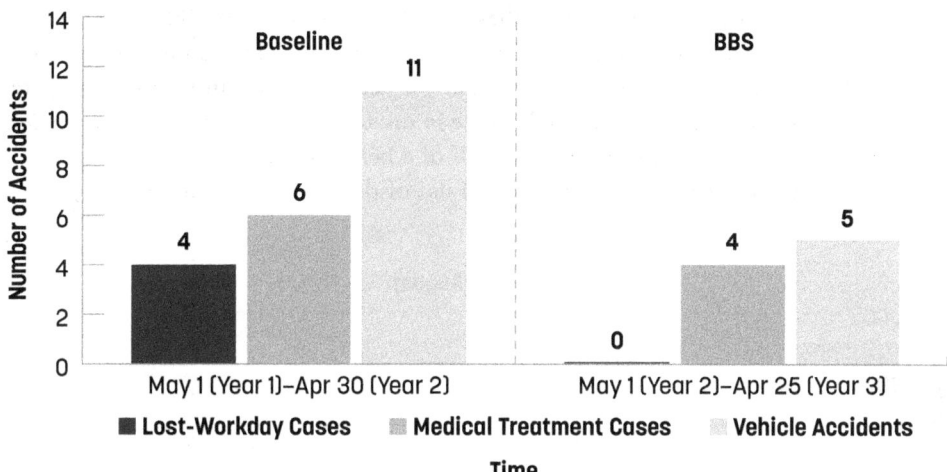

Figure 25.4. Self-observation BBS process in the pilot area at an electric utility helped eliminate lost-workday cases and significantly reduce minor injuries and vehicle accidents.

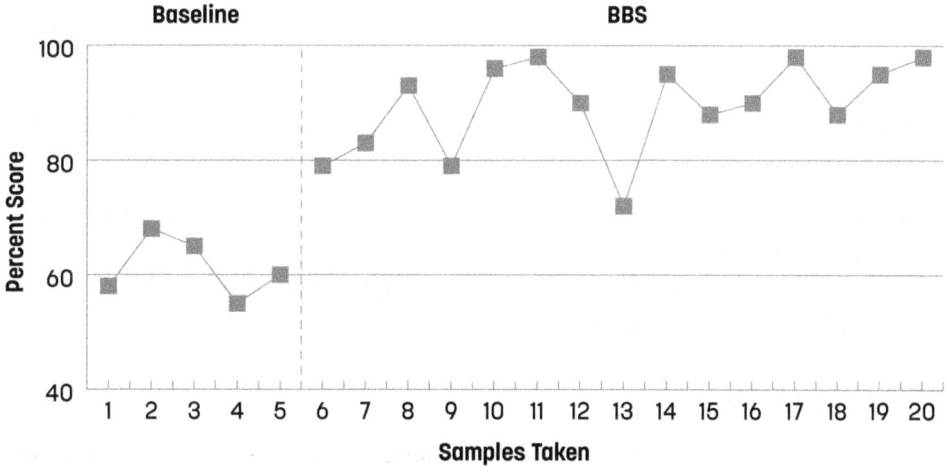

Figure 25.5. Self-observation safety scores before and after implementation.

significant decreases in lost-workday cases, injuries requiring medical treatment, and vehicle accidents after the behavioral implementation. Figure 25.5 illustrates the increase in safety scores after the intervention was implemented. The safety committee did not announce that employees were being observed while they collected the baseline data.

Baseline safety performance that had averaged 60% increased to an average of 90% after implementation of the BBS process.

Initially, safety implementation with the lineworkers was simply to be a pilot study, but as a result of word-of-mouth, maintenance personnel chose to implement the BBS process in their area as well. These employees were responsible for repairing the trucks used by the lineworkers. When word got around that the lineworkers were having so much fun and receiving treats and praise, they too wanted to participate. Figure 25.6 illustrates the substantial decrease in disabling injury severity that occurred throughout the entire organization as a result of a behavioral safety intervention in all areas. Due to the transportability and ease of use of the intervention developed for the

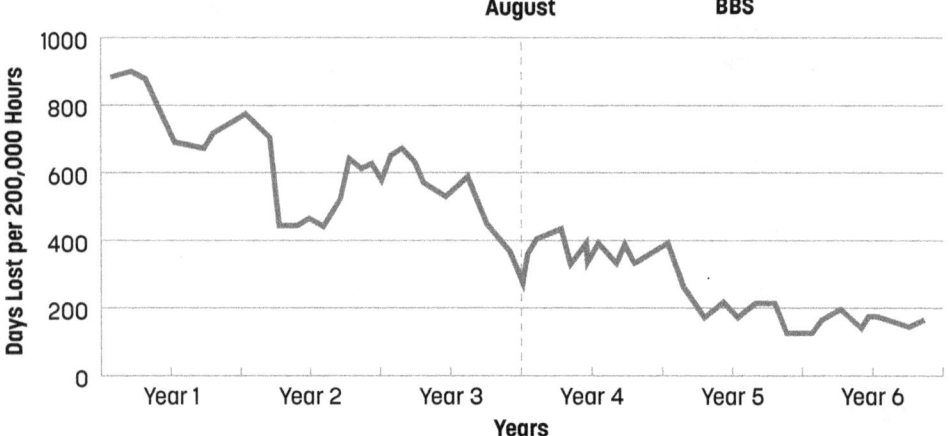

Figure 25.6. *Decrease in disabling injury severity after safety intervention at an electric utility.*

lineworkers, the maintenance department was able to implement its own safety process quickly and effectively.

Clearly, some organizations require only a quick, easy, and creative safety program to achieve dramatic positive results.

25.3 Logging Industry

Some organizations have a very tense and negative environment due to the extremely dangerous nature of the work involved and therefore do not welcome peer observations. Such was the case with an organization in the logging industry.

Loggers and fallers are responsible for cutting massive trees and harvesting immense amounts of wood. They work in isolated wooded areas surrounded by extremely hazardous conditions and *always* work with a partner. An initial examination suggested that a peer-to-peer observation system would best fit an organization without lone workers, but further investigation revealed otherwise.

First, relationships among employees were very tense and negative. Second, the organization was located in a state where employees would not be covered by disability if they were found responsible for an incident. Therefore, employees were extremely fearful and reluctant to participate in any program that would document their safety performance and could possibly link them to a hazardous action or, worse, a severe incident. As a result, employees took *extreme* caution in developing a data collection process that would ensure their anonymity and did not include peer-to-peer observation.

We began our consultation services with two divisions within the organization. Division 1 was comprised of fallers, those who worked up in the trees, and division 2 was largely made up of loggers, those who worked with the lumber on the ground. The implementation process was very similar for both divisions. It began with a 2-day training session attended by all management and a representative from each crew. As part of the training, representatives developed a sample safety index for their crew. Each index listed safe behaviors that were essential to performing their job without incident. Next, all employees attended a 3-hour "overview" session that outlined the safety process. At the end of the session, each crew elected whether or not to participate in the safety process. If the crew chose to participate, the safety consultant met with them to help build a specific safety index using the sample index as a guide.

The safety reps (employee volunteers) received more specific training concerning the rollout and maintenance of the process. First, the safety reps piloted the safety checklists and conducted several observations, thus allowing us to obtain baseline data. Next, they were trained on how to graph the safety data and reinforce participation and improvements in safety. Due to the existing tense environment, any amount of participation was initially reinforced. Unlike division 1, division 2 experienced a great deal of resistance to the safety process. Only two of the 30 employees initially volunteered, but by the end of the first quarter, 28 employees had volunteered to assist with the safety process. The specific reinforcement techniques used by the division 2 safety rep are discussed in further detail below.

Although the development of the safety indexes and management of the process were the same across both divisions, the observation system varied for each. Fallers initially engaged in peer prompts and self-observation. In other words, each employee would prompt their partner to conduct a self-observation using their *faller safety index*. The actual index form used by the fallers requires some further mention to help explain the caution taken to protect their anonymity. Fallers feared that they would be identified by their penmanship if their indexes required them to "mark off" items. Therefore, they developed a form that required them to punch holes next to each item. Using the end of their tape measurers, employees would punch a hole in the appropriate box for each item. After becoming familiar, and perhaps more comfortable, with the safety process, employees realized that their indexes were missing some critical ergonomic practices. Therefore, they developed another index that was then printed on the back of their existing index. At this time, division 1 moved into a combination of self-observation and peer-to-peer observation system. Employees realized that it was very difficult to self-observe the ergonomic items on the checklist and asked their peers to conduct observations on these items. The results of their unique observation system were substantial. Figure 25.7 on the following page displays division 1's recordable injury rate (RIR) before and after the behavioral safety intervention. Two quarters after the start of intervention, the RIR decreased almost 15 points.

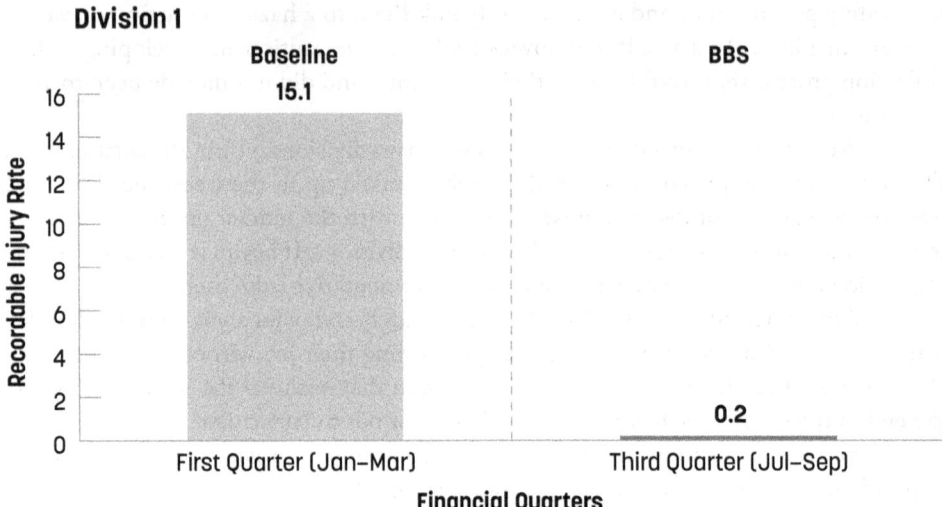

Figure 25.7. Recordable injury rates before and after implementing a behavioral self-observation process in division 1 of a logging operation.

Division 2 employees were prompted to conduct self-observations by three loud blasts emitted from the loudspeaker system. At this time, all employees would take a moment to conduct an observation using their specific index. The indexes were dropped off during their coffee break. The safety rep responsible for this division was faced with an extremely low participation rate and resistance to the process and therefore came up with creative ways to reinforce participation and safety improvements. One day, the safety rep went fishing and traded in his catch for some homemade pies. He brought in the pies to celebrate and encourage participation. Another time, the safety rep brought in a cake during a coffee break. The cake was decorated with a graph depicting the division's safety performance. These creative, personal, and thoughtful reinforcers played an important role in creating a more relaxed and positive culture, particularly regarding safety.

Figure 25.8 shows division 2's average safety and participation percentages after implementation. Note the initial drop in safety percentages after the start of publicly posting the scores. This drop is attributed to an initial inflation of scores. Employees reported being concerned about the public posting of data and inflated their scores. They felt more comfortable with the design after they saw the graphs and were able to observe everyone's reaction to the data. Thus, employees became more truthful when conducting self-observations and their safety scores slightly dropped. Another note should be made concerning the two data points that have an arrow pointed toward them.

These two points represent specific dates when the organization experienced union and management problems. Employees reported being upset and distracted on these specific dates and thus did not perform very safely. Figure 25.9 represents the substantial decreases in RIR after implementation of the BBS process.

Figure 25.8. Division 2: Safety and participation percentages.

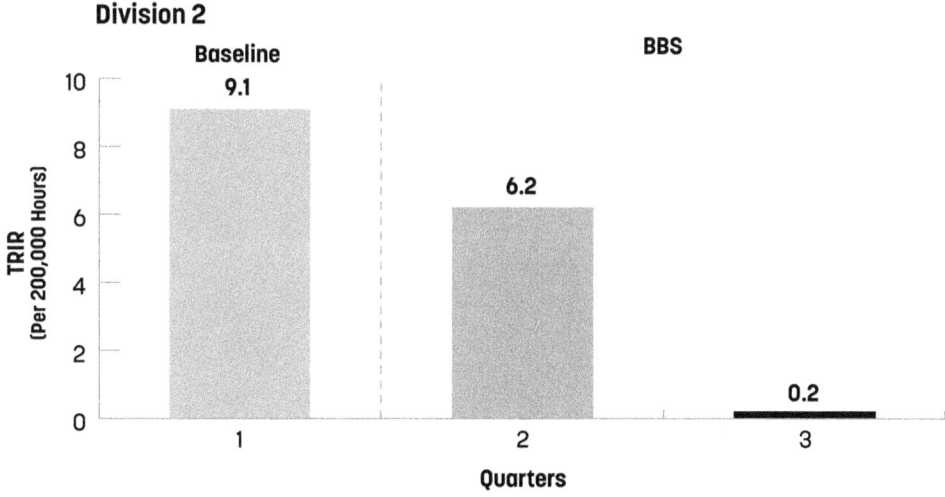

Figure 25.9. Division 2 achieved significant reductions in its total recordable incident rate (TRIR) after implementing a behavioral self-observation process.

Sometimes the best way to truly understand the impact a safety process has had on an organization's culture is through the actions and comments of its employees: One employee who had been in the logging industry for 35 years was vehemently against the BBS process. Until he conducted his first self-observation, he claimed there was no need for an observation system. Then he stated he was surprised at how much he had been doing unsafely. He became a safety rep and encouraged others to do the same.

A few years after implementation, a fatality occurred with a faller in a division of the company that had not implemented a BBS process. The employee who had once been opposed to the BBS process was most upset about the incident and volunteered to implement the safety process in the two divisions in which it had not yet been implemented. He was successful with his implementation efforts and continued to be a strong supporter for many years.

CHAPTER 26

Small-Company Case Studies

A question that often gets asked is whether Values-Based Safety (VBS) is appropriate for small organizations. Often the challenge is figuring out an implementation strategy that will work in such organizations. The following case studies show the potential effectiveness of a behavioral approach within small organizations, when the logistics can be addressed effectively.

26.1 Pipeline Company[12]

Monitoring the safety of employees who work in small, isolated groups poses a particular challenge for safety improvement efforts. Such was the case for an oil and gas company with which we consulted. Its pipeline maintenance employees worked in field groups of only a few people; their job was to maintain miles of pipeline in the so-called middle of nowhere. These workers were at risk not only for physical torque injuries and line-of-fire injuries from the energized systems they worked with but also for injuries from natural hazards (e.g., snakes) in the rough and remote territory in which they worked.

A team of seven workers from three different field crew locations and the district manager designed the safety process. They created a checklist that worked for all of the field groups and an additional one for administrative and office settings. The field checklist included items relating to body position, line of fire, general work conditions, and vehicle safety.

The safety process was designed much like the process detailed throughout this book and included peer-to-peer observations. All employees were asked to conduct one observation per month. Managers and supervisors conducted observations twice per month. Data were sent from the field locations to the steering committee for review and problem-solving. Summaries and trends were sent back to each location for field crews to discuss and plan their own safety action plans. In addition, locally planned celebrations were conducted based on the number of observations made, percentage of employee participation, and team achievements involving safety (there were no formal incentives based on accident statistics). To aid communication, the organization used both a newsletter and an online system. These tools provided a repository of information about safety accomplishments, ideas, and suggestions for improving safety.

After planning these elements of the process, the Quality Safety Edge (QSE) consultant conducted 4 hours of observer training for all employees across a 3-day period

---

12 Judith E. Stowe and Angelica Grindle made significant contributions to this section.

at three pipeline locations across the state. Immediately following training, the teams held kickoff barbecues at each location to celebrate the start-up of observations. After the safety process was implemented in 1996, 3 years passed without a lost-workday injury. It was still in place and functioning effectively as of 2000, when the company was reorganized as a result of a merger. The improvement in safety is shown in Figure 26.1.

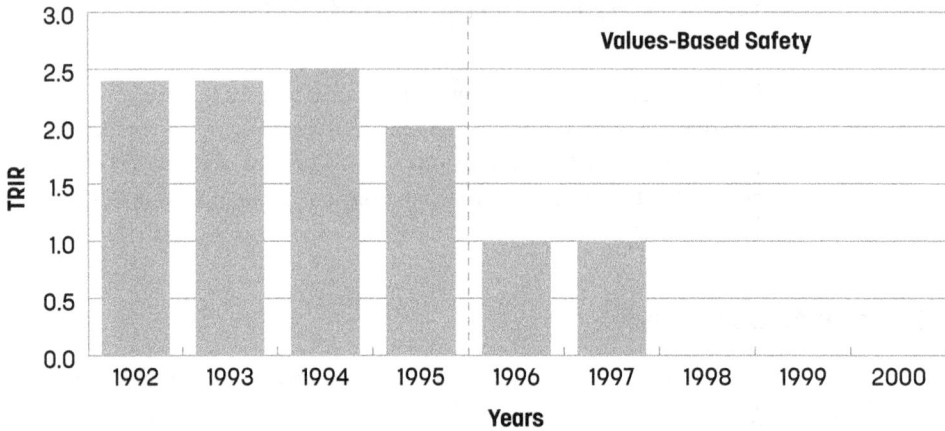

Figure 26.1. After implementing a VBS process, this pipeline company achieved significant reductions in its total recordable injury rates (TRIRs) and experienced zero injuries for 3 consecutive years.

Critical factors in the success of the Values-Based Safety (VBS) process were the strong support and involvement of the district manager and the development of trust between hourly workers and management. Given the nature of their jobs, people often relied on each other and therefore were completely open with each other about safety matters. As a result, all employees embraced the VBS process and were truly proud of their safety performance, to such an extent that, although this was a voluntary system, everyone conducted observations. Because of their success, BBS was also adopted at another pipeline district that had been working with one of our competitors.

26.2 Polyolefin Plant[13]

Obviously, concern about safety exists in small as well as large plants. However, small plants often do not have the resources to devote to an extended safety assessment and design phase. This was the case in a 100-employee plastic extrusion plant with which we consulted. To meet this plant's needs, we worked with a six-member design team in the planning of its safety process and kicked it off within 6 weeks. The safety process was designed as discussed throughout this book: primarily a system of employee-conducted safety observations together with incentives for individual participation,

---

13 Judith E. Stowe and Angelica Grindle made significant contributions to this section.

including such small items as hard-hat stickers, can coolers, and coffee mugs. Team and department process milestones were recognized with names on a plaque, inexpensive logo watches, and so on.

Shortly after the safety process was begun, some departments reached 97% participation from trained observers, and incentive milestones were rapidly attained. Despite this overwhelming level of participation, the expected safety performance improvements did not materialize. After careful examination we found two main problems. First, upper-level managers were pressuring supervisors, who in turn were pressuring hourly workers, to conduct observations, thereby effectively eliminating the concept of "voluntary" observations. Second, teams and departments were competing against each other to be the first to receive the seemingly modest incentives.

The solution to these problems was twofold. Once the plant manager was alerted to the consequences of his overly strong safety message, he instructed supervisors to stop pressuring employees to conduct safety observations. In addition, the incentive system was modified to eliminate potential competition between employees. Instead of group rewards, $1 went to a charity for every observation conducted, with employees nominating the charity after conducting an observation. The charity with the most nominations at the end of the month received the incentive money. The observation process got an added boost when charity representatives started coming into the plant to thank the employees. With these modifications, participation in the process dropped to about 60% but, interestingly, safety performance improved. Steering committee personnel reported that while employees were turning in fewer observation checklists each month, those checklists were higher quality. In other words, data from the observations were more likely to reflect activities observed in the workplace and less likely to be incentive-driven fabrications.

The safety process resulted in improved safety performance, as shown in Figure 26.2. The average annual number of total recordable unsafe incidents decreased from 17.9 prior to the implementation of the safety process to 3.4 after implementation.

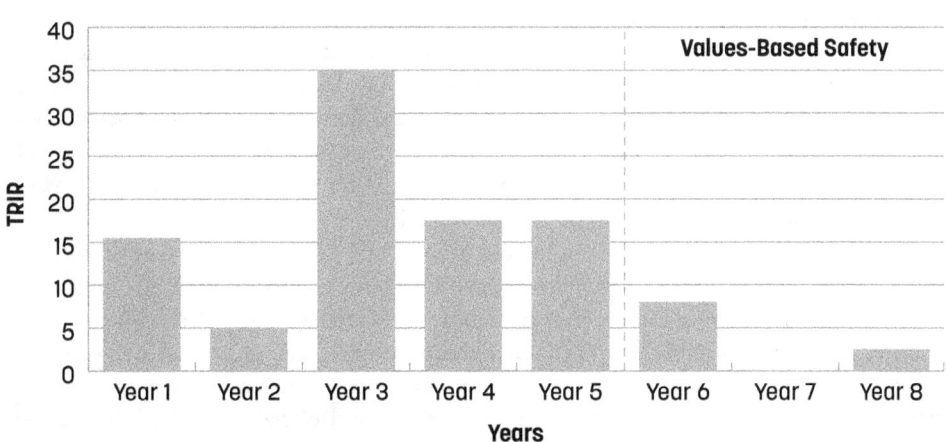

Figure 26.2. *This polyolefin plant achieved significant reductions in its total recordable injury rate (TRIR) after implementing a VBS process.*

As with most successful VBS processes, this one continued to evolve with the changing needs of the facility. The safety committee and management decided that participation in observations would become a job requirement and ended the monthly incentive program. Nonetheless, performance improvements continued. Does this suggest that incentives were not needed in the first place? No. The incentives served crucial purposes in that they

1. helped promote and sustain a high level of employee involvement
2. increased motivation concerning safety
3. helped overcome initial resistance to the process

Over time, employees lost interest in the charity donation program, which underscores the importance of keeping incentives fresh and tailoring them to the individual, as discussed in Chapter 13. Fortunately, by the time this occurred, conducting safety observations had become a job expectation at this plant, and participation continued to support a consistent level of safe work practices.

26.3 Food-Processing Plant[14]

This case study shows how the successful implementation of a VBS process can inadvertently and positively affect other aspects of an organization, ranging from increased attendance to changing a negative attitude about safety.

In 1999, a major rice manufacturer sought assistance in implementing a VBS process at their Louisiana plant. Three hundred employees worked in two main areas: "the mill" area (the mill, packaging, and shipping) and "the trucking area" (trucking, receiving, and drying). The trucking area manager did not wish to participate in implementing a VBS process. Therefore, implementation was initiated in the mill area, and by default, the trucking area served as a control group. The VBS process implementation followed the model presented in this book. Before it was implemented, the mill area reported up to seven lost-workday incidents per month. Within the first 6 months after implementation, a 50% reduction was achieved in lost-workday incidents, while the control group reported three major lost-workday incidents (Figure 26.3). The dramatic success of the VBS process in the mill area, along with continued occurrences of major incidents in the control group, helped the trucking area manager who was initially reluctant to become a strong supporter of the VBS process. Thus, the VBS process was soon implemented in the trucking area as well.

As a result of successful implementation of a VBS process, the Louisiana plant experienced a dramatic improvement in employee attendance. Previously, employees felt the organizational culture was very negative and management driven, which contributed to the low attendance rates. The employee-driven safety process helped create a more positive work environment and the site experienced noticeable improvement in attendance. Management also recognized the value and effectiveness of VBS process

---

14 Wanda Myers and Alicia M. Alvero made significant contributions to this section.

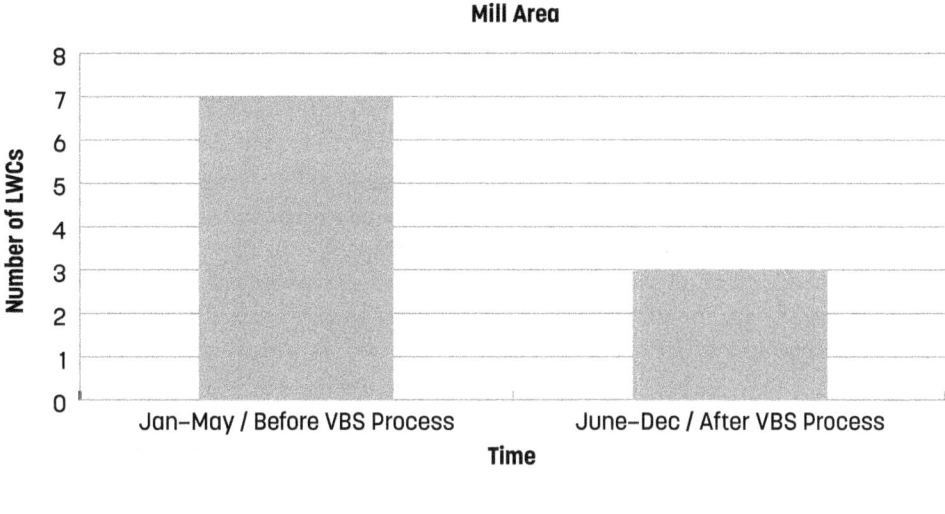

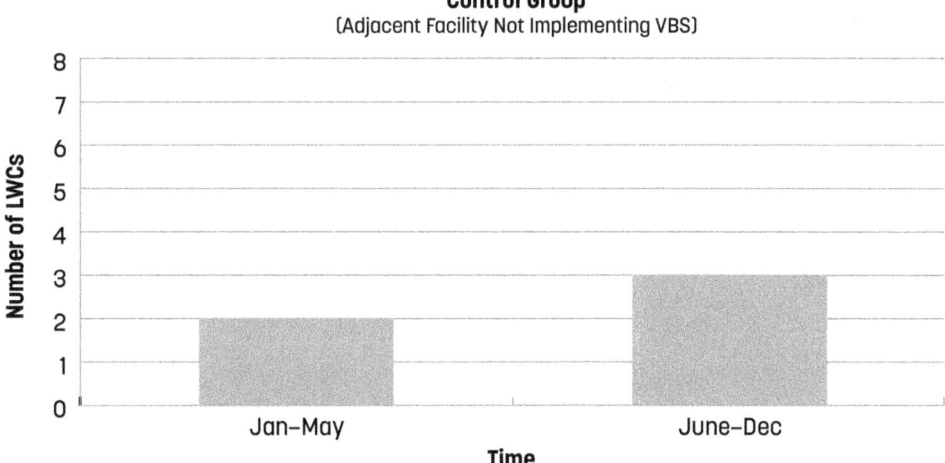

Figure 26.3. *This rice processing plant reduced lost-workday cases (LWCs) by 50% in the first 6 months while an adjacent area that elected not to participate in the behavioral process showed no improvement.*

concepts and requested assistance in implementing these concepts to help solve other work performance concerns.

In 2001 we were asked to assist a Texas plant with its struggling BBS program because of the significant safety improvements achieved in the Louisiana plant after VBS process implementation. This plant had approximately 250 employees and dealt mostly with instant rice. Another consulting firm had assisted with the initial BBS implementation at this location. But after 4 years, the site was experiencing three problems with their process:

1. Participation—defined as conducting at least two observations per month—was down to only 10%.
2. The steering committee was ineffective.
3. The process had not reduced injuries.

The steering committee was not effectively addressing safety issues and was not effective in promoting participation in the process. These problems were closely related in that employees did not participate because nothing was being done with the data. It was not used effectively for feedback or to identify and address safety issues or as the basis for recognition and celebrations. In short, employees had no reason to participate in the process. In addition, management had no formal role in the original process. To revive the process, a QSE consultant trained and coached the steering committee to manage the BBS process. They began to share the observation data and used the data to develop action plans that were routinely reviewed with employees in safety meetings. They also began to recognize individual participation and celebrate team successes. Once these issues were addressed, participation rose significantly, and both management and employees believed the process was functioning much more effectively. Furthermore, this site achieved a 65% reduction in injuries during the year following these enhancements.

CHAPTER 27

The Observer Effect[15]

Authors' note: This chapter explores Alicia M. Alvero and John Austin's research studies conducted in 2004. Their findings suggest that employees who observe safety practices tend to work more safely. The research also argues that more employee involvement in safety observations benefits organizations. As discussed earlier, more recent findings by Spigener and colleagues in 2022 favor fewer dedicated observers. However, we contend that some organizations can gain quicker culture shifts and fewer injuries with higher levels of employee participation. This chapter reinforces the view that serving as an observer positively influences an individual's safety behavior.

In the first edition of *The Values-Based Safety Process*, author Terry McSween wrote, "No one has yet conducted definitive research into the effects of employees conducting observations in their own work areas" (p. 24). We found this statement interesting and worthy of further investigation. On discussing the matter with other researchers and practitioners in the field, we decided that enough general interest existed to pursue additional research of the observation process. Many practitioners we approached felt that employees who conduct safety observations on the behavior of coworkers work more safely as a result of conducting those observations. However, this claim had not yet been scientifically tested. Both the feedback and observation processes are critical components of behavior-based safety (BBS), but interestingly, there are many studies on the effects of feedback, whereas studies of the observation process are almost nonexistent. These factors made our task both more interesting and even more challenging. So, with these considerations, we began our search to determine if employees who conduct safety observations do work more safely as a result of *conducting* these observations. We termed this hypothetical effect the *observer effect*.

Our first step was to determine whether to conduct the research in a real-world setting (an actual business) or in a laboratory setting. Ideally, we would have preferred a real-world setting, but practical advantages pointed toward the laboratory. First, we felt it would have been difficult to convince an organization to spend extended time and resources for the sole purpose of testing for the existence of an observer effect. Employees would need to be taken from their work to be trained as observers, and unless the

---

15 This chapter was written by Alicia M. Alvero and John Austin, during their time at Western Michigan University.

organization was interested in implementing a BBS process, it would have been difficult to get the employee buy-in that is so critical to the success of BBS. Further and most importantly, in a laboratory setting we would be able to eliminate the extraneous factors that would be present in an organization and therefore would be better able to attribute the effects, if any, to the intervention and not some other event within the organization. In this case, before trying this in an applied setting, we wanted to be sure that the behavior change of the observer was entirely due to conducting observations of coworker behavior. Based on these factors, we decided to begin our observer effect research in the laboratory.

Our university laboratory facilities are made up of two empty rooms, both equipped with a video camera mounted in the upper left corner of the room and a control room furnished with two televisions and VCRs (videocassette recorders) one of each connected to the empty laboratory rooms. For the purposes of our research, we furnished these two rooms with the following materials in order to simulate an office setting: a desk, chair, computer, telephone, cardboard box, and bookshelf. Both of the research studies discussed in this chapter were conducted in these facilities.

27.1 The First Study

For our first study we recruited 12 undergraduate students to serve as participants. Each student was randomly assigned to one of two groups, A or B, and given a list of instructions that described the work they would be asked to perform during the experiment. The work tasks were chosen to simulate the work of an office setting and involved lifting light objects, using a telephone, and typing. Participants were also informed that each session would be filmed so that data could be collected at a later time. Throughout all phases of the study, we measured safety performance on the following eight behaviors:

1. back posture during lifts
2. knee position during lifts
3. neck position while typing
4. wrist position while typing
5. back position when sitting
6. shoulder position when sitting
7. feet position when sitting
8. neck position when using the telephone

During the baseline condition (when no intervention was in effect), participants simply performed the office tasks described on the instruction sheet, and data were collected on their safety performance for the eight cited behaviors. The next phase of the experiment was an information phase. Participants were given a list of four behaviors that included a description of how to perform each one safely (group A participants were given the descriptions for behaviors 1–4 and group B for behaviors 5–8), and they were told these behaviors would be measured throughout the study.

The information on the four safety behaviors was given to them before every session during this phase. We decided to present them with the descriptions during a phase separate from the baseline phase to ensure that any effects we observed during the observation phase could be attributed to conducting observations and not to participants "figuring out" the safe way to do things. In other words, we wanted to ensure that any changes in safety performance were not occurring because participants learned from the descriptions provided on the safety checklist how to be safe. Interestingly, participants did not change their behavior just from knowing the definitions of *safe* and *at risk*. Safety performance did not increase significantly for most behaviors during the information phase.

Overall safety performance averaged 13.1% for group A and 10.1% for group B during this phase, increases of 6.4% and 0%, respectively, above the baseline averages. The position of the feet while sitting was the only behavior that increased significantly during the information phase. During baseline, overall feet position averaged 8.3% and increased to 84.1% for group B, which was comprised of the six participants who were presented with this safety description during the information phase. We speculate that this increase occurred because placing one's feet flat on the floor is perhaps the most easily understood and least effortful of the behaviors to perform safely.

During the observation phase, participants were asked to conduct safety observations while viewing a video of an associate (an "actor" who was instructed to perform the exact tasks the participants had been asked to perform in the same simulated office setting solely for the purpose of creating this "scoring" video). Participants were given an observation sheet containing a list of behaviors, descriptions of how to perform each behavior on the checklist safely, and columns to score each behavior as safe or unsafe. Safety observations were conducted immediately before participants began their "work" for the session. The observation sheets first given to each participant listed only the four behaviors for which they had received descriptions during the information phase (group A: behaviors 1–4; group B: behaviors 5–8.) The remaining four behaviors were added to the observation sheet at a later time. This allowed us to study the impact that conducting observations had on the behaviors that were not included on the observation sheets.

The effects of conducting safety observations on safety performance were substantial. Overall safety performance during the observation phase averaged 77.2% for group A and 74.4% for group B, increases of 70.5% and 64.4%, respectively, above the baseline averages. Figure 27.1, Figure 27.2, and Table 27.1 represent the safety percentages for each behavior averaged across all participants and phases. Figures 27.1 and 27.2 show the safety performance for groups A and B, respectively. Table 27.1 lists (a) the overall safety averages for each phase and (b) the safety averages for each group by behavior and phase.

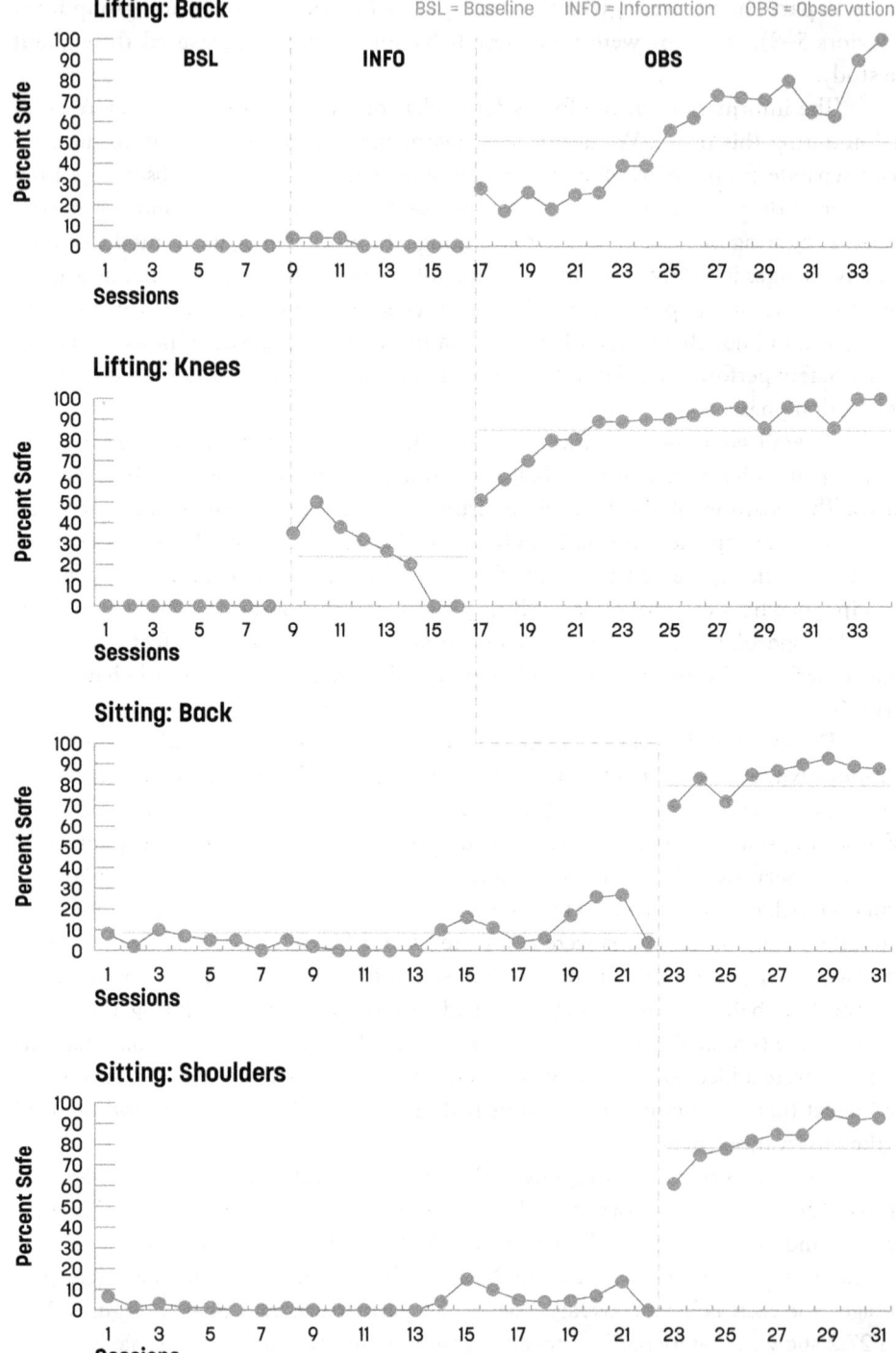

Figure 27.1. Safety performance data averaged across all participants in group A.

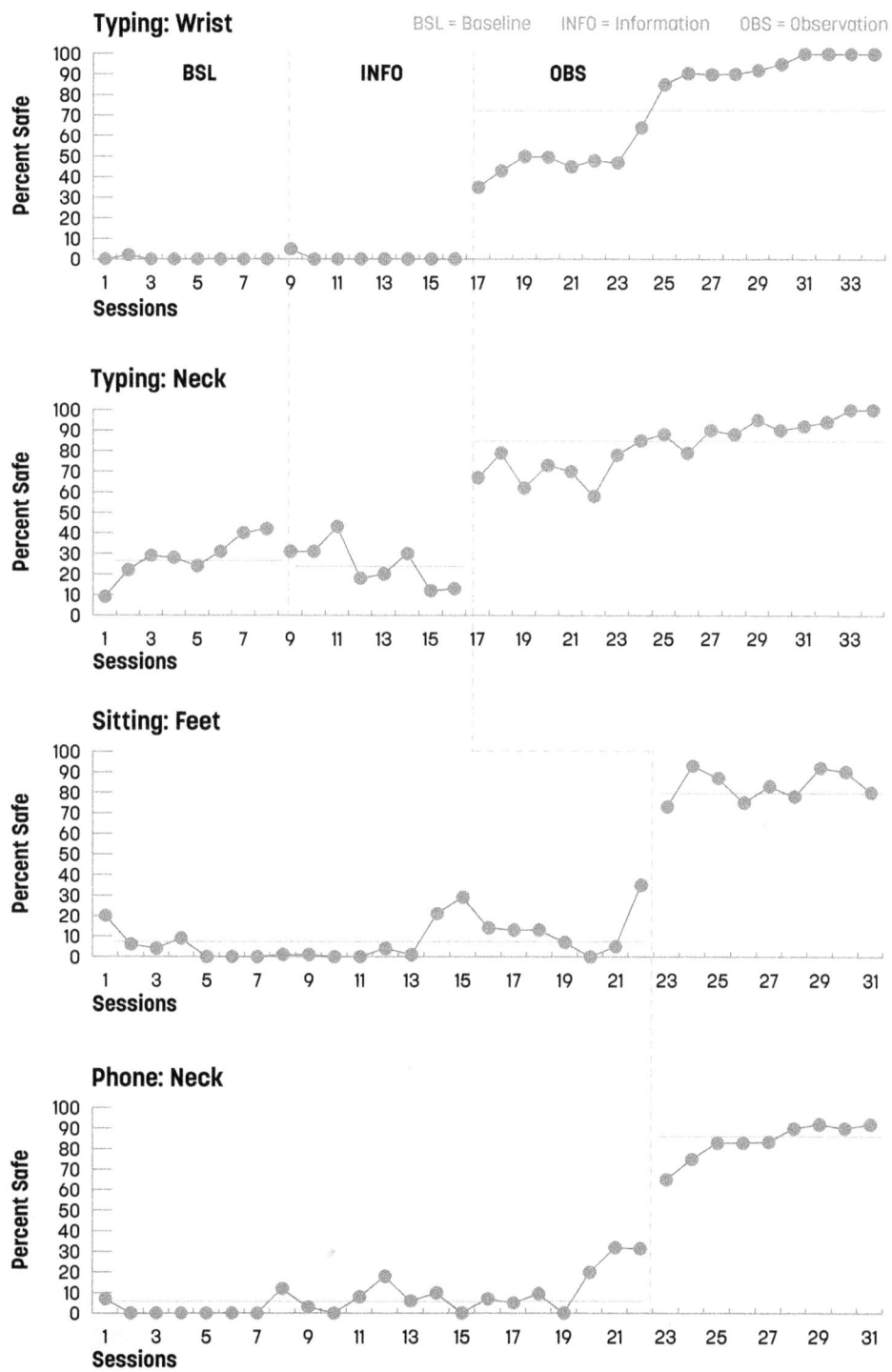

Figure 27.1. (Continued)

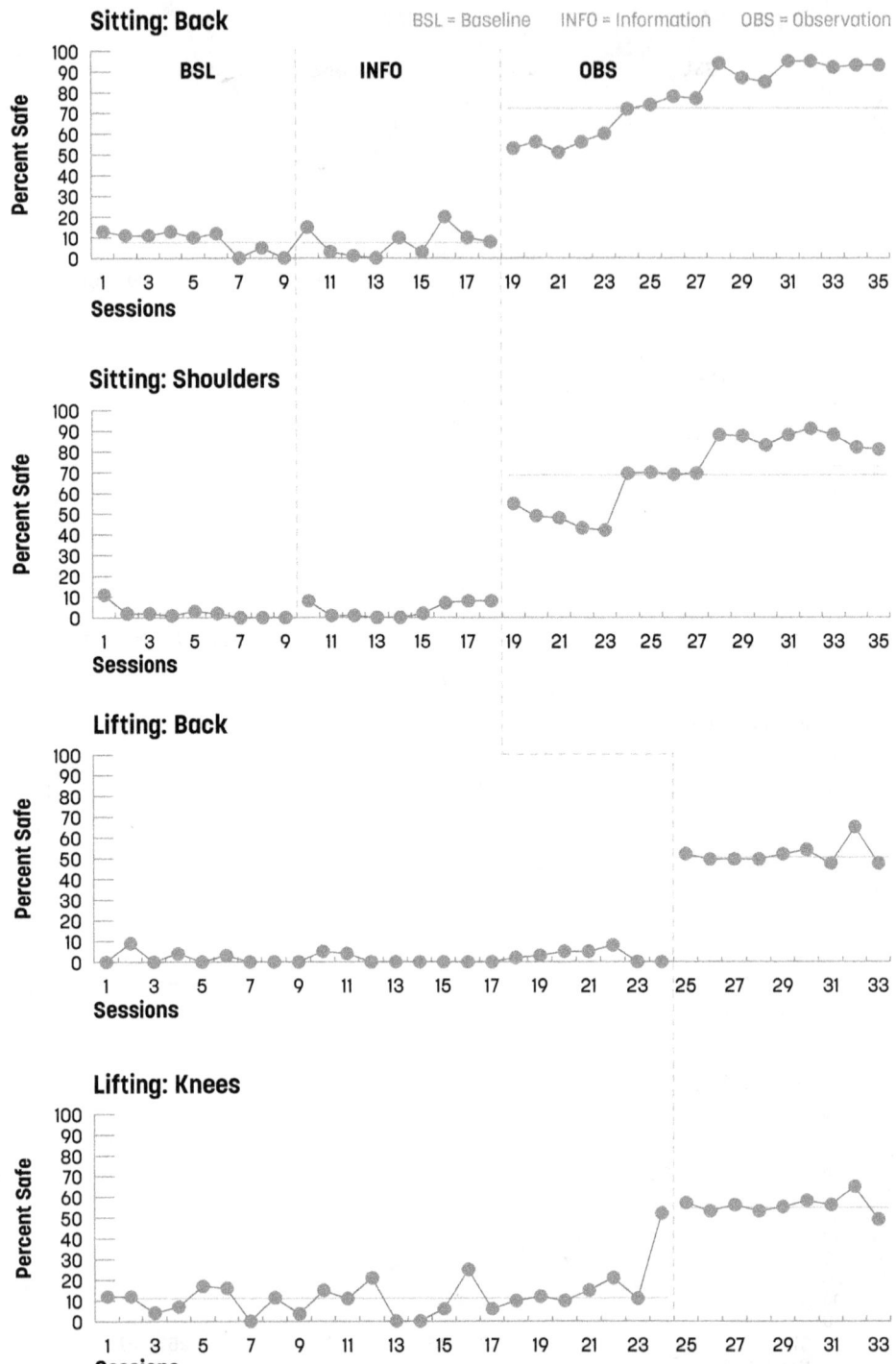

Figure 27.2. Safety performance data averaged across all participants in group B.

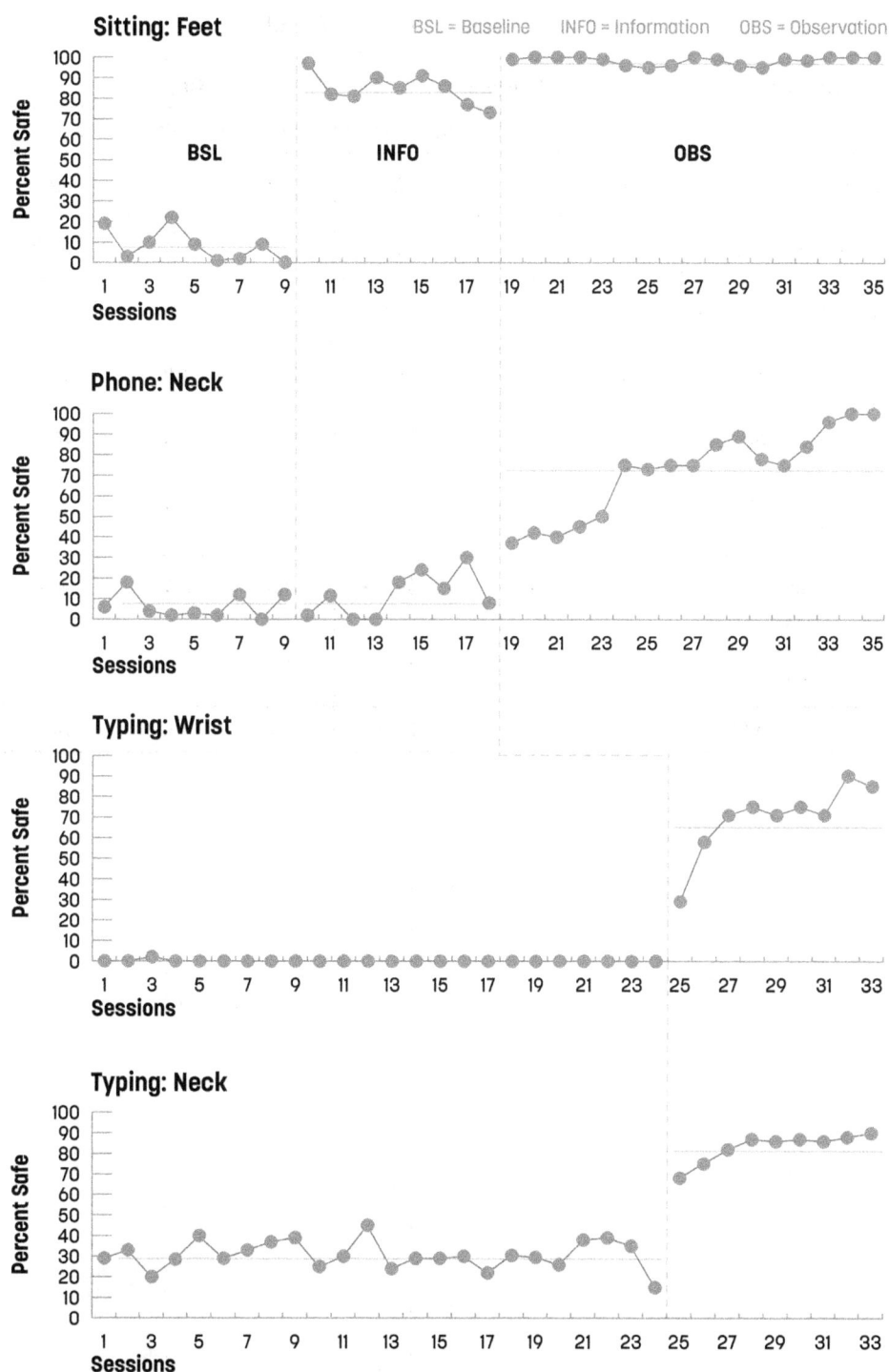

Figure 27.2. (Continued)

Table 27.1. Safety Performance Averages for Groups A and B

Behaviors	Group A			Group B		
	Baseline	Information	Observation	Baseline	Information	Observation
Back during lifts	0	1.2	53.1	2.2	n/a	52.9
Knees during lifts	0	24.9	85.9	12.7	n/a	56.2
Wrists while typing	0.2	0.7	73.6	0.1	n/a	68.5
Neck while typing	27.5	25.5	83	30.4	n/a	82.3
Back while sitting	6.9	n/a	83.4	8.9	7.8	76.9
Shoulders while sitting	3.3	n/a	83.3	2.1	3.6	70.6
Feet while sitting	8.3	n/a	83.3	8.3	84.1	98.6
Neck during phone use	7.8	n/a	84.7	6.7	12.2	71.7
OVERALL	**6.7**	**13.1**	**77.2**	**10**	**10.1**	**74.4**

27.2 A Second Study[16]

A second study on the observer effect, funded by the Cambridge Center for Behavioral Studies Safety Grant, compared the effects of conducting observations to those of feedback. The powerful effects of feedback have often been documented in both laboratory and applied settings. We wanted to know how the effects of conducting observations would compare to those of receiving feedback in our simulated office environment.

We recruited eight participants for the research. Four were assigned to the observation group and four to the feedback group. The setting and procedures for this study were identical to those of the study described above, with the exception of the feedback group. Participants in the feedback group were exposed to the same baseline and information phases as the observation group. During the feedback phase, immediately before they began each work session, participants received feedback (presented as written percentages) on their safety performance from the previous session. The description of how to perform each behavior safely was included on the feedback forms to ensure that feedback group participants had the necessary information to improve or maintain their safety performance. In addition, to ensure a well-designed study, we wanted to treat both groups the same, so we provided the descriptions of how to perform each behavior safely to both the feedback and observation groups.

The following are the findings for two participants, one from the observation group and the other from the feedback group, that are representative of the general findings of this study. Figure 27.3 shows the safety performance for the observation group participant and Figure 27.4 the safety performance for the feedback group participant. Table 27.2 lists safety performance averages for each behavior across each phase and includes the overall safety average for each phase. Information alone had the strongest effects on behaviors related to lifting for both participants. The effects of conducting safety observations and written feedback on safety performance were sizeable and very comparable. Overall safety performance averaged 86.7% during the observation phase and 88.9% during the feedback phase, increases of 77% and 68.1%, respectively, above the baseline averages. The results of this study seem to suggest that the effects of conducting observations are similar to those of written feedback within the context of a laboratory setting.

---

16 Alvero and Austin (2004).

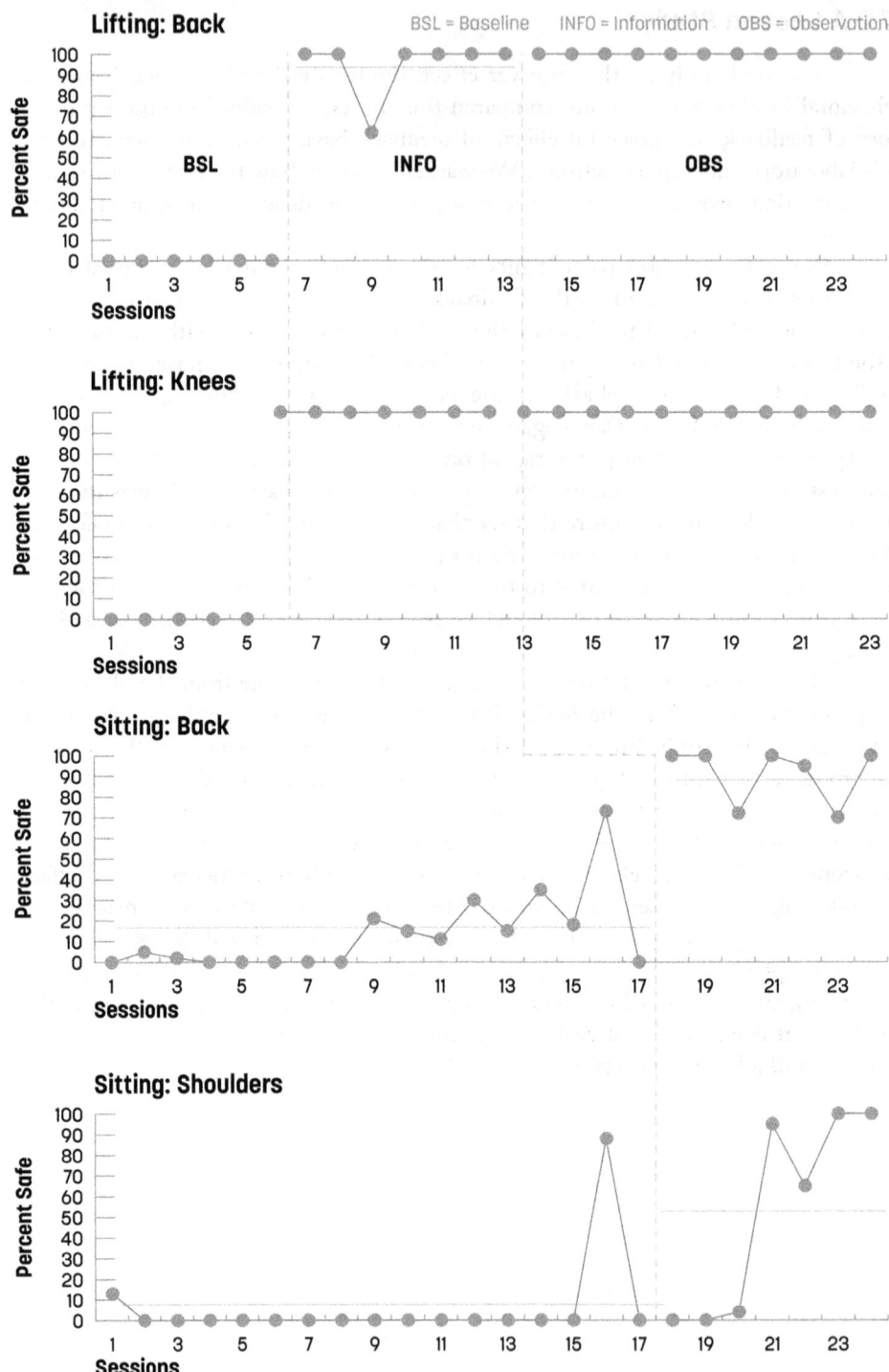

Figure 27.3. Safety performance for observation group participant.

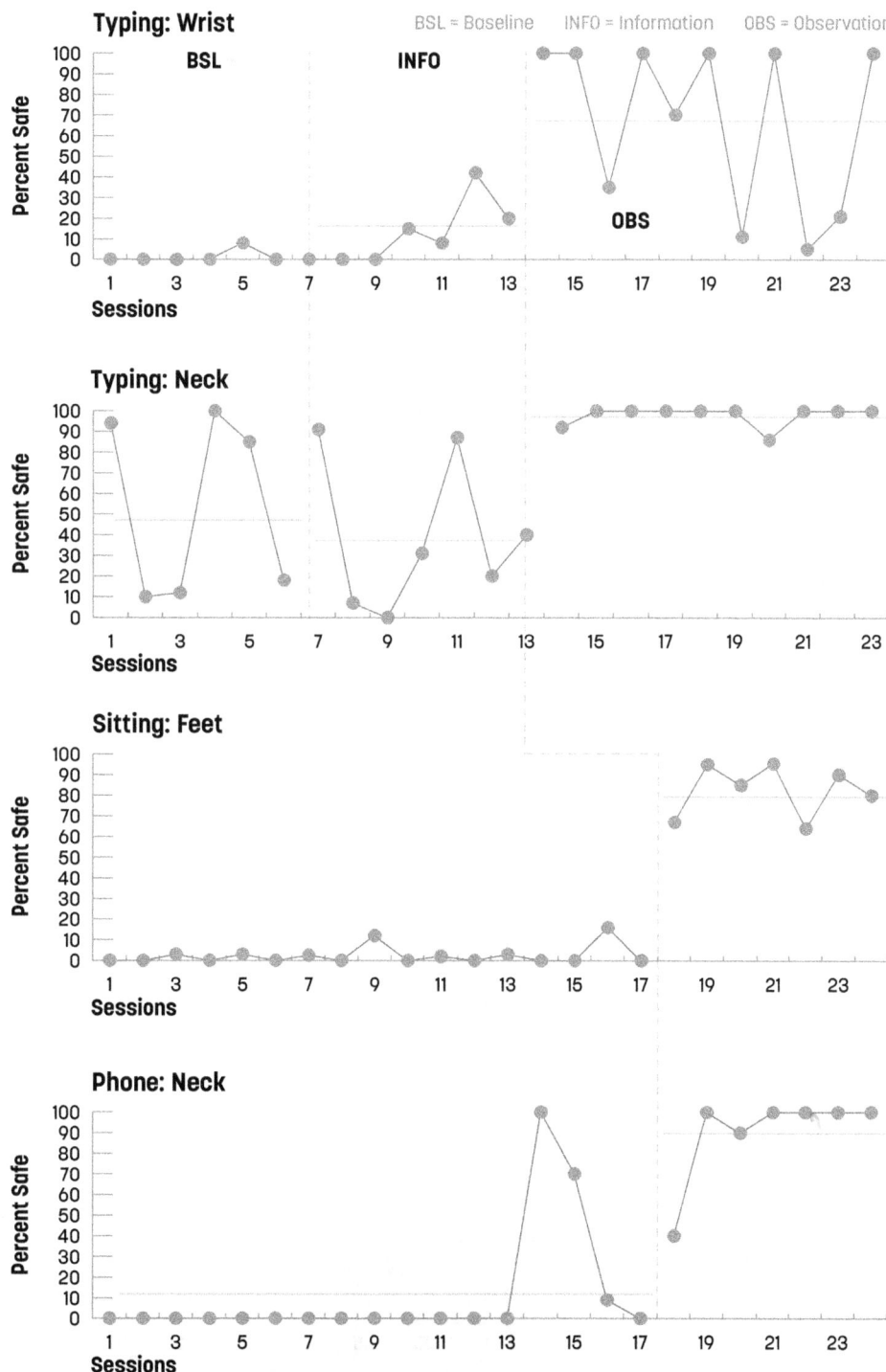

Figure 27.3. (Continued)

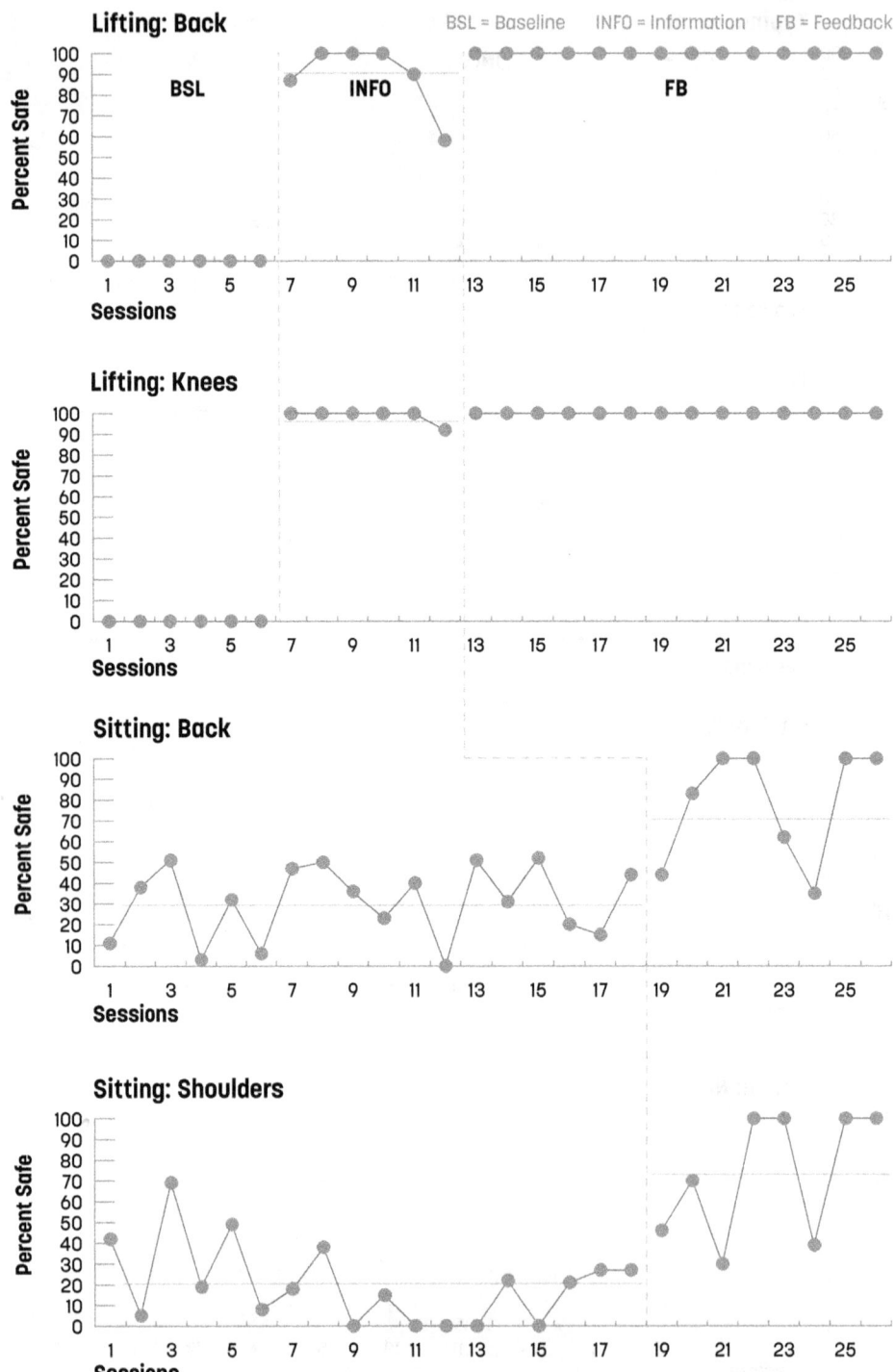

Figure 27.4. Safety performance for the feedback group participant.

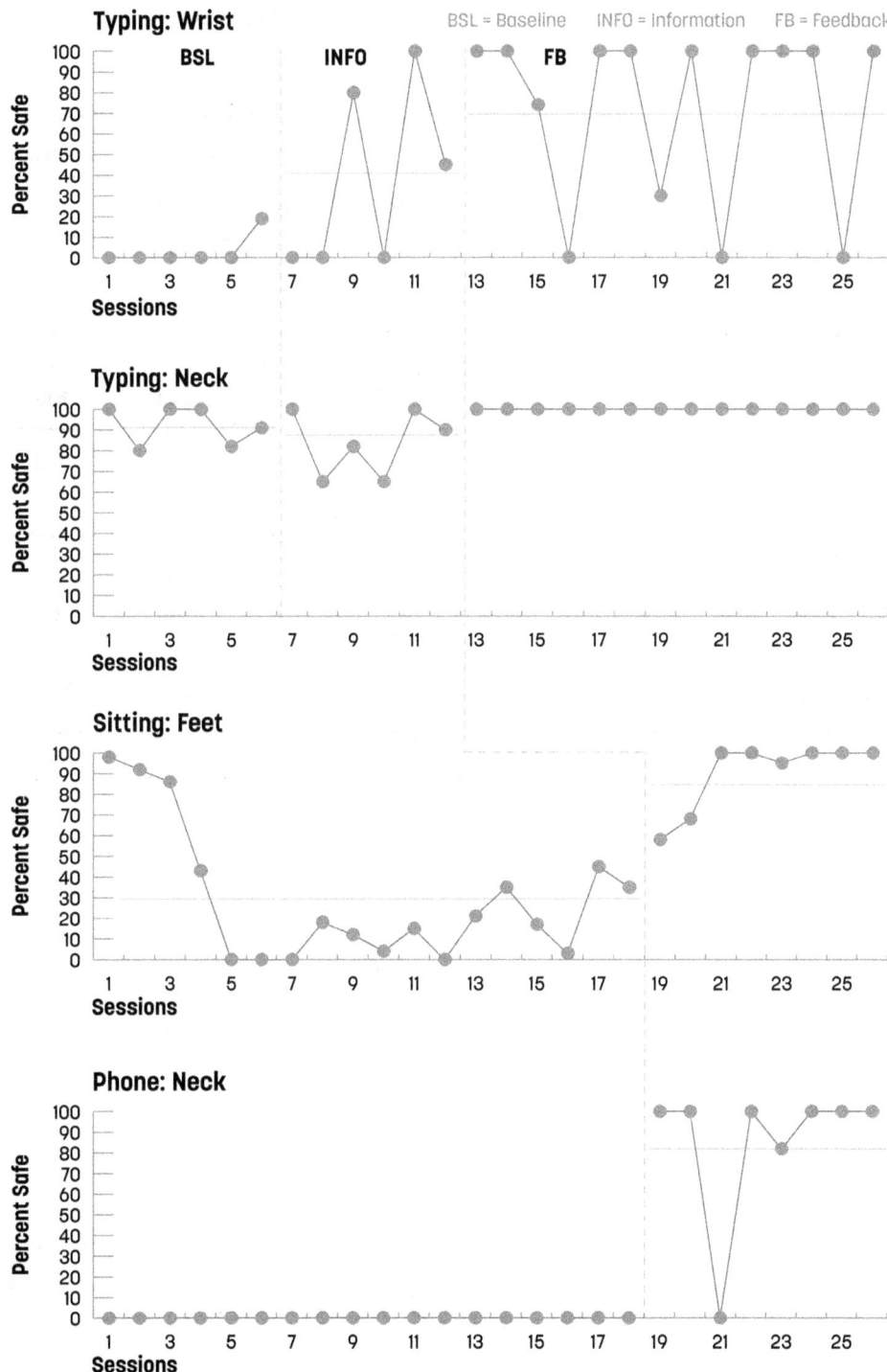

Figure 27.4. (Continued)

Table 27.2. Safety Performance Averages for Feedback and Observation Group Participants

Behaviors	Observation Participant			Feedback Participant		
	Baseline	Information	Observation	Baseline	Information	Feedback
Back during lifts	0	94.7	100	0	89.2	100
Knees during lifts	0	100	100	0	98.7	100
Wrists while typing	1.6	12.3	68	3	37.5	71.8
Neck while typing	45.4	38	98.2	92.3	84.5	100
Back while sitting	13	n/a	91	30.1	n/a	78.1
Shoulders while sitting	5.9	n/a	52.3	20	n/a	73.8
Feet while sitting	2.7	n/a	83	29.1	n/a	90.3
Neck during phone use	10.5	n/a	89.9	0	n/a	85.4
OVERALL	9.7	61.3	86.7	20.8	77.5	88.9

27.3 Conclusion

The results of these research studies provide preliminary evidence for the observer effect. In other words, the data indicate that in a laboratory setting persons who conduct safety observations do perform work more safely as a result of conducting observations.

It is important to note, however, that for several reasons we must exercise extreme caution when interpreting these data. First, these studies are the first to scientifically isolate and assess a main component of the observation process. Therefore, additional data and analysis of this effect are necessary to come to truly reliable conclusions about this component's possible implications for a BBS process. Second, because we isolated the observation process, we are unable to discuss any possible interactions with other components of the BBS process. Further, the observer effect was found to occur in a laboratory setting that lacked many common variables that may affect safety performance, such as social pressures and productivity demands. Therefore, we are unable to confirm that similar observer effect results will occur in a real-world setting. We do suggest that future research endeavors should attempt to replicate a similar study within an organization.

Caution should also be exercised when interpreting the effects of conducting observations versus receiving feedback. Although each component produced substantial effects on safety performance, we are not advocating the use of one component in lieu of the other or implying that one is more critical than the other. Nevertheless, these findings are interesting in suggesting that it may be beneficial to train all employees to be safety observers.

Further research will be conducted to determine why the behavior of an observer changes after conducting observations. One thing that these data suggest, however, is that the effect is more pronounced for some types of behavior than for others. We would guess that the effects of observing will be more pronounced when the observer is scoring hard-to-judge and hard-to-perform behavior, such as posture, lifting, and other ergonomically related behavior. A behavior such as hard-hat usage would be likely to produce a smaller observer effect, just because the observer already knows the rule of hard-hat usage (wear it or don't wear it). Seeing someone else wear a hard hat does not give the observer additional information about how to perform the behavior. However, actually seeing a person engage in a particular posture goes a long way toward clarifying the definitions discussed during training, and therefore it produces a larger observer effect.

References

Alavosius, M. P., & Burleigh, K. (2022). Behavior-based safety as a replicable technology. In R. A. Houmanfar, M. Fryling, & M. P. Alavosius (Eds.), *Applied behavior science in organizations* (pp. 21–63). Routledge. https://doi.org/10.4324/9781003198949-2

Alavosius, M. P., & Sulzer-Azaroff, B. (1986). The effects of performance feedback on the safety of client lifting and transfer. *Journal of Applied Behavior Analysis, 19*(3), 261–267. https://doi.org/10.1901/jaba.1986.19-261

Alvero, A. M., & Austin, J. (2004). The effects of conducting behavioral observations on the behavior of the observer. *Journal of Applied Behavior Analysis, 37*(4), 457–468. https://doi.org/10.1901/jaba.2004.37-457

Andrasik, T. (1980). Organizational behavior modification in business settings: A methodological and content review. *Journal of Organizational Behavior Management, 2*(2), 85–102. https://doi.org/10.1300/J075v02n02_02

Andrasik, T. (1991). A reinforcer profile in 8 easy steps. *Performance Management Magazine, 9*(2), 3–7. https://www.aubreydaniels.com/media-center/archive/performance-management-magazine-spring-summer-1991-vol-9-no-2

Burns, T. E. (2002). *Serious incident prevention: How to sustain accident-free operations in your plant or company* (2nd ed.). Gulf Professional Publishing.

Chhokar, S. J., & Wallin, J. A. (1984). Improving safety through applied behavior analysis. *Journal of Safety Research, 15*(4), 141–151. https://doi.org/10.1016/0022-4375(84)90045-8

Cook, S., & McSween, T. E. (2000). The role of supervisors in behavioral safety observations. *Professional Safety, 45*(10), 33–36. https://elcosh.org/record/document/1276/D000414.pdf

Cooper, M. D. (2006) Exploratory analyses of the effects of managerial support and feedback consequences on behavioral safety maintenance. *Journal of Organizational Behavior Management, 26*(3), 1–41.

Deming, W. E. (2018). *Out of the crisis*. The MIT Press.

DuPont. (n.d.). *Delivering world class health and safety performance*. https://www.dupont.com/about/sustainability/deliver-world-class-health-safety-performance.html.html

DuPont. (2019, May 22). *At our core: The historical origins of safety at DuPont*. https://www.dupont.com/news/safety-at-our-core.html

Fellner, D. J., & Sulzer-Azaroff, B. (1984). Increasing industrial safety practices and conditions through posted feedback. *Journal of Safety Research, 15*(1), 7–21. https://doi.org/10.1016/0022-4375(84)90026-4

Fellner, D. J., & Sulzer-Azaroff, B. (1985). Occupational safety: Assessing the impact of adding assigned or participative goalsetting. *Journal of Organizational Behavior Management, 7*(1–2), 3–24. https://doi.org/10.1300/J075v07n01_02

Fox, C. J., & Sulzer-Azaroff, B. (1990). The effectiveness of two different sources of feedback on staff teaching of fire evacuation skills. *Journal of Organizational Behavior Management, 10*(2), 19–36. https://doi.org/10.1300/J075v10n02_03

Fox, D. K., Hopkins, B. L., & Anger, W. K. (1987). The long-term effects of a token economy on safety performance in open-pit mining. *Journal of Applied Behavior Analysis, 20*, 215–224. https://doi.org/10.1901/jaba.1987.20-215

Frederiksen, L. W., & Sulzer-Azaroff, B. (1982). Behavioral approaches to occupational health and safety. In L. W. Frederiksen (Ed.), *Handbook of organizational behavior management* (pp. 505–538). Wiley.

Geller, E. S. (1984). A delayed reward strategy for large-scale motivation of safety belt use: A test of long-term impact. *Accident Analysis and Prevention, 16*(5–6), 457–463. https://doi.org/10.1016/0001-4575(84)90058-7

Geller, E. S. (1988). *Managing occupational health and safety*. Make-A-Difference, Inc.

Geller, E. S. (1989). *Managing occupational health and safety: Marketing and the human element* [Paper presentation]. Association for Behavior Analysis 15th Annual Convention, Milwaukee, WI, United States.

Geller, E. S. (1996). *The psychology of safety: How to improve behaviors and attitudes on the job*. Chilton Book Company.

Geller, E. S. (1997). The hammer misses the mark—Why punishment is most often counterproductive. *Industrial Safety & Hygiene News, 31*(11), 12–13.

Geller, E. S., & Hahn, H. A. (1984). Promoting safety belt use at industrial sites: An effective program for blue collar employees. *Professional Psychology, Research and Practice, 15*, 553–564. https://doi.org/10.1037/0735-7028.15.4.553

Geller, E. S., & Lehman, G. R. (1991). The buckle-up promise card: A versatile intervention for large-scale behavior change. *Journal of Applied Behavior Analysis, 24*, 91–94. https://doi.org/10.1901/jaba.1991.24-91

Glass v. Amber Inc., No. 01-00-00589-CV (Tex. Ct. App. 2001).

Hall, E. T. (1976). *Beyond culture*. Anchor Books.

Heinrich, H. W. (1931). *Industrial accident prevention: A scientific approach*. McGraw-Hill.

Heinrich, H. W. (1959). *Industrial incident prevention* (4th ed.). McGraw-Hill.

Hopkins, B. L., Conrad R. J., Dangle, R. F., Fitch, H. G., Smith, M. J., & Anger, W. K. (1986a). Behavioral technology for reducing occupational exposures to styrene. *Journal of Applied Behavior Analysis, 19*, 3–11. https://doi.org/10.1901/jaba.1986.19-3 PMID:3710946

Hopkins, B. L., Conard, R. J., & Smith, M. J. (1986b). Effective and reliable behavioral control technology. *American Industrial Hygiene Association Journal, 47*, 785–791. https://doi.org/10.1080/15298668691390665

Hughes Johnson, C. (2023). *Scaling people: Tactics for management and company building*. Stripe Press.

The Josh Bersin Company. (2022). *The big reset playbook: Organizational culture and performance*. https://joshbersin.com/the-big-reset-playbook-organizational-culture-and-performance/

Komaki, J. (1986). Toward effective supervision: An operant analysis and comparison of managers at work. *Journal of Applied Psychology, 71*(2), 270–279. https://doi.org/10.1037/0021-9010.71.2.270

Komaki, J. L. (1998). *Leadership from an operant perspective*. Routledge.

Komaki, J. L., Barwick, K. K., & Scott, L. R. (1978). A behavioral approach to occupational safety: Pinpointing and reinforcing safe performance in a food manufacturing plant. *Journal of Applied Psychology, 63*(4), 434–445. https://doi.org/10.1037/0021-9010.63.4.434

Komaki, J. L., Collins, R. L., & Penn, P. (1982). The role of performance antecedents and consequences in work motivation. *Journal of Applied Psychology, 67*(3), 334–340. https://doi.org/10.1037/0021-9010.67.3.334

Komaki, J. L., Desselles, M. L., & Bowman, E. D. (1989). Definitely not a breeze: Extending an operant model of effective supervision to teams. *Journal of Applied Psychology, 74*(3), 522–529. https://doi.org/10.1037/0021-9010.74.3.522

Komaki, J., Heinzmann, A. T., & Lawson, L. (1980). Effect of training and feedback: Component analysis of a behavioral safety program. *Journal of Applied Psychology, 65*, 261–270. https://doi.org/10.1037/0021-9010.65.3.261

Komaki, J. L., Zlotnick, S., & Jensen, M. (1986). Development of an operant-based taxonomy and observational index of supervisory behavior. *Journal of Applied Psychology, 71*(2), 260–269. https://doi.org/10.1037/0021-9010.71.2.260

Krause, T. R. (2012, October 29–30). *New perspectives in fatality and serious injury prevention* [Conference session]. Fatality Prevention Forum 2012, Coraopolis, PA, United States.

Krause, T. R., Hidley, J. H., & Hodson, S. J. (1996). *The behavior-based safety process* (2nd ed.). Wiley.

Krause, T. R., Hidley, J. H., & Lareau, W. (1984). Behavioral science applied to industrial incident prevention. *Professional Safety, 29*(7), 21–27.

Krause, T. R., Hidley, J. H., & Lareau, W. (1993). Implementing the behavior-based safety process in a union environment: A natural fit. *Professional Safety, 38*(6), 26–31.

Krause, T. R., & Murray, G. (2012, June 3–6). *On the prevention of serious injuries and fatalities* [Conference session]. ASSE Professional Development Conference and Exposition, Denver, CO, United States. https://aeasseincludes.assp.org/proceedings/2012/docs/564.pdf

Krause, T. R., Seymour, K. J., & Sloat, C. M. (1999). Long-term evaluation of behavior-based method for improving safety performance: A meta-analysis of 73 interrupted time-series replications. *Safety Science, 32*, 1–18. https://doi.org/10.1016/S0925-7535(99)00007-7

Malott, R. W. (1992a). Saving the world with contingency diagramming. *ABA Newsletter, 15*(1), 45.

Malott, R. W. (1992b). The three-contingency model of performance management. *ABA Newsletter, 15*(2), 6.

Malott, R. W., Malott, M. E., & Trojan, E. A. (2000). *Elementary principles of behavior* (4th ed.). Prentice-Hall.

McSween, T. E. (1990). Performance appraisal: What do we do instead? In G. N. McLean, S. R. Damme, & R. A. Swanson (Eds.), *Performance appraisal: Perspectives on a quality management approach* (pp. 96–101). American Society for Training and Development.

McSween, T. E. (1993a). Behavior and safety—the critical link. In *Performance Technology—1993 Selected Proceedings of the 31st NSPI Conference* (pp. 191–205). National Society for Performance and Instruction.

McSween, T. E. (1993b). Improve your safety program with a behavioral approach. *Hydrocarbon Processing, 72*(8), 119–128.

McSween, T. E. (1995). *The values-based safety process: Improving your safety culture with a behavioral approach* (1st ed.). Wiley.

McSween, T. E. (2003). *The values-based safety process: Improving your safety culture with behavior-based safety* (2nd ed.). Wiley.

McSween, T., & Moran, D. J. (2017). Assessing and preventing serious incidents with behavioral science: Enhancing Heinrich's triangle for the 21st century. *Journal of Organizational Behavior Management, 37*(3–4), 283–300.

McSween, T. E., Myers, W., & Kuchler, T. C. (1990). Getting buy-in at the executive level. In W. K. Redmon & A. M. Dickinson (Eds.), *Promoting excellence through performance management* (pp. 207–221). Haworth Press.

McSween, T. E. & Zaloom, V. (1990). Creating a positive work environment. *Chemical Engineering, 97*(6), 135–138.

Myers, W. V., McSween, T. E., Medina, R. E., Rost, K., & Alvero, A. M. (2010). The implementation and maintenance of a behavioral safety process in a petroleum refinery. *Journal of Organizational Behavior Management, 30*(4), 285-307. https://doi.org/10.1080/01608061.2010.499027

National Safety Council Injury Facts. (n.d.). Work-related incidence rate trends. https://injuryfacts.nsc.org/work/industry-incidence-rates/work-related-incident-rate-trends/#:~:text=The%20Bureau%20of%20Labor%20Statistics%20%28BLS%29%20reports%20that,increased%204.5%25%2C%20totaling%202.3%20million%20cases%20in%202022

Olson, R., & Austin, J. (2001). Behavior based safety and working alone: The effects of a self-monitoring package on the safe performance of bus operators. *Journal of Organizational Behavior Management, 21*(3), 5–43. https://doi.org/10.1300/J075v21n03_02

Paragon Hotel Corp. v. Ramirez, 783 S.W.2d 654 (Tex. Ct. App. 1990).

Peters, T. J., & Waterman, R. H. (1982). *In search of excellence: Lessons from America's best-run companies*. Harper & Row.

Peterson, D. (1984). An experiment in positive reinforcement. *Professional Safety, 29*(5), 30–35.

Reber, R. A., & Wallin, J. A. (1983). Validation of behavioral measures of occupational safety. *Journal of Organizational Behavior Management, 5*(2), 69–78. https://doi.org/10.1300/J075v05n02_04

Rhoton, W. W. (1980). A procedure to improve compliance with coal mine safety regulations. *Journal of Organizational Behavior Management, 2*(4), 243–249. https://doi.org/10.1300/J075v02n04_01

Sherman, S. J. (1980). On the self-erasing nature of errors of prediction. *Journal of Personality and Social Psychology, 39*, 211–221. https://doi.org/10.1037/0022-3514.39.2.211

Spigener, J., Lyon, G., & McSween, T. (2022). Behavior-based safety 2022: Today's evidence. *Journal of Organizational Behavior Management, 42*(4), 336–359. https://doi.org/10.1080/01608061.2022.2048943

Sulzer-Azaroff, B. (1987). The modification of occupational safety behavior. *Journal of Occupational Accidents, 9*(3), 177–197. https://doi.org/10.1016/0376-6349(87)90011-3

Sulzer-Azaroff, B., & Austin, J. A. (2000). Does BBS work: Behavior-based safety & injury reduction: a survey of the evidence. *Professional Safety 45*(7), 19–24.

Sulzer-Azaroff, B., & de Santamaria, M. C. (1980). Industrial safety hazard reduction through performance feedback. *Journal of Applied Behavior Analysis, 13*(2), 287–295. https://doi.org/10.1901/jaba.1980.13-287

Sulzer-Azaroff, B., & Fellner, D. J. (1984). Searching for performance targets in the behavioral analysis of occupational safety and health: An assessment strategy. *Journal of Organizational Behavior Management, 6*(2), 53–65. https://doi.org/10.1300/J075v06n02_09

Sulzer-Azaroff, B., Harris, T. C., & McCann, K. B. (1994). Beyond training: Organizational performance management techniques. *Occupational Medicine, 9*(2), 321–339.

Sulzer-Azaroff, B., Loafman, B., Merante, R. J., & Hlavacek, A. C. (1990). Improving occupational safety in a large industrial plant: A systematic replication. *Journal of Organizational Behavior Management, 11*(1), 99–120. https://doi.org/10.1300/J075v11n01_07

Tosti, D. T. (1993). *Performance technology applied to organizational culture and strategy* [Paper presentation]. NSPI Conference, Chicago, IL, United States.

U.S. Bureau of Labor Statistics. (2021, November 3). *Injuries, illnesses, and fatalities*. https://www.bls.gov/web/osh/summ1_00.htm

Index

A

ABC analysis, 235, 244–245. *See also* Antecedents, Behavior, Consequences
Accountability, 30, 49, 76, 216
    accountability systems, 64
Action plans, 51, 56, 66, 71, 77, 92, 130, 144, 151, 157, 164, 202, 229, 241, 251, 262, 277, 282
Alvero, Alicia M., 266, 280, 283–308
Antecedents, 230–231, 235–240, 242, 245–247
Assessment report, 56, 101–102, 111. *See also* Safety assessment
Austin, John, 37, 217, 266, 283–308
Awards programs, 32, 170–176, 203, 238. *See also* Celebrations, Recognition, Reinforcement
    awards program vs. awards process, 93, 174
    budget, 176, 184–185, 197–198, 220, 223, 269
    cash, 32, 186
    contest, 183, 251, 254, 260
    criteria, 126, 174–177, 182–184, 203, 220, 245, 263
    delivery of, 176, 183–184, 203–204, 267
    disadvantages of, 33–35, 153, 186
    general guidelines on, 187–188, 192, 203
    identifying potential awards and forms of recognition, 176
    internal marketing campaign for, 171
    lost-workday injuries, 131, 183, 187, 228
    lotteries, 183
    management and, 183, 184–186
    OSHA-recordable injuries and, 187, 234
    overview of, 172
    paid time off, 186, 263
    presentation to management, 99, 193, 196–198
    problems with, 31, 183–184, 187, 211
    recognition, 170–174, 176, 178–182
    rules of thumb on, 171
    simple and concurrent, 174–175
    tiered safety awards, 175–184
    tokens, 183–184, 189, 204, 256
    workers' compensation claims and, 186–187

B

Barriers to safety, 63–64
Behavior, 17, 20
    definition of, 233
    pinpointing, 36–37, 123–124, 135, 189, 233–234
    science, 18, 233–242
Behavior-based safety (BBS), 17–18, 20–29, 36–39, 266–276, 283–297. *See also* specific topics
Bersin, Josh, 44
Blame, minimizing, 35
Bureaucracy, creation of, 216
Burns, T. E., 80

C

Cards
    feedback support, 251, 255–256
    pledge, 251, 255
    thank-you, 204, 255–257
Cascading meetings, 65, 76–78
Case studies
    DuPont chemical plant, 24–29
    electric utility, 270–272
    food-processing plant, 280
    logging industry, 272–276
    long-term, 258–265
    ore-processing, 262–265
    paper mill, 128–161
    pipeline company, 266–269, 277–278
    pipeline operations, 85–89
    polyolefin plant, 278–280
    refinery, 258–261
    self-observation, 266–276
    small-company, 277–282
Cash awards, 32, 186
Catastrophic events, preventing, 80–89, 140–148, 227–228. *See also* Serious-incident prevention
Celebrations, 75, 88, 93, 105, 120, 170–190, 198, 203–204, 208, 210–211, 213, 219–220, 230–231, 249–250, 255, 263, 270
Checklists, safety observation
    creating, 131–133
    examples, 169, 187
    for different areas, 132–134
    questions that should be answered, 148–150

safety observation, 134, 138–143
  trial run of, 158–161
Chemical company, 25, 80–81
  case study of, 21–28
Chemical industry, accident rate in, 25
Classroom training, 216
Close call, 28–29, 105, 220
  program, 252
  reporting of, 34, 47, 50–55, 77–78, 88
Common problems with safety efforts, 31–33
Communication, 31, 45, 49, 53, 56, 62, 69–71, 91, 113, 123–125, 139, 260, 263, 269, 277
Compensation, safety incentive, 48–49, 120, 172, 178, 183–184, 185–187
Complacency, 20, 29, 151
Conferences, 185, 226
Consequences, 31, 50, 63, 75, 80, 129, 231, 235–242, 245–248. *See also* Awards programs, Celebrations, Punishment, Recognition, Reinforcement
  added consequences, 237
  built-in consequences, 236
  factors influencing effectiveness, 238
  self-provided consequences, 238
Consultants, 17, 97
Contests, 183–184, 251, 254, 257, 260
Contingency diagrams, 235–240
Contingency relationships, 235
Contract personnel, 150, 155
  observations and, 155–159
  orientations for, 168, 253–254
Cooperation, punishment and, 35
Corrective actions, 84–87
Corrective feedback, 35–36, 55, 76, 157, 238–240, 256
Crew safety representative, 263. *See also* employee safety representative
Criticism, impact of, 35, 237
Culture, 17–19, 37–39, 40–41, 44–79, 90–91, 107, 233. *See also* Organizational culture
  assessment, 49
    interviews, 51–56
    observations, 50
    process, 50
  elements of, 45
    mission, 45, 57
    purpose, 45, 57
    values, 45, 58
      clarifying, 122–123
      defined, 46
      discussion of, 125–126
      unstructured approach, 122
    vision, 45, 58
  iceberg, 44–45, 48
  report out, 56, 77

D

Declarations, public safety, 255
Delayed outcomes, 238–242
Deming, Edwards, 35
Design process, 114, 215. *See also* Design team and other specific topics
  employee involvement, 80, 83, 124, 228, 230, 269, 283
  marathon planning meetings, 118–119
  milestone schedule, 120, 126–127, 160, 184, 196–197
  objectives of, 114, 117
  periodic planning meetings, 118–120, 126–127, 160, 184, 200
  steering committee's role, 163–168, 172, 203–205
  steps in
    conducting management review, 196
    creating the safety observation process, 128
    designing feedback and involvement procedures, 162
    developing recognition and celebration plans, 170
    establishing mission, values, and milestone targets, 121
    planning training and kickoff meetings, 191
Design team, 92–93, 98. *See also* Design process
  implementation plan developed by, 101–102, 116–117
  kickoff meeting for, 114
  planning process and, 117–119
  safety assessment and, 99, 100–103
  structure of, 91–93
  workshop for, 114–115
Drilling company, 21–22
Drucker, Peter, 44
DuPont, 21, 24–28, 157, 256

E

Employee safety coordinator, 200–201
  in self-observations, 220, 222–223
Employees
  addressing concerns of, 210–211, 223
  design process and, 80, 83, 124, 228, 230, 269, 283
  individual learning history of, 239–241
  involving, 91, 228, 230, 250, 252–253, 254, 269
  kickoff meetings, 113, 120, 125–126, 193
  participation of, 70, 167, 211, 253, 265, 270, 283
  presentations by, 254

recognition preferences of, 176, 180–181, 203, 269
responsibility of, 35, 56, 93, 151
safety observation process and, 129–130, 151, 207
safety orientations for, 253–254
slogans and logos designed by, 183, 254
training of, 192, 194–195, 202, 216
values and, 124–126
working alone or in small groups in remote locations, 217–224
workshops for, 192, 265

F

False starts, 216
Feedback, 84, 156–158
appreciative, 164, 172–174, 207, 214
checklist for, 169
corrective, 35–36, 76, 157, 237–240, 256
example of, 42
importance of, 36–37, 43
management modeling of, 204–205, 207
thank-you cards, 172, 255–257
using graphs to provide, 163–166
verbal, 129, 255
Feedback support cards, 255–256
Follow-up, 64, 73, 254
Food-processing plant, 280–282
Formal systems, 44–45, 48–49, 58–59, 69–70

G

Geller, E. Scott, xiii, 28, 36, 251, 257
Goals, 166–168, 249–250
Graphs
posting, 163–164, 202–203, 220, 222–223
safety observation data, 144, 163–166
Great Plains Railroad, 47–48
Grindle, Angelica, xv, 277–278
Group discussions, 51, 114, 252, 254

H

Hall, Edward, 44
High-risk areas and activities, identifying, 100, 130–143
Hopkins, Bill, xv

I

Implementation plan, 118
safety leadership, 48–49, 76–78
Implementation process, 90–91
design team and, 92, 200–203
false starts and, 216

implementation plan and, 76–77, 118, 200–201, 205
management support for, 98, 101, 110
management's responsibilities, 151, 204–205
objectives of, 117
overview of, 90–91
planning and, 76–77, 118–119
process ownership and, 200–201
steps in, 120, 200
team structure for, 91–93, 101–102
time required for, 118–119
Improvement projects, 80–89, 228–231, 243–250
Incentive programs, 170–189
awards programs vs. awards process and, 93, 174–175
disadvantages of, 153, 171, 186
general guidelines on, 187–190
internal marketing campaign for, 171
overview of, 172
simple and concurrent safety awards, 173–175
tiered safety awards, 173–181
traditional compensation, 185
Incident investigation worksheet, 241–242
Individual learning history, 236–240, 242
Informal culture, 50, 58
Informal systems, 44, 48, 216
Injuries
causes of, 26–27
consequences of reporting, 31–34, 50
employee involvement in, 252–253
in chemical industry, 21–27, 80–81, 262
investigations of, 241–242, 252–253
lost-workday, 24, 28–29, 186–187, 264, 268, 271, 281
unsafe acts vs. unsafe conditions as cause of, 24, 28–29
Involvement procedures, 162–169

K

Kickoff meetings, 113–114, 125–126, 191–195, 202
Komaki, Judith, 36–37, 72, 129
Krause, Tom, 23, 37, 140

L

Labels, 135, 233–234
Layered safety audits, 24–25, 33
Leadership, 18, 40–41, 60, 76, 80. *See also* Management, Steering Committee
barriers to, 63–64, 70, 82
effective vs. ineffective, 72, 79
five categories of leadership behavior, 64–76
build support, 70–71

communicate, 69–70
create alignment, 64–69
manage the consequences, 75–79
study and review, 71–75
informal leaders, 50, 71, 114, 207, 224
leadership checklist, 68–69
monitoring, responsibility for, 64, 129
most important role, 129
new employee orientation, responsibility for, 68, 253–254
observations and, 62, 72–73, 100
phases, 91–92
positive questions, 63
reinforcement and, 70
special role, 65–67
three roles, 60–61
 executive, 60
 manager, 60–61
 supervisor, 61
Learning history, individual, 236–240, 242
Legal issues, 32, 171
Logos, design of, 254
Lost-workday injuries, 29, 131
 safety awards based on, 187
 statistics on, 20
Lotteries, 183

M

Maintenance of VBS process
 management and, 120, 213–214
 steering committee's responsibilities, 92–93, 207–213
Management, 62–63, 204–205, 213–214. See also specific topics.
 by exception, 64, 67, 79
 commitment, 82–83, 204–205
 expectations of, 53, 63, 125, 204–205
 implementation responsibilities, 204–205
 interview of, 52, 104
 involvement in safety process and, 24–25
 maintenance responsibilities, 213–214
 management review, 160–161, 196–197
 modeling observation and feedback practices, 65–66, 204–205
 monitoring, 64, 75, 129
 observation process and, 109, 160
 presentations or question-and-answer sessions, 257
 process- vs. results-oriented, 45–47
 purpose statement and, 56–57, 119, 121–122, 204
 responsibility of, 35, 151, 204–205, 213–214
 role of, 215–216
 safety awards and, 172–174
 steering committee, 200, 203–205, 213–214

support of, 97, 101, 110, 184–185, 202
training and, 113, 194–195
Management-based safety programs, 31–33
Management-employee relations
 in process-oriented organizations, 46–47
 in results-oriented organizations, 46
 punishment and, 33–36
 values statements and, 51, 56–59, 65
Management overview, 112–115
MasterBuild, 61–63
Matthews, Grainne, xv, 225, 243
Measurement and feedback systems, 84. See also Observation data
Monitoring, 21, 64, 73, 78, 85, 129, 218, 248, 266
Myers, Wanda, 258, 262, 280

N

Near miss. See Close call
New hire orientation, 68, 253–254

O

Observation data
 analysis of, 92, 105, 129, 145, 202–203, 212
 reviewing, 166
Observation process, 42, 109, 117, 128–161, 217. See also Observation data, Safety observations
 advantages of, 129–130
 checklists, 132–149
 common configurations, 158–159
 employee involvement in, 168–169, 228
 example of, 42–43
 feedback as part of, 156–158
 graphing of data, 163–166
 implementation of, 130
  analyzing past incidents and injuries, 130–133
  developing list of critical safe practices, 131–142
  drafting and revising checklists, 143–149
 importance of, 36–37, 40–43, 129–130
 management and, 60–61, 151–153
 management modeling of, 60–63, 204–205
 management review, 160–161, 204–205
 starting, 201–202
 trial run, 158–160
 uses of observation data, 80, 202–203, 211–212, 243
Observer effect, 283–297
Observer training, 126, 192–193, 208
Off-the-job safety programs, 21, 252, 256
Organizational culture
 alignment, 56–73
 changing, 46–47, 56

defined, 44–45
model, 45

P

Pareto
    analysis, 212, 243–244
    chart, 232, 243–244
    diagram, 212–213
Performance management, 80–82
Performance standards, 84
Pinney, Ann, 217, 266
Pinpointing, 123, 233–234
Pipeline company, 21, 23, 266–269, 277–278
    cause of pipeline accidents, 86, 266
    critical work practices, 87–88
    reinforcement plan, 89, 267
    serious incident prevention case study, 85–89, 266–269
Pledge cards, 255
    positive questions, 63
Problem-solving, 243–249
Process, overemphasis on, 46–47
Process owner, 200–201
Process safety reviews, 252
Programs vs. process, 93–94
Public declarations, 255
Punishment
    appropriate use of, 35–36
    problems with, 33–35

R

Recognition, 170–190, 203, 249–250. *See also* Awards programs
Recordable injury rate, 21, 173, 224, 264, 273–275, 278–279
Reinforcement, 84–85, 88–89
    reinforcers, 174–182, 267, 269, 274
Relationships, punishment and, 30, 33–35. *See also* Management-employee relations
Releases, preventing, 80–81
Reliability coefficient, 158–160
Results, overemphasis on, 46
Risk management practices, 82
Risks, identifying, 83

S

Safe-behavior pledge cards, 255
Safety as a team process, 29–31
Safety assessment, 95–111
    checklist for, 104–106
    definition of, 95–96
    interviews, 104–106
    objectives of, 96–101
    outcome of, 101–102
    participants in, 97–99
    purpose of, 96–97
    reporting on, 110–111
    safety audit vs., 95–96
    steps in, 102–110
        analysis and development of improvement plan, 108–110
        conduct interviews, 104–106
        final report and presentation, 110–111
        observation, 106–108
        review of safety data, 102–103
Safety awards. *See* Awards programs
Safety conference, 173, 178, 185, 226, 254
Safety index, in self-observations, 220–221
Safety observations, 37, 41–42, 51, 61–62, 72–73, 79, 104–105, 108–109, 128–161, 201, 205, 259, 270, 278–280, 283, 285, 291, 297. *See also* Observation process
    announcing of, 153
    contract personnel and, 155, 253–254
    feedback and, 156–158
    for employees who work alone or in small groups in remote locations, 217–224
    frequency of, 153
    participants in, 150–151
    procedure, 150–156
    reliability of, 158–159
    review of data, 166
    timing of, 153–155
    voluntary, 151–153
    who should conduct, 150–151
Safety Point of Contact, 70–71
Safety programs
    common problems with, 31–32
    components of, 20, 22, 36–37
    management based, 33
    management participation, 110–111
    mission statement for, 122
    naming of, 91, 254
    novelty of, 93, 173
    off-the-job, 252, 256
    pilot testing, 109, 118, 158
    punishment-based, 33
    traditional, 20–21
"Safety share" discussions, 256
Safety slogans, 254
Safety suggestions systems, 252–253
Safety triangle, 27–29
Say and do, 65–68, 78–79
Self-awareness, 63
Self-observations, 217–224
    celebrations, 223–224
    cheating, concerns about, 218
    crew safety representative, 220
    posting observation data, 222–223

prompting, 222
recognition, 223–224
safety index, 220–221
sample checklist, 219, 221
sampling process, 222
Serious-incident prevention, 80–89
   case study, 85
   elements of, 80–85
      building management commitment, 82–83
      establishing performance standards, 84
      identifying critical work, 83
      improving the process, 85
      involving employees, 83
      maintaining measurement and feedback systems, 84
      reinforcing and implementing corrective actions, 84–85
      understanding the risks, 83
Spills, preventing, 81
Steering committee, 225–232, 243–250
   addressing process integrity, 230–231
   common problems and, 211
   creating, 225–226
   implementation responsibilities, 207–211
   improvement targets, 231
   maintenance responsibilities, 207–210
   meetings, 209
   member responsibilities, 207–215
   problem solving steps, 243–250
   summary of responsibilities, 210
   training, 226
Stowe, Judith E., 277–278
Sulzer-Azaroff, Beth, 36–37, 128–130, 148, 167
Systematic desensitization, 29

T

Team structure, 91–92, 101–102
Training, 125–126, 192–193
   classroom, 216
   contract personnel, 253–254
   identifying the need for, 194–195
   introducing new values and, 125
   management, 205
   management and, 193–195
   new employee orientation, 253–254
   planning, 193–194
   steering committee, 195, 200–201, 226–232

V

Values-Based Safety (VBS), 18–19, 40–43, 90–94, 277–282. *See also* specific topics
   common configurations for, 158–159
   elements of, 90–92
   implementation phases, 92
   overview of, 90–91
   support groups, 257
   theory underlying, 194
Videos, observer training, 192

W

Walk-around, 72–73
Worker's compensation
   claims, 32
   safety awards based on, 186–187
Workshops, design team, 114–115

For more on the successful implementation and maintenance of a values-based, behavior-based safety (BBS) process, check out author Terry McSween's series of on-demand courses by ABA Technologies.

- BBS Essentials℠: **An Introduction to Safety Basics**
- Behavior-Based Safety: **Observations and Feedback**
- Behavior-Based Safety: **Visible Safety Leadership**
- Behavior-Based Safety: **Design Team**
- Behavior-Based Safety: **Steering Committee**

Save when you bundle all five courses!

abatechnologies.com/behavior-based-safety-series

www.ingramcontent.com/pod-product-compliance
Lightning Source LLC
Chambersburg PA
CBHW062122040426
42337CB00044B/3766